WOMEN IN NORDIC POLITICS

Women in Nordic Politics

Closing the Gap

Edited by

LAURI KARVONEN
and
PER SELLE

Ashgate

Aldershot • Brookfield USA • Singapore • Sydney

Published by
Ashgate Publishing Limited
Gower House
Croft Road
Aldershot, Hants
GU11 3HR
England

HQ
1236.5
.S34
W66
1995

Ashgate Publishing Company
Old Post Road
Brookfield
Vermont 05036
USA

Reprinted 1997, 1998

British Library Cataloguing in Publication Data
Women in Nordic Politics: Closing the Gap
  I. Karvonen, Lauri II. Selle, Per
  305.420948

Library of Congress Cataloging-in-Publication Data
Women in Nordic politics : closing the gap / [edited by] Lauri
  Karvonen, Per Selle.
    p. cm.
  ISBN 1-85521-533-0
    1. Women in politics–Scandinavia. 2. Women–Scandinavia–Social
  conditions. I. Karvonen, Lauri. II. Selle, Per.
  HQ1236.5.S34W66   1995
  320.948'082–dc20   95-101
                                                                         CIP

ISBN 1 85521 533 0

Reprinted 1997

Printed in Great Britain by Biddles Limited, Guildford and King's Lynn

Contents

Part II: Women as voters and party members

Part III: Organizational participation

Part IV: Public institutions

Part V: Attitudes and Symbols

Part VI: Beyond Scandinavia

Preface

The position of women in Scandinavia has long been regarded as something of a model by their politically active sisters elsewhere. Early female suffrage, an extensive involvement by women in the economy and an active female participation in all walks of social and political life seem to set Scandinavia apart even in a West European comparison.

To what extent are these alleged trends really fundamental features of the four Scandinavian societies? Can one speak of a linear trend towards an increasingly equal division of political power between men and women? Is the 'Gender Gap' narrowing down, or has there been a 'Backlash of the 1980s' in Scandinavia as well?

This volume seeks to provide a comprehensive answer to these questions. Its chapters address central fields of politics and social life, and they are based on extensive new primary research. Although by no means alien to theoretical reasoning, the various chapters share an orientation towards a firm empirical basis. If it is correct to speak of an ongoing reorientation in Scandinavian women's studies from theoretical research stressing marginalization and lack of political power to empirical investigations of women's political activity and influence, this volume can be seen as part of that reorientation.

The generous support of the Norwegian Centre for Management and Organization Research (LOS-senteret) was crucial to the success of this project. A grant from the Joint Committee of the Nordic Social Science Commissions (NOS-S) covered many of our overhead expenses. The Letterstedt Foundation generously supported one of our project meetings.

Individual colleagues and friends that have contributed to the project through comments, advice and criticism are too numerous to be listed here. Nevertheless, one person must be singled out: Maila Solheim. Without her professional skills and enthusiasm in the final editing of the book, the completion of the work would not have been possible.

Bergen, November 1994
Lauri Karvonen
Per Selle

Part I

Women in Nordic politics

Introduction:
Scandinavia: a case apart

Lauri Karvonen and Per Selle

Is the political gender gap really closing?

Women's political representation in Western democracies has been strengthened during recent decades. More women than previously take an active part in politics, more women gain elective office. On the other hand, this does not apply to all countries equally; some display a rapid growth, others practically no increase at all. Moreover, more often than not this increase has been painfully slow; the share of women obtaining representative and executive posts is still way below their share of the total population. 'With a very few and arguable exceptions among industrialised nations, women remain outside the centres of decision-making throughout the world and the forms of status, influence and power which are available to men continue to elude them. Cultural values continue to marginalise their identity and interests (even though commercial interests are only too eager and able to exploit them) and public policies continue to reflect the priorities of men', Jenny Chapman writes (1993, xi). By and large, politics is still a strongly male-dominated field.

Two fundamentally different basic interpretations of this situation can be discerned in the literature and the debate about the position of women in politics. Those who stress the *direction* of the change see the increases as indications of a persistent pattern which may finally bring about equal representation and influence in the future. This is often the mood of the 'official optimism' represented by government reports on equality and positive discrimination. Researchers and debaters connected with such government investigations often represent this view even more generally.

On the other hand, the slow and partial increase in women's representation has caused many to draw the conclusion that politics is indeed a man's world into which women are but infrequently admitted and which functions according to rules fundamentally alien to them. Women's participation is of little avail unless the basic nature of politics itself is made more compatible with those values and experiences that are unique to women. This is still an influential view within women's studies. Although comparatively few go as far as to suggest that women should turn their

3

4 *Women in Nordic Politics*

backs on politics altogether, there is fairly wide-spread scepticism as to what can be achieved solely by quantitative increases in women's representation.

To the 'optimists' as well as the 'pessimists', Scandinavia seems to offer a special case. Irrespective of what aspects of women's position or influence in society one looks at, Denmark, Finland, Norway and Sweden tend to be found at the top of the list. Consequently, many look to Scandinavia as a model worth striving for, a promise of a brighter future. Others tend to stress the unique character of the Scandinavian experience, a uniqueness based on shared cultural values and historical backgrounds, as well as political and social structures which set Scandinavia apart in an international comparison.

Looking at some of the central statistics, Scandinavia indeed seems different. By the early 1990s, the proportion of women in Scandinavian parliaments was more than 30 percent throughout the region; in Finland it was as high as 39 percent. The increase during the preceding decade was marked. Elsewhere in the Western world the level of women's representation was normally around 10-15 percent, in many cases even significantly lower. Interestingly enough, women's representation in continental Western Europe is in most cases stronger than in the Anglo-Saxon world; the Netherlands in fact comes close to a 'Scandinavian' level. In Great Britain and the USA, by contrast, still merely 9-10 percent of the legislators at the national level are women.

This pattern persists also in the executive branch of the government. In 1992, 37 percent of the cabinet ministers (all heads of government departments) in Scandinavia were women. In Norway, the figure was as high as 47 percent (9 out of 19 ministers), in Finland 44 percent, in Sweden 38 percent and in Denmark 21 percent; incidentally, the number of women doubled in the cabinet which succeeded the Schlüter cabinet in Denmark in 1993.

Meanwhile, merely 9 percent of the ministers in the rest of Western Europe were women. Again, there was some variation in this group (Germany and the Netherlands scoring highest, while Switzerland and Portugal had no women cabinet members at all). All in all, nevertheless, Scandinavia was sui generis here as well.

Equally significant, there was a clear difference between Scandinavia and the rest of Western Europe as concerns the distribution of cabinet seats between women and men ministers. Traditionally, those women that have obtained cabinet seats have been given the responsibility for matters related to social policy, family and youth issues, education and cultural policy. By contrast, ministers of finance, industry, justice, defense and foreign affairs have been men.

Looking at West European countries outside Scandinavia, this division of labour continues to apply almost without exception. As for Scandinavia, it is clear that women here as well are still more likely than men to be assigned cabinet posts connected to the 'welfare sector' perceived in general terms. However, among the Scandinavian women that held cabinet posts in 1992 there were also one prime minister, one minister of industry and energy, one minister of defense, one minister of environmental affairs, one minister of agriculture, one minister of labour, one minister of finance, one minister of foreign affairs, one minister of constitutional and civil law and - interestingly enough - three ministers of justice. In other words, the quantitative increases in women's share of political posts have begun to affect the division of labour between women and men in politics in substantive terms as well.

The growth of women's participation in Scandinavian politics is for all practical purposes a post-war phenomenon. With the partial exception of Finland, women were rare birds in representative assemblies before the second World War; in governments they were in practice absent altogether. By around 1970 the number of women in Scandinavian parliaments had roughly doubled, but the figure was still as low as 9 percent in Norway while Finland already had 22 percent women legislators. The following two decades witnessed an accelerated growth: between 1970 and the first parliamentary elections of the 1990s the rate of increase in women's share of parliamentary seats was 77 percent in Finland, 120 percent in Sweden, 209 percent in Denmark, and no less than 333 percent in Norway. Today, Finland and Norway have the highest proportion of women legislators (39 percent). The increase in Norway has occurred late and rapidly, whereas the Finnish case portrays a more gradual and steady development.

As for cabinets, the picture is largely similar. Since the early 1950s, most Scandinavian cabinets have contained at least one woman minister. Again, however, the change has been most marked during the last decade. Since the early 1980s, the share of women in Scandinavian cabinets has roughly doubled, and is nearly 40 percent today.

The same developmental pattern can be observed at other levels of government as well. In Denmark, Sweden and Norway (Finland has no elected assemblies at the regional level) women's representation in regional councils has risen to the same overall level as in national parliaments and cabinets. In all four countries, local representative assemblies have close to or around one-third women members. Again, the period since the 1970s marks an era of rapid growth.

However, political power and influence is, of course, a matter of much more than just parliamentary and cabinet seats. More detailed evidence which takes a broad view of things political is needed to substantiate any generalization about the Scandinavian situation. That is why this book contains comprehensive chapters on women's political representation also at the local level, within the trade union movement, the voluntary sector, and the corporate channel, as well as among employees in the public bureaucracy and the local adminstrative level, voters and party members. The overall picture is the same; a dramatic increase since the early 1970s. While the 1970s was mainly a period of increased political mobilization of women through the electoral channel, during the 1980s they increasingly penetrated the corporate channel and the public bureacracy. It is also in this last period we see a strong increase of women in leading positions.

The basic impression ought to be reasonably clear by now. In purely quantitative terms, women have made spectacular headway in Scandinavian politics during the last two decades. True, women's representation is still in most respects some distance away from a balanced situation. Nevertheless, growth rates of several hundred percent in the matter of a couple of decades are typical in most areas of politics in Scandinavia.

Rather than argue for or against any intrinsic differences between the situation of Scandinavian women and that of women in other regions, this book endeavors to provide a comprehensive analysis of what the position of women in Scandinavian politics today actually is. Whether one is an 'optimist' or 'pessimist' these chapters should help in clarifying the extent of the political space open to women in Scandinavia, and why it is so.

Perspective: numbers count and politics makes a difference

Several objections can readily be raised against any quantitative account of the kind presented above. Most of them are variations on the same theme: 'What difference do numbers make?'

To those arguing along these lines, one particular kind of evidence readily suggests itself. This has to do with the fact that Scandinavian women, while making rapid headway in the field of politics, still remain grossly under-represented in many other important areas. Thus, the extensive Swedish Commission of Inquiry into Democracy and Power revealed that while the power elite in the field of politics in Sweden in 1989 consisted of 31 percent women, the corresponding figure for the cultural sector was 23, for mass media 15 percent, for science and research 5 percent and for the business and industrial élites only one percent. Thus, it may well be argued that the increased political representation of women has not so far decisively helped them penetrate other important areas of social life.

Some stretch this argumentation even further by maintaining that the increased proportion of women in political office in itself presents evidence of the declining importance of politics at large. 'Where women go in, power goes out', is the well-known slogan with which this this theory of 'shrinking institutions' is often presented (e.g. Holter 1981).

Furthermore, it is of course pertinent to inquire about possible effects on the content of politics. Politics is, after all, not about representation and office for their own sake. Politics with a high degree of participation by women should produce an output which is significantly different from that accomplished by a strongly male-dominated political system. Many would argue that the output of the political system in Scandinavia still primarily reflects male values and experiences.

While these are serious viewpoints that cannot be dismissed lightly, they are at least equally difficult to substantiate in empirical terms. Whether politics will remain separate from, e.g., business and industry in terms of women's influence or whether these sectors will follow a similar course of development with a considerable time-lag only time can tell (we think it will). It is possible that the relative importance of political institutions has declined during recent years (we do not think it has) - although reliable measures of such a change seem exceedingly difficult to come by. Moreover, proponents of this 'shrinking institutions thesis' would be hard put to prove that, for instance, the Norwegian Prime Minister's Office has declined significantly in terms of power during the Gro Harlem Brundtland years, that the Swedish Minister of Finance has had less say since Anne Wibble assumed the job, or that the Bank of Finland has less influence since Sirkka Hämäläinen was appointed its Director General.

None of the above arguments against 'increasing numbers' should be rejected directly or belittled. Still, the burden of evidence should work both ways. The present volume looks less into the distant future than to the present situation and to the development leading up to it. In this context, we would argue that whatever the future position of politics at large may be, irrespective of whether or not women's participation and representation will continue to 'spill over' into other fields and whether or not the nature of politics will change with the increasing share of women (we think it will to some extent, however not in fundamental ways), the present internationally remarkable position of women in Scandinavian politics rests on several pillars that are so fundamental that the situation is largely irreversible.

Looking at the social, economic and political changes preceding or parallel to the rapid growth of women's representation in Scandinavian politics, various factors stand out as being of crucial importance: fundamental demographic changes, the growth of women's cultural, educational and economic resources, government policies and the achievements and influence of the women's movement. The crucial point is that all these factors have been operative side by side, and at the same time closely interconnected. Political changes have reflected demographic, social and economic transformations, but the causal link has functioned in the reverse direction as well; much of what might be termed structural changes is in fact the result of conscious policies on the part of governments and other political actors. The political sphere has had a decisive degree of autonomy.

Similar to their sisters throughout Europe, Scandinavian women have seen their role as childbearers and mothers change in the post-war era. Few women in Scandinavia give birth to more than 2-3 children; in fact, a family with three children is statistically rather uncommon today. Fertility rates have fallen dramatically since the first 'baby-boom' decades after the second World War. In Finland, the change came early, starting from a high level of fertility immediately after the war. In Sweden, the effects of the baby-boom were less marked; the main drop in fertility occurred from the 1960s on. Pretty much the same goes for Denmark as well. Norway displays a different pattern: fertility rates increased through the 1950s and then dropped dramatically from the 1960s on. Throughout the region, however, uniformly low fertility rates were the rule by the early 1980s.

As for labour market participation, the four countries are today characterized by high female labour force rates. Slightly under fifty percent of the total labour force throughout Scandinavia are women. A high proportion of women in the labour force has been the case ever since the First World War in Finland, whereas the growth in the three other countries has been most marked since the 1960s. In Norway, in fact, the bulk of the growth has occurred since 1970. Throughout the region however, the increased political representation of women has been paralleled by an ever more marked presence in the labour market.

Similarly, women's educational level is today entirely comparable with that of men. In fact, their propensity to acquire advanced education is even higher than among men; this is witnessed by the fact that universities throughout Scandinavia have female majorities among enrolled students. In Finland, the share of female university students was around 50 percent as early as in the late 1960s, while it took roughly another decade for the other three countries to catch up. Again, Norway displays a late and rapid growth pattern. All in all, women's educational resources are today equal or even better than those of men, although women are still clearly over-represented in welfare-related fields.

Equally important, several waves of political reforms have paved the way for the development described above. Starting with the 19th and early 20th Century reforms which gave women their basic individual and citizen's rights, continuing with the far-reaching social and family policies of the 1930s, 1940s and 1950s, and the equality legislation of the recent decades, legislators have sometimes boosted new advances for women, sometimes codified existing progress made by women unaided by formal political decisions. A central theme of this book is that political institutions and politics do make a difference (March and Olson 1989, Powell and DiMaggio 1991, Steinmo, Thelen and Longstreth 1992). Attained rights are guaranteed and legitimized by such institutions and this has been a crucial dimension in the improvement of the political position of women in the Nordic countries.

Of paramount importance is the fact that the role of the State in the Scandinavian societies has been so central for so long. Far from always having clear visions for the political empowerment of women, the State has contributed to a steady flow of reforms which have enhanced the participation of women in social, economic and political matters. This can not be explained only by the mobilization of women. Increased women's participation has sometimes been the goal; at other instances it can be viewed as an unintended consequence. At an early stage, traditional women's organizations could bring pressures to bear on the state to look into the conditions of women in different areas of social life (Blom 1982, Seip 1984, Kuhnle and Selle 1992). Later on, the international exchanges in which the states were involved - Nordic cooperation in particular - offered a channel through which issues important to women were brought directly into the politico-administrative machineries of the four states. In many areas, individual women as well as women's organizations have, thanks to the proliferation of the 'Strong State,' within a 'state-friendly' society had an influence over and above the numeric representation of women in political parties and elected assemblies.

True, political parties and ideological currents have been of importance for many crucial decisions. The role played by the social democrats in the introduction of the contemporary administrative structures and legal frameworks for the advancement of gender equality is a case in point. Nevertheless, seeing the State as merely a reflection of the parties that happen to be in power would be overly limiting as concerns the question of gender equality - as it indeed would be in most other important fields of Scandinavian politics (Baldwin 1990). There is, indeed, a need not only to 'bring the State back in' (Skocpol 1985), but to bring 'Society back in'

(Friedland and Alford 1991) in the present context as well. One needs to understand the special relationship between the State and the Civil Society in our 'state-friendly' society, i.e. the 'culture' of cooperation, in order to understand both the extent to which the State guarantees and supports attained rights at the same time as it is very open to pressure from below. This specific relationship makes it extremely difficult if not impossible to set up any clear boundaries between government and civil society in the Scandinavian context (Kuhnle and Selle 1992, Selle and Øymyr 1994). This relationship partly explains why, in a comparative perspective, it was easier for Scandinavian women both to gain access to politics and to get things through within the new and more positive ideological climate from the late 1960s.

Consequently, the interplay between 'political' and 'structural' factors should be stressed at all times. Far from belittling the role played by demographic, cultural and economic changes, this book emphasizes the role played by political decisions as determinants of such changes. It would be as unrealistic to expect the present economic crisis to sweep women out of the labour market back into the home as it would be oversimplistic to see their entry into the labour market and their concomitant political activation as simply a reflection of the growing need for labour. Both the 'demographic' and 'structural' changes and the increased women's representation in politics are to a decisive extent a result of conscious policies. These policies have aims far beyond the simple 'logic of the market'. There is a political will behind these changes, not just a passive adjustment to changes that are inevitable given structural shifts in the Scandinavian societies. In a word, women's position in politics is far from independent of the characteristics of political life at large.

Even as concerns the role of the State or the importance of political factors, however, interesting intra-regional variation can be noted in Scandinavia. These differences are by and large parallel to those noted above with a view to structural and demographic factors. Again, Finland and Norway represent the extremes, while Denmark and Sweden can be seen as intermediate cases.

In Finland, women's participation in the labour market, higher education and politics attained high levels at an early stage. The direct role played by the government or by political parties appears rather limited. Quotas for women's representation have virtually not been practiced at all. Women's representation in parliament and local assemblies is the result of elections where a candidate-centered electoral system, rather than ballots cast simply for parties, is employed.

In Norway, by contrast, the corresponding changes occurred later; once the transformation had begun, it took place unprecedentedly fast. The formal as well as informal quotas introduced to secure women's representation have rapidly given

Norwegian women a stronger overall representation in politics than anywhere else in the world. Norway rather than Finland today stands out as an example of the possibility of a rapid transformation of the role of women in politics, the labour market and in the educational system. The Norwegian case underlines the role that the 'art of the possible' may play in this process of transformation. The role played by the government and political parties in furthering women's representation has been crucial.

This way of understanding political change has gradually become influential also within Scandinavian Women's Studies. However, until the late 1980s most Scandinavian women's studies a priori accepted the abstract model of the patriarchical state, the dominating perspective of international women's studies. Within this perspective, influenced both by the liberal and marxist views, the State is per definition an enemy and suppressor. However, gradually a more context-dependent and 'state-friendly' view has emerged in sharp contrast to the dominating 'patriarchical' system perspective where the political space open to genuine women's interests is almost non-existent. A very influential work within the 'patriarchal' tradition from one of the 'heavyweights' of women's research is Carole Pateman's book, The Disorder of Women (1989). While versions of such a perspective are still dominant internationally, since the early 1990s we have seen even outside Scandinavia a move in the direction of a more 'state-friendly' view within women's studies, a view which de-emphasizes the marginalization of women and instead concentrates on the political space open to women (e.g. Piven 1990).

From the late 1980s some of the most influential Scandinavian women's studies scholars have questioned the 'patriarchal' perspective, ie the universal system perspective that a priori takes for granted that Scandinavian women are marginalized and excluded from the public sphere. It has became common to talk of 'state feminism' or of the 'women-friendly society'; i.e. that Government can be an important actor in promoting women's interests and the individual freedom of women in Scandinavia (Hernes 1987, Siim 1990, Dahlerup 1992, Skjeie 1992).

We support this reorientation and this work should be seen as part of it. Context is important and history counts. Furthermore, it is our view that women have played a significant role within important parts of civil society even before the 1970s, especially within the welfare and educational sectors (e.g. Selle 1994). Maybe that was an important and necessary precondition for the tremendous 'take off' in the political mobilization of Scandinavian women from the early 1970s. That 'take off', unknown in other parts of the world, has changed the whole political landscape in less than a generation.

Content: women in Nordic politics

The book is divided into six parts and contains 15 chapters. In addition to this general introduction, which discusses Scandinavia as a case apart both as regards the extent of change and the nature of the change (Chap. 1, by Lauri Karvonen and Per Selle), part I provides a broad bird's eye view of the changes in women's political participation and representation in all walks of political life during the last 20 years or so (Chap. 2, by Nina Raaum). This chapter shows quite clearly that it is not only in the electoral channel that the political gender gap is shrinking. Raaum argues that hypothesis concerning a hierarchical and functional marginalization of women in Nordic politics gain little empirical support today. The data confirms that women are best represented in sectors responsible for education, health and social services and cultural affairs, but there is no foundation for the claim that a gender-based division of labour is equivalent to a functional marginalization of women. The hierarchical division of labour has declined throughout the 1980s. The broad mobilization of women as ordinary representatives in the 1970s has continued in the 1980s through a relatively stronger mobilization of women to position of political leadership. The functional division of labour is declining as well. In the ten years between 1980 and 1990, the percentage of women increased most in policy areas in which women were least represented in the 1970s. Even if women are not equally represented, their extensive share in all fields of political life means that they are not any longer excluded from any part of the decision-making process.

From this broad and general level we move to what we consider to be the three main areas of political life; the voting and party arena (part II); the organizational society (part III), and the public institutions (part IV). So far we have emphasized the context and the fora into which women in increasing numbers gain positions. In part V we wish to examine some of the political effects of the growth of women's representation to see to what extent they can be expected to express attitudes and symbols different from those presented by men. Part VI, called Beyond Scandinavia, puts the Scandinavian case in perspective by contrasting it with the Nicaraguan situation.

Women as voters and party members

Here we survey women inside and outside of parties, as voters (Chap. 3, by Maria Oskarson) as well as party members (Chap. 4, by Jan Sundberg).

Maria Oskarson does not find the differences in the voting behaviour of women and men large enough to call it a gender gap. She underscores that increased education and labour market participation at the expense of family responsibility have made women more equal to men with regard to political resources. As a consequence, the predominance of women supporting those parties on the right which emphasize family values has clearly declined.

Even so, from the 1980s women to a larger extent than men vote for the parties on the left, especially the parties to the left of the social democratic parties. In general, women are somewhat over-represented in voting for the Christian parties, while the Conservative parties show a slight over-representation of men in their electorates. In the 'new' parties on the far right men are clearly in the majority.

Age has an effect. The gender difference is somewhat larger for those under 45 years of age. The 'socialist' side becomes more female, while older women are clearly the most conservative voters. Furthermore, there is an effect of public sector employment, however, it is not as strong as might have been expected. Women employed in the public sector are more inclined than men to vote for the socialist parties, and the gender difference is larger as compared to the voting pattern of those working in the private sector. Maria Oskarson concludes by saying that while the 'old' gender gap is closing, the increased differences between young men and women in Denmark, Norway and Sweeden in supporting the left parties may develop into a new gender gap.

Women have, in a historical perspective, to a much larger extent been marginalized as party members compared to as voters. Approaching the changes within party organizations (Chap. 4), Jan Sundberg emphasizes three features; female membership, the inclusion of women in the top of the party hierarchy, and the nomination of female candidates on the party lists. The gender differences were very extensive until the early 1970s, but have since diminished; first at the membership level, then from the 1980s at the leadership level as well.

Both the party politics and the internal party culture have in most parties been strongly male-oriented. That women are less eager to become party activists and not only members points in this direction. Gradually the internal and the external 'culture' has changed and by now Sundberg argues all moves against any demands from female members could violate the party image in the elections.

Today almost half of the party members are women, and in the social democratic parties there has been a sharp increase partly caused by the decline in collective membership, i.e trade union membership. Even so, the proportion of women in the Agrarian and Conservative parties exceeds those of the social democratic parties in some of the countries. However, like Oskarson, Sundberg finds generational effects indicating that perhaps women will gradually 'take over' the parties on the left, 'over-represented' as they already are by relatively young women. Norway leads the way towards increased gender equality, but the tendency is clearly the same in the other countries as well.

When it comes to the extent of the recruitment of women into the top party hierarchy, the increase of women in the higher electoral bodies has been very rapid. The change in Norway has been remarkable and here the influence of the quota rule saying that at least 40 percent of representatives to any elected body should be female (or male) has had a great effect.

The nomination process seems to be very open to women. Sundberg argues that this has been the easiest and most effective way for women to win political influence. Since close to half of the members are women and the party 'culture' has changed, it has started to become easy to be nominated, and in Norway the quota rule again is crucial in improving the representation of women.

Moreover, this section brings in the crucial issue facing all of Scandinavia today, the strategy of the dominant social democratic parties vis-a-vis the European Union (Chap. 5, by Ulf Lindström). Lindström shows quite clearly that women and men really differ in their view of the EU. Women are much more negative to joining than men. If it were up to the women of Finland, Norway and Sweden, the three countries would not become members of the EU after the referendums of 1994. Lindström suggests two reasons for this antipathy toward membership of the EU. First, Nordic women, empowered through public sector employment, do not believe that the welfare state is likely to survive a transmutation to Europe. Second, the social democratic parties, which hold the key to the outcome of the referendums, are unwilling to offer a gender-biased programme of public employment in exchange for providing Nordic capital full access to Europe.

Women in the organizational society

This section analyzes changes in women's participation in the organizational society. It starts by emphasizing that the massive move of women into the labour market has accentuated the importance of the trade union movement as an instrument for the social advancement of women (Chap. 6, by Lauri Karvonen). Women's participation in the labour market in Scandinavia has increased rapidly during recent decades; today, their share of the labour force is entirely comparable to that of men. Labour market organizations have, however, traditionally been more unwilling than political parties to let this be reflected in the composition of their representative and executive bodies. Nevertheless, the last two decades have witnessed a rapid growth of women's representation; if this trend continues women will soon gain the same degree of representation as in the parliamentary area.

In Norway, women's entry into the labour market occured late, whereas their share of the Finnish labour force has long been high. Comparing the two countries we see that the growth of women's representation in Norway has been indirectly aided by governmental intervention, whereas it is the result of more long-standing economic activity and union membership on the part of women in Finland. Thus, a more 'political' explanation of the increase would seem to apply to Norway than to Finland.

Women are clearly over-represented among public sector employees. It is perceivable that their demands for equal representation will be an ingredient in the demise of a centralized union movement, resulting in several separate national federations according to a sectoral division.

Two chapters analyze women within the voluntary sector; their role in the traditional voluntary sector, and within the 'new social movements'. Chapter 7 (by Per Selle and Bjarne Øymyr) analyzes sex segregation of the voluntary society and identifies crucial changes in the role of women within the voluntary sector making the voluntary sector less sex segregated. The gradual decline of the historically so important laymen and teetotal movements, in which women really dominated, and from the mid-1970s, the decline of the traditional social welfare organizations, which were almost completely dominated by women, means that women are gradually 'losing' their own organizational society.

On the other hand, we also see that women do not make up an equal part in the expanding organizational society related to leisure in the broad meaning of the word. Whether this can be explained by ideological differences, i.e. lack of interest, or by organizational structure and culture resulting in certain barriers against women's participation, we do not know. In other words, we do not know whether women gradually will increase their representation in such organizations so as to reflect their status in the labour market or in sports, or whether these organizations will continue to be dominated by men. However, women increasingly do take part in these 'modern' organizations, but it really is men that have so far been the driving force in 'modernizing' the voluntary sector.

These changes imply that the socalled 'complementary' role of women is in a process of decline, while the 'equality' role is increasingly expressed through the organizational society. The authors see the decline of the sex segregation in the voluntary sector as an accurate expression of the more overall changes in the relationship between the sexes.

Chapter 8 (by Kristin Morken and Per Selle) is about the development and change of the Women's Shelter Movement. The women's shelter movement is typical of an alternative welfare organization. The movement emerged primarily out of the feminist movement and is, in fact, the most important institutional expression of the modern women's movement. Typical of the organization of the women's shelter is the 'flat' structure, an organizational structure which does not set up clear divisions between users and staff. This implies that the organization, both ideologically and practically, breaks with the high degree of professionalism found in the welfare state, at the same time as it attempts to prevent both an oversized bureaucracy and strong centralization. Decentralization and proximity to the users are important values.

The women's shelter movement has played an important role in bringing the abuse of women to the public's attention and subsequently in lending legitimacy to the idea that abuse of women is a serious social problem which requires comprehensive government action. The welfare state presently regards abuse of women as a 'public' problem and attempts to solve or reduce the problem through an organization which is relatively removed from the welfare state, both ideologically and organizationally. Understanding the women's shelter movement's special relationship to the welfare state is the key to understanding the nature both of the movement and the welfare state. This relationship demonstrates the most typical aspect of the Scandinavian welfare state and also illustrates what it means to be an alternative movement in a 'state-friendly' society. This organization, as most alternative organizations in Scandinavia, turns towards rather than away from the welfare state. This is a very important feature, and it is necesary to understand its significance. Public financing is considered a right, an approval from the state that one's work is important to society, and consequently the autonomy of the organization is not an issue.

Women within public institutions

This part, approaching women within public institutions, starts by crossing the demarcation between voluntary (private) organizations and public institutions, i.e. women in the corporate channel (Chap. 9, by Christina Bergqvist). A clear pattern of growth is discernible, especially since the mid 1980s, and, futhermore, women are not only increasingly represented within the so-called 'soft' sector related to welfare and education, but there has been a strong increase of women even in corporate-related ministries like the Ministries of Foreign Affairs, Finance, Defence, Industry, and Agriculture as well. Women's overall representation in the corporate sector is still somewhat behind what we find in the electoral channel, but their share is by now as high as about 30 percent.

Bergqvist shows that the increase in women's representation is not only an effect of there being more women into the labour market and increased representation of women within interest organizations. It also has to do with changes in the selection procedures. Here the 'femocrats'; i.e. women bureaucrats with connections to the women's movement and in alliance with the top bureaucracy and female politicians, have been very influential. The so-called Commision on Women's Representation has played a crucial role in Sweden in increasing the representation of women. What we see is not at all passive adaption to external forces, but an active and visible political hand transforming one of the most politically important areas, which has, at the same time, traditionally been one of the most male-dominated arenas.

Chapter 10 (by Per Lægreid) emphasizes the tremendous increase in the number of women employees within the public bureaucracy, an increase which has by no means only been within the so-called 'soft' sectors, i.e welfare and education, even though the position of women is still the most comprehensive here. The increase has been so dramatic since the mid-1980s that it may be fair to characterize it as a silent revolution changing the face of the public bureaucracy; together with 'big business' the embodiment of male dominance. The feminization of the public bureaucracy has come furthest in Norway, but the transformation process is on its way in all the Nordic countries. Even if the increase so far has been most comprehensive at the lower and medium levels, the increase of women in leading positions has also been extensive. In seven of the Norwegian departments there are now more women than men in 'officer in charge' positions.

Lægreid does not find strong structural or cultural forces within the bureaucracy preventing female mobility, and argues that we shall soon see even more women in leading positions and a more equal gender representation across ministries.

Furthermore, and somewhat in contrast with Bergqvist's conclusion concerning corporative representation, Lægreid does not find an active and planned policy to increase women's representation. Rather he sees the changes as mainly externally generated, i.e. as a result of broad changes in women's education and occupational preferences.

This section also contains a chapter on women's participation and representation in local politics, as elected representatives and as leaders (Chap. 11, by Nina Raaum), showing the same extensive improvement in the representation of women. This chapter, together with Richard Matland's chapter on the electoral system (Chap. 12), strongly underscores the extent to which institutional solutions influence women's representation.

Nina Raaum goes beyond national average figures to analyze the extent to which local governments promote gender-equal citizenship, particularily emphasizing differences across regions and types of local governments. She argues that it is not sufficient to emphasize local policies that may empower women, because a main feature of democracy is to participate in local decision-making. She then analyzes the increases in women's representation within the local councils, the most important channel of local decision-making. The representation of women at the local level is, in general, somewhat lower as compared to the regional and national levels. Furthermore, there are still extensive differences between regions and within regions. While the tendency clearly goes in the direction of less difference across regions, there is in some regions a tendency towards increased difference beween central and peripheral local governments. Even so, also in the most 'backward' of these, the number of women councillors is increasing.

As late as in the mid-1950s, a majority of local councils lacked women representatives. However, the merging of local governments which started in the late 1950s and early 1960s increased the size of the local governments and resulted in an increase in the representation of women. This is partly exlained by the fact that this centralization resulted in an increased politicization of the local election. Party lists took over at the expense of local lists. From the end of the 1960s the new political mobilization resulted in another jump in women's representation. However, all throughout the 1970s women were highly underrepresented as leaders. However, during the 1980s we see a very extensive increase in the recruitment of women into élite positions (e.g. as mayors and committee leaders). Again it is interesting to note that this appears at the same time as the committee system becomes rationalized, and more than 50,000 political positions disappear. Centralization seems to empower women.

Raaum gives an uncommonly comprehensive picture of changes in women's representation in Norway, underscoring both structural (demographic, territorial, economic), cultural and political factors, and combinatorial effects. In general, centrality helps increase women's representation. However, the single most important factor is preferential voting, i.e. altering party lists. As many as 40 percent of the lists were altered in 1991, reducing the share of women councillors by between 5 and 10 percent as compared to if the party lists were left unaltered. Ever since 1957 preferential voting has been at women's expense.

Matland deals with a theme rarely perceived as a public institution, the electoral system. Well in line with Raaum's findings and with the general mood of the book, he shows that the electoral system can decisively affect female power. Matland's main argument is that the contours of the electoral system play a crucial role in women closing the representation gap. The political effects of electoral institutions are comprehensive and they are helping women to get represented. In the literature, there is a general acceptance of the fact that proportional representation results in a higher representation of women as compared to single member districts. However, Matland takes as his starting point the proportional system of Norway and emphasizes the consequences of district magnitude, which is the number of seats per district, and the candidate nomination process. The results show that a relatively high average district magnitude, in combination with a nomination process which is sufficiently open to allow for cohesive pressure groups to influence nomination procedures, both are important in understanding why women have been able to increase their representation in Norway so dramatically.

It has been very tempting to explain the high levels of women's representation (especially where equally high levels are found in all Nordic countries) as a reflection of a unique Nordic culture, a culture whose noted passion for equality also includes gender equality. This perspective often ends up by noting that the Nordic culture cannot be easily transplanted to other countries and therefore only provides limited guidance for those wishing to increase female representation in their own countries. The message of this chapter is that while culture may be part of the explanation it is surely not all of it.

Women's attitudes and symbols

Part V looks into the individual level, women as citizens and individual women politicians in an attempt to detect changes in the way women perceive the social environment and communicate with it. Lise Togeby (Chap. 13) shows dramatic changes in women's political tolerance since the 1970s making them much more similar to men. At the beginning of the 1970s there were major differences between women and men on most dimensions of political tolerance; women were less tolerant than men. By the late 1980s, however, this gap had completely vanished. The analysis shows that the gender gap found for the early 1970s could largely be attributed to differences in political involvement between women and men. It could therefore be seen as the result of differences in political socialization. However, part of the difference remains unchanged even when various background factors are controlled for. This 'unexplained difference' is interpreted as a result of a specific female culture.

Against this background it is remarkable that the gender differences in political tolerance had completely disappeared in a matter of merely a couple of decades. The author argues that a cultural shift has taken place during this period, merging female and male cultures and eliminating the previously 'unexplained' gender difference.

Chapter 14 (by Lauri Karvonen, Göran Djupsund and Tom Carlson) analyzes parliamentary speeches in Norway and election campaigns in Finland and seeks to map linguistic differences between male and female politicians over a period of thirty-forty years. Both substantive categories and the analytical content of their messages are analysed. The general expectation is that women politicians behave differently in a situation where they form a relatively large group (ie the 1990s) than several decades earlier, when their number was clearly more limited.

Both stable differences and a trend towards increased similarity were found in the data; the two data sets did not significantly differ from each other on these points. Women still bear the sole responsibility for placing 'women's issues' on the political agenda. They also retain their 'over-representation' with regard to issues related to welfare policies. It is they who to a large extent stand for 'soft' forms of political communication. At the same time they display activity in traditionally 'male' sectors and increasingly attempt to create an image of competence and toughness - typical 'male' forms of communication.

In a dualistic fashion, women therefore try to stand for those things that are normally associated with the traditional (male) role of a politician while simultaneously presenting issues and forms of communication that male politicians seldom touch upon. Indeed, women seem to be faced with a double workload in the world of political communication.

Beyond Scandinavia

Part VI contains only one chapter (Chap. 15, by Einar Berntzen) which offers a cultural contrast big enough to put the Scandinavian case in perspective and lift it out of the narrow West-European context, i.e. the case of Nicaragua. What this case clearly reveals is the role of political institutions in maintaining a steady pace in the political empowerment of women in Scandinavia. The chapter shows that stability matters. In the Nordic context the mobilization of women and the realization of their demands have become institutionalized. In the Nicaraguan context, by contrast, in spite of the revolution and considerable progress in the work to better the position of women, it was a consequence of the civil war rather than the revolution that led to a breakthrough for the political demands of women. However, this did not result in a permanent strengthening of a new political role for women measured in formal political positions as in the Nordic countries.

Furthermore, Berntzen also stresses that culture matters. The cultural impact of the Sandinista revolution was at best ambiguous with respect to the machismo dimension. The war certainly enhanced machismo, but also led to an increased emphasis on the importance of women, but then as mothers. With the virgin on their side, argues Berntzen, Nicaraguan women may have smashed the bourgeoisie to a certain extent, but they still seem to be trapped within the cultural tradition of Catholic marianisimo; i.e. the veneration of the traditional role of women as mothers.

Conclusion

In the Nordic countries, even if there are still important differences across countries and sectors, women are by now fully integrated in all main walks of public decision-making, even if not to an equal extent. The improvement of their position over the last two decades has been so dramatic that it has changed the whole face of politics. It is perhaps no exaggeration to say that the increased proportion of women in political life is the most important single change in Scandinavian social life in the post-war era.

Epilogue

The September 1994 parliamentary election in Sweden brought women's representation to a new all-time high of forty-one percent. In the social democratic cabinet that took office after the election, exactly half of the ministers were women.

References

Baldwin, P. (1990), *The Politics of Social Solidarity*. Cambridge: Cambridge University Press.

Blom, I. (1982), 'A Century of Organized Feminism in Norway'. *Women's Studies Int. Forum*, Vol. 5, No 6:569-574.

Chapman, J. (1993), *Politics, Feminism and the Reformation of Gender*. London: Routledge.

Dahlerup, D. (1992), 'Confusing concepts - confusing reality: a theoretical discussion of the patriarchal state', in Sasson, A. S. (ed.): *Women and the State*. London: Routledge.

Friedland, R. and Alford, R. R. (1991), 'Bringing Society Back In: Symbols, Practices, and Institutional Contradictions', in Powell, W. W. and DiMaggio, P. J. (eds): *The New Institutionalism in Organizational Analysis*. Chicago: University of Chicago Press.

Hernes, H. (1987), *Welfare State and Women Power: Essays in State Feminism*. Oslo: Norwegian University Press.

Holter, H. (1981), 'Om kvinneundertrykkelse, mannsundertrykkelse og herskerteknikker', in Andenæs, K. et al. (eds): *Maktens Ansikter*. Oslo: Gyldendal.

Kuhnle, S. and Selle, P. (1992), 'The Historical Precedent for Government-Nonprofit Cooperation in Norway', in Gidron, B., Kramer, R. M., and Salamon, L. M. (eds): *Government and the Third Sector. Emerging Relationships in Welfare States*. San Francisco: Jossey-Bass.

March, J. G. and Olsen, J. P. (1989), *Rediscovering Institutions*. New York: Free Press.

Pateman, C. (1989), The Disorder of Women: *Democracy, Feminism and Political Theory*. Cambridge: Polity Press.

Piven, F. P. (1990), 'Ideology and the State: Women, Power and the Welfare State', in Gordon, L. (ed.): *Woman, the State, and Welfare*. Madison: University of Wisconsin Press.

Powell, W. W. and DiMaggio, P. J. (1991), *The New Institutionalism in Organizational Analysis*. Chicago: University of Chicago Press.

Seip, A. L. (1984), *Sosialhjelpstaten blir til*. Oslo: Gyldendal.

Selle, P. (1994), 'Marginalisering eller kvinnemakt?', in *Syn og Segn*, No 3: 8-15.

Selle, P. and Øymyr, B. (1994), *Frå verdiorientering til tilbodsorientering. Organisasjonssamfunnet i djuptgripande endring 1940-1990*. Oslo: Samlaget.

Siim, B. (1990), 'Feministiska tolkningar av samspelet mellom kvinnor og välfärdsstaten', *Kvinnovetenskaplig Tidsskrift*, No. 2:13-25.

Skjeie, H. (1992), *Den politiske betydningen av kjønn: En studie av norsk topp-politikk*. Oslo: Institutt for samfunnsforsking.

Skocpol, T. (1985), 'Bringing the State Back In: Strategies of Analysis in Current Research, in Evans, P. et al. (eds): *Bringing the State Back In*. New York: Cambridge University Press.

Steinsmo, S., Thelen, K., Longstret, F. (eds) (1992), *Structuring Politics. Historical Institutionalism in Comparative Analysis*. Cambridge: Cambridge University Press. Analysis.

The political representation of women: a bird's eye view[1]

Nina Cecilie Raaum

Women and political power: what does the research tell us about women's political practice?

When we compare theories about women's political status with the data on women's political representation, we find a discrepancy between theory and practice. This discrepancy emerges, basically, from the fact that theory tends to focus on women's lack of authority and their institutional powerlessness, while women's political practice shows that they are to an increasing degree and very rapidly, being mobilized as decision-makers in public policy. For the most part, we have learned how women are alienated, made invisible and excluded from public decision-making processes; ie that women are marginalized in the political system. The political mobilization of Scandinavian women represents a sharp contrast to these powerlessness models. In 1986 Norway made history when a new Government, led by a female prime minister, was formed consisting of nearly 50 percent women. In 1991 a new record was set when half of the major political parties had an elected leader who was a woman (Skjeie 1992). After the 1993 election, 39.4 percent of the members of the Norwegian parliament, the Storting, were women, and in the system of government committees the percentage of women is approaching 40 percent. At the local and regional governmental levels, female representatives account for between 30 and 40 percent of all elected representatives, and at the most recent local election the number of female mayors was doubled.

The political status of women has changed dramatically in the course of the past two decades. In the early 1970s women were virtually absent from Scandinavian politics, while at the end of the 1980s their political presence was very apparent. It is in this area of political life, perhaps more than in any other area of society, that women have been willing and able to exercise power. For some reason, however,

[1] Thanks to Gunnar Grendstad, Knut Heidar, Ola Listhaug, Anne-Hilde Nagel, Per Selle, Hege Skjeie and Kristin Strømnes for useful comments.

there has been a striking lack of interest in studying this development empirically. Political scientists have not continued the tradition of earlier research on the mobilization of new voter groups among workers and women (Rokkan 1970), a process which after 1970 has primarily involved the mobilization of women. Research in women's studies, on the other hand, has been more concerned with the political consequences of social power relationships between the sexes than with the integration of women into positions in public decision-making fora. In Norway Heidar (1988) and Skjeie (1992) have carried out empirical studies of women's participation in top-level national politics (within the electoral channel) during the 1980s. With the exception of these two studies, Norwegian research in this area has primarily been based on data from the 1970s (Albrektsen 1977; Hellevik and Skard 1985; Hernes 1982; Haavio-Mannila 1985; Lafferty 1978, 1980; Means 1973 etc). In the other Nordic countries there are more recent empirical studies of women's political involvement (Andersen, Christensen, Langberg, Siim and Torpe 1993; Dahlerup 1989; SOU 1990:44; Togeby 1989). These studies, however, focus on the direct participation of women as fellow citizens, and provide little detailed information about women's political representation. With the exception of government statistics, which are somewhat general, we have little knowledge about women's position as decision-makers in the political institutions of today.[2] We know considerably more about women's powerlessness than about their power.

The question is whether our theoretical understanding of women and politics is in the process of becoming outdated. Have we become ensnared in *the myths* regarding women's traditional powerlessness which draw attention from the new power of women? Does existing research provide us with the 'cognitive glasses' which enable us to *see* women's political marginalization and *overlook* women's political integration and competence? Research in the field done in the late 1980s hints that the answer to the above is yes. Three Scandinavian contributions are of central importance here: Hernes (1987) and Siim (1988,1990) have indicated that the state can contribute to the realization of a woman-friendly society, and Skjeie (1992) has

---

[2] I have been in contact with the central bureaus of statistics and equal rights authorities in all of the Scandinavian countries in an attempt to gain detailed statistics on the political representation of women. Most countries only have systematic statistics covering female percentages of elected representatives at the national, regional and local levels. As for female representation in political bodies, which involves indirect elections (from among elected representatives) there is little data available. No complete surveys have been published, either by researchers or the authorities. We therefore have a relatively weak basis for the evaluation of women's integration into political leadership. As far as I know, Dahlerup (1989) is the only scholar who has published data of this kind for the Nordic countries from the 1980s, though this material also is mostly limited to relatively general surveys of female access to the base level in politics, ie representation in public bodies.

criticized the hypotheses concerning the political marginalization of women. In order to arrive at a deeper theoretical understanding of women and politics it is necessary to focus less on perspectives related to powerlessness, and to develop some of the finer points revealed by recent research in Scandinavian women's studies. We must confront existing theories on the political status and mobilization of women with the empirical data resulting from women's practice and experience by studying women's representation at various levels and areas of the political system over time. For this reason, I first discuss a number of central hypotheses regarding women's status as political representatives and decision-makers. Subsequently, I conduct an empirical analysis of women's entry into public decision-making bodies, ie elected bodies in the electoral channel and government committees in the corporative channel. For each of these areas, I present certain key figures for all of the Scandinavian countries. This data confirms the findings of previous studies which indicated a pattern of female mobilization shared by all the Nordic countries (Dahlerup 1989). I have thus chosen to delimit the more detailed empirical analysis to one country, Norway, both because there was more data available for this country (through the Norwegian Social Science Data Services) and because this allows for a more detailed analysis of women's political integration in the various levels and areas of the public decision-making system. The data was extracted from public election statistics, the state and local government committee archives.[3]

Ways of understanding women's political status

Research in women's studies inspired by the new women's movement in the early 1970s criticized political scientists for their lack of interest in the political significance of gender, and for their use of a narrowly defined and sexist definition of politics which excluded women. It was argued that *the personal is political* and

---

[3] The data has been prepared by the Norwegian Social Science Data Services (NSD) in Bergen. The database on government committees contains information on all government committees, executive committees, and councils which were active for one or more years in the period from 1980-1990. This corresponds to the data presented in Stortingsmelding (report to parliament) no. 7 and 7a for 1980-89. In accordance with a bill passed by the Storting in 1983 and the Norwegian Act pertaining to equal rights (Section 21) on gender representation on government committees, the Norwegian Central Bureau of Statistics has carried out comprehensive surveys of local and regional government elections starting in 1984. The statistical analyses of local and central government committees was done by John-Erik Ågotnes at NSD, but the presentation and interpretation of this data is my responsibility alone. NSD is in no way responsible for either the analysis or interpretation of the other data.

that power and democracy in all contexts, including private relations between the sexes, were important (Albrektsen 1977; Elsthain 1981; Jones and Jónasdóttir 1988; Jónasdóttir 1988, 1991; Halsaa 1992; Holter 1984; Okin 1991; Pateman 1983, 1989; Phillips 1991a, 1991b, 1992; Raaum and Skogerbø 1993; Stiehm 1984). Criticism was directed at the distinction between the public and private spheres which was inherent in liberalism. The exclusion of women from the public sphere, work and politics, and the subordination of the domestic sphere were the basis for characterizing society as a patriarchy, ie a system in which men have authority and power over women (Dahlerup 1987). This criticism also involved a categorical antipathy towards the state (Piven 1990), at the same time as it represented a rejection of the aims and procedures of representative democracy (Phillips 1992). In line with the women's movement's visions of a participant democracy, the woman-friendly society was portrayed as a nobler form of democracy in contrast to men's democracy of élites and competition. For that reason it was obvious that the finished democracy would be a completely different society than today's unfinished democracy, 'A society in which men and women share political representation is *naturally* quite different from our society today' (Dahlerup and Haavio-Mannila 1985:160, my emphasis). The road to real democracy lay outside routine politics, and focus was directed towards everyday life and women's alternative political actions and values (Jaquette 1974, 1984; Phillips 1991a,1992; Randall 1991; Stiehm 1984).

The political status of women has been studied using both macro- and micro-models. Macro-level approaches, most often based on different theoretical variations of patriarchy, have analyzed the influence on the state and society of masculine norms which suppress women. Studies at the meso- and micro-levels have been concerned with women's lack of political resources and competence, and the fact that women are excluded from politics by its content and the way it functions. Research in women's studies has raised fundamental questions which will have consequences for further research on democratic ideals and practice. Such research has provided insight into the conditions for the integration of new voter groups into the political decision-making processes, and the mutual relationship between democratization of the state and the society at large (Held 1991; Phillips 1992). However, the combination of skepticism vis a vis the state and enthusiasm for an extended political sphere has, paradoxically, led researchers away from conventional politics, towards the private lives of women and their participation *outside* the *public* and formal decision-making processes. This may explain the relative lack of interest in studying women's participation in political institutions which have the authority to make binding collective decisions. One may, of course, object, and argue that participation does not guarantee real influence. However, it is, if nothing else, a necessary prerequisite to influencing public policy.

Claims regarding marginalization come in basically two varieties. The first is that politics is less relevant for women than men, because the political agenda and the political processes reflect men's values and interests. As my intention is to illustrate women's entry into the decision-making bodies of the welfare state, I shall not consider the question of the relevance of politics for women. Instead, I shall focus on the other of the two varieties of marginalization, ie the issue of women's status and their possibility to have an influence as representatives, or decision-makers, in political institutions. Within this type, we find two types of marginalization, one related to the *vertical* and one to the *horizontal* division of labour between men and women in politics. The vertical division of labour is concerned with the position of men and women in political hierarchies, while the horizontal division of labour focuses on the various policy areas in which men and women work.

The *hierarchical* marginalization of women is visible in the decreasing number of women representatives as one progresses upwards in political hierarchies. The under-representation of women is not only reflected in the fact that the proportion of female representatives is lower than the proportion of women in the general population. We are dealing with a more dramatic effect in which this under-representation is amplified by the representatives' ability to influence political decisions. This reflects a phenomenon which Putnam (1976) called 'the law of increasing disproportion', which means that the disproportionate advantage of male, educated, high-status élites recruits increases as we move up the political stratification system. In Scandinavian research in women's studies, this phenomenon is reflected in the hypothesis concerning '*the iron law of politics*', ie 'the more the power, the fewer the women'. In other words, the proportion of women in political positions of power is lower than their proportion of ordinary representatives should imply (Dahlerup and Haavio-Mannila 1985). The political mobilization of women has thus been described, in relatively imprecise terms, as 'a development from powerlessness without participation, to relative powerlessness with participation' (Haavio-Mannila 1985), and 'power but not command' (Halsaa 1986:118).

When women, contrary to the predictions of the 'iron law', climbed quickly in the political hierarchies, the optimists were warned. It was claimed that women politicians were less representative of their gender than men (Sinkkonen 1985), and that women were being coopted in patriarchal bureaucracies (Randall 1990). Women were turning into 'men in skirts', and had to play down their identities as women.

For that reason it was seen as wasted energy to strive for increased female representation. 'The objective is not to gain a share of men's position of power, but to do away with all kinds of oppression, and that is why the [women's] movement has also started to use other organizational forms' (Dahlerup and Gulli 1985:25). Another objection was that the increasing proportion of women in politics would have marginal significance, because women were being integrated into *shrinking institutions*; women were going in where power was going out (Holter 1981:76). This hypothesis was primarily based on the growth of non-parliamentary decision-making bodies, and the establishment of corporatist decision-making structures which favored economic interests (Halsaa 1986). These interpretations have been criticized recently in light of new empirical findings. Skjeie (1992) emphasizes that there is not empirical support for the claim that parliaments are becoming less politically effective,[4] and Skjeie and Teigen (1993) illustrate that there is no basis for the claim that increased female participation leads to more uneven recruitment to, or lower competence in elected bodies.

The main problem with the iron law hypothesis is not its ability to characterize women's position in the political system at a given point in time. Its main weakness is that it is not suitable for diachronic analysis. The mobilization of new voter groups in political hierarchies goes through various stages and is subject to time-lags (Rokkan 1970). Therefore, there is good reason to believe that the broad mobilization of women representatives from the early 1970s is now continuing through the integration of women into new areas and levels in politics. In that case, it is more pertinent to talk about a *lag hypothesis* than an iron law hypothesis. In order to gain some insight into which of these hypotheses is most suitable, we must study the development over *time*, and map the proportion of women at *various levels* in the political hierarchies. If the iron law hypothesis holds true, then the relative under-representation of women upwards in the various strata will be maintained even though more women are recruited to political activity. The lag hypothesis, on the other hand, claims that the relative under-representation of women will decline over time.

---

[4] Skjeie emphasizes that 'the traditional preference for 'the decline of parliaments' thesis has recently been challenged by the new thesis on 'resurgence'. Majority governments have been replaced by minority governments: the trend in recent years is, furthermore, towards weaker minority governments. Governments cannot rely to the same extent on permanent support in parliament, but instead base their existence on insecure and shifting coalitions. Scandinavian parliaments have become forums for real bargaining, as witnessed in the growth of floor and committee activities. Thus long-term trends in the relationship of parliament to cabinet might more properly be characterized as one of 'ebb and flow'" (Skjeie 1992:72).

The *horizontal* division of labour in politics is expressed in the predominance of women within reproductive sectors such as education, health and social policy, the so-called 'soft' sectors, while men are more active in the productive or so-called 'hard' sectors (Hernes and Hänninen-Salmelin 1985). 'Soft' values are often described as 'weak' values, and the horizontal division of labour is thus presented as a *functional marginalization*, 'a process of their [women's] exclusion by the more influential men' (Dahlerup and Haavio-Mannila 1985:165). This presentation of functional forms of marginalization is highly problematic. First of all, we can hardly argue that women will change politics and at the same time maintain that they ought to have the same preferences as men. Secondly, it has been under-communicated that Nordic women are most active, and in the majority, in those policy areas and administrative levels which are responsible for the largest share of public expenditure: in education, and in health and social services, and at the local and regional level. The growth in the expenditure of the welfare state has primarily taken place at the local government level. In Norway expenditure on education and health and social services in 1990 accounted for more than 70 percent of total government expenditure (Central Bureau of Statistics 1992). From this point of view, women are being integrated into *expanding* political institutions.

Furthermore, Skjeie's studies of women's political integration into the Norwegian Storting and the Norwegian Government show that there is no empirical support for the hypothesis that women are in all respects and areas functionally marginalized. This hypothesis is only relevant if there is empirical documentation showing that women are excluded from those areas which are highly valued, *and* that this gender-based division of labour is contrary to what the women themselves want. The expressed preferences of Storting representatives indicate that there is no systematic support for this claim either in the distribution of ministerial positions or of committee memberships. There is, on the other hand, a certain functional division of labour among the parliamentary committees. Women are over-represented on the committees dealing with social services, church and education, and consumer and administrative affairs, while men are over-represented on the committees dealing with finance, transport, foreign affairs and agriculture. However, and this is an important reservation, politicians of both sexes place a high priority on the 'soft' policy areas, and the distribution of women and men does not provide a clear-cut indication of tendencies toward concentration in any particular policy area (Skjeie 1992:26). The growth in the welfare state has primarily represented an expansion of the so-called 'soft' policy areas in which women are best represented, and the 'softer' values and policy areas are certainly not synonymous with weak values and marginal issues which are being 'sidelined' in public policy. It must be emphasized that the distinction between 'soft' and 'hard' issues may be a bit confusing when used to characterize power relationships. This distinction does not allow for sector status, or for the nature of the decision-making process within the respective sectors. The so-called 'soft' sectors, which are responsible for the lion's share of the national budget, must make tough, if not virtually impossible, decisions on whether to give higher priority to, eg building more homes for care of the elderly, or building more daycare centers for children. Similarly, many of the decisions in the so-called 'hard' sectors pertain to issues which are vital in determining the quality of life for the population, eg creating and protecting a physical environment through planning and construction of good neighborhood environments, safe communications, and initiating environmental measures.

Skjeie's study strikes a powerful blow to the belief that it is difficult for women to gain access to important political positions. However, it is important to emphasize that Skjeie's conclusions are based on an analysis of relatively few representatives in the Norwegian Storting and the Norwegian Government at the end of the 1980s. Thus far, the marginalization hypothesis remains uncontested for all other areas of political life. It is thus crucial that Skjeie's research be carried on through studies of women's entry into decision-making bodies which comprise the vast majority of our political representatives: in elected bodies at the local and regional levels, and in the government committee system. This is an absolute necessity in order to make it possible to evaluate the nature of the political system as a whole. Furthermore, we must study the development over time, and evaluate both quantitative and qualitative aspects of women's representation. I shall therefore analyze the political mobilization of women along three dimensions which can illustrate the breadth, depth, and extent of this representation (Cohen 1971, Lafferty and Raaum 1990). *The breadth* is a quantitative question of the percentage of women among decision-makers. The *depth* of the mobilization is a qualitative question of how women representatives participate. Is the political system characterized by 'the iron law of politics' according to which under-representation of women is increased as one progresses up the political hierarchies, or are women mobilized at new levels through different stages of the mobilization process? The *extent* of the mobilization is an institutional question of where women participate. Is there still a functional division of labour which is expressed in the participation of men and women in different policy areas, or are women in the process of developing their own political space in which to act? I will analyze these questions of women's access to the system of public governance by looking at elected decision-making bodies on the basis of territorial representation and corporatist bodies on the basis of the representation of interested parties.

Territorial representation: elected bodies

A representative democracy comprises elected bodies at national, regional and local levels (in Norway, *stat, fylkeskommune* and *kommune*). First, I shall discuss a few basic features of women's participation in parliamentary decision-making bodies.[5] Subsequently, I shall concentrate on women's representation in local politics by studying women's integration at different levels and policy areas in Norwegian local government.

Scandinavia stands out in an international perspective in that there is a high percentage of women in the highest levels of political life. In 1991, the world average for women representatives in parliament was 11 percent. At the same time, the European average was 12.5 percent (IPU 1991). In the Nordic countries, women's parliamentary representation has grown steadily since the early 1970s. The percentage of women is highest in the Finnish and Norwegian parliaments (39 percent), and in Denmark and Sweden the percentages are 34 and 33 respectively. Iceland has had the lowest proportion of women throughout the period of mobilization. In the early 1970s women were less well represented in Governments than in parliament, but today the percentage of women in both institutions is nearly the same. The Icelandic Government, however, has relatively few women, and in Sweden and Norway the percentage of women in the Government is higher than that in the parliament. With the exception of Iceland, the 'iron law' hypothesis of increasing disproportion does not apply to national, top-level politics in the 1990s, as far as the relationship between parliaments and Governments is concerned.

The political parties have to varying degrees recruited female representatives to the parliaments. In the Norwegian Storting the percentage of women has been consistently highest in the socialist parties and lowest in the right-wing parties (see Table 2). The exception in this respect is the Norwegian Conservative party, in which the percentage of women has been constant since the mid-1970s, and the Socialist Left Party, in which the proportion of women has fallen following the

---

[5] For a closer look at women's political integration in the Norwegian Storting and Government see Skjeie (1991, 1992).

Table 1
Women in central government 1960-1994. Percent women (% W)

	1970s YEAR	%W	1980s YEAR	%W	1990s YEAR	%W
A. PARLIAMENT[1]						
- Denmark	1971	17	1984	26	1990	34
- Finland	1972	22	1983	31	1992	39
- Iceland	1971	5	1983	15	1991	24
- Norway	1973	24	1981	26	1993	39
- Sweden	1971	14	1982	28	1991	33[2]
B. MINISTERIAL POSITIONS[3]						
- Denmark	1971	11	1984	25	1994	32
- Finland	1972	6	1983	18	1992	35
- Iceland	1971	7	1983	10	1987	10
- Norway	1973	13	1982	24	1993	42
- Sweden	1971	11	1982	28	1991	38

Source: [1] 1970s and 1980s: Dahlerup (1989:20-21); 1990s: Amtrådsforeningen i Danmark; Equal Status Coucil, Helsiniki, 1994; Statistical Bureau of Iceland (1993): Elections to the Althing; Statistiska Centralbyrån: Statistiska Meddelanden (Be31SM9201). [2] At the last Swedish election in the 1980s, ie the 1988 election, women won 38% of the seats. Thus the 1991 figure shows a decline in the percentage of women in the Swedish parliament. [3] Haavio-Mannila (1985:180-183); Folketingets Præsidium (1991): Folketinget after the election of 12 December 1990.

party's growth in the Storting. Today three of the parties represented in the Storting have around 40 percent or more women representatives. In the social democratic Norwegian Labour party, which has the most members of parliament, half of the representatives are women. And in two of the liberal parties, the Centre party and the Christian People's party, there are 44 and 39 percent women representatives, respectively. Similar variations between the parties were found in all of the Nordic countries in the early 1980s (Haavio-Mannila et al. 1985), and official election statistics show that the partisan differences still remain. However, these variations do not show a systematic alignment along a socialist/non-socialist cleavage. In Sweden, as in Norway, the percentage of women is highest in the social democratic party. But in Iceland, Finland and Denmark it is the Conservative party

(SjalfstæÙisflokker), the Coalition party and the liberal Center Democrats respectively, which have most female members of parliament (Dahlerup 1989, Lovenduski and Norris 1993).

Table 2
Female Storting representatives by party. Elections of 1973 and 1981 excepted.
Percent women. (N=total number of seats)

Party	1969	1977	1985	1989	1993
The Socialist Left Party	- (0)	50 (2)	50 (6)	41 (17)	31 (13)
The Labour Party	15 (74)	26 (76)	42 (71)	51 (63)	49 (67)
The Left Party	- (13)	- (2)	- (0)	- (0)	- (1)
The Centre Party	- (20)	8 (12)	17 (12)	27 (11)	44 (32)
The Christian People's Party	7 (14)	14 (22)	25 (16)	36 (14)	39 (13)
The Conservative Party	7 (29)	29 (41)	30 (50)	30 (37)	29 (28)
The Progress Party	- (0)	- (0)	- (2)	5 (22)	10 (10)
Future for Finmark	*	*	*	- (0)	- (0)
The Red				- (1)	
Alliance	*	*	- (0)	- (0)	- (1)
Total	9 (150)	24(155)	34(157)	36(165)	39(165)

Source: Skjeie og Teigen (1993) and public election statistics.
* = No list entered.

The political mobilization of women in *local government* was a process which was parallel to that taking place in national politics. Table 3 shows the representation of Scandinavian women in elected bodies at *regional* and *local* levels. Iceland has no regional level of government and Finland does not have direct election of representatives at this level. In the other three countries women are better represented in elected bodies at regional than at local levels. This is particularly true of Norway

36   *Women in Nordic Politics*

and Sweden, where female representation is 10 percent higher at the regional than at the local level. In Norway, the main reason for this difference is preferential voting, ie the opportunity to change party lists at local elections. The percentage of women on the lists is equally high at both local and regional levels, but voters tend to alter party lists more often at local elections, and the result is often in women's

Table 3
Women in regional and local government 1970-1993. Percent women (%W)

	1970s[1]		1980s[1]		1990s[2]	
	Year	%W	Year	%W	Year	%W
A. REGIONAL COUNCILS						
- Denmark (amtsråd)	1974	8	1985	29	1993	32
- Norway (fylkesting)	1975	25	1983	33	1991	39
- Sweden (landsting)	1973	19	1985	37	1991	43
B. LOCAL COUNCILS						
- Denmark (kommunale råd)	1974	12	1985	24	1993	28
- Finland (kuunanvaltuusto)	1972	15	1988	27	1992	30
- Iceland (sveitsartjorn)	1974	4	1986	19	1990	22[3]
- Norway (kommunestyre)	1971	15	1987	31	1991	29
- Sweden (fullmäktig	1970	14	1985	30	1991	34

Sources: [1] Dahlerup (1989); Haavio-Manila (1985:87); Women and Men in Nordic Countries, Nordic Coucil of Ministers, Copenhagen 1989 [2] Denmark: Danske kommuner nr. 37/1993 (tillæg om kommunalvalget); Danmarks Amtsåd nr.17/93; Iceland: Statistical Abstracts of Iceland, Local Government Elections 1950-90 (Hagastofa Islands), Stefanìa Trasutaddòttir (1992) Verkaskipting ì sveitsarstjòrum (Jafneréttisrìd); Finland: Central Statistical Office of Finland, Municipal Elections 1992, Helsinki 1993. Norway: Local Elections 1991, Central Statistical Office of Norway; Sweden: Sweden: Central Statistical Office (Be 31SM 9201).
[3] Figure for 201 small councils. In the larger urban councils (N=31) the figure was 32% in 1990, 19% in 1982 and 8% in 1974.

disfavor (Hellevik and Bjørklund 1991). In spite of this tendency, the general trend is that women's proportion of the elected representatives has risen considerably in the last 20 years; first at the regional level, and somewhat later at the local level. In the early 1970s the proportion of women was lower than 15 percent in all Nordic countries, and in the mid-1980s the figure had reached nearly 25 percent or more in all countries except Iceland. A few years later, after the first elections of the 1990s, the figure has mounted to 30 percent or more in all countries, still with the exception of Iceland.

The question then becomes whether the relative under-representation of women is increasingly disproportionate in the higher levels of local government, in accordance with the iron law hypothesis, or whether women are gradually being integrated into local government leadership, as the lag hypothesis implies.[6] I shall consider this question in more detail on the basis of the Norwegian data. The elected, superordinate bodies of government at the local and regional levels are the local councils (*kommunestyrer)* at the local level, and the regional councils (*fylkesting*) at the regional level. The executive committees, the *formannskap* and *fylkesutvalg*, respectively, are elected indirectly from among the members of the local and regional councils. Most often, they are delegated considerable authority in local and regional policy matters. Mayors are elected by the members of the local and regional councils from among their members. They also chair the meetings of these councils. Both local and regional government also have *sektorutvalg* (sector committees) which are responsible for specific policy areas. The legal foundation for such committees is provided by the Norwegian Act pertaining to local government as well as additional legislation. The members are elected by the members of the local and regional councils.

With the exception of the sector committee members and mayors, the percentage of women is consistently higher in regional than local bodies. Relatively speaking, however, the increase has been equally great at both levels (Table 4). Some people have interpreted the slight decline in female representation after the last local election in 1991 as an expression of a 'political backlash', though there is hardly basis for such a conclusion. First of all, one election is not a sufficient basis from which to draw general conclusions regarding new developments. Secondly, we see that in the 1991 election female representation was strengthened in *all* areas other than regional and local councils. Women are still under-represented in elected bodies relative to their share of the general population, but after 1983 the 'iron law effect' disappears in the relationship between local councils and local executive committees. Women's representation in sector committees is strengthened evenly in both local and regional government. It is now approaching 40 percent, which is a higher percentage than

---

[6] Political leaders are representatives in the executive committees of regional and local councils, sector committee chairpersons, mayors and deputy mayors. Members of regional councils, regional sector committees, local councils, and local sector committees are designated as ordinary members.

Table 4
Percentage of women - regional and local government bodies. 1975-1991.
Percent women and number of representatives (N)

	1975	1979	1983	1987	1991
REGIONAL:					
- Regional council	24.9 (1099)	28.8 (1099)	32.8 (1101)	40.6 (1101)	38.6 (991)
- Regional council exec.committees	*	21.7	30.1	36.1 (226)	37.7 (220)
- Mayors	0 (18)	0 (18)	5.6 (18)	0 (18)	11.1 (18)
- Deputy Mayors	*	16.7 (18)	33.3 (18)	38.9 (18)	55.6 (18)
- Members of sector committees	*	*	29.9 (11085)	36.1 (5838)	37.1 (3896)
- Chairpersons - sector committees	*	*	21.5 (1840)	25.8 (898)	30.0 (583)
LOCAL:					
- Local councils	15.4 (13545)	22.8 (13772)	23.8 (13806)	31.2 (13648)	28.5 (13073)
- Local council exec. committees	*	15.3	22.0	28.0	28.0 (3347)
- Members of sector committees	*	*	31.2 (126537)	36.1 (93496)	36.4 (74798)
- Chairpersons - sector committees	*	*	16.2 (25833)	18.8 (15294)	19,6 (13626)
- Mayors	1.8 (445)	2.6 (454)	3.6 (454)	6.5 (438)	12.5 (439)
- Deputy Mayors	*	*	*	*	27.0 (439)

Source: Statistisk Sentralbyrå, electoral statistics.
* No data available.

in local councils.[7] One explanation for this might be that the members of the sector committees are chosen by the local council representatives following the recommendations of the political parties, ie without the candidate preferences of the voters influencing the result. There has also been a significant increase in the number of female committee chairpersons, though the percentage here is still lower than for committee members in general. The absence of women in leading positions is most obvious in the position of mayor. After the 1991 election, however, the number of female mayors doubled, and the percentage of women deputy mayors is now considerable. The iron law hypothesis still has empirical support in the area of recruitment of women as mayors, deputy mayors and committee chairpersons, ie in positions in which the leadership is individual, and not delegated to peer committees or representative bodies. This finding is in line with that revealed in comparative studies of national electoral systems, which show that the representation of women suffers considerably in systems involving majority vote in single-member constituencies (Lovenduski and Norris 1993, see also Matland in this volume). The fewer the number of representatives to be elected, and the fewer seats up for grabs, the slower the mobilization of new voter groups.

This picture may be elaborated on by taking a closer look at gender representation in the sector committees. To what degree does this reflect a functional division of labour between the sexes, and how does the recruitment of women vary between the different sectors? Table 5 shows women's percentage of members and chairpersons in sector committees at the *local* level, which include far more representatives than the sector committees at the regional level. From 1983 until 1991 the percentage of female representatives increased by five percent. This relatively slight increase must be seen in light of the local government reforms of the 1980s, which halved the number of local government committees from 23,833 to 13,262. The number of committee members was cut by over 50,000. This implies an average loss of more than 110 representatives in each Norwegian local government, which is a significant number considering that half of the Norwegian local governments in 1990 had fewer than 4300 inhabitants. We must also consider that the increase of five percent only covers the three last election periods. There is considerable reason to believe that the percentage of women was much lower in the 1970s, as in other local government

---

[7] The provisions of the Norwegian Act pertaining to Equal Rights which stipulate that at least 40 percent of the members of government committees must be female and at least 40 percent male can not be enforced with regard to *elected* committees as they can with *appointed* committees. These provisions, however, state that the 40 percent rule is meant to function as a guideline, and each year the state equal rights ombudsman publishes a list of local councils which fail to meet the requirement.

bodies. However, there is no data available to illustrate the development over a longer period of time.[8]

Table 5
Local govt. sector committees by area of responsibility. Election periods 1984-1987, 1988-1991 and 1992-1995. Number of committee members, percent women members and chairpersons

Area	Number of comm.members (N)			Percentage of female members			Percentage of female chairpersons		
	1983	1987	1991	1983	1987	1991	1983	1987	1991
Adm./ finance	17519	16247	15805	26	33	33	15	17	17
Edu- cation	8856	5726	4282	42	46	45	20	24	27
Health/ Social Services	15678	9451	9174	51	53	50	31	39	37
Church/ Cultural Affairs	12519	8529	7695	33	37	38	19	22	25
Techn. matters	13597	8795	7157	21	25	26	7	11	12
Public enterpr.	22612	17319	14159	20	26	27	5	7	8
Other (**)	35756	27428	16056	33	40	42	22	25	27
Sum	126537	93495	74798	31	36	36	15	19	20

Source: NSD: Data om kommunale og fylkeskommunale utvalg. (Data on local and regional committees).

* The committee chairperson's gender was not given for approx. one-third of the committees. In official statistics the percentage of women chairs is calculated on the basis of the total number of chairpersons. This means that the percentage of women chairpersons is underestimated. I have assumed for the purposes of this study that the 'not given' category reflects the same general distribution among the committees, and the percentage of female chairpersons has been calculated on the basis of the total number of chairpersons for which gender was given.
** Committee with several areas of responsibility, can not be placed in categories above.

---

[8] Official statistics are limited to the 1980s. Data registration was initiated by the national authorities in accordance with the requirements of the Norwegian Equal Rights Act, which stipulate that both sexes shall be represented in government bodies.

Local politics still shows signs of a gender-based functional division of labour. Women are best represented in committees responsible for education, health and social services, and cultural affairs. But committees with more varied responsibilities[9] also have a relatively high percentage of women members. Sector committees responsible for technical matters and public enterprises have relatively fewer female members. A similar pattern was found in the other Nordic countries (Dahlerup 1989). However, the functional division of labour declines over time; the increase in women's representation in the 1980s has been greatest in those areas in which women were originally least represented. The percentage of female committee members and chairpersons is, as previously mentioned, still disproportionate. Nevertheless, it ought to be mentioned that women are most often in charge of sector committees with a high percentage of female members, which illustrates the general lag tendency in the process of political mobilization. The under-representation of women in political leadership is thus not necessarily an expression of the existence of 'male' structures which bar women from politics. A simpler, more plausible explanation, which may be derived from the lag hypothesis, is that activation at lower levels must reach a certain point before there will be activation at the next level. Data from the Norwegian government committee archives confirms that the mobilization of female leaders increases considerably when the percentage of women among the representatives passes 30 percent (Raaum 1994).

The political mobilization of women goes through various *stages*. The mobilization of the 1970s broadened female representation, but women were still under-represented in leading positions in local and regional executive committees. During the following decade the depth of female representation was increased in that women were integrated into local political leadership. Women are still under-represented relative to their percentage of the general population, but women are being increasingly recruited to leading positions in regional and local government. In political positions such as mayor and committee chair women are still under-represented. In general, however, the lag hypothesis gains more empirical support than the iron law hypothesis when the development over time is considered. Whether women's real influence will increase in line with their relative number is, of course, another question. But there is no empirical evidence to suggest that women have less influence than men in comparable positions. Furthermore, in order to enlarge our

---

[9] The reorganization of the committee system and the loosening up of local government regulation has resulted in many local authorities choosing organizational models which are different from those used in the model with four or five committees. Committees with more varied responsibilities may thus also cover areas encompassed by the other categories in Table 5.

picture of women's political status, we must supplement this picture with data concerning the representation of women in the corporative system of government. Is mobilization in the corporative channel a parallel to that in the electoral channel, or does it show a part of the state where women are not allowed, as Hernes (1982) concluded in the early 1980s?

The corporative system of government: government committees

The corporative system of government consists of government committees, arrangements for public hearings, negotiations and various other informal forms of contact between public and private institutions and organizations. The corporatist networks are a supplement to elected government, and are especially directed towards those sectors of society in which the central government is reluctant to regulate activities through majority decisions. Examples of such areas might include the market and organizations in the voluntary sector, which would lose much of their respective uniqueness as 'market' and 'voluntary activity' if subjected to considerable government regulation. In Norwegian local government, as opposed to the central government, corporatist decision-making bodies are not highly institutionalized. The few local government committees which do have representatives from private business and organizations today are most often at the margins of the decision-making processes (Thorsteinsen 1992). The following analysis of women's representation in the corporative channel is therefore limited to the *central* government level, and to executive committees, councils, and committees, subsequently to be referred to as *committees*, as it is difficult to gain access to data on the other forms of contact. The committees in question have members from voluntary organizations, public and private institutions and businesses, local and regional government, government administration and parliament (Hult, Skeie and Ågotnes 1992). The number of committees has fallen considerably in the 1980s, from 1072 in 1980 to 656 in 1992. The majority of the committees (93 percent) are standing committees, and the remaining, ad hoc, committees are primarily responsible for investigation and reporting on specific issues. Furthermore, it is important to emphasize that the committee system is not peopled by only a few persons, the representatives normally sit on only one committee.[10]

---

[10] The 4542 committee positions existing in 1992 were filled by 4331 people.

The corporative channel has been the most male-dominated part of the political system. Early in the mid-1970s women represented only 10 percent of all committee members (Hernes 1982). In Norway, this figure grew rapidly to 27 percent in 1981, in contrast to the remaining Scandinavian countries, which lagged behind (Hernes and Hänninen-Salmelin 1985). During the 1980s, there was a relatively sizeable increase in women's corporative representation in all of the Scandinavian countries, but Norway is still ahead of the others in this respect (Table 6).

Table 6
Percentage of women (% W) in national committees

NORWAY YEAR %W	DENMARK YEAR %W	ICELAND YEAR %W	SWEDEN YEAR %W	FINLAND YEAR %W
1967 7	1965 5	1971 3	1965 6	1960 1
1977 24	1975 9	1979 6	1975 11	1975 9
1986 32	1985 16	1985 11	1985 23	1985 16
1992 38	1992 27	1990 17	1991 42	1992*

Source: 1960-85: Bergqvist 1994:84; Dahlerup (1989); Det statlige utvalgsarkivet 1994 (Governmental Committee Archive); Ligestillingsrådets årsberetning 1992 (Equality Status Council's yearly report 1992); Equal Status Council of Iceland 1993.
* Not available.

The under-representation of women has been explained with reference to the fact that they are only to a limited degree part of, and to an even smaller degree leaders of, those organizations and institutions which participate in the corporative decision-making process. Thus we are dealing with a structural phenomenon which reflects the weaker position and lack of élite status of women in economic life and in the public administration (Hernes 1982; Hernes and Hänninen-Salmelin 1985).

The existence of the government committee archives in Norway allows for more detailed analysis of women's positions in the committee system. The percentage of women in national government committees increased steadily throughout the 1980s (Table 7). Among members and deputy members, the increase was between 13 and 14 percent, and in early 1990 women represented nearly 40 percent of all committee members. When it comes to recruitment of women to leadership positions, the picture is more complex. During the 1980s the percentage of woman committee chairpersons increased by 11 percent, but compared with the percentage of women committee members, this figure still indicates an under-representation of women in such positions. Growth in the number of female deputy chairpersons, on the other

hand, has been quite considerable, an entire 22 percent, and in such positions women
are over-represented relative to their percentage of the general membership. If we
consider all government committees as a whole, there is no longer a basis for calling
the committee system male-dominated. The forces behind this development are many.
It is a reflection of, first of all, the general political mobilization of women. Second,
growth in female employment means that women to an increasing degree are part of
institutions which participate in government committees. Finally, the central
government has promoted an active equal rights policy aimed at increasing women's
representation. The Norwegian Equal Rights Act of 1981 stipulated that there should
be at least two representatives of each sex on each government committee. The law
was amended in 1987, the year after Norway's first 'female Government' was
formed, and the amended version calls for 40 percent of the representatives for each
sex. This requirement is nearly met if all committees are considered as a whole, but
there are considerable variations dependent on which bodies are represented on the
committees, the committees' geographic area of operation, and the committees'
specific tasks.

Table 7
Percentage of women members and chairpersons in government committees.
All existing committees in 1980, 1983, 1986, 1989 and 1992.
Percent women and number of chairpersons, deputy chairpersons,
members and deputy members (N)

Year	Chairpersons	Deputy Chairpersons	Members	Deputy members
1980	10 (963)	30 (367)	25 (6182)	19 (4164)
1983	14 (984)	32 (429)	28 (6140)	33 (4971)
1986	15 (907)	41 (380)	32 (5328)	36 (4697)
1989	19 (777)	48 (321)	37 (4490)	41 (4231)
1992	21 (768)	52 (309)	39 (4532)	42 (4106)

Source: Det statlige utvalgsarkivet. (Governmental Committee Archive).

The government committee archives do not have complete information on which
organizations or institutions the female committee members represent, but the
increase in the proportion of women seems to have been greatest among

Table 8
Government committees, exec. committees' councils; number of members (N)
and percentage of women members (M) and chairpersons (CH)

	1980 N	1980 M	1980 CH	1986 N	1986 M	1986 CH	1992 N	1992 M	1992 CH
Office of the Prime Minister	115	12	0	58	10	40	51	16	33
Foreign Affairs[1]	346	21	10	272	30	32	223	30	28
Church/Education/ Research[2]	1430	40	18	1190	46	23	990	51	26
Cultural Affairs[3]				84	39	20	159	49	33
Justice	414	32	9	348	40	10	334	41	7
Local Government[4]	501	29	16	497	33	26	361	45	27
Social Welfare (and Health)	873	36	10	873	42	14	835	46	24
Child and Family Affairs[5]							78	49	67
Commerce[6]	932	10	3	364	17	12	167	32	17
Fisheries	248	9	3	226	13	9	182	26	19
Agriculture	557	16	3	505	30	4	353	38	15
Transport and Communications	266	17	3	209	23	7	121	29	13
The Environment	159	18	18	174	25	20	111	36	23
Labour/ Administration	92	35	13	174	38	27	164	43	27
Finance	177	22	3	181	36	12	273	39	20
Defence	150	9	0	128	12	0	206	16	10
Petroleum/Energy	108	11	0	62	13	0	80	20	13

Source: Det statlige utvalgsarkivet (Governmental Committee Archive).
[1] The figures for 1986 include the Ministry of Foreign Aid, which was established in 1984 and dismantled in 1989.
[2 and 3] A pure ministry for cultural affairs was established in 1991, the 1980 and 1986 data are included under the Ministry of Church, Education and Research. This department has been subject to several reorganizations in recent years, including a two-department alternative with department for church/cultural affairs and one for education/research. Data for all the committees is included in this category.
[4] In the period from 1990-92 labour affairs were transferred to the Ministry of Labour and Administration.
[5] The Ministry of Child and Family Affairs was established in 1991. Data for earlier years is included under the Ministry of Labour and Administration.
[6] The Ministry of Commerce was established in 1988, and comprises the previous Ministry of Trade and Shipping. (As of January 1993, the Ministry of Commerce was merged with the Ministry of Energy.)

representatives of local and regional government. Here the increase was 26 percent from 1983 (23 percent) to 1989 (49 percent). For private businesses and institutions, which in relative terms had fewest female committee members in 1983, the proportion of women increased by 14 percent, to 25 percent in 1992. The percentage of women from parliament, public institutions and corporations, the central government administration, and voluntary organizations has increased by slightly over 10 percent in the last 10 years, and today is between 32 and 40 percent. The considerable growth in the percentage of women representatives from regional and local government is a reflection of the fact that the growth in women's employment has been particularly great in the local government sector. The same tendency is visible if we look at the committees' *geographical area of operation.* On committees which are internationally active or which operate in a Scandinavian arena, women representatives accounted for 19 and 21 percent, respectively, of the total committee membership in 1980, and 29 and 20 percent respectively in 1992.

In committees which were active at the regional and local levels, the percentage of women increased from 33 and 29 percent, respectively, in 1980, to 46 and 47 percent in 1992. This gender-based functional division of labour is even more obvious when we consider the committees' responsibilities. Table 8 shows that government ministries show varying practice in recruiting women as members and chairpersons of government committees. In 1980 committees under four ministries (Church, Education and Research, Justice, Social Welfare, and Labour and Administration) showed an average percentage of female members over 30 percent. The percentage of female chairpersons was on average below 20 percent for all ministries. In the mid-1980s committees under eight ministries had over 30 percent women members, and a percentage of women chairpersons over 20 percent. In 1992 committees under 11 ministries had over 30 percent women members and in 10 of these the percentage of women among committee chairpersons was above 20 percent. Today the Equal Rights Act's 40 percent quota for both sexes has been met in the following ministries: Church, Education and Research, Cultural Affairs, Social Welfare, Justice, Local Government, Labour and Administration. Committees under the ministries of Finance, the Environment, and Agriculture are approaching the 40 percent quota, while committees under the Office of the Prime Minister and the Ministry of Defence stand apart in that 20 percent or fewer of the members are women. It is also interesting to note that there is a higher percentage of women chairpersons than women members in committees under the Office of the Prime Minister and the Ministry of Child and Family Affairs. This uneven representation of women reflects a functional division of labour between women and men, but the differences have become far smaller than they were in the 1970s (Hernes 1982). Furthermore, it is important to remember that there is no basis for considering a division of labour to be a marginalization of female representatives. Such a claim must be proven empirically though studies of the committee members' own preferences, and such data is not available.

The percentage of women committee *chairpersons* is highest, between 30 and 40 percent, in committees under the ministries of Child and Family Affairs, the Office of the Prime Minister, the Ministries of Cultural Affairs, Foreign Affairs, Church, Education and Research, Local Government, and Labour and Administration. Committees under the Ministries of Justice, Defence, Petroleum and Energy, and Agriculture have fewest female committee chairpersons. In committees under four of these ministries women are still highly under-represented as committee chairpersons relative to their proportion of the general membership. These four are Justice, Church, Education and Research, Agriculture, and Social Welfare, and the difference between the percentage of women members and committee chairpersons for these committees exceeds 20 percent.

The lag hypothesis implies that both the hierarchical and the functional division of labour between the sexes decline over time. This also gives reason to believe that the mobilization of women is particularly strong in policy areas where women traditionally have been absent. In Table 9 Norwegian ministries are ranked according to growth in women's representation among members and chairpersons from 1980 until 1992. This material clearly supports the lag hypothesis as growth, with few exceptions, has been greatest in those areas in which women originally had little representation, and which hardly can be said to be primarily concerned with women's interests, ie in committees responsible for production, infrastructure, and coordination of government activities. Committees under the Ministries of Finance and Fisheries have had considerable growth in both the number of women members and women chairpersons. The general tendency, however, is that recruitment of women leaders does not come until a few years after the recruitment of women members.

Thus far we have studied all existing committees at a given point in time. As most of the government committees are standing committees, this data only provides us with a limited look at how the central government's recruitment of women has changed over time. In order to gain a better overview of the development, we may study how the percentage of women varies in committees according to the year in which the committee was founded. Table 10 shows the percentage of women in government committees established in 1981, 1985, and 1992. Starting in the 1980s the percentage of women members increased slightly, but steadily, from 30 percent in committees established in 1981, to 38 percent in committees established in 1992. Recruitment of female committee chairpersons has increased somewhat more, from

15 percent in committees established in 1981, to 28 percent in committees formed in 1992. Parallel to the representative democracy, we see that the mobilization of women from the mid-1980s has primarily been aimed at leading positions in politics. This leads us to believe that the under-representation of women in leading positions in politics will decline throughout the 1990s.

In conclusion, it is clear that the corporative committee system is still characterized by a gender-based division of labour which is both hierarchical and functional, though both types are declining over time. In the early 1980s, government committees were described as a part of the state where women had no access (Hernes 1982). A mere ten years later representation of women is

Table 9
Ministries ranked by increase in percentage of women members and chairpersons
in government committees from 1980 to 1992.
Percentage increase for the period

Ministry:	Increase
Percentage of women among committee members:	
• Commerce, Agriculture	22
• the Environment	18
• Fisheries, Finance	17
• Local Government	16
• Transport and Communications	12
Percentage of women among Chairpersons:	
• Office of the Prime Minister	33
• Foreign Affairs	18
• Finance	17
• Fisheries	16
• Social Welfare, Labour and Administration	14

Source: Det statlige utvalgsarkivet (Governmental Committee Archive).

Table 10
Number of committee members (N) and percent women in government
committees appointed in 1981, 1985 and 1992

Position	Appointed 1981 N	Appointed 1981 %W	Appointed 1985 N	Appointed 1985 %W	Appointed 1992 N	Appointed 1992 %W
Chairpersons	81	15	42	15	18	28
Member	544	30	216	33	138	38

Source: Det statlige utvalgsarkivet (Governmental Committee Archive).

significantly improved, and the mobilization of women throughout the 1980s has been particularly great in areas in which women have traditionally been absent. Women have thus gained access to the corporative state, and are in the process of enlarging their political space.

Summary and further challenges

In 1973 Ingun Norderval Means wrote, 'In all parts of the world women legislators are so rare a species that they ought to have inspired our researchers to serious efforts ... Who are these deviants from the traditional female role patterns' (Means 1973:13). Twenty years later, women are in central positions as political decision-makers in all areas and at all levels in the political system, but we have *not* made a serious effort to study the Scandinavian development. In spite of the fact that Scandinavia leads the world in women's representation, research on women and politics has only to a minor degree been concerned with women's representation in political decision-making bodies. Theories focusing on the political marginalization of women have influenced our understanding of women's political citizenship, and they have not been confronted with the criticism which, quite simply, is apparent in women's political practice.

Hypotheses concerning a hierarchical and functional marginalization of women in politics gain little empirical support today. I have argued for the view that functional marginalization expresses myths about the importance or lack of importance of various policy areas. The data confirms that women are best represented in sectors responsible for education, health and social services and cultural affairs, but there is no foundation for the claim that *a gender-based division of labour* is equivalent to a functional marginalization of women. The hierarchical division of labour has declined throughout the 1980s. The broad mobilization of women as ordinary representatives in the 1970s has continued in the 1980s through a relatively stronger mobilization of women to positions of political leadership. The functional division of labour is declining as well. In the ten years between 1980 and 1990, the percentage of women increased most in policy areas in which women were least represented in the 1970s. The time-lag, which Rokkan has documented for the mobilization of new voter groups up to the end of the 1950s, is also evident in the recruitment of women into politics after 1970. The empirical analysis shows that the decision-making bodies of the welfare state still reflect a hierarchical and functional division of labour between the sexes, but both forms are diminishing over time. The political mobilization of Scandinavian women from 1970 until 1990 may best be described as a 'silent revolution'. It has its expression in the breadth, depth, and extent of women's political representation. It still remains, as we saw, to integrate more women into local councils and leadership positions in which only one person is elected, ie mayors, and committee chairpersons. However, from a historical perspective, it is the speed of the development which is unique for the political mobilization of Scandinavian women.

There is very little disagreement about whether women have had, or currently have, less power than men. The most important challenges in the years to come are, nevertheless: (1) To gain greater insight into women's participation in various institutions linked to the political processes, and (2) to analyze whether, and if so how, women behave differently than men in politics. The first of these two challenges is concerned with filling the empirical space which remains open in relation to women's participation in organizational life, ie voluntary organizations, political parties and the labour movement. We must also study the territorial patterns in political mobilization in order to reveal and interpret any local variations which may be concealed by the national averages presented in this chapter. The second challenge concerns women's political values and behavior. The extensive mobilization of women leaves us with little doubt as to their political competence or their willingness to assume positions of power. It also largely puts to shame speculation that a patriarchal authority, through political marginalization, is keeping women out of politics. On the contrary, the mobilization of women opens for studies of more interesting problems which have a greater potential for enriching our understanding of gender and politics. There is still much to be done in research on the gender gap. Do women have 'softer' values and a 'softer' style than men? Do men and women have different motives for participating in politics? Are there gender-specific features of the political learning process which affect women's and men's political citizenship and values? Does the presence of women influence the form or content of politics? Empirical studies of these questions are necessary in order to supplement, and critically evaluate, existing theories on the political involvement of women.

References

Albrektsen, B. H. (1977), *Kvinner og politisk deltakelse*. Oslo: Universitetforlaget.

Andersen, J., Christensen, A. D., Langberg, K., Siim, B. and Torpe, L. (1993), *Medborgerskapet. Demokrati og Politisk Deltakelse*. Herning: Systime.

Bergqvist, C. (1994): *Måns makt och kvinnors interessen*. Uppsala: Uppsala University, Department of Government.

Bjørklund, T. and Hellevik, O. (1987), *Barrierer mot kvinners deltakelse i lokalpolitikken. Valgordning, motivasjon og perifieriens normtrykk*. Rapport, nr. 11. Oslo: Institutt for samfunnsforskning.

Borchorst, A. and Siim, B. (1986), Woman and the Welfare State: A New Form of Patriarchal Power, in Sassoon. A. S. (ed.): *Women and the Welfare State*. London: Hutchinson.

Cohen, C. (1971), *Democracy*. New York: Free Press.

Dahlerup, D. (1987), Confusing concepts - confusing reality: a theoretical discussion of the partiarchal state, in Sassoon, A. (ed.): *Women and the State*. London: Routledge.

Dahlerup, D. (1989), *Vi har ventet lenge nok- håndbok i kvinnerepresentasjon*. København: Nordisk Ministerråd.

Dahlerup, D. and Haavio-Mannila, E. (1985), 'Summary', in Haavio-Mannila, E. et.al. (eds): *Unfinished Democracy. Women in Nordic Politics*. Oxford:: Pergamon Press.

Dahlerup, D. and Gulli, B. (1985), 'Women's organizations in the Nordic Countries: Lack of Force or Counterforce?', in Haavio-Mannila, E. et.al. (eds): *Unfinished Democracy. Women in Nordic Politics*. Oxford: Pergamon Press.

Elsthain, J. B. (1981), *Public Man, Private Woman: Women in Social and Political Thought*. Princeton: Princeton University Press.

Haavio-Mannila, E. et. al. (1985) (eds), *Unfinished Democracy. Women in Nordic Politics*. Oxford: Pergamon Press.

Halsaa, B. (1986), 'Kvinner og politisk deltakelse - etter kvinne-tiåret', in Kuhnle, S. (ed.): *Det politiske samfunn. Linjer i norsk statvitenskap*. Oslo: Tano.

Halsaa, B. (1992), 'Kjønn og statsvitenskap', in Widerberg, K. and Taksdal, A. (eds): *Forståelser av kjønn i samfunnsvitenskapenes fag og kvinneforskning*. Oslo: Ad Notam.

Heidar, K. (1988), *Partidemokrati på prøve*. Oslo: Universitetsforlaget.

Held, D. (1987), *Models of democracy*. Cambridge: Polity Press.

Held, D. (1991), 'Between State and Civil Society', in Andrew, G. (ed.): *Citizenship*. London: Lawrence & Wishart.

Hellevik, O. and Bjørklund, T. (1991), *Retting på stemmeseddelen ved kommunevalg og rettingens effekt på rekrutteringen av kvinner*. Rapport, nr. 10. Oslo: Institutt for samfunnsforskning.

Hellevik, O. and Skard, T. (1985), *Norske kommunestyrer - plass for kvinner?* Oslo: Universitetsforlaget.

Hernes, H. M. (1982), *Staten - kvinner ingen adgang?* Oslo: Universitetsforlaget.

Hernes, H. M. (1984), 'Women and the welfare state: the transition fram private to public dependence', in Sasson, A. S. (ed.): *Women and the State*. London: Routledge.

Hernes, H. M. (1987): *Welfare State and Woman Power: Essays in State Feminism.* Oslo: Universitetsforlaget.

Hernes, H. and Hänninen-Salmelin, E. (1985), 'Women in the Corporate System', in Haavio-Mannila, E. et.al.: *Unfinished Democracy. Women in Nordic Politics*. Oxford: Pergamon Press.

Hirdman, Y. (1987), 'Makt och kön', in Petersson, O. (ed.): *Maktbegreppet*. Stockholm: Carlssons.

Holter, H. (1981), 'Om kvinneundertrykkelse, mannsundertrykkelse og herseteknikker', in Andenæs, K. et. al (ed.): *Maktens ansikter*. Oslo: Gyldendal.

Holter, H. (ed.) (1982), *Kvinner i fellesskap*. Oslo: Universitetsforlaget.

Holter, H. (ed.) (1984), *Patriarchy in a Welfare Society*. Oslo: Universitetsforlaget.

Hult, S. R., Skeie, H. and Ågotnes, J.-E. (1992), *Utvalgsarkivet. Kodebok med dokumentasjon og eksempler på informasjon*. Rapport nr. 96. Bergen: Norsk Samfunnsvitenskapelig Datatjeneste.

IPU - Interparliamentary Union (1991), *Distribution of seats between men and women in national parliaments.* Série 'Rapports et documents', no.18. Genève.

Jaquette, J. S. (ed.) (1974), *Women in Politics.* New York: John Wiley.

Jaquette, J. S. (1984), 'Power as Ideology: A Feminist Analysis', in Stiehm, J.H. (ed.): *Women's Views of the Political World of Men.* New York: Transnational Publishers.

Jónasdóttir, A. G. (1988), 'Sex/Gender, Power and Politics: Towards a Theory of Patriarchy in the Formally Equal Society', *Acta Sociologica*, 31 (2):157-74.

Jónasdóttir, A. G. (1991), Love Power and Political Interest. Örebro: Örebro Studies.

Jones, K. (1990), 'Citizenship in a woman-friendly polity', *Signs*, 15, 4:781-812.

Jones, K. B. and Jónasdóttir, E. G. (eds) (1988), *The Political Interest of Gender.* London: Sage Publications.

Katzenstein, M.F. and Skjeie, H. (eds): *Going Public. National Histories of Women's Enfranchisement and Women's Participation within State Institutions.* Rapport nr. 4. Oslo: Institutt for samfunnforskning.

Lafferty, W. (1978), Social Development and Political Participation: Class, Organization and Sex', *Scandinavian Political Studies*, Vol. 2. New Series, No. 4:233-254.

Lafferty, W. (1980): 'Sex and Political Participation: An Exploratory Analysis of the 'Female Culture'', *European Journal of Political Research*, No. 8:323-347.

Lafferty, W. and Raaum, N. (1990), *Makt og politikk med en annen røst? Perspektiver på politisk læring hos kvinner og menn.* Institutt for statsvitenskap, Universitetet i Oslo.

Lovenduski, J. and Norris, P. (1993), *Gender and Party Politics.* London: Sage Publications.

Matland, R. (1995): 'How the election system structure has helped women close the representation gap', in Karvonen, L. and Selle, P. (eds): *Women in Nordic Politics: Closing the Gap.* Aldershot: Dartmouth.

Means, I. N. (1973), *Kvinner i norsk politikk.* Oslo: Cappelen.

Okin, S. M. (1991), 'Gender, the Public and the Private', in Held, D. (ed.): *Political Theory Today.* Cambridge: Polity Press.

Pateman, C. (1983), 'Feminist Critiques of the public/private dichotomy', in Benn, G. F. & Gaus, S. I. (eds): *Public and Private in Social Life.* London: Groom Helm.

Pateman, C. (1989), *The Disorder of Women.* Cambridge: Polity Press.

Petersson, O., Westholm, A. amd Blomberg, G. (1989), *Medborgarnas makt*. Stockholm: Carlssons.

Phillips, A. (1991a), *Engendering Democracy*. Cambridge: Polity Press.

Phillips, A. (1991b), 'Citizenship and Feminist Theory', in Andrews, G. (ed.): *Citizenship*. London: Lawrence & Wishart.

Phillips, A. (1992), 'Must Feminists Give Up on Liberal Democracy?', *Political Studies*, XL, Special Issue: 68-82.

Piven, F. Fox (1990), 'Ideology and the State: Women, Power, and the Welfare State', in Gordon, L. (ed.): *Women, the State, and Welfare*. Madison: University of Wisconsin Press.

Putnam, R. O. (1976), The Comparative Study of Political Elites. Englewood Cliffs, New Jersey: Prentice Hall.

Raaum, N. and Skogerbø, E. (1993), 'Statsvitenskap og politisk (s)kjønn', *Norsk Statsvitenskapelig Tidsskrift*, nr. 3: 201-218.

Raaum, N. (1994), 'Politisk mobilisering i velferdsstaten: Mannefall og kvinnekall', in Nagel, A.H. (ed.): *Kjønn og velferdsstat*. Bergen: Alma Mater (Forthcoming).

Raaum, N. (1995), 'Women in local democracy', in Karvonen, L. and Selle, P. (eds): *Women in Nordic Politics: Closing the Gap*. Aldershot: Dartmouth.

Randall, V. (1982), *Women and Politics*. London and Basingstoke: MacMillan.

Randall, V. (1990), 'Do Women Politicans make a Difference?', in Katzenstein, M. F. and Skjeie, H. (eds): *Going Public. National Histories of Women's Enfrachicement and Women's Participation within State Institutions*. Rapport nr. 4. Oslo: Institutt for samfunnforskning.

Randall, V. (1991): 'Feminism and Poltiival Analysis', *Political Studies*, XXXIX: 513-532.

Rokkan, S. (1970), 'The Mobilization of the Periphery', in Rokkan, S.: *Citizens, Elections, Parties*. Oslo: Universitetsforlaget.

Rosaldo, M. Z. and Lamphere, L. (1974), *Women, Culture and Society*. Stanford: Standford University Press.

Rose, L. L. and Waldahl, R. (1982), 'The Distribution of Political Participation in Norway. Alternative Perspectives on a Problem of Democratic Theory', *Scandinavian Political Studies*, Vol. 5, New Series-No. 4:283-314.

Schive, J. van der Ros (1981), 'Kvinners representasjonsvilkår i norske kommunestyrer', *Tidsskrift for samfunnsforskning*, Vol. 22:87-101.

Selle, P. and Øymyr, B. (1995), 'The changing role of women within local voluntary organization: sex segregation in the voluntary sector', in Karvonen, L. and Selle, P. (eds): *Women in Nordic Politics: Closing the Gap.* Aldershot: Dartmouth.

Siim, B. (1988), 'Towards a Feminist Rethinking of the Welfare State', in Jones, K. B. og Jònasdòttir, E. G. (eds): *The Political Interests of Gender.* London: Sage Publications.

Siim, B. (1990), 'Feministiska tolkningar av samspelet mellom kvinnor och välfärdsstaten', *Kvinnovetenskaplig Tidsskrift* nr. 2:13-25.

Sinkkonen, S. (1985), 'Women in Local Politics', in Haavio-Mannila et.al.: *Unfinished Democracy. Women in Nordic Politics.* Oxford: Pergamon Press.

Skard, T. and Haavio-Mannila, E. (1985), 'Women in Parliament', in Haavio-Mannila, E. et al. (eds): *Unfinished Democracy. Women in Nordic Politics.* Oxford: Pergamon Press.

Skjeie, H. (1991): 'The Uneven Advance of Norwegian Women', New Left *Rewiev,* No. 187:79-102.

Skjeie, H. (1992), *Den politiske betydningen av kjønn: En studie av norsk topp-politikk.* Doktoravhandling. Rapport nr. 11, Oslo: Institutt for samfunnsforskning.

Skjeie, H. and Teigen, M. (1993), 'Kvinnenes inntog i topp-politikken: et uttrykk for politikkens marginalisering?', in Rasch, B. E. (ed.): *Symbolpolitikk og parlamentarisk styring.* Oslo: Universitetsforlaget.

SOU - Statens Offentliga Utredningar (1990): Demokrati och makt i Svergie. SOU nr. 44.

Statistisk Sentralbyrå (1992): *Statistisk ukehefte,* nr. 20.

Stiehm, J. H. (ed.) (1984), *Women's Views of the Political World of Men.* New York: Transnational Publishers.

Thorsteinsen, H. (1992), 'Lokal organisasjoners innflytelse i kommunepolitikken', *Norsk Statvitenskapelig Tidsskrift,* No. 2:113-132.

Togeby, L. (1989), *Ens og forskellig. Græsrotdeltagelse i Norden.* Århus: Politica.

Part II

Women as voters and party members

Gender gaps in Nordic voting behaviour

Maria Oskarson

Gender and voting

Studies from some of the Nordic countries, as well as from other western countries, have shown that women during the 1980's became more inclined than men to vote for parties to the left on the ideological spectrum. Studies have also shown that women's attitudes towards environmental and welfare issues on the average differ substantially from those of men (Norris 1988). The general term for this pattern is *gender gap*.

Gender gap as a term was introduced in the United States in the aftermath of the 1980 presidential election, when the support for Ronald Reagan was found to be significantly stronger among men than among women. The American political scientist Pamela Johnston Conover divides the concept into four aspects: gender differences in participation, in attitudes, in party identification and in voting. The term gender gap indicates substantial differences between men and women, which is why I prefer to use the term *gender difference* in most of the chapter.

In this chapter gender differences in voting behaviour in the Nordic countries will be explored - are there any differences between Nordic men and women when it comes to voting in parliamentary elections? Whether there exist gender differences large and consistent enough to be labelled a gender gap is an empirical question to which I return in the end of the chapter (Conover 1988:985f.)[1]

There are two central aspects of gender differences regarding political behaviour which are relevant as a framework for this analysis. The first has to do with political resources and political representation, and the second with interests, attitudes and party choice.

---

[1] For a more extensive discussion of the concept of gender gap, see also Mueller (1991); Mansbridge (1985).

Traditionally, the political resources of women have been weaker than those of men, in the Nordic countries as in others. Women as a group used to have less education, a lower self-reported interest in politics and also a low labour force participation compared to men. Women were confined to family and household, where daily life had little to do with politics. Among other consequences, the lack of political resources among women resulted in a lower voting turnout than men and low political activity (Haavio-Mannila et al 1985; Lovenduski and Hills 1981).

Today, women in the Nordic countries have substantially increased political resources. The average educational level has increased, as well as the labour force participation. This is also reflected in voting turnout - several of the Nordic countries have shown a higher voting turnout among women than among men in recent years. Studies have also shown higher participation rates among women than men in different sorts of 'grass root politics' (Togeby 1993a,1984; Petersson, Westholm and Blomberg 1989:145-154).

The other central aspect of gender differences in political behaviour is differences in political interests, attitudes and eventually party choice. Gender differences in political attitudes and opinions are often traced to different interests. There has been an intense academic discussion about whether there is any such thing as 'women's interests', discernable from 'men's interests'. Today, however, there is widespread agreement that it is in all women's interest, regardless of time and place, not to be discriminated against and also not to be sexually exploited. Issues concerning these interests can, at least theoretically, unite all women. Apart from this there are special interests involved in women's positions and role in society, such as how to combine being a mother and also being vocationally active. What form and expression these special interests take is highly dependent on the actual social and political context (Jónasdóttir 1988;Togeby 1989,1993b).

In this second regard, the Nordic countries form a specific context, different from most other countries, due to the characteristic Nordic welfare state and the position of women within this welfare state.

A significant trait of the Nordic welfare states is the central role played by the public sector. During the first decades after world war II the Nordic countries all developed the 'Nordic welfare state', with a large public sector providing welfare services such as child care, education, social welfare, health care and care of the old. The 'Nordic welfare state' also includes different transfers to citizens, such as pensions and child allowances, which guarantee a basic living standard.

This transformation of the societies is closely connected to the entrance of women into the labour market, since many of the traditional female tasks conducted in the home were transferred to the public sector - a development sometimes described as 'the family going public'. This transformation also produced a lot of new employment opportunities within the public sector, which were mainly filled by women. All in all, the expansion of the welfare state resulted in a switch in dependence for women - from being dependent on the individual man to a dependence on the collective public sector, both as an employee and as a service-taker (Hernes 1987:31-49). The implication of this development is, besides the fact that many citizens have a self-interest in the public sector, that many questions which formerly, and also in other countries, were regarded to be non-political are now explicitly political in the Nordic countries. It is often stated that this development has given rise to a new political dividing line, and that men and women in many cases split differently along this dividing line.

The two aspects of aggregate gender differences in political behaviour can be combined to a four-fold table describing different societies.

Figure 1
Four different stages of a Gender Gap

		Gender neutral	Gender specific
Political resources	Equal	No gender differences in participation, preferences or party choice	No gender differences in participation. Gender differences in preferences and party choice
	Not equal	Gender differences in participation, but not in preferences or party choice	Gender differences in participation and in preferences. Passivity

The traditional pattern of gender differences in political behaviour has been a lower participation rate among women, and gender differences in opinions, especially regarding moral questions. Often women have voted for conservative or Christian parties to a higher degree than men, which has generally been explained with reference to women's responsibility for home and family, as well as women's religiousness. During the 1970's the gender differences in voting became less pronounced, as women's traditional role as housewives was gradually replaced by gainful employment. This led to a situation where the gender specific interests as mothers and wives were relevant especially for older women.

What has happened in the Nordic countries during the last decades is that the political resources of women have increased. At the same time the inequality in the labour market and in the reproductive responsibility in the family has not disappeared. Nordic women in general are more often than men employed in low-paying jobs, employed in the public sector and working part time.[2] And still women in most cases bear the main responsibility for home and family. The question at stake is then whether there are any gender differences in interests, and whether these interests are formulated into political opinions influencing party choice.

Gender differences in general are most probable where there are no differences in political resources between men and women, but substantial differences in interests. In this situation women have the ability to realize their specific interests and formulate them into political issues and demands. But this is usually not enough. In order to make these issues of any political importance and eventually to have an impact on the party choice, it is necessary that the parties take a stand - that the issues are politicized. The probability of this happening is, of course, higher where women have a high representation in the political parties and in parliament.[3]

The five Nordic countries can today be characterized by far-reaching equality between men and women with regard to political resources, and also a comparatively high political representation. At the same time there are a lot differences in the daily life of men and women. Women are to a higher degree than men publicly employed, employed in service and reproduction sectors, in subordinate positions with low pay. Still, however, women have the main responsibility for children and household work.

The dividing line between public and private sector, as well as between what kind of welfare services the state should provide, what is the responsibility of the family and how the welfare should be financed, has been central in the political debate at the end of the 1980's. Generally in the debate, the dividing line between public and

---

[2] Finland is partly an exception from this, since Finnish women are publicly employed to a lower degree than, for example, Swedish women, and Finnish women also work full-time to a higher degree.

[3] See Lovenduski and Norris (1993) for a discussion of female political representation

private coincides with the political left-right dimension, with the parties to the left more positive to a large public sector. This has often been put forward as an explanation of why women today vote for the left parties to a higher degree then men do.

Given the framework described above as a background, the question is whether this situation has led to a gender gap in political preferences, manifested in party choice, in the five Nordic countries. That is, are there any gender gaps in Nordic voting behaviour?[4]

Figure 2 describes left voting among men and women over a longer period of time.[5] The first comment to be made is that there are no major gender gaps in Nordic voting behaviour, with the possible exception of Iceland. The differences in left voting between men and women are slight, rarely over 5 percentage points.[6] Compared to the most powerful social characteristic explaining party choice in the Nordic countries, the respondents' class, the gender cleavage is dismissable.

However, to say that there are no differences in party choice between men and women is also an exaggeration. In Denmark the socialist parties have received more votes from female than from male voters in every election since 1981, and not since 1971 have more men than women voted socialist. In Norway the socialist parties were stronger among men than among women up until the 1985 election, when the gender difference changed sign and 5 percent more women than men voted socialist - a gender difference which remained the same in the 1989 election. Gender differences in Sweden show a pattern quite similar to the Norwegian. Up until the 1985 election there were either no gender differences in socialist voting or a stronger support among men. In the 1985 and 1988 elections, on the other hand, the socialist bloc received stronger support among women (4 and 5 percentage points respectively (Oskarson 1990; Gilljam and Holmberg 1993:185-190). In the latest election, 1991, this gender difference disappeared. The Finnish pattern is different from that seen

---

[4] The analysis is based on national election studies conducted in the Nordic countries in connection with parliamentary elections. Material for this analysis has been provided by Lise Togeby (Denmark), Sami Borg (Finland), Ólafur Th. Hardarson (Iceland) and Ola Listhaug (Norway). The analysis of the Swedish election study is my own.

[5] The election studies started in Sweden 1956, Norway 1957, Denmark 1964, Finland 1983 and Iceland 1983. The figures for 1966 are from Pesonen (1972) and figures for 1975 from the Political Action I project).

[6] The Icelandic gender gap is almost completely attributed to the women's party. The grounds for characterizing this party as a left party are discussed later in the text.

Figure 2: Socialist voting by gender. Percent.

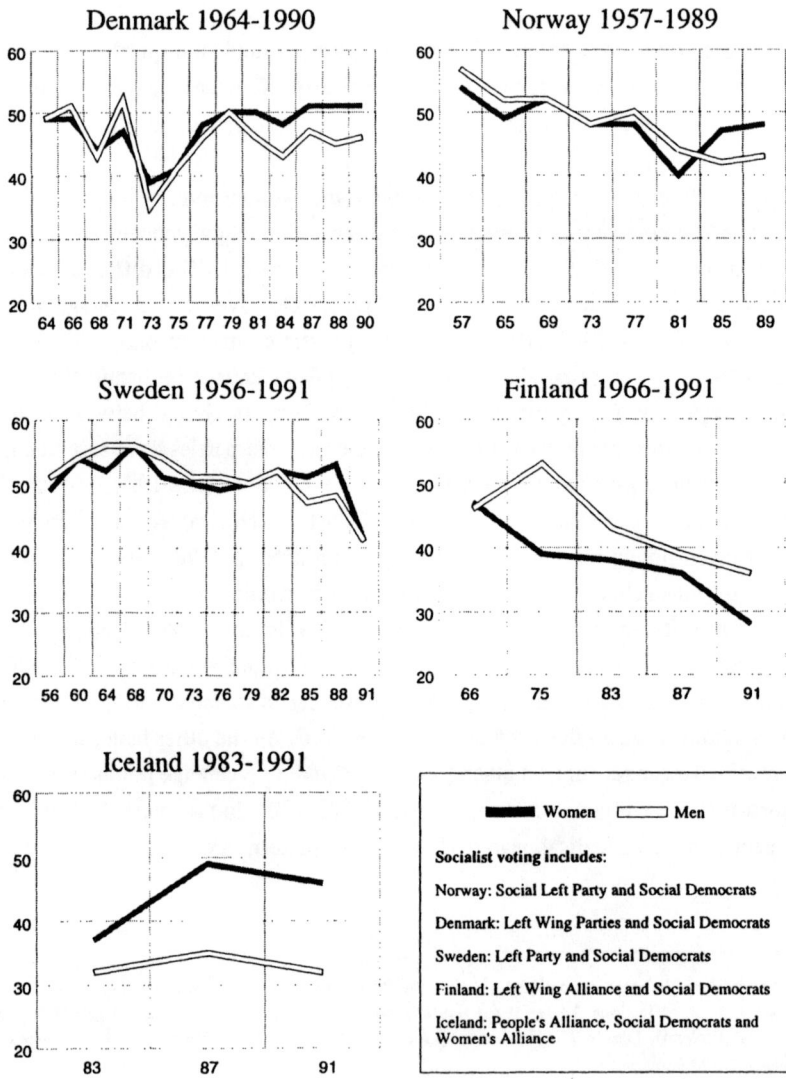

Denmark 1964-1990

Norway 1957-1989

Sweden 1956-1991

Finland 1966-1991

Iceland 1983-1991

Women   Men

Socialist voting includes:

Norway: Social Left Party and Social Democrats

Denmark: Left Wing Parties and Social Democrats

Sweden: Left Party and Social Democrats

Finland: Left Wing Alliance and Social Democrats

Iceland: People's Alliance, Social Democrats and Women's Alliance

NSD Grafikk

in the other countries, since the socialist bloc has continuously been strongest among male voters. As for Iceland it is not as easy or natural to split the party system into two blocs. The parties, especially the social democrats and the progressive party, have been cooperating with all other parties, which blurs the dividing lines. If the social democrats, the people's alliance and the women's alliance are taken together to form a left bloc in Icelandic politics, there is a gender gap leaning to the left in Iceland.[7] However, it is fully attributable to the women's alliance.

To give a more comprehensive answer to the question of whether there is a gender gap in Nordic voting behaviour, it is necessary to go beyond the simple dichotomization of the party systems into left and right. A dichotomization of the party systems might hide significant gender differences in support for single parties. There might for instance be gender differences in support for the different non-socialist parties - gender differences that 'even out' when the non-socialist bloc is analyzed as a whole.

The Nordic party systems

The party systems in the five Nordic countries share many basic traits. The Norwegian political scientist Stein Rokkan once characterized the typical Nordic party systems as based on two cleavage lines - the working class/middle class cleavage and the rural/urban cleavage. These two cleavage lines have given rise to a basic five-party system, with from the left a Communist Party, a Social Democratic Party (together forming a socialist bloc), a Center Party (agrarian/rural), a Liberal Party and a Conservative Party (together forming a non-socialist bloc). Table 1 presents the party systems of the five Nordic countries in the early 1990's organized through an ideological typologisation of the parties. This typologisation will be used throughout this chapter in analysing the voting.[8]

---

[7] The Women's Alliance is further discussed below.

[8] The typologisation is originally presented in Petersson (1994: table 3.1).

Table 1
The Political Parties

	Denmark	Finland	Iceland	Norway	Sweden
Communists and left socialists	Socialist People's Party 1959 Left Socialist Party 1967	Left Wing Alliance 1944	People's Alliance 1956	Socialist Left Party 1975-(1961)	Left Party 1917
Social Democrats	Social Democrats 1871	Social Democrats 1899	Social Democrats 1916	Labour Party 1887	Social Democrats 1889
Centrist and agrarian parties	Liberals 1870	Centre Party 1906	Progressive 1916	Centre Party 1920	Centre Party 1910
Liberal Parties	Social Liberals 1905	Swedish People's Party 1906 Liberal Party 1894		Liberals 1883	Liberals 1934
Christian Parties	Christian People's Party 1970	Christian League 1958		Christian Democratic Party 1933	Christian Democrats 1964
Other Centrist Parties	Centre Democrats 1973				
Conservative parties	Conservatives 1916	Coalition Party 1918	Independence Party 1929	Conservatives 1884	Conservatives 1904
Protest parties	Progress Party 1972	Rural Party 1959		Progress Party 1973	New Democracy 1991
Environmental and women parties	Green Party 1983	Green League 1988	Women's Alliance 1986	The Greens 1988	Ecological 1981

Source: Petersson (1994): *The Government and Politics of the Nordic Countries*, table 3.1. The years indicated are the years of formation.

For a long time the basic five-party structure in the Nordic party systems was 'frozen', and not much changed. Since the mid-seventies, however, certain changes have occurred, giving rise to more fragmented party systems - different from earlier years and also somewhat different between the countries.[9] Three new types of parties emerged in all of the countries except Iceland, namely Christian parties, Protest parties and Green parties. In Denmark there is also a new centre party, the Centre Democrats, a splinter party from the Social Democrats established in 1973 as a protest party.

In Iceland the only 'new' party is the Women's Alliance, formed mainly out of discontent with the low political representation of women in Iceland. Ever since it started the Women's Alliance has been hesitant to be placed under any ideological labels such as left or right. However, when the Icelandic voters are asked to place the party on a left-right scale, the party is placed clearly left, which is also where the Women's Alliance voters place themselves. Also, in policies the party is closest to the People's Alliance (Hardarsson and Kristinsson 1987:223).[10]

Party choice of men and women

The five Nordic countries do not show an identical pattern of gender differences in voting, which is shown below. Table 2 presents the party choice of men and women at the elections held around 1990 in the five Nordic countries. The figures are from the election studies - national interview studies held in connection with each election.[11]

---

[9] Petersson (1994: chapter 3) gives an overview of the party systems in the Nordic countries.

[10] The Icelandic elections are also discussed in Kristinsson (1991); Hardarsson (1992). About the Women's Alliance, see also Styrkársdottir (1986); Ehinger and Nilausen (1989); Sigurbjarnardóttir (1992).

[11] In Norway the latest election was held in September 1993. The Norwegian election study for 1993 has not been completed at the present time, which is why the analysis here is based on the 1989 election study.

Table 2
Voting by Gender in the Nordic Countries 1989-1991

	Denmark 1990			Finland 1991			Iceland 1991			Norway 1989			Sweden 1991		
	M	F	diff	M	F	diff	M	F	diff	M	F	diff	M	F	diff
Communists and left socialists	9	12	-3	14	6	+8	14	13	+1	10	14	-4	4	4	±0
Social democrats	37	39	-2	22	22	±0	15	16	-1	33	34	-1	37	37	±0
Centrist and agrarian parties	15	17	-2	25	25	±0	18	17	+1	6	6	±0	8	10	-2
Liberal parties	4	3	+1	6	5	+1				5	4	+1	8	10	-2
Christian parties	2	2	±0	2	4	-2				8	10	-2	7	9	-2
Other centrist parties	4	5	-1												
Conservative parties	16	14	+2	17	21	-4	47	33	+14	23	22	-1	24	19	+5
Protest parties	6	3	+3	6	4	+2				14	9	+5	9	5	+4
Environment. parties and woman parties	1	0	+1	5	8	-3	3	17	-14				2	5	-3
Other parties	6	5	+1	3	4	-1	3	4		1	1	±0	1	1	±0
Index of Gender Difference			1.6			1.8			5.3			2.0			2.3
Total percentage	100	100		100	100		100	100		100	100		100	100	
Number interviewed	399	418		522	472		579	586		911	908		1212	1159	

Source: The results are from The Election Studies from each country, and were provided by researchers in each respective country. Index of Gender Difference stands for the average gender difference.

The gender differences in party choice are in most cases modest also when the single parties are analyzed.[12] The Index of Gender Difference is over 5 percentage points only in Iceland.

The Social Democratic parties show no significant gender differences in any of the countries; whether there is a gender gap to the left is rather dependent on what kind of party there is left of the social democrats. In Denmark and Norway there are rather large socialist parties, formed without ties to the former Soviet union, but rather with a clear 'post-materialist' and 'green' profile. In Denmark the difference between female and male support for the Socialist People's party was 3 percentage points, with female support the higher. For the Social Democrats the female lead was 2 percentage points. The Norwegian Socialist Left party showed a difference of 4 percentage points, with more of the women's votes than of the men's and the Social Democrats had a difference of one percentage point. The Swedish Left Party is now, in the beginning of the 1990's, in the process of liberating itself from its 'communist' past.[13] The party has, in spite of its ideological ties, been rather succesful among young people and students, especially between the mid-seventies and the mid-eighties, but has always remained one of the smallest parties in Sweden.

The Finnish Left Wing Alliance is a left party of a different character than the others, with stronger ties to the former Soviet Communist Party than any of the other left wing parties analysed here. Also, memories of the civil war of 1918 have been vivid in Finnish society, even though the cooperation between left and right after world war II united the nation. The Left Wing Alliance is, and has always been, significantly stronger among men than among women. The Finnish Social Democratic party showed no gender difference in the 1991 election.

The agrarian parties show no major gender differences, even though the Center party of Sweden and the Liberals in Denmark both showed differences of two percentage points, with more of the female votes than of the male. The liberal parties in Denmark, Finland and Norway are slightly stronger among men than women, while the Swedish Liberal Party traditionally has been somewhat stronger among women.

---

[12] Whether the gender differences are significant or not depends both on the sample size of the study and on the size of the party. As a general rule a difference of 6 percentage points is significant when the sample is around 1000 persons, 8 percentage points with a sample of 500, and 12 percentage points with a sample size of 250 persons.

[13] The Swedish left party changed its name in 1990 from the left party communists to only the left party.

Christian parties exist in all of the Nordic party systems except the Icelandic. However, only in Norway has the Christian Democratic Party been one of the 'major' parties in the party system. The Danish and Finnish parties have always been small, albeit represented in parliament since 1973 and 1970 respectively. The Swedish Christian Democrats did not reach the four-percent threshold for representation until the 1991 election.

Christian parties are generally stronger among women than men, which is mostly explained by the parties' emphasis on the traditional family. This is the case in the Nordic countries as well. In Norway the gender difference in support for the Christian Democrats in 1989 was small compared to prior elections. All through the 1957-1989 period there were only two elections in which female support for the party was less than five percentage points higher than the male, i.e. the elections of 1965 and 1989.

The conservative parties are stronger among men than women in Denmark, Iceland and Sweden. The Icelandic conservative party - The Independence Party - showed a difference of an entire 14 percentage points, which turns the party into the mirror image of the Women's Alliance. In Sweden the gender difference in conservative voting is smaller, 5 percentage points, but the Conservative Party has had more men than women in its electorate in every election since 1973. The Danish Conservatives show a 2 percentage point gender difference with stronger support among men in the 1990 election - in the two preceeding elections there were no gender differences at all and before that the party generally received stronger support from women than from men.

The Norwegian Conservatives showed a difference of one percentage point, indicating stronger support among men then among women in the 1989 election. In every election since 1969 the party has received most of its votes from men. The largest gender differences were found in the 1977 and the 1985 elections - 5 percentage points. In Finland the conservative Coalition Party's support among women was 4 percentage points higher than that among men, which was twice as much as in the 1987 election. There seems to have been an overflow of female voters from the Centre party to the Coalition Party in 1987. One reason for this might be that the Coalition Party for the first time was considered as a candidate for government, and this affected women more than men (Berglund 1987:271).[14]

Right-wing protest parties exist in four of the five Nordic countries (Iceland is the exception), and gain more support from men than women in all four. One

---

[14] See also Berglund (1991) about the latest Finnish election.

explanation for this might be that the Nordic protest parties strongly criticize high taxes, which puts them in opposition to the traditional 'welfare state' built up around a large, and expensive, public sector.

The Green parties of Sweden and Finland have more women than men in their electorates, while the smaller Green Party of Denmark was slightly stronger among men. This general pattern is in accordance with women's strong concern about environmental issues.

Gender differences among young and old voters

The situation of women in the Nordic countries has changed quite drastically during the post-war period, with an increased educational level and labour force participation. The life situation for women has changed from one generation of women to the next, which might have given rise to differences in political attitudes between older and younger women. A gender gap in voting behaviour is, considering the importance of political resources, most probable among younger voters. Table 3 shows party choice in the Nordic countries among men and women under the age of 45 years, and Table 4 among older voters.[15]

First of all, in four out of five countries gender differences in party choice are larger among voters under the age of 45 than among older voters. The only exception is Norway, where the Index of Gender Differences is 3.0 percent in both age groups. However, among Norwegian voters under 30 years of age, women have been voting socialist to a higher degree than men ever since the mid-sixties.[16] Of course, the results have to be interpreted with caution, since the number of interviews is limited, especially for Denmark, Norway and Finland.

In Denmark, Norway and Sweden the parties to the left have more female than male voters under 45 years of age, while there are more men than women in the age group over 46 years. The gender difference accordingly has opposite signs in the two groups.

---

[15] For Denmark, Finland and Sweden young voters consist of the age group 18-44, and for Norway and Iceland 18-45.

[16] Aardal and Valen (1988:250); Listhaug, Miller and Valen (1985:193); Björklund (1986:438); Valen (1992).

Table 3
Voting by Gender among Voters 18-45 Years of Age in the Nordic Countries 1989-1991

	Denmark 1990			Finland 1991			Iceland 1991			Norway 1989			Sweden 1991		
	M	F	diff	M	F	diff	M	F	diff	M	F	diff	M	F	diff
Communists and left socialists	13	20	-7	15	7	+8	13	12	+1	12	20	-8	4	5	-1
Social democrats	31	42	-11	18	19	-1	16	15	+1	29	31	-2	32	34	-2
Centrist and agrarian parties	15	11	+4	23	21	+2	15	16	-1	5	5	±0	6	9	-3
Liberal parties	4	3	+1	12	8	+4				6	4	+2	9	11	-2
Christian parties	0	2	-2	1	4	-3				5	6	-1	5	8	-3
Other centrist parties	4	3	+1												
Conservative parties	15	10	+5	19	24	-5	47	31	+16	26	21	+5	29	19	+10
Protest parties	7	3	+4							16	11	+5	11	6	+5
Environmental and women parties	3	1	+2	9	14	-5	4	21	-17				3	7	-4
Other parties	8	5	+3	3	3	±0	4	5	-1	1	2	-1	1	1	±0
Index of Gender Difference		3.8			3.5			6.2			3.0			3.3	
Total percent	100	100		100	100		100	100		100	100		100	100	
Number interviewed	199	225		276	276		361	391		552	391		605	607	

Source: The results are from The Election Studies from each country, and were provided by researchers in each respective country.

Table 4
Voting by Gender among Voters 45-80 Years of Age in the Nordic Countries 1989-1991

	Denmark 1990			Finland 1991			Iceland			Norway 1989			Sweden 1991		
	M	F	diff	M	F	diff	M	F	diff	M	F	diff	M	F	diff
Communist and left socialists	6	2	+4	12	6	+6	15	14	+1	8	5	+3	3	2	+1
Social democrats	43	36	+7	28	26	+2	12	18	-6	41	40	+1	43	42	+1
Centrist and agrarian parties	15	24	-9	27	29	-2	24	21	+3	8	7	+1	9	10	-1
Liberal parties	4	4	±0	11	9	+2				4	3	+1	8	8	±0
Christian parties	2	2	±0	3	5	-2				11	15	-4	8	10	-2
Other centrist parties	4	8	-4												
Conservative parties	17	18	-1	16	17	-1	46	37	+9	16	23	-7	20	20	±0
Protest parties	6	2	+4							12	6	+6	6	5	+1
Environment. parties and women parties	0	0		2	1	+1	2	9	-7				2	3	-1
Other parties	3	4	-1	2	7	-5	1	1	±0	0	1	-1	1	0	+1
Index of gender diff.			3.2			2.4			4.3			3.0			0.8
Total percent	100	100		100	100		100	100		100	100		100	100	
Number interviewed	200	193		245	208		218	195		359	388		581	578	

Source: The results are from The Election Studies from each country, and were provided by researchers in each respective country.

The same is the case for the Conservative parties in the three countries, but here the direction is the opposite. The Conservative parties of Denmark, Norway and Sweden are stronger among men in the younger age group, but among women in the older (in Sweden there is no gender difference).

In Iceland the Social Democrats have a female majority in the older age group, while the party is one percentage point ahead among men in the younger age group. Also, among voters aged over 46 the male dominance in vote for the Conservative Party is much smaller than among younger voters - 9 percentage points compared to 16 percentage points among the younger.

In Finland the Social Democrats have a small over-representation of men among their older voters; among younger the gender difference is in the opposite direction. The differences are very small though. A somewhat larger difference is found in support for the Centre Party (male among young and female among old) and the Conservative Party. The latter is strongest among young voters, and there is also a larger gender difference found in the female direction.

For three of the five countries the expected pattern was found. The gender differences in the direction of women voting left to a higher degree than men are more pronounced among younger voters. Among older voters more of the 'traditional' pattern of more conservative women is found. Finland and Iceland differ from this pattern.

In Finland there is a male dominance in support for the socialist bloc regardless, in both age groups. This can be explained especially by the former stalinist ties of the Left Wing Alliance. The Icelandic case is, as discussed earlier, rather complicated. If the Women's Alliance is put together with the People's Alliance and the Social Democrats as a left bloc, then there is a gender gap with the expected direction among women in Iceland, and this gender gap is somewhat more pronounced among voters under the age of 45 years. However, among the young voters this is wholly due to the strong position of the Womens's Alliance among younger women. Both the People's Alliance and the Social Democrats are slightly stronger among men. Among women over the age of 45 years the Women's Alliance is weaker, and instead there is a female majority among the voters of the Social Democratic party. The conclusion is thus dependent on how the Women's Alliance is treated.

Gender differences and the public sector

The changes in women's lives are closely connected to the expansion of the public sector, which is why the gender differences might be different among public and private employees. The effect of sector employment can, however, take either direction, i.e. increase or decrease the gender differences. If the explanation for women voting left to a higher degree than men is that they more often are publicly employed, then the gender differences are expected to disappear when the analysis is made separate for the two sectors. On the other hand, it is also possible that the gender differences increase when the control is introduced. The explanation for this would be that especially women in the public sector are aware of their specific interests connected with this position. Tables 5 and 6 present party choice among men and women separately for the public and private sectors.

In Denmark, Finland and Iceland the Index of Gender Difference is higher among voters in the public sector than in the private, while the opposite is the case in Sweden. In Norway the index is identical.

In Denmark, Finland and Norway gender differences in left voting are most pronounced in the public sector. In Iceland the gender differences in voting for the conservative party and the Women's Alliance are most pronounced among public employees. In Sweden the strength of the difference is the same, but the direction is the opposite in the public and the private sectors. Among publicly employed there are more women than men who vote for the Social Democrats, in the private sector there is no difference in voting for the Social Democrats. Instead, there is a slight male dominance in votes for the Left Party.

Thus, there is a slight tendency towards larger gender differences in the public sector than in the private, especially in voting for the left bloc.

Conclusion: is there any gender gap?

At the beginning of this chapter gender gap was defined as a substantial difference between men and women, and the differences explored here are differences in party choice between men and women in the five Nordic countries. Usually when gender gap in voting is discussed, it indicates that women vote left to a higher degree than men do. Table 7 summarizes the findings of the chapter regarding the situation at the latest election held in each of the Nordic countries, and shows the average gender

Table 5
Voting by Gender in the Public Sector in the Nordic Countries 1989-1991

	Denmark 1990			Finland 1991			Iceland 1991			Norway 1989			Sweden 1991		
	M	F	diff	M	F	diff	M	F	diff	M	F	diff	M	F	diff
Communists and left socialists	15	23	-8	16	8	+8	12	12	-0	16	24	-8	5	5	±0
Social democrats	36	42	-6	27	24	+3	20	17	+3	37	30	+7	38	41	-3
Centrist and agrarian parties	6	9	-3	16	24	-8	15	14	+1	3	4	-1	8	9	-1
Liberal parties	12	3	+9	3	5	-2				7	4	+3	11	10	+1
Christian parties	1	2	-1	2	6	-4				10	8	+2	6	9	-3
Other centr. parties	4	6	-2												
Conservative parties	13	7	+6	18	22	-4	47	26	+21	18	22	-4	18	14	+4
Protest parties	4	0	+4	9	2	+7				8	5	+3	7	5	+2
Environment. and women parties	1	0	+1	6	5	+1	4	25	-21	6	6	±0			
Other parties	8	8	±0	3	4	-1	2	6	-4	1	3	-2	1	0	+1
Index of Gender Diff.		*4.0*			*3.76*			*8.3*			*3.75*			*1.67*	
Total percent	100	100		100	100		100	100		100	100		100	100	
Number interviewed	78	135		134	175		133	201		196	267		249	443	

Source: The results are from The Election Studies from each country, and were provided by researchers in each respective country.

Table 6
Voting by Gender in the Private Sector in the Nordic Countries 1989-1991

	Denmark 1990			Finland 1991			Iceland 1991			Norway 1989			Sweden 1991		
	M	F	diff	M	F	diff	M	F	diff	M	F	diff	M	F	diff
Communists and left socialists	7	9	-2	12	7	+5	14	12	+2	8	16	-8	3	1	+2
Social democrats	35	34	+1	22	23	-1	13	15	-2	32	33	-1	33	33	±0
Centrist and agrarian parties	18	25	-7	30	24	+6	20	21	-1	4	7	-3	7	9	-2
Liberal parties	1	1	±0	6	6	±0				5	3	+2	8	11	-3
Christian parties	1	1	±0	2	6	-4				4	7	-3	6	7	-1
Other centrist parties	5	9	-4												
Conservative parties	19	1	±0	16	22	-6	47	34	+13	26	21	+5	30	26	+4
Protest parties	7	2	+5	5	4	+1				29	21	+8	11	7	+4
Environment. and women parties	2	0	+2	5	9	-4	3	15	-12				1	6	-5
Other parties	5	0	+5	3	4	-1	3	3	±0	1	1	±0	1	0	+1
Index of Gender diff.	2.6			2.78			5.0			3.75			2.44		
Total percent	100	100		100	100		100	100		100	100		100	100	
Number interviewed	202	130		328	203		417	262		330	180		649	322	

Source: The results are from The Election Studies from each country, and were provided by researchers in each respective country.

Table 7
Gender Differences in Voting in the Nordic Countries around 1990

	Denmark 1990	Finland 1991	Iceland 1991	Norway 1989	Sweden 1991
Index of Gender Difference/Gender Difference in Left Voting					
Population	1.6 / -5	2.6 / +8	5.3 / -14	2.0 / -5	2.3 / ±0
Age					
18-45	3.8 / -18	3.5 / +7	6.2 / -15	3.0 / -10	3.3 / -3
46-	3.2 / +11	2.4 / +8	4.3 / -12	3.0 / +4	0.8 / +2
Sector					
Public	4.0 / -14	3.8 / +12	8.3 / -18	3.8 / -1	1.7 / -3
Private	2.6 / -1	2.8 / +4	5.0 / -12	3.8 / -9	2.4 / +2

Comment: The index of Gender Difference is derived from the average differences in party choice between men and women. Gender Difference in Left Voting is the difference between the proportion of men and the proportion of women voting for the left bloc. A negative sign indicates that women voted left to a higher degree than men. All figures have been presented in Tables 2-6. The figures for Iceland are based on the classification of the Women's Alliance as a left party.

difference in the party system (Index of Gender Difference), as well as the gender difference in left voting.

The average gender differences in party choice are modest; only in Iceland, where the Women's Alliance is heavily female-dominated and the conservative Independence Party heavily male-dominated, is the index more than 5 percentage points. The lowest average difference is found in Denmark, followed by Norway, Sweden and Finland.

The Index of Gender Differences is higher among voters younger than 45 years of age (except Norway), which is in accordance with earlier findings. The largest difference between the two age groups is found in Iceland, followed by Sweden, Finland and Denmark). The average gender difference is higher for voters occupied in the public sector in Denmark and Finland, while there is no difference between the sectors in Norway, and in Sweden there is a larger average difference in the private sector.

The fact that the gender differences in voting not only goes between the two blocs in the party system (socialist versus bourgeois) is evident when gender differences in left voting is used for comparison. In the population as a whole, the gender difference in left voting is largest in Iceland. This is wholly because the Women's

Alliance has been classified as a left party, a decision which is not self-evident. If this party is left out, there is no gender difference in left voting on Iceland. The second largest gender difference in left voting is found in Finland, but with more men than women voting left; that is the opposite pattern from that expected. This was earlier explained by the specific traits of the Finnish party system, with a traditionally more 'communist' left party than in the other Nordic countries.[17] In Denmark and Norway there is a difference between female and male voters of 5 percentage points, with more women than men voting for the left bloc, and in Sweden there was no difference in the 1991 election. The two previous elections, however, showed an equivalent gender difference as Denmark and Norway.

The differences in left voting between men and women are largest among the younger voters in Denmark, Norway and Sweden. In these three countries the left-biased gender difference only exists among voters under the age of 45 years - among older voters there are more men than women voting for the left parties. In Denmark and Finland, finally, the gender difference is stronger in the public sector than in the private, albeit in opposite directions in the two countries. In Denmark the gender difference with more women than men is almost exclusively found in the public sector. In Finland on the other hand it is mainly in the public sector men vote left to a higher degree than women. In Norway the gender difference is most marked in the private sector. In Sweden the gender differences in left voting are slight in both sectors. However, in the public sector women vote more left than men, while in the private sector the opposite is true - men vote for the socialist bloc to a higher degree than women.

From this analysis it is hardly possible to conclude that there is a general gender gap in voting behaviour in the Nordic countries - the gender differences are quite modest and also do not follow the same pattern in the five countries. The Finnish pattern differs a lot from the other Nordic countries, as Finnish gender differences have the opposite sign from the other countries, especially among the young. Iceland is very special, since it is the only country with a Women's Party which gives a very specific pattern of gender differences.

However, there are some indications that at least in Denmark, Norway and Sweden there might be an emerging gender gap. Among the younger voters the differences in party choice are larger than among older voters - young women vote left to a higher degree than young men do. Also, the gender differences are related

---

[17] Since around 1990 however, the Finnish People's Alliance has been undergoing a transformation towards a more general left party, more similar to those of the other Nordic countries.

80   *Women in Nordic Politics*

to the public/private sector division, even if the direction of this relation differs between the countries. The hypothesis that gender gaps in political preferences and party choice are most probable among the young and that women's interests are related to the public/private split in society seems to find support in these results. What this conclusion might imply for the future in terms of gender and politics is still to early to predict.

References

Aardal, B. and Valen, H. (1988), *Velgere, partier og politisk avstand*. Oslo: Statistisk Sentralbyrå.

Berglund, S. (1987), 'The Finnish General Election of 1987', *Electoral Studies*, 3: 271-273.

Berglund, S. (1991), 'The Finnish Parliamentary Election of 1991', *Electoral Studies*, 10, 3:256-261.

Björklund, T. (1986), 'Kvinners og Menns partipreferanse', *Tidsskrift for samfunnsforskning*, 27:417-443.

Conover, P.J. (1988), 'Feminists and the Gender Gap', *Journal of Politics*, Vol. 50, No 4:985-1010.

Ehinger, Å. and Nilausen, J. (1989), 'Kan politikens villkor förändras inifrån? Ett reportage om Kvennalistinn, Islands kvinnoparti', *Zenit*, 1:5-14.

Gilljam, M. och Holmberg, S. (1993), *Väljarna inför 90-talet* Stockholm: Norstedts juridik.

Haavio-Mannila, E. et al. (1985), *Unfinished Democracy. Women in Nordic Politics*. Oxford: Pergamon Press.

Hardarsson, O. Th. (1992), 'Iceland', *European Journal of Political Research*, Vol. 22: 429-435.

Hardarsson, O. Th. and Kristinsson, G. H. (1987), 'The Icelandic Parliamentary Election of 1987', *Electoral Studies* Vol. 6, 3:219-234.

Hernes, H. M. (1987), *Welfare State and Women Power. Essays in State Feminism*. Oslo: Universitetsforlaget.

Jónasdóttir, A. (1988), 'On the Concept of Interest, Women's Interests, and the Limitations of Interest Theory', in Jones, K. and Jónasdóttir, A. (eds): *The Politics of Gender*. London: Sage.

Kristinsson, G. H. (1991), 'The Icelandic Election of 1991' *Electoral Studies*, 10, Vol. 3: 262-266.

Listhaug, O., Miller, A.H. and Valen, H. (1985), 'The Gender Gap in Norwegian Voting Behaviour', *Scandinavian Political Studies*, Vol. 8, 3:187-206.

Lovenduski, J. and Hills J. (eds) (1981), *The Politics of the Second Electorate. Women and Political Participation* London: Routledge & Kegan Paul.

Lovenduski, J. and Norris, P. (eds) (1993), *Gender and Party Politics*. London: Sage.

Mueller, C. M. (ed.) (1991), *The Politics of the Gender Gap. The Social Construction of Political Influence*. Beverly Hills: Sage.

Mansbridge, J. J. (1985), 'Myth and Reality: The ERA and the Gender Gap in the 1980 Election', *Public Opinion Quarterly*, Vol. 49:1:164-177.

Norris, P. (1988), 'The Gender Gap: A Cross-National Trend', in Mueller, C.M. (ed.): *The Politics of the Gender Gap*. Newbury Park: SAGE.

Oskarson, M. (1990), 'Klassröstning på reträtt', in Gilljam, M. and Holmberg, S. (eds): *Rött Blått Grönt. En bok om 1988 års riksdagsval*. Stockholm: Bonniers.

Pesonen, P. (1972), 'Suomen puolueiden kannatuspohja', in Pesonen, P. (ed.): *Protestivaalit, nuorisovaalit*. Tampere: Gaudeamus.

Petersson, O., Westholm, A. and Blomberg, G. (1989), *Medborgarnas makt*. Stockholm: Carlssons bokförlag.

Petersson, O. (1994), *Government and Politics of the Nordic Countries*. Stockholm: Publica.

Slgurbjarnardóttir, S. H. (1992), 'Kvinnelisten i Island. Underveis fra kvinnepolitikk til feministisk politikk?' Hovedoppgave i sosiologi. Institutt for sosiologi. University of Oslo.

Styrkársdottir, A. (1986), 'From social movement to political party: the new women's movement in Iceland', in Dahlerup, D. (ed.): *The New Women's Movement*. London: Sage.

Togeby, L. (1984), *Politik - også en kvindesag*. Aarhus: Politica.

Togeby, L. (1989), 'Politiseringen af kvinder og af kvindespörgsmålet', in Elklit, J. and Tonsgaard, O. (eds): *To folketingsvalg*. Aarhus: Politica.

Togeby, L. (1993a), 'Grass roots participation in the Nordic countries', *European Journal of Political Research*, Vol. 24, 2:159-175.

Togeby, L. (1993b), 'Feminist Attitudes: Social Interests or Political Ideology'. Draft provided by the author.

Valen, H. (1992), *Valg og Politikk - et samfunn i endring*, 2nd edition. Oslo: NKS-Forlaget.

Women in Scandinavian party organizations[1]

Jan Sundberg

The problem

According to the Swedish political scientist Maud Eduards, the level of abstraction in political studies has become so high that the existence of human beings can no longer be identified. Instead of studying the sentiments and intuitions of women and men in political life, researchers prefer to construct sexless models of rationality totally divorced from their bodies and emotions (Eduards 1993:99-108). This general remark on the state of political science captures very well what has been elaborated in party research up until now. Briefly, theories of party growth characterized parties as a function of a social class, denominational group, ethnic group or the like. When the social base was growing, it automatically resulted in a corresponding party growth (Michels 1925; Duverger 1978). No place was given to women in the classical studies of the growing mass organizations, either on the grass roots level or in the party leadership. In addition, when party growth was seen as determined by democratic integration (where the party incorporated the individual to the community through the enlarging governmental functions) women were excluded as an important category of incorporation (Neumann 1956:395-421).

Similarly, more recent studies of party decline are faulted by the neglect of female members. According to the functionalist view, parties decline when the original social base fades as a source of change and expansion (Kirchheimer 1966:177-200; Panebianco 1988). Parties are seen as a mirror of the social forces and not as an independent group of female and male actors, who can affect their environment. Following a different argumentation, the application of public choice theory on party research likewise results in party decline. According to this theory, all forms of

[1] The author is indebted to Drude Dahlerup and Lise Togeby of the University of Aarhus for their help in providing the data and studies relevant to this article, and to the Norwegian Social Science Data Service (NSD), the Danish Data Archive (DDA), and the Swedish Social Science Data Service (SSD) for the computer runs. Finally, Ingela Carlsson of the Swedish Social Democratic Party (SAP) helped me on the way to find the hidden women in the party records.

party activity are exclusively driven by the selfish interest to win seats in elections or other material rewards provided by the party (Epstein 1967; Wright 1971:17-54; Schlesinger 1984:369-400). All types of informal female networks, female solidarity, party loyalty, compassion, or formal rules and routines are unheard of. In short, the dominant party theories from past and present provide little, if any, guidelines in understanding and explaining the forms and content of female membership in political parties.

However, female party membership is older than all the theories discussed above, it dates its origin to the suffrage issue which was raised at the turn of this century when women in all Scandinavian countries were mobilized to pursue their aims. It was the liberal parties and the labour movement that paved the way to suffrage for men and women. The dominance of men in politics continued with the same strength after the enfrachisement of women. When the female participation in elections approached the level of men, the gap of dominance shrank only slightly. Similarly, the male members dominated the party organizations from the day women were given the right to become members. No signs of change in the strong male dominance appeared until the 1970s; since then, however, the inclusion of women has radically changed the proportion of gender at all levels in Scandinavian parties. Unfortunately, very little has been done to analyse why women in Scandinavian parties - in contrast to women in the rest of Europe - have managed to increase their influence radically.

The aim of this paper is to evaluate and compare the proportion of female party membership in four Scandinavian countries, the inclusion of women in the top of the party hierarchy, and the nomination of female candidates on the party lists. Traditionally, the low inclusion of women in politics has been explained in terms of diverging female interests that do not fit the male dominated politics. It has been assumed that women prefer to abstain rather than to waste all their strength to start a long uncertain struggle for change of the content of politics (Eduards, Gustafsson and Jónasdóttir 1989:25-52; Hedlund 1988:79-105; Miller, Hildreth, and Simmons 1988:106-134). The notion of interest is problematic in general terms as well as in a female context. Starting with the latter, women's interests are not clear, and have been given different theoretical and empirical meanings. Women's interests can empirically be stated by statistics. If women are under-represented (in terms of representation), it is a women's interest to politicize the issue. This does not always happen, and the perceptions about the interests often fall apart. Theoretical definitions also fall apart as some researchers claim that the individual's relation to reproduction is a women's interest, while others claim that it is the politicization of gender/sexual relations, or try to differentiate between objective and subjective interests (Sapiro 1981:701-716; Jónasdóttir 1988:33-65; Diamond and Hartsock 1981: 717-721). One way of defining interest is to relate the concept to social relations, and assume that a person's interest will be formed on the basis of his/her position in society.

Taking the concept of female interest as a point of departure, it is a female interest to be included in balanced proportions as members and representatives at all levels in the party hierarchy. The path to equal representation in all party bodies is by no means an easy one. It is one thing to heighten political consciousness among women, to make them want to become members, and to get positions in the party organization. It is another thing to deal with the hindrances women face in the contest for positions at all levels of the party hierarchy. These two processes can be seen as causal and the former feeds the latter. In other words, a large female membership is necessary to break through the organizational barriers to promotion.

In this paper we follow a similar idea. Starting with the pioneering role of the social democratic parties who actively encouraged women to join the party in the first wave of female mobilization, we will compare the proportion of female membership today in the largest Scandinavian parties. This discussion is followed by a presentation of the party hierarchy and those hindrances women meet in the four different Scandinavian countries. Finally we examine the electoral channel to power and influence that parties formally provide through the nomination process to all its members in the subnational party. A total of 20 established parties are investigated, all with a long heritage and an ideological resemblance to parties in the other countries included.

The pioneering role of female members in the social democratic parties

Female enfranchisement was a great victory for the early women's movement. Women were given full political citizenship but the female response to this formal equality was met with caution for many years to come. One of the main functions of the local branches and their members was to mobilize the enfranchised citizens to vote. A low voter turnout was commonly seen as a greater threat than low party loyalty. However, as the parties were totally dominated by men, the campaign to mobilize the citizens to vote initially appealed to the male and not to the female electorate. To break the male hegemony where male party members mobilized the electorate to vote for male candidates, female activists came together to organize women's associations linked to the party. One of their first missions was to mobilize the female electorate to vote.

The concept of membership was by no means clear in the Scandinavian parties when the first women were politically organized. The non-socialist party records were often incomplete as there was not much activity between elections, and the difference between formal membership and party adherents was unclear. It was the Scandinavian social democratic parties that started to formalize the membership, as the well-structured and organized party machine needed a clear overview over those who ran the activity. For this reason, the social democrats in Scandinavia have always put more effort than most other parties into proper membership records. In addition, as votes and members were extremely important for the offensive worker's movement, also women had to be included early on in the loyal electorate, but also in the party machine. The first women's associations were created even before the enfranchisement of women (1900 in Finland and 1901 in Norway). In Sweden the women's association was founded in 1920, directly after their enfranchisement. Only in Denmark did the social democratic party actively oppose a separate women's organization. Not until 1929 was a national committee founded, and 40 years later it was dissolved in the name of equality (Dahlerup 1979b:138-141; Dahlerup 1979a: 5-35; Dahlerup 1979b:111-149). All members of the four women's associations were members of the party as well. In Denmark the women's committees had no members. Their role was to deal with female issues. In all Scandinavian countries, perhaps with the exception of Denmark, the social democratic women's associations were pioneers in politicizing the female electorate. As to formal membership, the social democats were also pioneers in recruiting female members to their ranks.

Although the social democrats put much effort into keeping proper membership records, the periodical lack of valid information on female membership is striking. Generally, the female membership is better emphasized in the party records before World War II than after. In Norway, female membership was systematically recorded from 1911 to 1939. After the war no systematic data has been gathered on the female members. From the beginning of the 1990s a separation of women and men can be achieved through the computerization of the membership records, but the figures are not published in the annual reports. Similarly, in Finland excellent membership records from the beginning of this century were carefully kept. After World War II, the accuracy decreased considerably (due to internal party conflicts) and no information on female membership size was documented until 1977. At that time data became available thanks to the computerization of the record functions in

1974. Unfortunately, there is no systematic documentation in the annual reports on the female membership.

In Denmark the female membership is properly documented in the annual reports from 1915 until the early 1960s. The annual reports from 1963 and 1965 to 1969 lack membership data (available in the party archive) and after 1969 the registration of female membership was terminated. Not until the 1990s, when the registration process was computerized, could a break-down of membership by gender be achieved. Finally, in Sweden no systematic time series data on female membership are available in the annual reports. However, as the annual reports include detailed membership data on the female members, among other things, a time series can be constructed by investigating every annual report back to 1923, when the first membership figures were differentiated by sex.

Given the status of the annual reports as the most important official document of the internal party life, it seems evident, on the basis of registration and documentation policy, that female party membership was more important before World War II than after. Only by promoting/enlisting women as party members, or more generally, as political citizens could they be mobilized to participate in elections. From the first election when women were enfranchised, voter turnout has accurately been documented by sex in the official statistics. The low female turnout in elections must have been considered a painful waste of mandates of power in parliament. Supposing that women had party preferences similar to men's (or their husbands'), the mobilizing function grew extremely important. Studies show that a large membership plays an important role where there is a strong need to mobilize voters (von Beyme 1985:167-188). Unfortunately, very little has been done to show the mobilizing effect of a large female membership on female voting. The social democrats, however, realized that a large female membership was a necessity in order to mobilize women to vote when the campaign work relied heavily on mass membership involvement.

In addition, the enfranchisement of women gave them a political citizenship with formally equal political rights to men and the inclusion of women as party members integrated them into political work and at least implicitly prepared them to take office in the future. At these times a majority of women were economically dependent on their husbands. Only a minority of women were employed, but their incomes lagged far behind the male employees'. The social democratic parties recruited their members from the proletariat, which included a large group of people, from those with practically no incomes to skilled labourers with relatively good incomes. Therefore the social democrats adopted a gradual subscription system based on ability to pay. This arrangement effectively diminished the economic barriers to the female members' joining the party. Either the female members paid their subscription according to their level of income like the male members, or they were all put in the same low paying category labelled women. Moreover, to enlarge the female membership the social democratic party in Denmark turned to its male members, offering their wives full membership at a symbolic price of subscription (Dahlerup 1979a:9-10). As female employment increased, the reduced subscription for all women was phased out. However, even in the late 1960s, the Danish female members paid half subscription. After 1969 they followed the same system as the male members, which made it impossible to identify the members according to sex.

One of the most striking features of the early female membership can be found in the figures from Denmark and Finland prior to women's enfranchisement. More than 20 percent of the members were women, though they had no right to vote in parliamentary elections. In addition, as the Social Democratic party was the leading political force in the enfranchisement issue, the female members could not escape being politicized and mobilized. The share of female members increased rapidly in Denmark and in the beginning of World War II about 40 percent of all members were women. Since then, only small changes in the gender proportions have taken place. The growth in numbers was even greater as the party tripled its membership during the period from 1917 to 1939. A separate women's association seems in this context superfluous. When the Danish women's association was founded, female members exceeded 30 percent of all party members. In Finland, the proportion of women was lower than in Denmark, but the mass organization was much smaller and badly hurt by the civil war and the violent pressure from the right. Nevertheless, the proportion of women exceeded 30 percent shortly after World War II and since then the changes have been minor.

The figures show that the proportion of women is considerably lower in Norway compared to Denmark and Finland. During the rapid growth of the organization in the 1920s and 1930s, the share of women in the Norwegian Labour party never came close to 20 percent. No signs of an increase in the female membership are visible during this period. In Sweden, the proportion of female membership shows a close resemblance to the Norwegian case during the same period. The proportion of women increased very slowly during the post-War period. In a 45-year period

Table 1
The proportion of female members in social democratic parties in
four Scandinavian countries

	Denmark Members N	Women %		Finland Members N	Women %		Norway Members N	Women %
Year			Year			Year		
1915	60.112	17	1900	9165	18	1911	36073	12
1920	126568	27	1905	45298	21	1915	62952	13
1925	143203	31	1910	52076	23	1920	97585	16
1930	171055	34	1915	51821	21	1925	40874	18
1935	195142	35	1920	49830	30	1930	80177	17
1939	206995	35	1925	27268	27	1935	122007	15
1945	243532	39	1930	28701	26	1939	170889	15
1949	294969	41	1935	28243	27			
1955	278299	41	1939	32897	26			
1960	253855	40	1945	61816	30			
1965	223977	38	1950	67946	30			
1969	179907	33						
			1977	101388	34			
			1980	99484	35			
			1983	95785	36			
			1986	90115	38			
1993	90000	38	1992	78247	38	1993	115000	38

Sweden Year	Members N	Women %
1923	138510	14
1930	277017	14
1935	338482	16
1939	458831	17
1945	563981	23
1950	722073	25
1956	777860	27
1960	801068	27
1965	873024	27
1969	907502	25
1974	1001406	29
1980	1205252	34
1985	1215250	35
1990	837870	33
1992	262089	41

Source: Denmark, Dahlerup 1979a:5-35; Documents available at Arbeiderbevaegelsens Bibliotek og Arkiv; Finland, SDP Puoluetilastot 1899-1942, Annual Reports 1943-1950; Computer lists for 1977-1992 available at the party office; Norway, DNA Annual Reports 1911-1939; Sweden, Annual Reports 1923-1992.

(1945-1990) the increase was only about 10 percent. The total number of female members increased rapidly during this period, from 128 026 in 1945 to 422 695 in 1985. In 1990 the party underwent a fundamental organizational change, when the system of collective membership (Labour union and party) was abolished. As a result, the membership declined from one million members down to fewer than 300 000 members. After this membership exit, the share of female members was strengthened from 33 percent in late 1990 to 41 percent in late 1992. The labour union federation, LO, has a strong heritage of male dominance. In 1945 only 17 percent of its members were female but the share increased rapidly in the 1970s and

1980s to 45 percent in 1990 (Bergqvist 1991:107-125; Bergqvist 1993). However, only about one third of the LO members were collectively affiliated because the decision of affiliation was made by the local branch units.

The figures in Table 1 show that the male dominated units were more likely to be collectively affiliated than those units dominated by women. In addition, the low share of female members in the Norwegian Labour party is highly dependent on the close relationship between the party and the 'masculine' labour unions in the first half of this century. The relation between union and party is commonly seen as most developed in Sweden and most problematic in Denmark (Elvander 1980:171-181). Following our argumentation the increase in female membership is dependent on the degree of connection between union and party and the degree of male dominance in the union. Given this statement, the low share of female members in the Norwegian Labour party can be better understood. During the early years of this century the Norwegian Labour party was something between an interest organization and a political party. Because of the electoral system, the pay-off in elections was meagre and the party became increasingly suspicious of the parliamentary channel (Ryssevik 1991:15-48). During these years the Labour party was strongly radicalized and deeply tied to the labour union. The radicalism faded long ago, but the ties to the unions are still strong. According to a 1969 survey, only 11 percent of the collectively affilated membes were women compared to 32 percent of the individually affiliated members (NSD 1969). Now the percentage of women is 38 percent in the Norwegian Labour party. In Denmark and Finland the ties to the unions have always been looser. The internal conflicts and differentiation within the Danish union movement are usually seen as the major deteminants, whereas in Finland the constant political power struggle in the unions between the social democrats and the communists effectively hindered a deep social democratic union connection. All in all, after the breakthrough of individual membership as a dominant form of party affiliation, the proportions of female members in the Scandinavian Social democratic parties of today are more similar than ever before in their documented history.

Female membership in Scandinavian parties at large

A systematic time series of female party membership, even for a short period, is not possible for most Scandinavian parties as women have not been considered a category of interest. The calculation of female membership proved to be more problematic than expected in the social democratic parties. The lack of accuracy and systematic time series are the most common shortcomings in the party records. The lack of accuracy usually appears in the form of approximated totals and as a difference between formal membership registered by parties and membership figures presented in surveys. The latter problem is most striking among parties with collective membership and the former among some non-socialist parties (especially the Finnish Center and the populist parties).

One way of coping with this problem is to use available survey data. The first opinion polls date back to the 1940s and 1950s, but systematic data on party membership is more commonly documented in electoral studies from the 1960s. The validity problem is common to most of the surveys, as the samples are relatively small, the number of parties large, and the percentage of party members low. As a result, it is only possible to document the share of female members for the largest parties in those surveys with the highest number of observations. A breakdown of membership in parties is not possible in Denmark and Finland, either because the connection between party and membership cannot be identified, or because the validity requirements are severely violated. In Finland the surveys count less than half the number of respondents answering yes on the question of party membership in Sweden. As the number of surveys is higher and the number of observations larger, data from Norway and Sweden can be broken down for the largest parties and included in the table below.

According to the results of 18 surveys, the proportion of female party members in the four Scandinavian countries has grown steadily. Figures show a very rapid increase in the female representation in Denmark and Norway, whereas the development has been slower in Finland and Sweden. The 1970s seems to be a very important decade for the rising of political consciousness among women. However, the wave of politicization was not a phenomenon visible in parties alone. Perhaps the largest visible participation was channelled into different forms of alternative politics including demonstrations/protests, grass-roots movements and networks, which are all slightly dominated by women (Togeby 1989a:63-66). Totalling all forms of political involvement, the female influx was therefore much more comprehensive than the party membership figures indicate. A high proportion of female party members does not determine a similar high proportion among party activists. Studies show that women are less active than men in the traditional forms of politics including party activities (Petersson, Westholm, and Blomberg 1989:145-154).

The increase of female members is not linear according to the figures in Table 2. In the case of Finland there is an increase of female members from 36 percent to 44 percent in 1987, and in 1991 the proportion is back where it started. The data for 1991 seems less reliable than the 1987 figures. A large welfare suvery with a sample of about 13,000 respondents in 1986 supports the results of the 1987 survey. No signs of a drastic decline since then are visible, and it seems more likely that the shift is determined by shortcomings in the interview data. Similarly, the figures show a drastic decline in the Swedish data for 1979. As in the Finnish case, no signs of a sudden decline can be distinguished in the Swedish parties during the late 1970s. It is more likely that the decline is determined by shortcomings in the interview data.

Table 2
The proportion of female members in a selection of Scandinavian parties

Denmark Year	Women %	Men %	Total N
1971	38	62	218
1979	39	61	215
1987	47	53	287

Finland Year	Women %	Men %	Total N
1975	36	64	97
1987	44	56	167
1991	36	64	164

Norway Year	DNA %	SP %	H %	N for all parties	Women %	Men %
1965	25	29	58	264	35	65
1969	26	31	47	258	33	67
1977	24	43	42	219	36	64
1981	40	44	41	224	42	58
1985	40	44	41	224	42	58
1989	40	40	54	274	48	52

Sweden Year	SAP %	CP %	M %	N for all parties	Women %	Men %
1964	23	40	54	496	33	67
1970	31	44	44	177	37	63
1979	32	22	37	395	30	70
1985	40	30	42	426	36	64
1988	32	37	43	335	35	65

Source, Denmark: DDA, Finland: University of Tampere (Risto Sänkiaho and Sami Borg), Norway: NSD (Henry Valen), Sweden: SSD (Bo Särlvik, Olof Johansson and Sören Holmberg).
Abbrevations, DNA: Labour party, SP: Center party, H: Conservative party, SAP: Social Democratic party, CP: Center party, M: Conservative party.

As the number of observations allows us to break down the party membership shares for the largest parties in Norway and Sweden, comparisons can be made between the Social Democratic party and the two main non-socialist parties. For both countries, the agrarian Center and the Conservative party on the right have memberships large enough to appear in Table 2. The figures from the beginning of the period systematically show a higher share of female members in the two non-socialist parties compared to the Social Democratic party. A comparison between the social democratic parties and other parties in Norway and Sweden cannot, however, be made without reservations. Collective membership disadvantages female membership and compared to the individual membership in the non-socialist parties the difference becomes large in both countries. In addition, the difference is also determined by how the question is formulated in the questionnaire. In many of the surveys, the respondents are asked to answer on a question of party membership or political organization. Treating these two categories as one will have an effect on the result that can substantially differ from the official party records. The notion of a political organization includes both affiliated and associated organizations to the party. Including all members with ties to a party can have a considerable effect on the proportion of women as compared to the proportion exclusively in the party organization. The proportion of female members in the Swedish Center party is very high in the beginning of the period. Also the shares from the two Conservative parties are very high in the beginning of the period, showing a female proportion over 50 percent. The latest measures show a share of around 40 percent, which seems more reasonable. No sudden changes have taken place and therefore the drop of the female membership in the Swedish Center party from 44 percent in 1970 to 22 percent in 1979 is determined by factors of measurement and not reality. All in all, the surveys used here are not very accurate on party membership, although the results have been extensively used in many electoral studies.

The survey results from the Norwegian electoral studies show a very rapid increase in the share of female members in the Labour party. As no figures are available from the party records, no comparisons can be made as to when the proportion of women started to increase rapidly. The current figures from the party records correspond with the survey measure from 1989. Thus, the influx of women into the party can therefore on relatively valid grounds, be dated to the late 1970s, although the figures in the survey may well overestimate the proportions. The agrarian Center party shows a very high proportion of women since the late 1970s and in the conservative Høyre, the proportion of women exceeds 40 percent during the whole period. As in the case of the Labour party, no comparisons can be made with official party records; but the overall trend in Norway seems to be that women have been included as party members to a higher degree than in the rest of Scandinavia since the early 1980s.

Female power in Scandinavian parties

The most powerful positions in a party organization are by no means unproblematic to detect, as the party is hierarchially organized around units with different functions. Starting from the base line, every branch is hierarchially organized with a board and a chairman. The organizational model follows similar patterns at the constituency level, in which all branches in the geographical area are included. At the national level, the party congress is formally the highest decision-making unit in the entire party organization. Perhaps for that reason participants in the congress are sometimes seen as belonging to the party élite (Heidar 1988). The party congress, however, at the most meets annually, in some cases only every fourth year. As several hundred delegates participate in the congress it resembles the function of an annual meeting of shareholders. During the past 30 years, the flow of motions raised by the delegates has remarkably increased, and the variety of issues is larger than ever before. Also the number of issues raised by female activists has shown a remarkable increase since the early 1970s (Ramstedt-Silén 1990:95-129; Heidar 1990:131-149; Pierre 1990:151-166; Pierre and Widfeldt 1992). Though the delegates show an impressive activity, very few motions have a fair chance of being adopted in the program, and the chances are microscopic that a motion would ever be materialized through the party's activity in cabinet and parliament.

The regular meetings of the party executive are more important in terms of pushing power and influence than the large party congresses or the smaller party council, which meet more frequently than the congress but less frequently than the executive. Thus, it is in the executive that important decisions are made on internal organizational affairs and on the daily party policy in cabinet and parliament. To be effective, the party executive has to be relatively manageable. It has relatively few members and they must be ready to make considerable efforts for the party. However, if the executive has a large membership it can be an indication that the real power is delegated to a smaller body, named a working committee or national committee. In the table below, the percentages of female representatives are listed from 20 different Scandinavian parties, grouped in five categories according to the common left - right dimension in all four countries.

Compared to the share of female members in the parties, the proportion of women included in the executive is ill-balanced. The phenomenon is well known from other voluntary and professional organizations. There are no systematic differences between the parties on that point, perhaps with the exception that the parties on the right in Norway and Sweden have included women to a larger extent than the Social Democrats. Thus, the male dominance was as well established among the members in the branches as among the elected positions in the executives. However, a remarkable change took place in the Norwegian Labour party in the early 1970s, when the proportion of women included in the executive was doubled in a period of five years. Since then, the change has been small and now about half of the executive members are women. With this rapid change the Norwegian Labour party has achieved a considerably higher proportion of women in its executive than any other social democratic party in Scandinavia.

Also the socialist parties left of the social democrats, in Denmark, Finland and Sweden have greatly increased the inclusion of women in their executives. The big change in Denmark and Sweden came in the late 1970s, and about ten years later in Finland. As no figures are available from the early period in the Norwegian Socialist party, no conclusions can be made; but the figures from 1971 and onwards show an inclusion of women at a constant high level. All in all, the socialist parties today

Table 3
Representation of women on National Party Executives in Scandinavia 1960-1990 (five year averages)

Den-mark	SF	SF	SD	SD	RV	RV	V	V	KF	KF
Year	All Exec	Wo-men %	All Exec	Wo-men %	All Exec	Wo-men %	All Exec	Wo-men %	All Exec	Wo-men %
1960 -65	29	8					75	3		
1966 -70	38	12					69	3		
1971 -75	36	14	53	9			60	7		
1976 -80	41	36	50	10			60	13		
1981 -85	39	36	49	20	105	26	60	15	88	15
1986 -89	39	36	51	30	105	28	60	18	75	16

Fin-land	SKDL	SKDL	SDP	SDP	SFP	SFP	Kesk	Kesk	Kok	Kok
Year	All Exec	Wo-men %	All Exec	Wo-men %	All Exec	Wo-men %	All Exec	Wo-men %	All Exec	Wo-men %
1960 - 65	28	20	14	11	26	10	16	13	12	18
1966 -70	29	16	12	17	27	7	19	11	12	10
1971 -75	25	10	13	8	28	9	23	12	17	14
1976 -80	24	15	13	8	29	19	25	14	17	14
1981 -85	24	19	13	15	29	27	30	17	19	21
1986 -90	14	39	13	19	29	28	31	16	23	14

Nor-way	SV	SV	DNA	DNA	V	V	SP	SP	H	H
Year	All Exec	Wo-men %	All Exec	Wo-men %	All Exec	Wo-men %	All Exec	Wo-men %	All Exec	Wo-men %
1960 -65			15	16	14	7	11	24	14	22
1966 -70			15	23	7	19	11	23	10	13
1971 -75	15	47	15	40	7	36	11	36	5	0
1976 -80	15	47	15	40	8	43	11	36	7	19
1981 -85	15	47	15	45	9	50	11	46	8	38
1986 -90	15	47	15	47	10	45	11	55	8	38

Swe-den	VPK	VPK	S	S	FP	FP	C	C	M	M
Year	All Exec	Wo-men %	All Exec	Wo-men %	All Exec	Wo-men %	All Exec	Wo-men %	All Exec	Wo-men %
1960 -65	60	10	56	10	42	17	31	10	21	28
1966 -70	46	13	56	8	42	18	32	14	22	24
1971 -75	45	18	57	11	41	26	31	26	19	27
1976 -80	48	27	57	23	43	36	31	26	19	38
1981 -85	50	36	57	27	42	44	31	32	19	42
1986 -90	50	47	57	29	43	48	33	35	18	43

Source: Bille 1992:258-259; Sundberg and Gylling 1992:306-308; Svåsand 1992:772-773; Pierre and Widfeldt 1992:822-823

Abbrevations:
Denmark, SF: Socialist People's Party; SD: Social Democrats; RV: Social Liberals; V: Liberal Party;
KF: Conservative People's Party
Finland, SKDL: Finnish People's Democratic League; SDP: Social Democratic Party; SFP: Swedish
People's Party; Kesk.: Centre Party; Kok.: National Coalition
Norway, SV: Socialist Left Party; DNA: Labour Party; V: Liberal Party; SP: Centre Party; H:
Conservative Party
Sweden, VPK: Left Party Communists; S: Social Democratic Party; FP: People's Party; C: Centre Party;
M: Moderate Unity Party

show a much smaller variation in the proportion of female executives than ten years ago. Compared to the social democratic parties, the socialist parties seem generally to maintain a higher proportion of female representatives.

In the non-socialist block, the liberal parties in Denmark and Finland (Swedish People's Party) have increased their inclusion of women, but their share is still under 30 percent. In Norway and Sweden the increase during the three decades has been considerable and now the share of women and men is balanced in the executive. The variation is larger between the agrarian Centre parties (Liberal Party in Denmark), which have a heritage of supporting traditional family views. The figures for female inclusion show sluggish changes in that respect in Denmark and Finland. In both countries the agrarian executives are heavily dominated by men. Though the changes have been slow in Finland and in Denmark, the total male dominance was to some extent relaxed during the late 1970s. However, the break with the old male dominance is most prominent in the Norwegian Centre party, followed by the Swedish agrarians. In Norway, the executive is now slightly dominated by women and in Sweden the strong male dominance was broken by the early 1970s. Finally, among the conservative parties nothing has changed drastically in Denmark and Finland, i.e. the male dominance is strong and almost unchanged. In Norway and Sweden, the trend is the same as for other parties. The male dominance has been broken in the Swedish Conservative party since the late 1970s followed by the Norwegian Conservative party in the early 1980s.

Comparing parties across the nations seems to give less variance than comparing nations, as parties in Norway and Sweden generally tend to include higher proportions of women than parties in Denmark and Finland. The country differences were substantially smaller in the beginning of the period, indicating that the party executives very early become the target of change for the female members in these two countries. One institutional reform is important in this context as all Norwegian parties have adopted a general quota of a minimum of 40 percent of each sex in elected party bodies with the exception of the conservative Høyre. The quota rule seems to have an important role in attracting women to high positions. According to the quota rule, the female positions can be filled without competition with male candidates. This change in culture towards more solidarity and cooperation contributes considerably to making the high party positions more attractive to women. The Swedish case shows that a high inclusion of women is possible without quota rules if there is a social pressure towards promoting women in society. The most efficient way, however, is a combination of quota and pressure as the figures from Norway indicate.

Denmark and Finland score very low in comparison with Norway and Sweden but this does not necessarily mean that the problems are identical. Studies show that the Danish women are less oriented towards the traditional channels in pursuing their aims (Togeby 1989a; Togeby 1989b:227-254). As the pattern is the opposite in Finland, the low shares can instead be understood in cultural terms. Thus, it seems more probable that the Danish female party members put less emphasis on winning influence through the executive than through other non-traditional channels like grass-roots movements and protests. In Finland, on the other hand, these channels are poorly utilized, and therefore the bulk of political activities are still monopolized by parties. This general pattern is the same for Finnish women as for men, and therefore the arena for channeling one's political aims is much narrower in Finland, not exclusively compared to Denmark but also to Norway and Sweden. Studies show that the party organizations in Finland are much more externally controlled and regulated by public authorities than parties in the rest of Scandinavia (Sundberg 1994). Hence, the Finnish parties have a much more authoritative party culture and in combination with poor alternative political channels, the female party members in Finland have few other choices than pursuing their aims through the party. One of them is the executive which is still heavily male dominated, the other is the electoral channel at the subnational level (to be discussed in the next section).

In addition, comparing party executives the way we have done here is somewhat problematic as their functions are not identical. In Norway the party executives are small, indicating that it is the real executive where important decisions are made. This also indicates that the members are full or part-time politicians, as the meetings are long and frequent. By a professional politician we mean an MP, cabinet member, or an elected professional in a county or municipal leadership. A part-time professional is a politician that works for a party, an ancillary organization, an affiliated organization, a connected labour union, producer's organization or the like. By making this distinction we want to make it clear that the inner circle of power today is to a high degree professionalized. Though this pattern is most prominent in Norway, the same tendency is evident in Finland as well. In Sweden the executives are larger and in Denmark the largest executive counts over one hundred members. In fact, the important decisions are not made in these large organizational bodies, but in small committees. These working executives are much smaller and open only to a small minority of professional politicans, like in Norway and Finland. No systematic differences between the size of the executive and the share of women positions can be found. Whether we count the share of women in the inner circle of power or the circle close to it, the female politicians in Norway always appear to be best represented. All in all, with the exception of Norway and partly of Sweden, women systematically fail to be equally represented.

The nomination of female candidates

The party executive is the most important unit concerning power and influence in the organization. Political parties are complex organizations, giving their members options to utilize other more direct forms of power and influence. One of the most rational ways for female party members to pursue their aims is to be nominated in parliamentary elections. The prospect of getting an issue raised and accepted at a party congress and implemented via the active work of the party executive and the parliamentary party is very small. A much more efficient way for the active member to pursue an aim is to be nominated in a constituency by the subnational party, and via the elections work for the aim directly in parliament. With this strategy the female member does not need to compete on the positions up in the party hierarchy. In contrast, the nomination process is much closer to the party grass roots, as the decisions are made at the constituency level. In addition, either the branch or single members have the right to nominate a candidate. The variation of the membership influence in the nomination process between Scandinavian parties is narrow, giving the female members almost equal opportunities to nominate and choose their candidates (Sundberg 1993). Thus, the party rules include no formal hindrances to prevent the female members in the subnational party from becoming candidates.

The electoral laws, in contrast, differ considerably between the Scandinavian multi-party systems. Finland has the most candidate-centered system, as the candidate lists have no ranking order. It is the voters who choose their individual candidates from the list nominated by by the party members in alphabetic order. In Sweden, at the other extreme, it is the party which ranks the candidates, and the voters decide how many candidates from each party will be elected. Similarly to Sweden, the Norwegian voters have very little opportunity to change the ranking order on lists made up by the party. The Danish system, or rather systems, allow the voters to make individual choices if they wish, or alternatively to follow the ranking order made by the party (less common today). By the individual option the Danish system comes somewhere between the two extremes on the dichotomy (Elklit and Pade 1991:18-20; Tonsgaard 1984:369-382; Törnudd 1968:80-128; Tarasti 1987:284-323; Valen 1988:210-235; Valen 1985:46-56; Holmberg and Stjernquist 1988:65-81; Ricknell 1975:42-57; Birgersson and Westerståhl 1982:126-139). Thus, the nomination situation for women is considerably different between the two extreme types of systems in Scandinavia. In Finland women have to recruit a great number of female nominees to fill the party list with sufficient candidates. A large supply of female candidates is the most efficient way of facilitating a natural choice of a woman. In the three other Scandinavian countries, the first stage of getting sufficient female nominees is equally important. More important, in Norway and Sweden female party activists also have to ensure that women are highly ranked on the candidate list in order to have a fair chance of being elected. As the voter only chooses the share of mandates between parties, much more effort is put on the women's own party work in the nomination process.

In the following table the shares of female candidates and elected representatives are compared. Unfortunately, no candidates are included from Sweden as the public records do not provide such data.

The electoral channel is the most efficient way for women today to win political influence. It is relatively easy for women to become nominated, as almost half of the membership are women. A large female membership increases the potential supply of candidates and composes a viable platform for the nominees. However, in the beginning of the period the share of female candidates was low in all three countries. As the voters can choose among the candidates in Finland the effect is much different from that in Norway. The few female candidates in Norway were also ranked low on the party list, which hindered them greatly from being elected. The Danish electoral alternative seems not to be a barrier to female candidates as the Norwegian case is, since the share of female candidates has strongly increased. In Finland the share of female candidates reached a level of around 40 percent in the late 1980s and in Norway the same share was reached as early as ten years earlier. Finally, in Denmark the share of female candidates is at a lower level, though the proportion of women has increased steadily.

In addition, the increase in the number of female candidates in Norway during the 1970s follows the same trend of heightened female consciousness that can be observed in other party functions discussed above. A high proportion of female

Table 4
The share of female candidates (C) and elected representatives (E) in Scandinavia 1960-1990

Denmark Year	SF Tot % N	SD Tot % N	RV Tot % N	V Tot % N	KF Tot % N
1960 C:	10 91	6 124	20 116	9 122	13 114
E:	0 11	9 76	18 11	5 38	19 32
1964 C:	13 113	6 124	16 116	9 122	14 116
E:	10 10	9 76	20 10	3 38	17 36
1966 C:	14 122	7 126	17 117	9 124	16 121
E:	15 20	7 69	23 13	3 35	18 34
1968 C:	15 120	6 126	16 117	13 128	16 120
E:	9 11	5 62	19 27	9 34	16 37
1971 C:	17 107	13 104	18 102	17 113	19 93
E:	24 17	14 70	22 27	3 30	23 31
1973 C:	15 104	16 104	18 100	19 108	21 95
E:	27 11	13 46	25 20	14 22	13 16
1975 C:	22 104	15 104	23 99	18 106	21 96
E:	22 9	11 53	31 13	17 42	20 10
1977 C:	23 104	14 104	21 99	19 102	24 90
E:	29 7	18 65	17 6	10 21	27 15
1979 C:	25 103	16 104	24 98	18 98	17 86
E:	64 11	24 68	30 10	14 22	32 22
1981 C:	22 99	22 105	30 98	20 95	23 88
E:	43 21	19 59	33 9	5 20	35 26
1984 C:	28 102	23 104	29 99	23 96	21 103
E:	43 21	18 56	20 10	27 22	13 42
1987 C:	35 103	28 104	29 101	26 96	20 104
E:	33 27	24 54	45 11	11 19	34 38
1988 C:	37 105	29 104	30 100	29 98	23 103
E:	33 24	33 55	50 10	14 22	31 35

Finland Year	SKDL/VAS Tot % N	SDP Tot % N	Kesk. Tot % N	SFP Tot % N	Kok. Tot % N
1962 C:	19 200	11 199	12 156	4 51	21 183
E:	19 47	16 38	8 53	0 14	13 32
1966 C:	17 178	14 199	14 184	11 53	20 186
E:	17 41	16 55	12 49	0 12	19 26
1970 C:	22 178	20 199	15 192	13 55	22 193
E:	28 36	25 52	17 36	8 12	27 37
1972 C:	21 186	19 199	19 171	22 51	25 199
E:	24 37	27 55	17 35	10 10	21 34
1975 C:	26 209	25 224	26 151	16 38	28 179
E:	23 40	24 54	18 39	20 10	25 36
1979 C:	26 220	31 225	23 185	21 57	28 226
E:	31 35	31 52	14 36	20 10	28 47
1983 C:	33 227	33 227	31 199	34 65	30 227
E:	38 26	32 57	24 38	18 11	41 44
1987 C:	37 229	40 229	37 177	36 61	35 229
E:	31 16	32 56	28 40	8 13	42 53
1991 C:	43 230	42 230	38 215	39 71	43 230
E:	26 19	46 48	27 55	25 12	50 40

candidates does not automatically result in a high proportion of elected representatives. The table shows that it is the Socialist left party and the Labour party that provided the best chances for their female candidates by giving them high positions in the ranking order. In the agrarian Center party and in the Conservative party the share of female candidates is equally high, but the proportion of those elected is much lower. Thus, in these two parties the male candidates are given higher priority by ranking them high on the party list. In other words, the subnational party culture differs from the central party culture. The Party executive is under more pressure to have balanced proportions between gender if the demand for equality is strongly emphasized in the political culture. Moreover, the party leadership must by virtue of their position be open for changes in the political culture. Therefore, the executive is one of the first units to be formed according to the new demands. The subnational party, in contrast, is not formally directed by the national party in the nomination process. In the first instance, the subnational party is responsible to its members in the constituency.

Norway Year	SV Tot		DNA Tot		V Tot		SP Tot		H Tot	
	%	N	%	N	%	N	%	N	%	N
1961 C:	16	86	19	270	21	206	17	218	22	270
E:	0	2	1	74	0	14	6	16	3	29
1965 C:	13	269	19	270	26	212	17	217	23	270
E:	0	2	13	68	0	18	0	18	3	31
1969 C:	10	270	22	270	21	270	24	190	23	270
E:			15	74	15	13	0	20	7	29
1973 C:	34	235	28	268	25	152	29	269	27	269
E:	19	16	19	62	0	2	14	21	17	29
1977 C:	46	268	37	269	43	209	37	217	30	269
E:	50	2	26	76	0	2	8	12	29	41
1981 C:	48	267	41	269	46	209	39	263	36	269
E:	50	4	33	66	0	2	18	11	25	53
1985 C:	50	271	46	271	49	271	42	271	41	271
E:	50	6	42	71			17	12	30	50
1989 C:	49	271	48	271	48	271	46	268	43	271
E:	41	17	51	63			27	11	24	37

Source: Bille 1992:258-259; Sundberg and Gylling 1992:306-308; Svåsand 1992:772-773; Pierre and Widfeldt 1992:822-823.

Only in Finland has the party executive a formal right to diverge from the nomination result in the constituencies. In contrast to Finland, the subnational party rules in Denmark, Norway and Sweden often differ within the party, which further emphasizes their independence from the party leadership (Sundberg 1993). Hence, the subnational parties can independently decide the number of female candidates and their ranking order on the party list. As the political culture may differ considerably in the constituencies, also the ranking order of female candidates can vary from one constituency to another. The Finnish experience shows that the party executive most commonly diverges when the subnational party neglects to nominate a sufficient number of female candidates. However, proportional barriers can relatively easily be won when the demands of change are commonly accepted in the party, and when the influx of more female candidates has a marginal effect on the electoral results. By increasing the influx of female candidates, the subnational party can, with an easier conscience, ignore them in the ranking process. Tactics of that type have been used, but the Scandinavian case also shows a remarkable readiness for fundamental change in the relationship between women and men in organizational work, a readiness which is unheard of in the rest of Europe.

The silent revolution revised

Political scientists have put much effort into identifying and explaining fundamental transitions in our social and political life. The extensive research into changing political values from materialism to post-materialism in the wake of the rapidly growing information society belongs to this tradition (Inglehart 1977). Unfortunately very little, if any, attention is paid to the changing role of women in politics in this context. However, changes in values and beliefs are largely a result of how the observations are measured, and the findings are therefore open to criticism. Thus it is remarkable that the revolutionary influx of women in Scandinavian politics is not paid sufficient attention. Women are easy to observe and easy to count, which releases us from long discussions of method and validity demands.

On the basis of this study we can, however, conclude that one of the simplest things, like counting women and men in the party organization, is neglected when considered unimportant. Counting women and incorporating them as full members was considered extremely important in the first half of this century, when the female voter turnout was far below the level of male voting. The importance was underscored by the fact that although women did not pay full fees there was no formal difference between female and male members. However, when the difference between female and male voting diminished, women were paid less attention in the organizational work. A new recognition grew with the female demand for shared power and influence in the party organization as well as in candidate selection. Women struggled for visible positions to motivate more women to compete for high positions in the party and to become elected. No formal barriers existed in the party rules for women to be nominated as candidates or to be elected as members to the party executive. The change was made possible by their own activity, the demand from the voters, and the lack of strong resistance from the party élite.

This silent revolution was structurally based on the massive increase in female employment and level of education. Politically it was a result of the long process of female politicization which made women conscious of their own interests. This increasing female consiousness was as well developed among party members as among the voters. In the competition for votes and mandates all moves against any demands from the female members could violate the party image in elections. To maximize votes and seats the party élite had to be very sensitive to opinions in the party organization and among the electorate. As almost half of the members were female and half of the electorate were female there was no base for active resistance from the male members. All actions in that direction would have hurt the idea of equality which at that time was deeply rooted in Scandinavia. Thus, the female revolution could proceed silently in parties and elections paving the way to a unique balance between women and men in Scandinavian parties.

Moreover, our study also shows that parties not simply mirror their environments. If that were the case it would be very difficult to explain the difference in female representation between parties in the four Scandinavian countries. Parties have the ability to act independently and they have more power than any other voluntary organization to affect the political environment. The quota rule adopted by most Norwegian parties had a larger effect on the political culture around parties than any other single decision to promote female representation. By raising quotas within the party organization, it forces the male members to reflect on gender proportions in any public assembly where candidates are nominated or elected, regardless of whether quota rules are formalized in them or not. Although the quota rules are the most effective instrument to promote female members, other means have also proved to be efficient. As the Swedish case shows, a change in the proportion of gender in the party leadership can be obtained with relatively little effort, provided that the female members come together and give it a high priority. In Denmark and Finland a similar change is within reach, but here the content of politics has been given more attention by female members than formal representation. The choice of priority seems, however, to be different among women in Denmark and Finland. In Denmark women utilize a broad arena of options (grass roots movements and protests) to pursue their political aims. The party option is one among many and for that reason female members often prefer to find political means of influence outside the party organization. In Finland, by contrast, the options are far fewer, as the party channel in practice is the sole way of pursuing one's political aims. Within this channel the electoral option is more efficient for women, as the nominees are selected at the subnational level and the electoral system gives the female voters a free choice to support female candidates.

References

Bergqvist, C. (1993), 'De organiserade intressena, staten och kvinnorna'. University of Uppsala, Department of Government. Working paper.

Bergqvist, C. (1991), 'Corporatism and gender equality. A comparative study of two Swedish labour market organisations', *European Journal of Political Research*, Vol. 20:107-125.

von Beyme, K. (1985), *Political Parties in Western Democracies*. Gower: Aldershot.

Bille, L. (1992), 'Denmark', in Katz, R. and Mair, P. (eds): *Party Organizations*. London: Sage.

Birgersson, B. O. and Westerståhl, J. (1982), *Den svenska folkstyrelsen*. Stockholm: Liber Förlag.

Dahlerup, D. (1979a), 'Kvinders organisering i det danske Socialdemokrati 1908-69. For og imod en selvstaendig socialistisk kvindebevaegelse', *Meddelelser om Forskning i Arbeiderbeaegelsens Historie*. Rapport nr. 13.

Dahlerup, D. (1979b), 'Udviklingslinier i kvinders politiske deltagelse og representation i Danmark', in Pedersen, M. N. (ed.): *Dansk politik i 1970'erne*. København: Safundsvidenskabeligt Forlag.

Dahlerup, D. and Gulli, B. (1983), 'Kvinneorganisationerne i Norden: Avmagt eller modmagt?', in Haavio-Mannila, E. et al. (red.): *Det uferdige demokratiet*. Oslo: Nordisk ministerråd.

Diamond, I. and Hartsock, N. (1981), 'Beyond Interests in Politics: A Comment on Virginia Sapiro's: When are Interests Interesting? The Problem of Political Representation of Women', *The American Political Science Review*, Vol. 75:717-721.

Duverger, M. (1978), *Political Parties*. London: Methuen.

Eduards, M. (1993),'Politiken förkroppsligad', in v. Sydow, B., Wallin, G. and Wiitrock, B. (eds): *Politikens väsen*. Stockholm: Tidens Förlag.

Eduards, M., Gustafsson, G., and Jónasdóttir, A. (1989), 'Könsmakt och maktlöshet i nationalstaten', in: *Kvinnors makt och inflytande, Delegationen för jämställdhetsforskning*. Rapport nr 15. Stockholm.

Elklit, J. and Pade, A. B. (1991), *Election Administration in Denmark*. Copenhagen: Ministry of the Interior.

Elvander, N. (1980), *Skandinavisk arbetarrörelse*. Stockholm: Liber förlag.

Epstein, L. D. (1967), *Political Parties in Western Democracies*. New York: Praeger.

Haavio-Mannila, E. et. al. (eds): *(1983), Det uferdige demokratiet.* Oslo: Nordisk ministerråd.

Hedlund, G. (1988), 'Women's Interests in Local Politics', in Jones, K. and Jónasdóttir, A. (eds): The Political Interests of Gender. Sage: London.

Heidar, K. (1990), 'Landsmotepolitikk: På verkstedsgolvet i Det Norske Arbeiderparti', in Djupsund, G. & Svåsand, L. (eds): *Partiorganisasjoner: studier i strukturer og processer i finske, norske og svenske partier.* Åbo: Åbo Akademis Förlag.

Heidar, K. (1988), *Partidemokrati på prøve.* Oslo: Universitetsforlaget.

Holmberg, E. and Stjernquist, N. (1988), *Vår författning.* Stockholm: Norstedts.

Inglehart, R. (1977), *The Silent Revolution.* Princeton: Princeton University Press.

Jónasdóttir, A. (1988), 'On the Concept of Interest, Women's Interests, and the Limitation of Interest Theory', in Jones, K. and Jónasdóttir, A. (eds): *The Political Interests of Gender.* London: Sage.

Kirchheimer, O. (1966), 'The Transformation of the Western European Party System', in LaPalombara, J. and Weiner, M. (eds): *Political Parties and Political Development.* Princeton: Princeton University Press.

Michels, R. (1962), *Political Parties.* New York: The Free Press.

Miller, A., Hildreth, A. and Simmons, G. (1988), 'The Mobilization of Gender Group Consciousness', in Jones, K. and Jónasdóttir, A. (eds): *The Political Interests of Gender.* London: Sage.

Mills, A. and Tancred, P. (eds) (1992), *Gendering Organizational Analysis.* London: Sage.

Neumann, S. (1956), 'Towards a Comparative Study of Political Parties', in Neumann, S. (ed.): *Modern Political Parties.* Chicago: University of Chicago Press.

Panebianco, A. (1988), *Political Parties: Organization and Power.* Cambridge Cambridge University Press.

Petersson, O., Westholm, A. and Blomberg, G. (1989), *Medborgarnas makt.* Stockholm: Carlsson Bokförlag.

Pierre, J. (1990), 'Rörelsens parlament eller partioligarkins fikonlöv?', i Djupsund, G. & Svåsand, L.: *Partiorganisasjoner: studier i strukturer og processer i finske, norske og svenske partier.* Åbo: Åbo Akademis Förlag.

Pierre, J. and Widfeldt, A. (1992), 'Sweden', in Katz, R. and Mair, P. (eds): *Party Organizations.* London: Sage.

Ramstedt-Silén, V. (1990), 'Högt i tak och brett mellan väggarna!', i Djupsund, G. & Svåsand, L.: *Partiorganisasjoner: studier i strukturer og processer i finske, norske og svenske partier.* Åbo: Akademis Förlag.

Ricknell, L. (1975), *Hur vårt statsskick fungerar.* Stockholm: Prisma.

Ryssevik, J. (1991), 'Party vs. Parliament. Contrasting Configurations of Electoral and Ministerial Socialism in Scandinavia', in Karvonen, L. and Sundberg, J. (eds.): *Social Democracy in Transition.* Aldershot: Dartmouth.

Sapiro, V. (1981), 'Research Frontier Essay: When are Interests Interesting? The Problem of Political Representation of Women', *The American Political Science Review,* Vol. 75:701-716.

Schlesinger, J.A. (1984), 'On the Theory of Party Organization', *The Journal of Politics,* Vol. 46:369-400.

Skard, T. and Haavio-Mannila, E. (1983), 'Kvinner i parlamentene', i Haavio-Mannila, E. et. al. (red.): *Det uferdige demokratiet.* Oslo: Nordisk ministerråd.

Sundberg, J. (1993), 'Frihet och förmynderskap: två dominerande organisationskulturer i nordiskt partiliv', i Engman, M. & Stenius, H. (eds): *Svenskt föreingsliv i Finland, Svenska Litteratursällskapet i Finland.* Helsingfors (forthcoming).

Sundberg, J. and Gylling, C. (1992), 'Finland', in Katz, R. and Mair, P. (eds): *Party Organizations.* London: Sage.

Svåsand, L. (1992), 'Norway', in Katz, R. and Mair, P. (eds), *Party Organizations.* London: Sage.

Tarasti, L. (1987), Suomen vaalilainsäädäntö. Helsinki: Kunnallispaino.

Togeby, L. (1989a), *Ens og forskellig. Graesrodsdeltagels. i Norden.* Århus: Forlaget Politica.

Togeby, L. (1989b), 'Politiseringen av kvinder og af kvindesporgsmålet', in Elklit, J. & Tonsgaard (red.): *To folketingsvalg.* Århus: Forlaget Politica.

Tonsgaard, O. (1984), 'Valglovgivningen - en kritisk granskning', in Elklit, J. and Tonsgaard, O. (eds): *Val og vaelgeradfaerd.* Århus: Forlaget Politica.

Törnudd, K. (1968), *The Electoral System of Finland.* London: Hugh Evelyn.

Valen, H. (1985), 'Valgsystemet', in Nordby, T. (ed.): *Storting og regjering 1945-1985.* Oslo: Kunskapsforlaget.

Valen, H. (1988), 'Norway: decentralization and group representation', in Gallagher, M. & Marsh, M. (eds): *Candidate Selection in Comparative Perspective.* London: Sage.

Wright, W.E. (1971), 'Comparative Party Models: Rational-Efficient and Party Democracy', in Wright, W. E. (ed.): *A Comparative Study of Party Organization.* Columbus: Charles E. Merrill.

Part III

Organizational
participation

Social democracy, women, and the European union

Ulf Lindström

The problem

Scandinavia, as evidenced by Denmark's popular rejection of the Maastricht Treaty in 1992 and approval of the 'opt-out' Edinburgh Agreement in 1993, is reluctant about joining the new Europe. Finland, Norway, and Sweden might well decline the European Union (EU) option in the referenda on membership that are scheduled for 1994.

Now more than ever - and until referendum night - the Social Democratic parties and their constituencies hold the key to the European issue in Scandinavia (cf. Tables 1 and 2). If the leaders of the Social Democratic parties fail to mitigate the resistance to membership among their voters - among whom women public employees are prominent - a plurality of votes in favor of joining the EU is not within reach (Lindström 1993).

This paper offers an account of the structural forces that make Nordic women resent membership of the new Europe. As a corollary, the paper suggests that the dilemma of the Social Democratic parties is self-inflicted. It reflects the parties' unwillingness to allow gender-perspectives bear on the issue of Nordic membership of the EU.

Theoretical framework

The EU is a project of and for *individual* Europeans already in possession of economic, cultural, and political resources, or European *states* collectively within *reach* thereof. Mixes and imbalances between these extreme historical configurations- a situation in which sections of the population (e.g. males in the private sector) can be accused of confusing their personal/ sectarian interest with that of the nation - spell popular conflict over the issue of membership.

The following account of the predicament of the Scandinavian Social Democratic parties starts by returning to mainstream political sociology. It assumes:

• that there are contextual regularities and contradictions that apply exclusively to how Social Democratic constituents come to form their perception of EU membership;

• that these regularities vary among the Nordic countries. They reflect an increasingly complex area in terms of both economic and political relations to the outside world.

• In effect, the Nordic Social Democratic leaders and cadres have to penetrate public contexts that, once sources of class-based loyalty and later supplemented by arenas of public policy trade-offs, have turned away from things political and evolved into compartments in possession of relative autonomy vis-à-vis matters of public concern. The means of penetrating these public contexts in order to break the resistance/ reluctance to membership of the EU are limited. In essence, the Social Democratic rationale for joining the EU is about the safeguarding of national growth and jobs.

Table 1
Denmark's Vote on Edinburgh Agreement (1993), and
national opinion distribution on EU membership, by gender.
(Percentages)

	Denmark			Finland			Norway			Sweden		
	Women		Men	Women		Men	Women		Men	Women		Men
For	52	57	63	36	42	47	20	25	30	27	34	42
Against	48	43	37	37	35	33	42	41	39	42	39	36
No opinion/ don't know				27	23	20	31	34	38	32	27	22

Sources: Denmark: Nielsen, H.J., *EF på valg*: 59 (Copenhagen: Columbus, 1993). Finland: Suomen Gallup Oy, Survey 27-30 December, 1993, courtesy of the editors of *Ilta-Sanomat*. Norway: *MMI-Barometer*, January, 1994, courtesy of the MMI. Sweden: *Göteborgs-Posten*, 16 January, 1994.

Table 2
Party support and vote against Maastricht Treaty and Edinburgh
Agreement in Danish referenda; party support and opinion on
EU membership in Finland, Norway, and Sweden.
(Percentages)

DENMARK (Vote on Maastricht, June 1992)

	Soc.P.P.	SD	Center p*	Agr.Lib.	Cons.	Progr.
No	89	67	37	11	21	67

DENMARK (Vote on Edinburgh, May 1993)

	Soc.P.P.	SD	Center p*	Agr.Lib.	Cons.	Progr.
No	85	50	31	11	14	55

FINLAND (27-30 Dec, 1993)

	Left	SD	Green	Agr.	Cons.
For	24	51	58	26	70
Against	60	29	23	47	17
Others	16	21	20	28	13

NORWAY (January, 1994)

	Soc.Left	SD	Lib.(Green)	Agr.	Chr.	Cons.	Progr.
For	9	29	31	2	8	58	31
Against	72	29	34	92	63	11	28
Others	19	42	35	6	29	31	41

SWEDEN (January, 1994)

	Left	SD	Green	Lib.	Agr.	Chr.	Cons.	New Dem.
For	13	22	16	57	32	34	75	54
Against	66	50	78	19	44	42	7	32
Others	21	29	5	24	24	24	18	14

Sources: See Table 1 above (Nielsen 1993:55).
* Includes the Radical Liberal party, Christian People's party, and the Center Democrats.

However, with the massive entry of women into the labour market, in particular the
public sector - and as a result of the subsequent political resources women have

invested in this sector - the 'relative automony' of the households has increased substantially. Granted a number of social rights by the state, these empowered households now form a cluster of microcosms that challenges the original Social Democratic macrocosm, the one that was based on the obsolete 'market-patriarchate household.' Obviously, 'public households,' i.e. households in which both breadwinners are employed by the public sector in professional positions, are replacing those in which the male breadwinner employed in manufacturing industry looked upon the wife's part-time job with local government as a source of pocket-money for the household.

The social democratic impasse

As was brought out by tables 1 and 2 above, the citizens (and Social Democratic voters in particular) of two of the three nations applying for membership of the EU are liable to vote 'No' in the referendum. The resistance to membership in Norway and Sweden was only marginally reduced by Brussels coming forward to accommodate Nordic interests in the rounds of negotiations on the terms of membership that were concluded shortly before Christmas 1993. Also, the much talked about 'Zhirinovsky-effect' - the threat to the Nordic countries by the rise of Russian chauvinism - could be registered only in Finnish opinion. In the Danish vote on the Edinburgh Agreement, as well as in each of the three applicant countries, there is a gap between women and men in the opinion distribution on membership of about ten percentage points. A multivariate approach to this gap suggests that it should be accounted for by structural regularities.

Table 3 shows Norwegian and Swedish opinion on membership in two contexts defined according to (i) gender, (ii) sector and (iii) geography. Whereas about 50 percent of men employed in the private sector and living in the urban areas of the south said they would cast a vote in favor of Norwegian and Swedish membership of the EU, less than 10 to 15 percent of women employed in the public sector and living in the northern half of the countries would vote 'Yes' to membership. (As for the large Swedish proportion of those who have not made up their minds among the latter category, more than two out of three tend to go against membership.)

Table 3
Norwegian and Swedish Opinion on EC/EU Membership in two Contexts (defined by a three-fold dichotomy). Percentages. Surveys conducted continuously 1992-1993 in Norway, and November 1992 in Sweden

	Male Private Sector Empl. Urban South*		Female Public Sector Empl. The North**	
	Norway	Sweden	Norway	Sweden
For	52.7	46.9	14.9	9.8
Against	25.9	31.0	56.6	52.7
Don't know/ other answers	20.6	22.1	26.2	37.5

Note: While not identical, the questions put to the respondents in Norway and Sweden respectively are comparable.
* Norway: Residents of Trondheim, Bergen, Stavanger, Kristiansand, Drammen, and Oslo. Sweden: Stockholm, Göteborg, and the 'Four Cities' (Malmö, Lund, Helsingborg, and Landskrona).
** Norway: The counties north of and including Sør-Trøndelag. Sweden: Norrland.
Source: Norsk Gallup A/S 'Forbruker & Media', 1992-1993. The survey was based on a sample of 13,417 citizens. SCB (Statistics Sweden), 'Party Sympathy Survey,' November 1992. The survey was based on a sample of 9,200 citizens.
Ms Bente Pettersen of Norsk Gallup A/S and Mr Staffan Sollander and Ms Marie Uhlén of SCB kindly forwarded the data to the author. They bear no responsibility for the interpretation of the data.

There is reason to believe that similar findings would be obtained in Finland too. About 7 out of 10 women in Denmark and Sweden are employed outside the household. Finnish and Norwegian women trail their Nordic sisters by almost 10 percentage points. Table 4 also brings out the causal background of these differences. More than anything else, it has been the growth of the public sector that has brought women into the labour market. Of all employed women in Sweden, 56 percent occupy public positions. Finland is the only country where the majority of employed women are still in the private sector.

If qualified geographically, these data would most likely show that peripheral areas, not least the far north, offer very little in the way of employment opportunities for women other than positions in the public sector (including *government* misuse of early retirement programs).

Table 4
Female labour force rate (FLFR) and proportion employed
in public sector (PPS*), 1972-1991

	Denmark		Finland		Norway		Sweden	
	FLFR	PPS	FLFR	PPS	FLFR	PPS	FLFR	PPS
1972	53.5		55.5		44.8		54.7	
1981	62.5		60.0		56.3		65.7	
1991	69.7	52.3	63.1	43.6	62.3	51.0	70.7	56.2

Sources: Yearbook of Nordic Statistics (1982), Table 42 (1992), Tables 46-47 (1993) Table 48.
* 1990.

The Social Democratic parties are disproportionately favored by women in general and those employed in the public sector in particular, partly because women in the public sector are more likely to be unionized than are those in the private. However, women employed in the public sector are also a prominent part of the Radical Left constituencies. In Norway, 44 percent of women (20-44 years old) with an academic diploma holding full-time positions in the public sector support the anti-EU Socialist Left party (Hines 1993:182). Especially in Denmark, Norway, and Sweden, the Radical Left is the prime opponent of the Social Democratic endorsement of EU membership, and the decisive battle is expected to be fought precisely over the vote of women public employees in the Norwegian and Swedish referenda. As the two Danish referenda show, women as opposed to men, and public as opposed to private employees were slow to come out in support of the less far-reaching Edinburgh Agreement (Nielsen 1993:57ff).

Social democracy, Europe and the world according to the market-patriarchate, public, and tripod households

The classic rhetoric of the Social Democrats about the primacy of economic growth for maintaining full employment and the welfare society, one that bears on the very rationale of social democracy, is becoming less meaningful to listeners. More important, it is a theme met with conditional acceptance, particularly when it entails a trade-off of national sovereignty for market access. The simple reason for·this reluctance is that the Social Democratic *constituents* in Denmark, Finland, Norway, and Sweden evidently live in many different worlds than that of the 'market-patriarchate household,' and this shapes their perceptions of EU membership differently.

The 1950s was a time when the message of economic growth was instantly received and understood, and responded to accordingly. During this period second-thoughts among the grass-roots voters - from the objections on principle to the innumerable petty details about discomfort - were suppressed. It was a time when *social democratic* Scandinavia bought the bad with the good. If necessary they committed themselves to international regimes that did not arouse much enthusiasm among the cadres, let alone the rank-and-file. For instance, Nordic membership in EFTA never caused any popular conflict.

But loyalty carried a different meaning when social democracy was still understood primarily in the red *Lager* context. For about 15 years after WW II, this context remained fixed in the minds of the less 'proletarian' allies within the labour movement and furnished the Social Democratic parties with answers to the issues of the day (Sejersted 1984). It was from this milieu, and in particular the new cooperative housing neighborhoods in suburbia - *the* source of pride and self-confidence for a labour movement tied to a culture that has been preoccupied with the standards of domestic life - that the cadres were recruited (Ambjörnsson 1988)

These neighborhoods set the example for social democratic excellence until, in the 1960s, publicly financed high-rise apartment buildings and, later, market-financed one-family houses dimmed the landscape in more senses than one. Labour-saving facilities were designed and installed for wives, who were *not* supposed to work outside the household (Lund 1991, Hirdman 1990, Saarikangas 1993).

What is it today that makes the economic dimension - 'growth and jobs require membership of the EU' - carry different connotations and provoke different responses? Pursuing this task in the standard fashion would mean offering an in-depth account of the labour market and class relations, not least the de-industrialization process. The following analysis turns elsewhere: nothing brings out the profound changes of society like revisiting the Scandinavian Social Democrats *at home*.

A changing family structure has accompanied the emergence of, for want of a better term, the post-industrial society. A new household economy has furthered a more composite view of what growth and jobs really mean. The typical household of the 1960s, as part of the red *Lager* and its cultural features, saw the male breadwinner working in the private sector and the wife, if employed at all, holding a part-time position in the public sector (Moqvist 1990:125).

Normally, material improvement was a matter of the single breadwinner's local trade-union signing a new contract. But sometimes it was a matter of accepting a better-paying job, even if doing so meant moving to another town. Job opportunities for the wife and day-care for the children, aspects that are part of the overall family perspective that must be considered today, were secondary. Pay rises and promotions are still welcome, but now they have to appeal to *both* breadwinners, and if opportunities come with drawbacks they are not worth the trouble (or are looked upon as sour grapes). A double income means twice as much frustration over material concerns since the mere thought of losing one source of income evokes pictures of losing vital *social* connections.

Indeed, there is more to double-income households than the pay. Adapting the common usage of 'households' from economics to political sociology in general and the European issue in particular means introducing a microcosm different from individual voters. Households relate to the outside world in a more multi-faceted way than do individuals; household members are in possession of more or less autonomy vis-à-vis the outside world according to the composition of the household.

A referendum, unlike a regular - and recurrent - parliamentary election, offers only two choices, yes or no. A referendum of this calibre, yes or no to the surrendering of national self-determination, is a definite choice. This brings a unique psychology to bear on individual behavior.

'Microcosm voting,' households casting a uniform vote, will be likely according to the well-known cross-pressure hypothesis. In particular, one-party households - more than three-fourths of all households in Sweden (Petersson, et al 1989)) - but also those that have become accustomed to a domesticized multi-party pluralism, will be wary not to split the vote so as to turn the kitchen-table into a place of family feuding.

Save for single-person households, the sharpest increase over the last 20 years is the number of 'public households' in which *both* the man and woman are gainfully employed in the public sector in professional positions. Of all public employees, almost 75 percent occupy positions serving the tasks of a modern welfare state (Goul Andersen 1992).

Extrapolations from Table 4 suggest that the proportion of public households is highest in Sweden, followed by Denmark. Differences between Norway and Finland are difficult to detect. The proportion of women working *full-time* in the public sector is likely to show a similar rank-ordering. However, Norwegian women are exceptional for their extensive part-time employment.

But Norway in general is an odd country, largely because of an intact, scattered settlement structure that has been paid for with petroleum revenues. Typical to the Norwegian household economy outside the larger cities is the multitude of, and popular attitude to, its sources. The household commonly draws also on income from a small enterprise, whether smallholding, fishing boat, aquafarm, camping site, etc. There is reason to suspect that women prefer, or are expected by the surrounding community to prefer, part-time jobs with the local government so that they will find time to attend the household's small business on the side. In any case, two pay-checks and whatever the household can earn on the side is what constitutes a so-called 'tripod household.'

This means that the fight between the market and state for hegemony over agenda-setting no longer has an unspoiled arena in which the orthodox Social Democratic growth-and-jobs worldview can be made to rule.

The decline, if not extinction, of 'market-patriarchate households,' more common among the working-class than the middle-class in terms of both numbers and mentality, has left its mark on Scandinavian politics in at least three ways. First and most obvious, it has done away with a larger number of loyal Social Democratic microcosms relative to bourgeois. Secondly, a public household doubles the politicization of the kitchen-table. It turns into a platform from which restrictions felt to be imposed by, as well as opportunities offered through, public employment intercept the unlimited opportunities of the market. Third, the new household structure and the numbers of women ascending to middle-level executive positions, furthering professionalization in addition to more militant unionization, have expanded the parameters of the political agenda:...'the most significant contrasts in [Danish] voting patterns today are found between 20-29-year-old male employees in the private sector (among whom only one fifth vote for socialist parties) and 30-39-year-old female employees in the public sector (among whom four fifths vote socialist).' (Goul Andersen 1992).

A post-industrial society, one in which the macrocosm of manufacturing industry is edged out of the center of the political stage without the two other 'worlds' (private service industry and the public sector) moving to fully *intermingle* with each other, throws additional light on what it is that impedes the Scandinavian Social Democrats' attempts to get the nations' support for joining the EU by using the classic growth-and-jobs argument to sway the parties' grass-roots.

Public households will be more prone to cast a uniform vote than market and, above all, mixed ones. While a mixed household can always find a straightforward rationalization for splitting the vote by externalizing the issue, i.e. referring to legitimate sector interests, the market household is liable to defy its source of livelihood for ideological reasons. In sum, the aggregate effect of the modernization of household structure increases the likelihood of depriving the Social Democrats of *two* votes. In some cases three or more votes will be lost if the microcosm includes parents as well as offspring who are entitled to vote and residing in the household.

In normal circumstances, or during the mobilization of the constituency before parliamentary elections, the second-best watering hole of the Social Democratic party - the community of public households - is a source of support for the leadership. A community drawing on the memory and experience of the Social Democrats' Golden Era, it has been serviced on the basis of a contract that gives priority to economic growth in return for increased appropriations to the public sector.

In effect, people no longer readily recognize themselves when exposed to the Social Democratic *Europeanized* growth-and-jobs argument, if indeed it reaches them at all amidst a world of omnipresent airwaves, a world asking for full-time attention to market and government opportunities.

A concrete example may be in order. A married woman with pre-school children employed at the senior-citizens' home in northern Norway is against membership of the EU partly because she is Norwegian and thus belongs to a context not constantly harassed by the market. But her colleagues immediately across the border in Finland and Sweden - and in far away Copenhagen - are almost as certain as she is about declining membership of the EU. These sisters-in-arms, as part of a public or tripod household, rarely intermingle with households exposed to market forces, and when they do, the habit and mentality associated with producer economism and an administrative culture marked by cost-benefit hegemony do not leave *lasting* imprints. Contexts and institutional changes are responsible for having made some people more aware, ignorant, or puzzled than others about where national wealth originally came from and how easily it once used to plummet at the whim of the market forces and through administrative negligence.

The Danish SD, led by Copenhagen (one-third of the national population), is undermined by public household radical leftism, even a neo-liberalism that appeals to the working-class vote. Norway, save for a few cities inside a triangle covering the Oslo region, is marked by petroleum-inflicted localistic *Verzuiling*. An extensive tripod economy among hinterland households produces local contexts that challenge the world views of the DNA leadership. Sweden and, above all, Finland, on account of industry's politico-cultural supremacy, are closer to the once congenial context of social democracy. However, owing to the influx of immigrant labour into Swedish manufacturing industry, this dominance has been tempered by the public households' orbiting farther out from the core of the country's traditional economy and its world views. The SAP is thus in a precarious position. The party is facing a substantial community of women public employees capable of severely hurting the leadership by robbing the party of *two* votes in the referendum through 'microcosm voting.'

In Sweden, more than in Finland, conversion capability conveying the original market-patriarchate world according to the Social Democratic leaderships lies dormant at best. In Norway - where conversion capability is badly needed to confront voters who remember having declined membership in the EC (1972) - it is about to disappear altogether.

In search of social democratic Europe

If there really is an exclusive Social Democratic reason for supporting membership, it would be presumptuous to imagine that the leaderships of four of the world's most renowned Social Democratic parties do not possess the faculty to discover that unique cause. And it would be conspiratorial thinking to believe that three of them knew the secret formula to Euro-consensus but forgot to tell the Danish leaders before the June referendum of 1992.

The Social Democratic party is cornered by its intimate ties to a benevolent nation-state, an institutional link that is not compatible with the liberalism, and union-busting, of a European common market or the conservatism, and gender traditionalism, of a European Union diluted by the subsidiarity principle. The Scandinavian labour movement is not cut out to make Nordic membership of the new Europe a smooth transition.

The Movement, close as it is to public administration - inseparable, some would say, in Sweden - is caught in a vicious circle. For each word of praise in favor of membership uttered by the Social Democratic élites, for each step closer to Brussels, the tens of thousands of cadres become even more preoccupied with the institutions of the nation-state that they believe they have sired, raised, and inherited and are now about to see abandoned. Features of the welfare state which were earlier taken for granted are suddenly bestowed with elabourate ideological meaning and, despite recent cuts in provisions, said to contrast favorably to those found in the EC countries.

Of course, European social democratic ideologues, for example a Rocard or a Glotz, would have no problem in refuting arguments to the effect that membership in the EU entails risks of trade-unions losing out against capital and women being pushed back toward the household.

What was unique to the Nordic working-class movement, coordinating its industrial and political branches, was the mobilization, integration, and accommodation of labour that elsewhere in Europe was often left behind. Scandinavia certainly knows of backbreaking unskilled labour, but not of a *Lumpenproletariat*, male or female, in the politico-cultural sense. While the free labour market is no threat to the interests of professional manpower like air-traffic controllers, the trade-unions organizing unskilled manpower need the backing of pan-European labour legislation. Thus, while close relations to the Social Democratic party are becoming more and more expendable to some unions, others fear the party is no longer in a position to help them fight the specter of social dumping.

More than other European nationals, Scandinavian women politicians, public executives and leaders of voluntary associations concerned with issues of equality view EU legislation as inferior to that of domestic public policy on *every single* count in terms of provisions to the benefit of women.

Being allied with the political right, whose excitement about future membership at times gets out of hand, the Social Democratic parties appear to use a foreign vocabulary about EU membership. To the grass-roots, it is indistinguishable from the one espoused by both Latin European visionaries and the homegrown hard-core activists in favor of membership. The infallibility of the EU as subscribed to among the Scandinavian activists repels others.

Failing to get through on the message that is of vital concern to Nordic women - jobs and welfare-state provisions - this is fellow-travelling speak. It is a language adopted from Latins who relate to the *reality* of poverty, religious intolerance, and even dictatorship. But past wrongdoings, like Galician poverty, Andalusian intolerance, and Castillian dictatorship, are no excuse for Nordic women activists to accept a less ambitious policy in creating new jobs and upholding programs that enable women to make use of the opportunities for employment. Latinized arguments for joining the EU provoke the rank-and-file Social Democrats: it is not a language that covers the 'real interest' of the Scandinavian business community. And the lingo of the stock exchanges, alien to the everyday experience of the traditional industrial milieu of the Nordic countries, is an insult. It is a language that does not relate to the floor of the workshop, let alone to the hospital staff canteens. It is a language that does not communicate with the public households or the tripod households of Norway's periphery. The bottom line of the Social Democratic rhetoric is suddenly too close to a world view of society that still regards the services of the public sector as something really not productive.

Nurses and others returning home to a public or tripod household after having served eight hours for a good cause on behalf of a good-natured state rather than for private or denomination interests at homes for the elderly, etc., have never been willing to accept the idea that only industrial workers contribute to the wealth-creating process.

As contributors to, rather than depleters of, national resources, nurses would like to be shown some respect for their toil. However, there is an important reason why the contributions of public employees are neglected: they do not fit the language of market shares. Scandinavian industry needs to increase its market shares inside the EU; Scandinavian nurses do not. Goods, services, and capital need unrestricted access to an open European market whereas, if only because of language barriers, the bulk of manpower would be well advised to stay put in the national labour market.

The EU can easily be made to look like the alien that will rip the Scandinavian way of life apart at its very heart: the household, its closest circles, and the neighborhood.

Out of the impasse: the Euro-contract?

The single most effective message of the Social Democratic platform for the referenda would be - if fellow social democrats in the European Parliament could only get Brussels to go along with it - a 'country-back guarantee': to the capitalist his markets, to the politicians their gavels, but, if unemployment is not down to less than 3 percent five years after joining, Nordic membership will be declared null and void.

The vote of the community of women public employees could deny the Scandinavian business community political rearguard support inside the EEA; in preventive response the business community may threaten that public employees will end up taking care of a poor state no longer able to foot the bill of a generous welfare society. A prologue to a contest of chicken, this calls for a political leadership that sees to it that a head-on collision is avoided.

Is this a setting that calls for the Social Democratic parties to provide national leadership? The party's long-standing record, which is fondly cultivated among the leadership, is one of offering comparatively reliable leadership in times when momentous issues confront the nation. Or is the idea of a Euro-contract merely a historical inversion of the red-green crisis agreements of the 1930s, a red-blue *rapprochement* that would bring Scandinavia back to Europe?

It was Denmark that, under a Social Democratic cabinet, pioneered the red-green option in 1933. Later, in 1992, under a Conservative-led cabinet, Denmark proved what a failed contract means. Finally, in 1993, under a Social Democratic coalition cabinet, the notion of Scandinavia not being able to resolve serious issues without the Social Democratic parties' taking the lead received new support.

Public employees now hold a grudge against legislative assemblies. More importantly, the very rationale of the unions of public employees is to keep discontent sizzling. The salaried officials of these unions are aware that they possess a blackmail potential over Scandinavia's future position in Europe. If they do not keep this in mind, the Radical Left parties, operating from a position of relative strength among public households and inside public workplaces, will remind them, as will the No-to-the-EU movements.

Indicative, perhaps even representative, of the worldview among Nordic public employees is the demand put forward by the journal of Sweden's local government employees' trade-union, *Kommunalarbetaren* (largest of all trade-union journals), in 1992: it is the duty of the elected body (read: parliament) unilaterally to fix interest rates and exchange rates! As international political economy is unintelligible to all but a few, this is one demand among many that refuse to submit to the realities of an open economy. These demands are instantly adopted by the Scandinavian Radical Left as a means of fuelling discontent among public employees. The post-1989 fiscal populism among the Radical Left is also a remedy for the internal conflicts that are likely to grow as a consequence of socialism having lost its historical identity and sense of direction.

A contract tempers the stupidity of a referendum by extending its split-second timeframe to one that may span years. Only a contract offers an attractive package to fit the identity of Scandinavian political culture (and the image of this as upheld by the international social science community).

However, sober assessments of the preconditions of a Euro-contract say it will not hold water. With the well-known corporate channel in Scandinavian politics more or less closed, the weak link is the business community and, on the receiving end of the contract, women public employees, in particular those who are part of public and tripod households. In addition to the 50-55 percent of women directly employed in the public sector, another 10-20 percent are immediately dependent on transfers through this sector. This means that no more than 25 percent of women employees are mentally integrated in the market economy. Unionization and professionalization, in particular among women in executive public positions, will also make it less easy than before to ignore demands that are put forward from a gender perspective. Still, in the negotiations on the terms of Nordic membership, fish and farms were of more concern to the Scandinavian statesmen than their women.

Business executives, whether prominent representatives of the Employers' Confederation or not, may well pledge allegiance to the flag. Alas, this is of little help in a market that knows no borders. An offer extended by each of the three business communities to create 100,000 new jobs in the industrial sectors exposed to global competition has to be examined in the light of on-line, split-second transfers of capital to wherever in the world marginal dividends seem to have the edge for the next few weeks. One single successful transaction on the international money market is worth more to the company than its annual earnings from doing what it was meant to do.

So, whether the business community likes it or not - and unless politicians and women public employees are willing to let themselves be duped - it has nothing but the means of coercion at its disposal as it relates to the general public on the issue of EU membership. This places the ball in the government's court: since business cannot deliver, it leaves government to see to it that business delivers.

On the face of it, a Social Democratic commitment to find 100,000 [*sic!*] new jobs and create another 100,000 public positions earmarked for women, in exchange for public employees' support for the 'Yes'-ticket, is not to be ruled out. Once membership of the EU is achieved, such a pledge cannot become subject to an auditor's review and therefore held accountable before a judicial body. This makes a Social Democratic commitment too vague, too easy to break, and hence too tempting to offer as referendum day grows closer.

Corollary

Few surprises other than the raising of voices to a furious pitch will come from the side of the Social Democratic leaders in the final weeks before the referenda in Finland, Sweden, and Norway. Indeed, the Nordic negotiations with the EU were set in a framework of vulgar Marxism; the terms reached for the regulation of *commodities*, like fish, liquor, and long-haul vehicles are expected to change the home opinion on membership.

What if the Social Democratic party finally realized that women - unlike fish - are a part of microcosms that are entitled to vote? What if the parties perceived women as an untapped well of a multitude of resources that could serve as a contribution to the *community* rather than to the separate markets of Europe, those arenas in which businessmen, academics, soccer-players and opera singers are incorporated as part of the EEA? What if the party was to approach the European issue from a demystified gender-perspective that addressed the sources rather than the prejudice of women's resentment about membership? (The notion of 'irrational emotional biases' interfering with the issue has an unmistakably sexist touch.) What if that approach told the party it was to drop the whole idea of trying to make the nation part of the EU or, if not, to offer the microcosms something in the way of a gender-biased contract for new jobs in return for 'Yes' to membership as well as the substantial contributions and commitments beyond referendum night? Will the female executive of the retirement home, unable to free herself from the worries about the economic impact of a popular 'No' in the referendum be overcome by doubt that changes her mind in favor of membership? Will colleagues, friends, and neighbors start to listen, wonder, and perhaps even reconsider their own standpoint?

References

Ambjörnsson, R. (1988), *Den skötsamme arbetaren*. Stockholm: Carlssons.

Goul Andersen, J. (1992), 'The Decline of Class Voting Revisited,' in Gundelach & Siune (eds): *From Voters to Participants*. Aarhus: Politica.

Hines, K. (1993), 'SVs velgeroppslutning - sektor-, generasjons- eller kjønnsbestemt?,' *Norsk Statsvitenskapelig Tidsskrift*, Vol. 9:171-189.

Hirdman, Y. (1990), *Att lägga livet till rätta*. Stockholm: Carlssons.

Lindström, U. (1993), *Euro-Consent, Euro-Contract, or Euro-Coercion? Scandinavian Social Democracy, the European Impasse, and the Abolition of Things Political*. Oslo: Scandinavian University Press.

Lund, N-O. (1991), *Nordisk arkitektur*. København: Arkitektens forlag.

Moqvist, I. (1990), 'Familjen - beständig och föränderlig,' in Åberg, R. (ed.): *Industrisamhälle i omvandling*. Stockholm: Carlssons.

Nielsen, H. J. (1993), *EF på valg*. Copenhagen: Columbus.

Petersson, O., Westholm, A. & Blomberg, G. (1989), *Medborgarnas makt.* Stockholm: Carlssons.

Saarikangas, K. (1993), *Model Houses for Model Families. Gender, Ideology and the Modern Dwellings.* Helsinki: SHS.

Sejersted, F. (1984), 'Opposisjon og posisjon,' *Høyres historie*, Vol. 3. Oslo: Cappelen.

Trade unions and the feminization of the labour market in Scandinavia[1]

Lauri Karvonen

Introduction

It is commonly held that labour market policies belong to the core of the Scandinavian model of welfare state. A high degree of unionization and a centralized organization of the unions on the one hand, and a tradition of comprehensive agreements based on consensus with the employers on the other hand have provided a stable basis for economic efficiency as well as for the continued development of welfare policies. Ethno-social homogeneity and the strong allegiance of the working class to the social democratic parties have boosted central union power. Where exceptions to this rule have occurred, the development of the welfare state has been affected: the politically determined division of the Finnish labour union movement up until the late 1960s partly explains why the Finnish welfare state emerged somewhat later than in the neighboring countries and why welfare spending has remained on a somewhat lower level.

The politics of Scandinavian labour markets have, however, been subjected to various pressures of change during recent years. The focus of the present study is on what we believe to be one important factor behind these changes: *the increased proportion of women in the labour force and in the unions.* As will be shown below, the share of women in the labour force has increased rapidly since the 1970s throughout Scandinavia. All the same, the labour market remains strongly skewed in the sense that traditionally male-dominated fields and professions largely continue

[1] I would like to record my thanks to the individuals and institutions who have been of assistance: Christina Bergqvist (University of Uppsala, Department of Government), Ulla Aitta (AKAVA, Helsinki), Marja-Liisa Anttalainen (Council for Equality, Helsinki), Hege Skjeie (Institute for Social Research, Oslo), Riitta Partinen (SAK, Helsinki), Jostein Ryssevik (Norwegian Social Science Data Services, Bergen), Gunilla Lyngfelt (SACO, Stockholm) and Jorunn Christensen (LO, Oslo).

to be so, as the influx of women into the labour market still primarily affects 'female' sectors and occupations.

How has the unionization of women evolved in Scandinavia in the past couple of decades? To what extent has the entry of women into the labour market entailed a concomitant share of union power, i.e. women's representation in those arenas where decisions are made in the unions? How can the 'feminization' of the labour market affect the unions and the relations between them? Are women a risk or a resource from the point of view of centralized union power? Figure 1 depicts these questions in the form of a hypothetical chain of causality.

Figure 1
Women and unions: a causal model

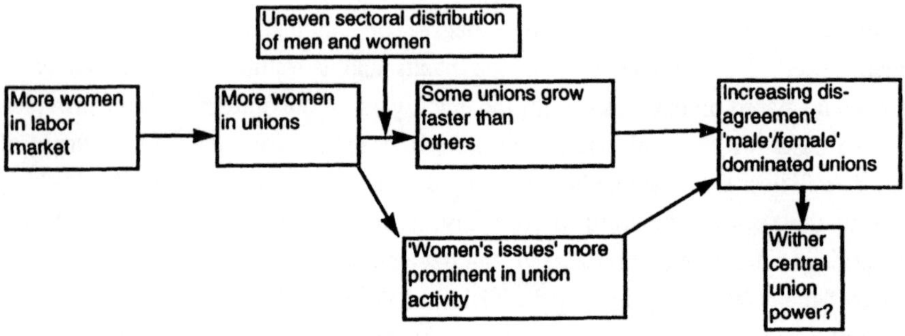

It need not be stressed that the model omits a number of important structural and historical factors: the emergence and development of the welfare state, economic growth and stagnation, level of unemployment etc. The increased number of women in the labour market is in itself a consequence of a number of developments of an economic, as well as of a political nature. Conflicts of interest related to gender need not only be a consequence of the increased number of women in labour unions; economic stagnation, unemployment and the increasingly critical attitude towards the welfare state can have similar effects. Most importantly, the increased female involvement in the labour market and in the unions will not as such be sufficient to bring about the demise of centralized union power. Rather, it stands out as one of many potential factors which may contribute to such an outcome.

The present study focuses to a large extent on women's representation as such; to date there is no comprehensive comparative study of the position of women in this important field of Scandinavian politics. Nevertheless, the central perspective is that of the unions as organizations and actors: how have unions dealt with the rising share of women among their members and the growing demands for representation and power inside the unions? What does the rapid and massive entry of women into the labour market and the unions mean from the point of view of the individual unions and the labour policy area at large?

Women in the work force

The growth of the share of women in the Scandinavian labour market has been impressive in the past decades. However, it is interesting to note that the immediate post-WWII decades witnessed a temporary *drop* in women's involvement in the non-agricultural work force except in the case of Finland (Haavio-Mannila 1981:558). Nevertheless, since then the growth has been rapid, which is apparent from Table 1.

Table 1
Proportion of women of total work force in Scandinavia, 1960-1991. Percentages

Year	Denmark	Finland	Norway	Sweden
1960	30	39	23	30
1970	37	42	28	35
1982	45	48	41	47
1987	46	48	44	48
1991	46	49	46	48

Sources: for 1960-1970, *Yearbook of Nordic Statistics 1972*, for 1982-1991, *Aktuell nordisk statistik, Oktober 1992*.

As early as 1960, almost forty percent of the Finnish work force were women, while the corresponding figures for the other three countries, Norway in particular, were considerably lower. Today, however, nearly half of the Scandinavian labour force is female. True, some minor differences remain between the countries, but the general picture is clear: the Scandinavian labour market consists of men and women to almost equal degrees.

One major difference between Finland and the other other three countries remains, however: *Finnish women have full-time jobs, while their Scandinavian sisters to a much greater extent work part-time.* Eleven percent of the Finnish women (and around five percent of the men) have part-time jobs, while 30-50 percent of the female work force elsewhere in Scandinavia is employed on a part-time basis. At the same time, there are no significant differences between men in different Scandinavian countries in this regard (Nord 1988, 58:79; Tasa-arvoselonteko, 1991:12).

If the number of women in the work force is almost equal to the men, major differences continue to exist as regards economic *sector*. It has become commonplace to speak of a 'segregated labour market'; Table 2 does, at least, not refute such a notion. For the sake of comparison, the table lists the sectoral distribution of the male labour force in 1991.

The general course of development over the thirty-year period is strikingly similar throughout Scandinavia: 1) the importance of the primary and secondary sectors for women's employment has declined; 2) the non-public tertiary sector has retained its role throughout the period, employing close to a third of the female work force; 3) the public sector has become increasingly dominant as a source of employment for Scandinavian women.

At the same time, throughout Scandinavia men 1) retain a somewhat higher involvement in the primary sector; 2) are significantly more dependent on the secondary sector for employment, and; 3) are dramatically *less* dependent on the public sector than are women. The non-public tertiary sector is of about equal importance for men and women.

Again, certain differences between the countries can be noted, despite the generally similar course. In Finland, the importance of the primary sector has declined dramatically, whereas the decline for the secondary sector is less marked than that in Norway and Sweden particularly. By the same token, the public sector continues to employ a lower share of the women in Finland than in the other countries, Sweden in particular.

An important aspect which cannot be overlooked in this context is the amount of money made by women and men. The income levels of women still lag behind those of men. In Finland, the average hourly earnings of women employed in manufacturing still amount to less than eighty percent of those of male workers. Sweden is the other extreme with women's earnings close to ninety percent of those of men.

Norway tails closely behind Sweden, whereas Denmark is an intermediate case (Yearbook of Nordic Statistics 1993:238). However, looking at men and women across all occupational categories, Norway lags behind the other countries (Nord 1988:58, 94).

Table 2
The sectoral distrubution of the female labour force in Scandinavia, 1960-1991.
Percentages

	Primary	Secondary	Tertiary		Public
			Sector		
	Primary	Secondary	Tertiary		Public
Denmark					
1960	5	25		68	
1976	5	19	28		48
1982	4	14	28		53
1987	3	15	30		52
1991	3	16	28		53
(Men					
1991	8	39	32		23)
Finland					
1960	32	22		46	
1976	14	24	30		30
1982	11	22	29		38
1987	8	19	31		43
1991	6	16	34		44
(Men					
1991	10	41	32		16)
Norway					
1960	4	22		74	
1976	8	15	33		44
1982	6	13	34		48
1987	4	12	35		48
1991	3	10	34		53
(Men					
1991	8	34	33		25)
Sweden					
1960	4	27		67	
1976	3	18	28		50
1982	3	15	27		56
1987	2	14	27		56
1991	2	13	28		57
(Men					
1991	5	42	32		21)

Sources: for 1960, *Yearbook of Nordic Statistics 1972*, for 1976, *Yearbook of Nordic Statistics 1985*, for 1982-91, *Aktuell nordisk statistik, Oktober 1992*. Primary sector = agriculture, forestry, fishing; Secondary = manufacturing, construction, mining; Tertiary = commerce, transport, banking; Public = public adm., community services. N.B. Row totals may not add up to 100 percent

In sum, the levelling-off of the differences between men and women as regards participation in the labour market has not entailed a more even sectoral distribution. On the contrary, in many fields the influx of women into the labour market has accentuated the differences between men and women. The increased dependence of the women on the public sector as a source of employment is the most conspicuous factor in this regard.

Women in Scandinavian trade unions

In an international comparison, the organizational structures of the Scandinavian labour markets certainly display more similarities than differences. The strong position of the National Federations of Labour (LO in Denmark, Norway and Sweden, SAK in Finland) is a central feature; given weak or non-existent ethnic and religious cleavages among the working class, these central organizations represent eighty to ninety percent of the workers. Today, there are also central organizations for functionaries[2] and professional ('academic') employees. However, the actual degree of centralization varies to a large extent here; traditionally, Denmark has been characterized by a lower degree of centralization than the other countries, Sweden in particular.

As for unionization, Denmark, Finland and Sweden have long had the highest levels in the Western world (over 80 percent in the late 1980s). With a level of unionization around 60 percent, Norway clearly lags behind its three neighbors. Nevertheless, it still belongs to those Western countries where unionization can be said to be high (Petersson 1991:103).

In sum, the position of the unions can generally be characterized as strong in Scandinavia.

Membership

Again, we can note some differences between the countries. For one, the proportion of women among the members of the Finnish SAK was more than 30 percent in 1970, while the corresponding figure for Norway was almost ten percentage points lower; this corresponds to differences between the countries concerning the share of women in the labour market. Similarly, Norway still lags behind the other *countries* to a certain extent, although the difference is less marked than it was 20 years ago.

---

[2] The central organization of the Finnish functionaries (TVK) was dissolved in 1992 after having gone bankrupt (sic); most of its member unions have joined the Central Federation of Technical Functionaries, which therefore today has a dramatically increased female membership.

Table 3
Percentage of female members in unions belonging to the Central Federations of
Labour[1] in Scandinavia. Selected years

Year	Denmark	Finland	Norway	Sweden
1970/71[2]	28	32	23	30
1982	43	43	33	42
1990/91[3]	48	45	41	45

1) LO in Denmark, Norway and Sweden, SAK in Finland
2) For Denmark, Finland and Norway, 1970, for Sweden, 1971
3) For Sweden and Norway, 1990, for Denmark and Finland, 1991

Sources: For Denmark, Pedersen 1988:52 and *Statistisk Årbog 1992*; For Finland, Valkonen 1989:71 and data provided by Riitta Partinen (SAK); for Norway, data provided by Jostein Ryssevik of the Norwegian Social Science Data Services (NSD) and Hernes & Hänninen-Salmelin 1983, p.177; for Sweden *Kvinnor i facket 1988*:7 and *Statistisk Årsbok 1992*.

Most significantly, however, in all countries union membership has undergone a dramatic 'feminization' in the past two decades. In fact, women account for the lion's share of the growth of unions throughout Scandinavia. In Denmark, union membership rose by almost 550,000 from 1970 to 1991; the increase in the number of women members was roughly 440,000, corresponding to 81 percent of the total growth. The figures for the other countries are: Finland, 284,000, 65 percent, Norway, 182,000 or 96 percent and Sweden, 487,000, i.e. no less than 98 percent.

Among the member unions, this massive growth has brought about an uneven pattern of change. Due to the sectoral imbalance between men and women in the labour market, some unions have experienced a dramatic growth thanks to the influx of women into the labour market, while others display stagnation. The Finnish case, where the change in many ways has been least dramatic in the past couple of decades, is used below to depict a pattern which is common to the entire region. Table 4 comprises four of the largest unions under the SAK; two of these are strongly male-dominated, while the two others have a clear majority of women. The table shows how the total membership has evolved during the period, and what the significance of the growth of female membership has been.

Table 4
The growth of four major unions under the Finnish Federation of Labour; the impact of 'feminization'

Union	Year	Members	Women %	Growth % 1974-91 (all)	Growth % 1974-91 (women)
Construct.	1974	99,192	9	3	-40
	1991	102,421	5		
Metal	1974	134,024	17	6	27
	1991	141,1886	21		
Commerce	1974	75,814	78	62	70
	1991	122,461	82		
Municipal	1974	91,633	56	125	184
	1991	206,000	70		

Sources: For 1974, *Statistics about the position of women in Finland*, 1991:91, data provided by Riitta Partinen (SAK).

The message conveyed by Table 4 is reasonably clear: it is the female-dominated unions that have grown, and this growth is the result of more women in these unions. The traditionally dominant unions of metal and construction workers display little in the way of an increase (and the the case of Metal what growth there is is explicable in terms of increased numbers of women). The Union of Municipal Workers has undergone dramatic growth and is today by far the largest single union within the realm of the SAK. Its rise to prominence is for all practical purposes the result of its further 'feminization'. Clearly, the influx of women into the unions has created new centers of gravity within the labour union movement.

The Central Federations of Labour are by far the largest central employee organizations in Scandinavia. There are, however, several other large central associations of particular importance to our topic. The federations of functionaries ('salaried employees') are the second largest of these central organizations; the share of women has long been higher in these organizations than in any other federation.

Table 5
'Feminization' of unions belonging to The Central Federations of Functionaries[1] in Finland and Sweden. Selected years

		1974	1988	Growth 1974-88 (%)
Finland	All members	211,286	370,600	75.4
	Women (%)	69	85	115
		1975	*1985*	*Growth 1975-85 (%)*
Sweden	All members	880,589	1108,463	26
	Women (%)	49	57	46

1) In Finland, TVK, in Sweden TCO.

Sources: Finland 1974, *Statistics about the position of women in Finland*:94, Finland 1988, Valkonen 1989:71 and *Olennainen työssä*:33, Sweden, Bergqvist 1991:111.

The membership of Scandinavian federations of employees is today at a much higher level thanks to the entry of women into the labour market and the unions. At the same time, it is apparent that the concentration of women in jobs in the public sector has altered the numeric relationships of strength between traditional blue-collar unions and unions representing municipal and other public sector employees.

Table 5 contains basic data on the Finnish and Swedish federations.

Partly due to a somewhat different structure of member unions, the Finnish federation has at all times had a greater share of women than its Swedish counterpart; by the end of the 1980s, TVK stood out as a very 'female' federation indeed. Nevertheless the pattern of growth in both countries is similar, and the influx of

142   *Women in Nordic Politics*

women members largely accounts for the growth of both federations in the 1970s and 1980s.

The picture is similar when looking at the Federations of Professional Employees (*akademiker* in the Scandinavian usage). Again, the Finnish and Swedish federations are used as representative examples for Scandinavia at large.

These data again confirm the basic conclusion apparent from the earlier tables: it is the influx of women that largely accounts for union growth, whether these are unions of workers, functionaries or professional employees.

Table 6
'Feminization' of unions belonging to the Central Federations of Professional Employees[1] in Finland and Sweden. Selected years

		All members	Women (%)	Total growth 1968-90 (%)[2]	Growth women
Sweden	1968	103,379	28		
	1976	178,403	32	244	428
	1992	356,012	43		
		All members	Women (%)	Total growth 1978-92 (%)	Growth women
	1978	150,177	ca 40	93	ca 125
Finland	1992	290,408	47		

1) AKAVA in Finland, SACO in Sweden
2) Growth 1968-76 73 percent, for women 98 percent; 1976-1992 100 and 166 percent, respectively

Sources: For Finland, data provided by Ulla Aitta (AKAVA), for Sweden, Eduards 1977, p.56 and data provided by Gunilla Lyngfelt (SACO).

Representation

Most central federations have basically a three-layered decision-making structure. The Congress, which assembles bi- or tri-annually, is formally the highest decision-making body. Between congresses, the Council or General Assembly comprised of somewhat fewer member union representatives than the Congress, has the power to make important policy decisions. The Executive Board elected by the Congress is, of course, in many ways the most influential single body in determining the day-to-day policy course. Many member unions of the central federations have a similar internal structure.

Table 7
Women's representation in decision-making bodies of the Finnish, Norwegian and Swedish Central Federations of Labour (%). Selected years

		Board	Assembly	Congress
Finland	1974	4	15	23[1]
	1986	15	30	33
	1993	22	41	37[2]
Norway	1969	0	N.A	6
	1981	7	13	18
	1985	20	19	26
	1989	20	24	31
	1993	20	29	36
Sweden	1972	0	2	13
	1988	7	19	27[3]
	1992	13	25	26[4]

1) Congress held in 1976 2) 1991 3) 1986 4) 1991

Sources: Finland 1974, *Nainen SAK:laisessa ammattiyhdistysliikkeessä*:15, Finland 1986, *Olennainen työssä*:65, Finland 1993, data provided by the SAK; Norway, Skjeie 1989, data provided by Jostein Ryssevik and Jorunn Christensen; Sweden, *Kvinnor i facket 1992*:18

Some data at the *level of member unions* in Sweden and Finland can also be presented to make the picture more complete. In 1972, eleven percent of the congress delegates of the various LO unions in Sweden were women; in 1991 their share had risen to 24 percent. For general assemblies, the corresponding figures were nine and 21 percent, respectively. On the boards of the member unions, six percent of the seats were held by women in 1972, 20 percent in 1991. The variation from union to union was enormous. For instance, at the 1991 congresses of the Union of Construction Workers and the Union of Commercial Employees, the shares of women delegates were zero and 68 percent, respectively (*Kvinnor i facket 1993*:28-30).

Again, a similar picture emerges in Finland. Thirty percent of the delegates at member union congresses were women in 1986; their representation had doubled since 1974. The growth ratio was exactly the same for the general assemblies and boards of the member unions: the shares of women in 1986 were 25 and 22 percent, respectively (*Statistics about the position of women in Finland*:92; Mikkonen 1987, Appendices 1.2 - 1.4).

All in all, it is apparent that the representation of women in the decision-making bodies of the labour union movement has lagged behind their numeric share of the membership. It is particularly striking that there are still only two women among the fifteen members the Central Board (*landssekretariatet*) of the Swedish LO. All the same, the *ratio of growth* of women's representation is well abreast of the increase of the share of women among the members.

As for the other central federations, the Finnish Federation of Functionaries TVK is (or rather *was*, as it was dissolved in 1992) in a way, a unique case. In 1988, 65 percent of the congress delegates, 68 percent of the general assembly members, and 57 percent of the board members were women. Still it should not be disregarded that all of 85 percent of the membership were women. Even considering this, however, TVK compared favorably with its Swedish sister organization. In 1985, TCO had a female membership of 57 percent; still only 18 percent of the board members were women, and there was *no growth at all in this share* in the post-war period (Bergqvist 1991:114). Bergqvist attributes part of this development to the decrease in the number of member unions; this led to the disappearance of completely 'female' member unions and thus reduced the number of 'guaranteed' female delegates, seats etc. (ibid. 117-118).[3] The Norwegian Conferederation of Vocational Unions (YSF) had around seventy percent women members in 1992; 26 percent of the Board members were women (Skjeie 1992:89).

As for the Federations of Professional Employees, Swedish SACO had approximately 35 percent women members in the early 1980s, while twenty percent of the board members were women. Ten years later, with 41 percent women members, SACO's Board included 32 percent women (data provided by SACO). Finnish AKAVA had 44 percent female members in 1988; that same year, 35 percent of the congress delegates and 19 percent of the board members were women (*Olennainen työssä*:65). By 1992, incidentally, women board members were down to three, or fourteen percent (data provided by Ulla Aitta). AF, their Norwegian sister federation, displayed a much more balanced structure in 1992:40 percent women members and 38 percent women on the Board (Skjeie 1992:89).

---

[3]   By 1993 this share had risen slightly to 21 percent (*Dagens Nyheter* 16.5.1993).

Comments

The growth in the female membership of the main unions is impressive; the level of women's representation is far less impressive, although the overall growth pattern is similar. The following reflections seem to suggest themselves.

An *optimistic* interpretation would point to the overall growth ratio in women's representation. 'One cannot expect those in power to give up their positions over night'. It will take some years until the massive influx of women will fully manifest itself in decision-making bodies through a process of 'orderly and natural succession'. The fact that women's representation seems to be highest in Finland, where female union membership has been substantial longer than in the other countries, would seem to support this gradualist view.

Moreover, this interpretation could point to comparable developments in other fields, parliamentary politics in particular. Here, women's representation in cabinets lagged behind the share of women among the members of parliament for quite some time. Having risen to around 30 percent in the course of the 1980s, female representation in parliament gave rise to a rapid increase in the number of women even in the executive branch. Today, the share of women cabinet members in Scandinavia is as high as the female share of parliamentary seats. In a word, 'critical masses' seem to make a difference.

The *pessimist* can point to several features. For one, there are some notable imbalances in the growth pattern, particularly in the Swedish case. Moreover, Bergqvist's observation about *structural changes* (centralization) as an obstacle to increased representation of women is particularly noteworthy. Amalgamation of unions creates a heightened rivalry for representative posts; women's interests and representation may be the first to lose from such a development. It is, consequently, quite imaginable that such changes can slow down, if not entirely stop, the growth of women's representation (Bergqvist 1991:114-119).

Impact

Assessing the impact of the 'feminization' of the labour market and the unions is, of course, a demanding task. For one thing, any major change occurring in the labour relations field is likely to reflect a number of parallel processes, among which the position of women is but one, albeit certainly an important one. Attempts to relate the position of women to other explanatory factors, such as the present economic crisis, would most likely render the causal discussion extremely complicated.

Moreover, much of the growth in the position of women is of such recent origin that it is simply too early yet to really speak of any definite impact. The discussion therefore unavoidably assumes a somewhat speculative character.

Be that as it may, it is clear from the quantitative overview that the feminization of the labour market represents a classical *dilemma* (in the correct sense of the word) to the central federations. Women are the only major growth potential available to them. At the same time, if the influx of women is allowed to be reflected in the representation and power patterns of the federations without restraint, the character and orientation of the federations is likely to undergo a change. Women will then tip the balance in the favor of unions representing public sector employees. What strategies will the federations opt for?

It may very well be that the differences between the countries noted above may come into play and produce varying outcomes. Finland and Norway represent the extremes. The following final discussion uses these cases in an attempt to illustrate the dynamics of the processes depicted above and the strategic choices available to the unions.

Two different roads: Finland and Norway

Finland displays an early and gradual process of 'feminization' in the labour market as well as in the unions. The share of women working part-time has remained low, and employment in the public sector, although very important, has remained somewhat lower than elsewhere in Scandinavia. The SAK has for several decades faced competition from central federations of functionaries and professional employees. At the same time, and paradoxically from the point of view of the early involvement of women in the labour market, the wage gap between women and men in the industrial sector has remained larger than elsewhere in Scandinavia.

In Norway, by contrast, women entered the labour market late and suddenly: the 1970s were a period of dramatic 'feminization' in the Norwegian labour market. Typically, the Norwegian woman employee works in the public sector; in approximately fifty percent of the cases, the work is on a part-time basis. Another important difference is that up until the 1980s, LO had somewhat of a monopoly as a central federation in the labour union field. Since then, however, it faces considerable competition from new central organizations largely representing functionaries and public sector employees.

In the light of these differences, it is interesting to note that the emphasis in the debate seems to have been on different aspects of gender equality in the two countries. In Finland, much of the discussion has concentrated on the *substance* of labour market policies: wages, vacations, various social policy aspects. In the General Program of the SAK adopted in 1991, no specific mention is made of the position or representation of women in the federation (SAK:n periaateohjelma 1991). In the more concrete Goal Agenda for 1991-96 there is similarly no separate discussion on the question of gender equality in the federation itself. Instead, the equality of job opportunities, the importance of shared responsibility for child care, and the principle of equal pay for equal work are mentioned in the list of demands on the part of the federation (Tavoiteohjelma:6-9).

In terms of practical policies, the SAK has largely followed a similar course. The federation has refrained from any quotas for women's representation or from changes in statutes entailing such measures (although two member unions have chosen to make such changes in their statutes). Instead, the emphasis has been on changes in the substance of labour market agreements. The solidaristic wage policy pursued by the SAK has in itself been instrumental to the reduction of wage differences between men and women. As social policy 'packages' have been a distinct feature of Finnish incomes policy, many reforms of primary importance to women have been implemented in this way. Nevertheless, it is important to note that these improvements have been 'side-effects' of a centralized union policy, the primary object of which has been to promote wage increases in (male-dominated) export industries. Women have benefited from the centralized system of wage agreements, but their role has been that of 'second-class free-riders'.

Potentially much more important is the fact that the central wage agreements have since 1988 included an 'equality rate', a bonus favoring those sectors where the share of women is highest and the wage-level is lowest. The impact of this bonus on the total cost of the wage agreements has so far been limited: 0.1 percent in 1988 and 0.5 percent in 1990. However, as a concrete sign of the recognition of the special needs of women employees in this very hard core of union policy, its value should not be underestimated (Tasa-arvoselonteko:8-12).

In Norway, much more attention has been paid to the 'rules of the game' within LO itself. The 1980s were a period of conflict over women's quotas in the federation. Clear and definite quotas were not achieved, but in 1989 the statutes were changed so as to include passages to the effect that the top leadership must include both women and men, and that the committees and boards of the federation must reflect the gender division of the membership. This complemented the previously adopted clause stipulating that there should be women as well as men among the leading functionaries of LO congresses. Moreover, a new clause was added to the general objectives of the federation, in which LO proclaims its intention to fight 'all forms of negative discrimination on the basis of gender, sexual inclination, race, outlook on life or cultural attitudes'. Equality between men and women within the realm of the federation, as well as in society at large, had been included among the basic goals at an earlier stage (Vedtekter:6-14).

As for the question of gender quotas, Hege Skjeie points out that LO opted for a strategy of 'supplementation' in order to avoid tipping the balance of power among its member unions. Instead of redistributing seats so as to give female-dominated unions more central power, a new seat in the Secretariat was created and earmarked for a woman. Skjeie also notes that the opinions among LO members concerning women's quotas not only diverged according to gender but according to the public/private sector division, 'Men in the public sector not only took a clearly more positive attitude to quotas than did men in the private sector; they were also more positive than women in the private sector' (Skjeie 1989:89).

The issue of wages was addressed in connection with the introduction of the Equal Status Act (adopted in 1978), which involved a confrontation in which LO stood out as a conservative bastion. The Labour Party originally wanted this legislation to contain effective instruments by which wage negotiations could be influenced to bring about equality between women and men. LO strongly resisted, claiming that such instruments would entail undue political encroachment upon collective bargaining, which should be left to the representatives of employers and employees. A compromise was finally reached so that the general clauses of the Act pointed to the use of positive discrimination in favor of women as a possible instrument; at the same time, no specific regulation of wage settlements was included (Skjeie 1992:77-79).

The question of wage policies in Norway is complicated by the trend towards decentralization evident in collective bargaining since the early 1980s. Most wage agreements have since then been based on separate deals on the level of the member unions of the LO. The government has at times used its legally sanctioned powers by intervening to produce centralized agreements. This has contributed to the reluctance of the LO to allow wage settlements to be part of the general political agenda. The Norwegian picture indeed offers a clear contrast to the situation in Finland, where broad central agreements containing comprehensive social policy reforms, in addition to wage norms, were the rule from the late 1960s through most of the 1980s (Elvander 1988:13-15).

Politics vs economy?

Women's representation in Norwegian and Finnish unions is today of roughly equal size. In a broader international comparison, both countries stand out as societies where women have made considerable headway in union politics. Still, it would appear as if the seemingly identical development might be based on quite different mechanisms in the two countries.

In the Norwegian case, political and ideological factors have come into play to a much larger extent than in Finland. To begin with, the fact that the share of women in the labour market rose so rapidly from the early 1970s on was in itself partly a result of a conscious policy on the part of the government, the Labour Party in particular. The policy resulted in the creation of a great number of new jobs in the public sector, many of them on a part-time basis.

Moreover, as the case of the Equal Status Act indicates, there has been an active attempt on the part of the Labour Party to influence the principles for wage settlements in the Norwegian labour market in order to bring about wage equality between women and men. These attempts have not met with enthusiasm among the LO leadership, who generally dislike the legal right of the government to intervene in the wage negotiation process in Norway.

The Norwegian emphasis on gender quotas for representative posts in LO clearly reflects the parallel course characteristic of the political parties, the socialist parties in particular. The fact that gender quotas have become such a central issue in the debate about the position of women in the labour union movement can be seen as a 'spill-over effect' from the party political arena. Quotas have simply become an established instrument for equality in politics; it seems natural to extend them to other areas as well. (Interestingly enough, in Finland the absence of gender quotas in the SAK is matched by the lack of such quotas among political parties - see Sundberg's contribution to this volume).

This 'primacy of party politics' is clearly not present in the Finnish case. In fact, the position of the Social Democratic Party vis-à-vis the unions has been weaker than elsewhere in Scandinavia due to traditionally stronger competition from the extreme left. Moreover, the government lacks the strong legal instruments available in Norway to intervene in wage settlements.

In Finland, the SAK has not only been a central actor in the wage negotiation process. Due to the relative weakness of the political left among the parties, the Central Federation of Labour has shouldered a major responsibility for social policy reforms. Much of the advancement in the area of welfare policies is the result of the comprehensive agreements in the labour market. The SAK has not only presented wage demands to the employers; to an equal extent it has presented demands for social policy reforms to the government. The 'soft packages' included in the settlements have meant two things. On the one hand, the government, not the employers, has financed this part of the gains made by the unions. On the other hand, the unions have acted as an engine behind reforms that the social democrats on their own would have been too weak to force their government coalition partners to accept.

Although basically 'gender neutral', these social policy reforms have been more crucial to women than men in working life. Extended paid maternity leaves, a comprehensive system of public daycare centers and increased oppportunities for continued training and education have primarily enhanced the professional position of women. Although still of minor economic significance, the 'equality rates' included in the most recent central wage agreements show that women's interests have started to affect the very hard core of collective bargaining. All of this seems to have taken place without decisive involvement on the part of political parties.

It is possible that the longer involvement of Finnish women in the labour market and in the unions, their somewhat higher dependence on competitive sectors and their involvement in full-time work has directed their attention primarily to the substance of wage agreements rather than to the internal 'rules of the game' of the organizations. The high degree of female participation in the labour market and the unions is a result primarily of 'economic' rather than 'political' factors. Increased membership and women's representation reflect the increased role of women in working life. It is difficult to point to any government action which would have decisively enhanced this growth. Just like in the party political arena, women have to fight for their share of power largely unaided by externally determined rules and regulations.

In Norway, by contrast, the growth of women's representation is part of a rapid development since the 1970s by which the idea of women's quotas became more or less generally accepted in social and political life. It was by no means a simple task to establish these principles, but the composition of governments, public commissions and most party executives today demonstrates that the drive has been successful. LO has, as Skjeie has put it (1989), been somewhat of a 'final bastion' trying to resist regulated women's representation. The step taken towards women's quotas in 1985 was a partial one. Still, given the proportion of women among LO members today, it is hardly an exaggeration to call it a decisive one: it will bring about an increase of women's representation similar to that of political parties.

Conclusion

The rapid increase in the share of women in the total work force during the last three decades is one of the most fundamental changes in Scandinavian societies. By the same token, it has transformed the membership of Scandinavian trade unions.

In the representation of the citizens' interests, parties and parliaments are closer to the 'immaterial' and trade unions to the 'material' side of the interest spectrum. It is a well-known fact that where important questions of money are decided, women tend to be absent. Consequently, women's representation has been strengthened more rapidly in the party political field than in the decision-making bodies of the unions. The process of a growing women's representation is, however, under way, and it is difficult to see why women, given the membership potential they represent to the unions, would allow it to be halted. Whether the result of quota policies or a 'natural transformation', women's representation has begun on an upward trend which is largely irreversible.

What is more uncertain is the future of the trade union movement at large. Today, centralized union politics and other fundamental features of the labour market system are under increased pressure due to the economic crisis, growing unemployment and calls for privatization of public welfare functions. In Sweden and Finland, where central federations of labour still claim the importance of centralized wage settlements, there have been increasing indications that the employers are about to succeed in creating a more decentralized - and less solidaristic - system of wage policies. In Denmark and Norway, this has already been a fact for many years.

Just as male-dominated unions in export-oriented sectors may grow impatient with 'bearing the burdens of public-sector workers', women may grow tired of supplying the federations with their membership growth while having their claims for representation voted down by the traditionally dominant unions. In such a situation, a fundamental realignment in the labour market along the public/private sector distinction is not out of the question.

References

Official documents and publications
Aktuell nordisk statistik, oktober 1992.

Nord 1988:58, *Kvinnor och män i Norden. Fakta om jämställdheten 1988.* Nordic Council of Ministers.

Olennainen työssä. Sosiaali- ja terveysministeriö: tasa-arvojulkaisuja, sarja B: Tiedotteita 2/1989, Helsinki 1989.

Statistics about the position of women in Finland, Council for Equality, Publications of the Prime Minister's Office 1975:5, Helsinki 1975.

Statistisk Årbog 1992 (Denmark).

Statistisk Årsbok 1992 (Sweden).

Yearbook of Nordic Statistics 1972, 1985 and 1993.

Other written sources

Bergqvist, C. (1991), 'Corporatism and Gender equality. A Comparative Study of two Swedish labour market organizations', *European Journal of Political Research,* 20:107-125.

Elvander, N. (1988) (ed), *Förhandlingssystem, inkomstpolitik och arbetskonflikter i Norden.* Stockholm: Norstedts.

Haavio-Mannila, E. (1981), 'The Position of Women', in Allardt, E. et al. (eds): *Nordic Democracy.* Copenhagen: Det Danske Selskab.

Hernes, H.M. and Hänninen-Salmelin, E. (1983), 'Kvinners representation i det korporative system', in Haavio-mannila, E. et al. (eds): *Det uferdige demokratiet. Kvinner i nordisk politikk.* Oslo: Nordisk Ministerråd.

Kvinnor i facket (1988), *Undersökning om kvinnorepresentation inom LO och förbunden.* Published by LO, Sweden.

Kvinnor i facket (1993), *En undersökning om kvinnorepresentation inom LO och förbunden 1992.* LO: Löne- och arbetslivsenheten.

Mikkonen, E. (1987), *Minäkö SAKissa? Tutkimus SAK:n naisjäsenistöstä,* Helsinki: SAK:n järjestötutkimusprojekti.

Nainen SAK:laisessa ammattiyhdistysliikkeessä, Jyväskylä 1980: SAK.

Pedersen, J. C. (1988), 'Overenskomstforhandlinger og indkomstpolitik i Danmark', in Elvander, N. (ed.): *Förhandlingssystem, inkomstpolitik och arbetskonflikter i Norden.* Stockholm: Norstedts.

Petersson, O. (1991), *Nordisk politik.* Stockholm: Allmänna förlaget.

SAK:n periaateohjelma. SAK:n 14. edustajakokous 17.-20.6 1991.

Skjeie, H. (1989), 'Rapport fra en siste skanse: Kvinnerepresentasjon i fagbevegelsen', *Arbeierbevegelsens Arkiv og Bibliotek: Arbeiderhistorie 1989.*

Skjeie, H. (1992), *Den politiske betydningen av kjønn. En studie av norsk topp-politikk.* Oslo: Institutt for samfunnsforskning.

Tasa-arvoselonteko. SAK:n hallitus 6.5. 1991.

Tavoiteohjelma 1991-1996. SAK:n edustajakokous 17.-20.6. 1991.

Valkonen, M. (1989), *Suomen Ammattiliittojen Keskusjärjestö SAK r.y. 1907-87,* Helsinki: SAK.

Vedtekter for Landsorganisasjonen (med endringer vedtatt på kongressen i 1989), Oslo 1989: LO.

Unpublished sources are indicated in the text.

The changing role of women within local voluntary organizations: sex segregation in the voluntary sector[1]

Per Selle and Bjarne Øymyr

Introduction

Women have always played a crucial role within the voluntary sector and within certain historically very important organizational types like the laymen movement and the teetotal movement, and among social and humanitarian organizations they have dominated. In organizing activities for children and youth, women have also been far more important than men. The ongoing transformation of the women's role within this organizational society does not only mean a different organizational life, but, also a different society to live in.

Local voluntary organizations, at least in Norway, are rather easy to build and quite often they do not live for a long time, i.e. the local organizational society is quite dynamic. Our study of organizational change in a specific region in Norway from 1940-1980 concluded that as many as 78 percent of the organizations existing in 1980 were founded after 1940. Furthermore, as many as 64 percent of the organizations existing in 1940 had disappeared. Even if there is extensive variation across organizational types, an extinction rate below 50 percent is unusual (Brandal and Selle 1983).

Since 40 years is quite a long period, what about short-term change? From the 1980s we know that as many as 13.8 percent of the organizations existing in 1980 had already ceased to exist in 1988 and 17.5 percent of the organizations in 1988 had appeared after 1980 (Selle and Øymyr 1992). Furthermore, 80 percent of all Norwegians between 16 and 79 years of age are members of at least one voluntary

[1] We thank Nina Raaum for comments. An earlier version of this paper was presented at the Third International Research Conference on Non-Profit Organizations and Philanthropy, Indianapolis, 11-13 March 1992.

155

organization, one out of three Norwegians are members of three or more such organizations; 50 percent of all members define themselves as 'active', i.e. they do more than just pay the yearly fees (St. meld. nr. 83, 1984-85:257). This means that quite a large number of people are constantly entering and leaving organizations, leaving either because their organization ceases to exist, or making an individual exit. The local voluntary sector is a continuously changing and rather *open* and dynamic sector.

Changes in the *population of voluntary organizations* and of *organizational forms* within such an open and dynamic sector we argue, are - in an *organizational society* like Norway - one of the best places to get hold of and understand more genuine societal transformation. It is our point of view that local organizational change really *reflects* more general societal change. The position of women within the organizational society at any point in time is an important expression of the society's view of women and the role of women within that same society.

This chapter looks into the transformation of the role of women within the local voluntary sector. We shall distinguish between organizations *only* for women, i.e. closed organizations, and organizations *dominated* by women. We define an organization as dominated by women when two out of three members are women. The first group of organizations serves as the pure organizational society for women per definition. It tells us at any given time what *the general society* defines as a pure women's role, i.e. *what ought to be sex specific*. Organizations dominated by women on the other hand, show the more accurate *sexual division of labour* within the voluntary sector.

In the first section we approach changes in the population of voluntary organizations since World War II, particularily emphasizing changes in the sex composition. Then we move on to take a closer look at the dynamics of the 1980s, comparing main characteristics of organizations that have disappeared with those of old ones surviving and new ones emerging since 1980.

This chapter identifies crucial changes in the role of women within the voluntary sector. The gradual decline of the historically so important mass movements (the laymen movement and the teetotal movement) in which women really dominated, and from the mid 1970s, the decline in the traditional social welfare organizations, almost completely dominated by women, means that women are 'losing' their own organizational society. In most of the new types of organizations appearing, related to leisure in the broad meaning of the word, men dominate. Having 'lost' their own organizational society, women have so far not been able to become an equal part within most 'modern' parts of the voluntary sector. However, women are increasing their share even within these types of organizations.

Growth and transformation[2]

Organizational growth

Changes in the population of voluntary organizations have a direct effect upon the sex composition of the organizational society. Therefore we ask the questions: what types of organizations have been founded in different periods of time and what is the sex composition within these organizations? We do not have complete information about every organization that has been founded through history,[3] and we have no information about the sex composition at the time of founding. What we do know is the sex composition of the organizations existing in 1980 and their year of founding.

Figure 1 shows the sex composition of organizations established in different time periods. When pure women's organizations have the highest founding rate we see an extensive growth in missionary organizations and in social and humanitarian organizations. The first comprehensive growth period of more mixed organizations corresponds to the first important founding period of organizations for children and youth, i.e. from 1890 to 1920. Mixed organizations make up a growing share from the 1960s, i.e. the major founding period of song and music organizations, and culture and leisure organizations. It is an interesting and important finding that during the 1980s there is a rather strong increase in the founding rate of organizations with *only men as members*, even if these organizations are open to women. This is an important and *new structural characteristic* of the Norwegian voluntary society. What this may indicate, we shall return to later on. Furthermore, the figure shows that while mixed organizations constitute the largest group of

---

[2] This project contains not only a total registration of VO's in a Norwegian region (county) (Hordaland) at three different points in time, it also contains a total registration of VO's in two other Norwegian regions (Buskerud and Finnmark) in 1941 and 1988. (The registration of 1941 was done by the Norwegian Nazis, and as far as we know Norway was the only western country in which the Nazis accomplished such a registration). Furthermore, in Hordaland in 1980 we did not only register organizations, but we distributed an extensive questionnaire as well, i.e. we have extensive information about organizational age, geographical space, organizational networks, contact with public authorities, membership and leadership structure, level of and types of activity, economy, etc. For more information about the project and about methodological problems, see Brandal and Selle, 1983; Leipart and Selle, 1984; Selle and Øymyr, 1989.

[3] For possible consequences, see Selle and Øymyr, 1992.

organizations that is also growing, the group of male-dominated organizations is more comprehensive than the group of female-dominated organizations. We also see that the group of female-dominated organizations is decreasing while the male-dominated group is rather stable.

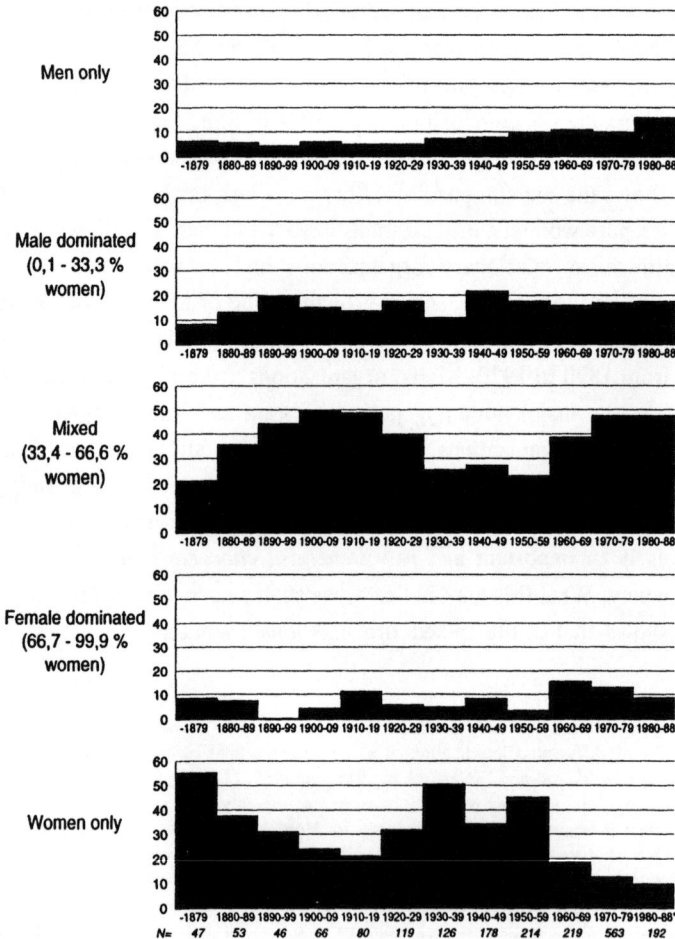

Figure 1: Sex composition and year of founding

Figure showing the sex composition of organizations founded in different time periods.

Let us look closer at changes in the population of organizations since World War II. Table 1 displays the population of organizations in a given Norwegian region in 1941, 1980 and 1988. The *number* of organizations has increased substantially, from about 3000 in 1941 to almost 6,000 in 1988. So has the organizational *density*. In 1941 we find one organization for every 49 inhabitants while the number in 1988 is 33 (Selle and Øymyr 1989:16). More interesting is the changing *composition* of the organizational population. Two main groups of organizations show a dramatic decline, and both of these are strongly dominated by women; missionary organizations and teetotal organizations. Both of these types belong historically to strong mass movements, and their decline continues during the 1980s.

Furthermore, as regards the total percentage of religious organizations (including missionary organizations) these amounted to an impressing 58 percent in 1941, but have decreased to 34 percent of all organizations in 1988, which is a very substantial decline. However, we see that religious organizations still play an important role, especially in the group of organizations for children and youth. More important here is the fact that the relative importance of organizations that are *only for women* declines in relative terms, and during the 1980s we even find a substantial decline in the total number of such organizations. This development is partly explained by the decrease in missionary organizations, since organizations only for women dominate within this category. But as we shall see, that is not the whole story.

Table 1: Changes in the population of VO's in a Norwegian Province (Hordaland) 1940-1990												
	1941		1980		1988		1941-80		1980-88		1941-88	
	N	%	N	%	N	%	N	%	N	%	N	%
Economic	401	13.3	604	11.0	670	11.4	203	-2.3	66	0.4	269	-1.9
Political*	1	.0	291	5.3	289	4.9	290	5.3	-2	-.4	288	4.9
Sport	115	3.8	349	6.4	390	6.7	234	2.6	41	.3	275	2.9
Language	19	.6	32	.6	38	.6	13	.0	6	.0	19	.0
Teetotal	207	6.9	122	2.2	106	1.8	-85	-4.7	-16	-.4	-101	-5.1
Missionary	1327	44.1	902	16.5	837	14.3	-425	-27.6	-65	-2.2	-490	-29.8
Youth	631	21.0	1268	23.2	1316	22.4	637	2.2	48	-0.8	685	1.4
Song/Music	45	1.5	619	11.3	678	11.6	574	9.8	59	.3	633	10.1
Humanitarian	237	7.9	586	10.7	596	10.2	349	2.8	10	-.5	359	2.3
Culture/Leisure	25	.8	698	12.8	943	16.1	673	12.0	245	3.3	918	15.3
N=	3008	100	5471	100	5863	100	2463	-	392	-	2855	-
Women	657	21.8	846	15.5	773	13.2	189	-6.3	-73	-2.3	116	-8.6
Youth	697	23.2	1654	30.2	1708	29.1	957	7.0	54	-1.1	1011	5.9
Christian	1745	58.0	2109	38.6	2037	34.7	364	-19.4	-72	-3.9	292	-23.3
*)Political organizations were banned by the Nazis in 1941.												

There is a dramatic increase in the group of culture and leisure organizations and of song and music organizations. In 1941 these groups amounted to only 2.7 percent of the organizational population while their percentage in 1988 is 27.7. While the growth in song and music organizations came to an end during the 1980s, the culture and leisure type organizations continue their dramatic growth, both in real numbers and in their relative part of the organizational society, even if the increase slows down at the end of the 1980s. We also see that the number of sports organizations have increased substantially, an increase that continues during the 1980s. As already indicated by Figure 1, in most of the expanding organizational types, *men dominate*, even if these organizations are open to women. The combination of male dominance in 'modern' and expanding organizations and the decline within the organizational society for women only is really transforming the role of women within the organizational society. One of the most important characeristics of the organizational society, that men and women have complementary organizations, i.e. complementary roles in society, is in a process of decline. This mirrors crucial change in the relationship between the sexes in the society at large.

Organizational transformation and the changing sex composition of the voluntary society[4]

Even if the traditional women's organizations are in a process of decline, surveys on participation in voluntary organizations show that there is no general decline in female membership in the voluntary sector. Furthermore, women's overall membership rate is *as high* as that of men (NOU 1988:17). Thus, we must determine what types of organizations women are turning to. Our descriptive organizational typology used in Table 1 consists of 10 main categories. To study change in more detail, we have divided these categories into new subgroups, containing 19 types of organizations (See Appendix A). Figure 2 shows sex composition, membership figures, year of founding and the turnover rate for these organizational types.

---

[4] Throughout this paper we are using different typologies showing the sex composition of different organizational types. In this section, when comparing the structure at different points in time we use a typology based on the dominating sex composition within each type (subgroup) of organizations. Therefore we speak of a e.g. male-dominated *type* of organization. In the section that deals with characteristics of the 'surviving' and 'dead' organizations in the period 1980-88 we use the *sex composition of each single organization*.

Figure 2: Sex, Size, Age and Turnover

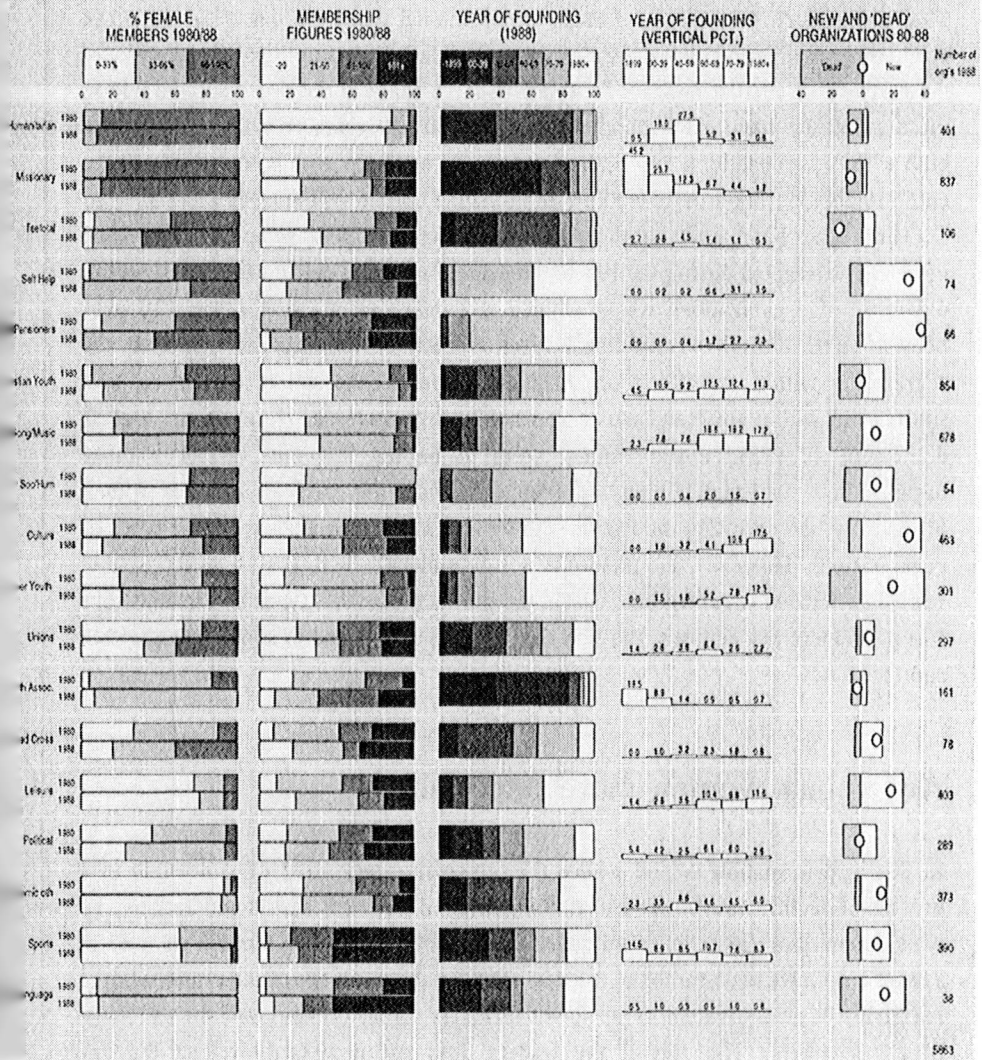

Looking at sex composition we see that of the social and humanitarian organizations and the missionary organizations, close to 90 percent are dominated by women. Furthermore, their extinction rate is much higher than their founding rate. Seven of the 19 organizational types in Figure 2 have to some degree become less sex segregated during the 1980s, i.e. the share of mixed organizations has increased. Two common characteristics of these organizational types are that they are either stable or growing, and except for the youth associations and political organizations, these are rather new organizational types. A large share of the organizations within these categories have been founded during the last 20 years. We find this picture both within organizations for children and youth, self help groups, political parties, culture/neighbourhood organizations and to some degree within trade unions.

On the other hand, seven of the organizational types have to some degree become more sex segregated during the 1980s. This development is evident first of all within old types of organizations where women now make up a larger share than ever before. These are all organizational types in decline. We also see increased sex segregation within expanding organizational types in the sphere of leisure, like sports, and within song and music and hobby organizations. Here we see a clear dominance of men. While women seem to be the last ones to leave those organizations that are declining, but even so has been the most important to women historically, they are also the last ones to move into the new and expanding types of organizations. However, the picture is not only black. There is also an increase in female dominated organizations within the growing or stable types of organizations like pensioners associations, the Red Cross, trade unions and to some extent within sports.

Are young women more like men?

In this transformation period where the 'complementary' role of women is in a process of decline, maybe we will find important differences across generations. To what extent does age seem to influence the type of organization women choose? In Figure 3 we have been forced to use data showing the mean age of the organizational leadership as an equivalent to the age of members, as we do not know the exact age of the members. The age of the leaders does not necessarily reflect the age composition of the members, e.g. it is quite common for children and youth organizations to have adult leaders. Still, we hold that in general the age composition gives an indication of the age of the members in most organizational types, even if the common member in most cases will be somewhat younger. In Figure 3 we categorize the average age of the leadership, i.e. the members, into four groups. The figure shows the percentage of organizations with an average age of leaders and members below 30 years, 31-40 years, 41-50 years and above 50 years of age. We see a clear difference between the female-dominated organizations and the others. Apart from the female leisure organizations (a group which consists of only eight organizations) the majority of the leaders and members within the female-dominated organizations are more than 40 years of age, and, furthermore, leaders above 50 years of age are the largest group except within the group of social and humanitarian organizations.

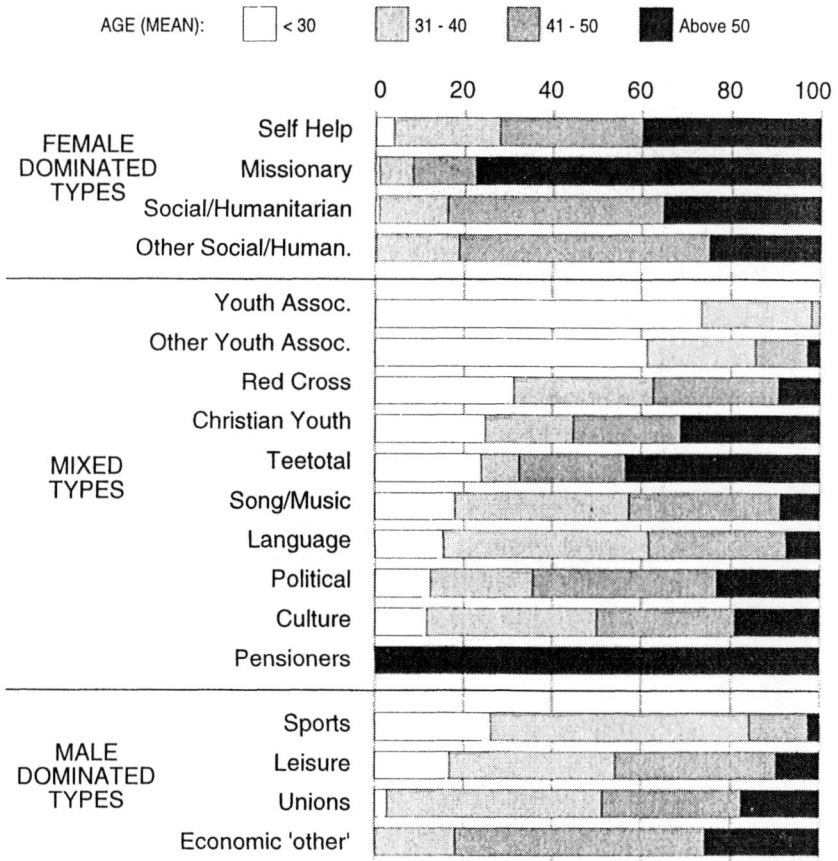

Figure 3: Age (mean) by type of organization

In general, we find that organizations related to sports, leisure and youth associations have the youngest leaders and members, while missionary organizations, teetotal organizations and traditional social welfare organizations have the oldest leaders and members, i.e. all organizational types in which women dominate.

Table 2 systematizes the relationship between age and sex composition. We see a clear-cut difference between organizations dominated by different age groups. Close to two-thirds of the organizations with an average age of leaders and members above 50 are dominated by women, while only 24 percent of the organizations dominated

Table 2: Sex composition by age. Percentage.				
	Age (mean)			
	<30	31-40	41-50	51+
Male Dominated	36.2	46.9	38.6	22.2
Mixed	39.9	28.0	21.8	16.6
Female Dominated	23.9	25.1	39.6	61.2
Sum	*100.0*	*100.0*	*100.0*	*100.0*
N=	401	586	624	613

by leaders and members below 30 are female-dominated organizations. The structural picture is quite clear: the proportion of female-dominated organizations *increases* with age, the proportion of mixed organizations decreases with age, while the proportion of male-dominated organizations is largest where the average leader and member are between 30 and 50 years of age.

In order to take a closer look into long-term changes, we have compared two Norwegian surveys on participation in voluntary organizations,[5] one from 1957, the other from 1986, to grasp more in detail changes over time in the types of organizations to which different age groups belong.[6]

---

[5] Valgundersøkelsen, 1957 [Election Survey, 1957] and Undersøkelse om deltaking i frivillige organisasjoner [Survey on participation in voluntary organizations, 1986]. Central Bureau of Statistics/Norwegian Social Science Data Services.

[6] The respondents are members in a varying number of organizations, with a maximum of 15 different membership. Each membership is registered as one case. In Figure 4, the unit is membership.

Figure 4: Membership by age and sex 1957 and 1986. (Percent).

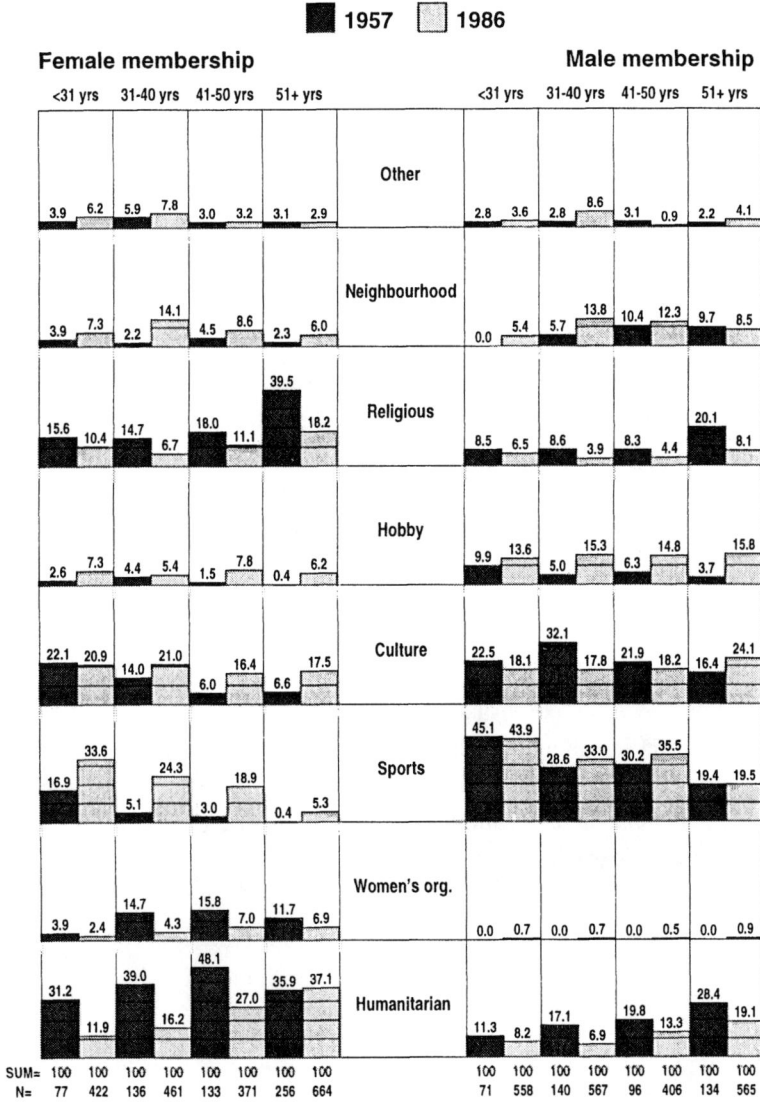

■ 1957   □ 1986

Female membership — columns: <31 yrs, 31-40 yrs, 41-50 yrs, 51+ yrs
Male membership — columns: <31 yrs, 31-40 yrs, 41-50 yrs, 51+ yrs

Category	F <31 (57,86)	F 31-40	F 41-50	F 51+	M <31	M 31-40	M 41-50	M 51+
Other	3.9, 6.2	5.9, 7.8	3.0, 3.2	3.1, 2.9	2.8, 3.6	2.8, 8.6	3.1, 0.9	2.2, 4.1
Neighbourhood	3.9, 7.3	2.2, 14.1	4.5, 8.6	2.3, 6.0	0.0, 5.4	5.7, 13.8	10.4, 12.3	9.7, 8.5
Religious	15.6, 10.4	14.7, 6.7	18.0, 11.1	39.5, 18.2	8.5, 6.5	8.6, 3.9	8.3, 4.4	20.1, 8.1
Hobby	2.6, 7.3	4.4, 5.4	1.5, 7.8	0.4, 6.2	9.9, 13.6	15.3, 5.0	14.8, 6.3	15.8, 3.7
Culture	22.1, 20.9	14.0, 21.0	6.0, 16.4	6.6, 17.5	22.5, 18.1	32.1, 17.8	21.9, 18.2	16.4, 24.1
Sports	16.9, 33.6	5.1, 24.3	3.0, 18.9	0.4, 5.3	45.1, 43.9	28.6, 33.0	30.2, 35.5	19.4, 19.5
Women's org.	3.9, 2.4	14.7, 4.3	15.8, 7.0	11.7, 6.9	0.0, 0.7	0.0, 0.7	0.0, 0.5	0.0, 0.9
Humanitarian	31.2, 11.9	39.0, 16.2	48.1, 27.0	35.9, 37.1	11.3, 8.2	17.1, 6.9	19.8, 13.3	28.4, 19.1
SUM=	100, 100	100, 100	100, 100	100, 100	100, 100	100, 100	100, 100	100, 100
N=	77, 422	136, 461	133, 371	256, 664	71, 558	140, 567	96, 406	134, 565

Source: Election Survey, 1957 and Survey on participation in voluntary organizations, 1986 (SSB/NSD).

Figure 4 shows strong differences over time.[7] The most dramatic change is to be found within the religious and social and humanitarian organizations, and within women's organizations. Within these categories we find a strong overall decline in membership. However, there is one important difference between these types of organizations. For those above 50 years of age, membership in religious organizations has, in relative terms, been more than halved between 1957 and 1986, both for men and women. However, within this age group there is *no* such decrease in women's participation in humanitarian organizations.

Male membership in religious organizations has in the same period been reduced from 28.4 to 19.1 percent. We find the strongest relative increase in female membership within sports, and we should note that also women above 30 increasingly find their place within sports organizations. There is also an increase in female participation within neighbourhood, hobby and culture organizations. The strongest growth in male membership is to be found within hobby clubs.

Two more important observations appear from Figure 4. The *changes* in membership patterns seem to be less dramatic for men than for women. Furthermore, we see that in 1986 the *membership pattern of young women* (below 40 years of age) *is closer to the overall male membership pattern than to the membership patterns of women above 50*. That means that today there exists more of a generation gap than a gender gap.

Furthermore, missionary organizations, which had their peak early in this century, are not only in a process of decline, but the membership rates are declining within *all* age groups. Humanitarian organizations, which had their major founding period between 1945 and 1960, are losing in importance within all age groups except for women above 50 years of age. We know that some of the most important subgroups within this organizational type really have difficulties in recruiting new members. This *could* imply that these organizations will continue to decline as the members are gradually getting older (and dying).

---

[7] The categories in Figure 4 have been defined and coded by Statistisk Sentralbyrå (Central Bureau of Statistics), and are not fully comparable with our categories. Economic and political organizations are not included in these surveys.

Characteristics of the dead, the new and the surviving organizations in the 1980s

The 'dead' versus the 'surviving' organizations

To dig deeper into the transformation process we compare those organizations that disappeared during the 1980s with those that survived.[8] The figures have been broken down and categorised to show the sex composition of the members within the organizations; male-dominated means 0-33.3 percent female members, 'mixed' means 33.3-66.6 percent female members while female-dominated means 66,7-100 percent female members.

Including the year of founding adds important new information about the organizational transformation. Within the 'dead' male-dominated and mixed organizations we find a higher proportion of newly built organizations, i.e. organizations established in the periods after 1974, as compared to the surviving organizations. Almost half of the 'dead' mixed organizations were established between 1975 and 1980, and more than 25 percent of the male organizations that have disappeared were established in the same period. This shows that older organizations within these categories seem to be the most stable. For female-dominated organizations the situation is really different. They have a higher proportion of old organizations among the dead organizations as compared to the surviving ones. As many as 35 percent of the dead female organizations were established before the turn of the century, and as high a proportion as 56 percent was established before 1920. Even if these figures may not be completely accurate, they illustrate quite clearly the transformation of the female-dominated part of the organizational society. This implies that the 'liability of newness' (e.g. Stinchcombe 1965, Freeman, Carroll and Hannan 1983, Hannan and Freeman 1984, Aldrich and Marsden 1988) is found within the male-dominated and mixed organizations, but not at all within the female-dominated organizations.

---

[8] In the 1988 registration the organizations that had ceased to exist during the 1980-88 period were registered. Thus we have traced these organizations back to the 1980 survey. We found that 255 of the 'dead' organizations had answered the survey back in 1980. However, not all of these organizations have answered all the questions, and the tables represent those organizations that did answer the relevant questions. There is no major skewness between the main categories of organizations answering the survey in 1980 (Selle and Øymyr 1992). Still, there is some skewness concerning subgroups. We know, for instance, that among the traditional missionary organizations the reply percentage is low. To correct for this the organizations have been weighted.

Table 3: Characteristics of the 'surviving' and 'dead' organizations 1980-88.					
	Male Dominated		Mixed		Female Dominated
PROBLEMS	Surv.	Dead	Surv.	Dead	Surv.	Dead
Economy	11,1	2,4	8,4	0,0	2,7	1,4
Recruitment of members	7,3	6,1	7,4	10,9	11,8	13,0
Recruitment of leaders	7,5	8,1	8,7	6,4	4,5	4,3
Activity level	8,4	6,2	8,8	10,3	3,7	2,0
N=	*359*	*33*	*502*	*51*	*549*	*92*
YEAR OF FOUNDING	Surv.	Dead	Surv.	Dead	Surv.	Dead
1847-1890	3,9	2,4	4,3	0,0	7,4	35,0
1891-1900	2,3	0,0	3,5	5,7	1,5	0,4
1901-1920	7,0	4,8	13,5	1,4	9,1	20,6
1921-1944	14,4	4,7	13,0	4,8	18,0	13,6
1945-1960	22,3	27,6	12,9	9,2	23,7	8,8
1961-1974	31,3	34,4	24,2	32,3	26,5	10,4
1975-1980	18,8	26,1	28,5	46,7	13,9	11,1
N=	*336*	*29*	*465*	*51*	*515*	*84*
MEMBERSHIP FIGURES	Surv.	Dead	Surv.	Dead	Surv.	Dead
20 or less	19,3	59,3	16,4	25,9	62,3	78,3
21 to 50	40,6	27,5	42,7	39,1	25,5	14,1
51 to 100	22,4	11,2	23,5	16,5	6,6	4,6
101 to 200	8,9	0,0	8,7	17,2	3,6	0,0
More than 200	8,8	2,1	8,7	1,4	2,1	3,0
N=	*342*	*30*	*468*	*48*	*501*	*82*
ECONOMY	Surv.	Dead	Surv.	Dead	Surv.	Dead
Budget > 10,000 NOK (1980)	38,2	13,4	32,8	15,1	11,6	22,2
Satisfactory econ,	72,5	53,7	77,3	79,9	82,7	80,1
Public finance	57,6	58,4	81,6	86,1	55,9	49,8
INTERNAL ACTIVITY	Surv.	Dead	Surv.	Dead	Surv.	Dead
Meetings at least once a month	25,5	34,7	39,5	39,7	66,5	63,2
Members participating:						
< 33 %	24,3	9,5	18,1	22,1	5,7	2,4
33 - 50 %	30,9	26,5	27,3	29,7	12,8	5,0
> 50 %	44,8	64,0	54,6	48,2	81,5	92,6
N=	*339*	*29*	*449*	*47*	*508*	*77*
EXTROVERT ACTIVITY INDEX	Surv.	Dead	Surv.	Dead	Surv.	Dead
Zero	37,9	37,9	59,7	67,1	73,2	89,4
Low	22,3	17,2	18,2	2,9	15,2	6,0
Medium	23,9	33,0	10,7	8,7	7,1	3,4
High	15,9	10,1	11,4	21,3	4,4	1,2
N=	*359*	*33*	*502*	*51*	*549*	*92*
GEOGRAPHICAL SPACE	Surv.	Dead	Surv.	Dead	Surv.	Dead
Village	42,9	56,8	76,5	69,5	76,8	70,7
Municipality	40,8	43,2	20,9	26,9	21,1	29,3
Larger areas	16,3	0,0	2,6	3,6	2,1	0,0
N=	*357*	*33*	*502*	*51*	*549*	*92*
ORG. NETWORK	Surv.	Dead	Surv.	Dead	Surv.	Dead
Hold sub groups	6,8	4,2	8,1	10,1	3,9	3,4
Reg. motherorg.,	74,1	58,1	64,5	53,9	55,4	49,6
Nat. motherorg.	83,5	65,6	65,1	61,4	58,5	50,5
Coop. council	25,7	13,9	18,4	17,8	11,6	7,8
N=	*336*	*31*	*453*	*44*	*464*	*79*

Furthermore, the table shows quite clearly that a larger proportion of female-dominated organizations are small in size as compared to male-dominated and mixed organizations. However, the 'dead' organizations are in general smaller than the surviving ones. More than three out of four female organizations that ceased to exist during the 1980s had fewer than 20 members. When it comes to the dead male-dominated organizations, close to six out of ten organizations had such low membership figures, while the percentage for the mixed organizations was 25.9.

There are strong differences between the male-dominated, mixed and female-dominated organizations when it comes to the frequency of membership meetings,[9] but it is only within the male-dominated category that we find significant differences between the 'dead' and 'surviving' organizations. About two-thirds of the female-dominated organizations have meetings at least once a month, while the same may be said of four out of ten mixed organizations. Female-dominated organizations seem to disappear independently of the frequency of meetings. Within the male dominant category the figures are 34.7 and 25.5 percent for the dead and surviving organizations respectively. Concerning the extent to which members take part in such meetings, a surprising picture appears. It seems that those organizations which disappeared during the 1980s had a larger proportion of their members participating back in 1980. This is so both within the group of male-dominated and female-dominated organizations. We do not find this tendency among mixed organizations. It is important to note that in general, the female-dominated organizations, whether surviving or not, have a higher membership participation as compared to the male-dominated and mixed organizations, while at the same time they have a higher turnover-rate. This implies that those organizational types with the highest turnover rate had the highest level of *introvert* activity. That the female-dominated organizations in general have a higher level of membership participation than mixed and male-dominated organizations might be partly explained by size, but it also has to do with organizational culture. Small membership-based organizations require that a high proportion of members do take part in order to keep a certain level of activity going. But it might also be that members of old and traditional organizations feel more obliged to take part, i.e. they are part of a 'participation culture'. However, to the surprise of some, social and cultural density do not prevent organizational extinction.

---

[9] We have to stress that these figures do not necessarily contain information on all the "internal" activities. Organizational types having membership meetings as their main activity (e.g. missionary organizations) will necessarily have a higher score on this question than e.g. sports organizations, where members often meet to practice sports, but only have membership meetings a few times a year.

Looking into the index showing the degree of *extrovert* activities[10] we find that within the male-dominated and mixed categories a higher proportion of the 'dead' as compared to the surviving ones have a low score on this index. However, much more important is the fact that *the female-dominated organizations are less engaged in extrovert activities* than the mixed and male-dominated organizations. This is the case both for the surviving and 'dead' organizations. It is a very important finding that the 'dead' organizations seem to be less integrated into overall organizational networks, and that within the female-dominated and mixed categories, few of the organizations that have disappeared hold a high level of *extrovert* activity. Extrovert activity seems to be much more important for organizational survival as compared to introvert activity.

Concerning organizational networks, the general picture is that the 'dead' organizations to a lesser degree maintain subgroups, are part of national organizational networks, or participate in co-operating councils within their municipalities. We also see that male dominated organizations seem to be the most integrated into extensive organizational networks, *while the female-dominated organizations are the least so*. Those organizations with a high level of extrovert activity which are an integrated part of organizational networks definitely have the highest possibility of survival.

Differences between the 'surviving', the 'dead' and the new organizations of the 1980s

So far we have compared the organizations that have disappeared with those that have survived, but we have not given any information about main characteristics of the new ones emerging (except organizational type). However, even if we do not have any comprehensive survey to add to our registration in 1988, we do have some important *structural* information about the organizations founded during the 1980s. We are able to compare them with the 'dead' and the surviving ones on such important variables as geographical space, membership figures and sex composition.

---

[10] The index shows the degree of engagement in public affairs. It is based on the following variables: the number of engagements, whether the organizations have arranged meetings about public matters, whether they have sent notes/letters to the authorities or taken personal contact with officials.

Table 4[11] shows *strong* and very *crucial* differences. Both within male-dominated and mixed organizations we find that the surviving organizations are larger than both the new and the 'dead' ones. There are no major differences in size between the 'dead' and the new organizations. New organizations are already as big as those going out of existence. Looking at the female-dominated organizations, the picture is very different. Here we find that new organizations relatively are already larger than both the surviving and the dead organizations.[12] Furthermore the size of the 'dead' female-dominated organizations clearly differs, with eight out of ten organizations having fewer than 20 members. It is the old and small neighbourhood organizations working where people live that are really disappearing. These are the organizational types in which women historically have dominated, but in the centralization and professionalization process of today these organizational types have become old fashioned, because the neighbourhoods themselves have lost most of their old functions (Selle and Øymyr 1994).

Table 4: The new organizations of the 1980s compared with the 'dead' and 'surviving' organizations*.

	Male Dominated			Mixed			Female dominated		
MEMBERSHIP FIGURES	Surv.	Dead	New	Surv.	Dead	New	Surv.	Dead	New
< 20	23,8	57,8	49,4	14,7	26,2	23,9	56,9	81,8	47,4
21 to 50	36,7	31,8	39,2	37,5	47,2	45,1	27,8	12,3	34,2
51 to 100	21,6	7,8	5,1	24,5	13,5	22,5	8,0	3,0	15,8
More than 100	18,0	2,5	6,3	23,2	13,1	8,5	7,3	2,9	2,6
N=	370	28	79	707	80	71	557	83	38
GEOGRAPHICAL AREA	Surv.	Dead	New	Surv.	Dead	New	Surv.	Dead	New
Village	60,2	45,9	52,6	71,3	62,1	63,4	87,7	80,1	50,0
Municipality	27,9	54,1	35,9	25,5	34,5	23,9	11,2	19,9	44,4
Larger areas	11,9	0,0	11,5	3,2	3,5	12,7	1,1	0,0	5,6
N=	413	34	78	797	89	71	598	98	36

*)Surviving and dead organizations: data from 1980, new organizations: data from 1988

Looking into the geographical space from which the organizations recruit their members, we find a mixed picture. A new tendency is that new organizations more often organize to cover larger geographical areas as compared to the 'dead' and 'surviving' ones. Breaking down this variable by sex adds important new

---

[11] The figures are somewhat uncertain, partly since N is low and there is some statistical skewness on these variables. Still we argue that the extensive differences express *real* differences.

[12] Still, there are more surviving organizations with more than 100 members as compared to new ones.

information. We do not find that the new male-dominated organizations cover larger areas than the 'dead' and 'surviving' organizations do, and we find only small differences within the group of mixed organizations. On the other hand, there is a rather strong tendency in this direction within the female-dominated organizations. Here only half of the new organizations are organized as 'neighbourhood-organizations' while between 80 and 90 percent of the 'surviving' and 'dead' organizations are organized in this way.

Both in terms of size and geographical space new female-dominated organizations are highly 'modern', i.e. rather large in size and covering the whole local authority area. The majority of the female-dominated organizations which are disappearing, on the other hand, are as previously mentioned of the *old* and *traditional* type, i.e. small and neighbourhood-based. This implies that some of the most crucial structural changes within the organizational society are taking place within the female-dominated part of the organizational society. The modernization of the organizational society means not only increased centralization and professionalization, but also a larger concentration of organizations working for their own members at the expense of the society at large (e.g. Selle and Øymyr 1992, Selle and Øymyr 1994), which means that crucial features of the traditional organizational society of women have lost touch with their environment.

Discussion and conclusion

The sex composition of the local organizational society has changed in fundamental ways after World War II. *Women have to a much lesser degree an organizational society of their own*, and the organizational society they still have is one in continuous decline. Furthermore, we have seen that the development of the 1980s quite clearly goes in the direction of a *less sex segregated organizational society*. Small and introvert organizations (in activity, but to some extent also in ideology) most often dominated by women are in a process of decline, i.e. their extinction rate is substantially higher than their founding rate. Furthermore, looking into the dynamics of the organizational society of the 1980s (and probably the 1990s) *we do not see the contours of any new type of organizational society for women only or even strongly dominated by women*. We understand this to be a strong organizational expression of a general ideological or cognitive move from viewing women mainly as complementary to men, i.e. different from men in fundamental ways, to being understood as equal. If there is a new development in the direction of sex segregated organizations these are rather organizations with only men as members.

So far so good, if one thinks women should be equal to men. But as we have seen, even if the increase in women's employment rate and in their participation in traditional male activities, like for instance sports, has been comprehensive, their new role in the labour market and within sports is not at all fully reflected organizationally. Even if these organizations are open to women, and women do take part, they are clearly dominated by men. Whether this means that modern women are less 'interested' in the 'new' and dominant 'leisure and market-ideology' of these organizations (Selle and Svåsand 1987), i.e. that these organizations mainly express a male-dominated value system, or that the lack of female participation is best explained by internal organizational characteristics of these organizations, making it difficult to be a woman within them, we can not really tell (Kanter 1977). However, what we can tell is that as a whole, this means that during this transformation period the organizational society has become increasingly dominated by men. To some extent at least, we can say that women have become more *invisible* in the local organizational society.

Whether this will be a more permanent structural characteristic within the more 'equal' society or whether it is only a question of time before women become really 'integrated' into the 'modern' organizational types is an important societal question and will therefore be an important research question in the near future. However, structural characteristics of women's participation in organizations of the 1980s point in the direction of women's integration in the overall organizational society. While the old gender gap is closing down because women are 'losing' their own organizational society, we doubt that a new organizational gender gap will develop in the near future. The 'old' society is gradually 'disappearing' from the voluntary sector and men are the main organizational modernizers in this transformation process. However, we believe women are on their way to take equal part.

References

Aldrich, H. E. and Marsden, P. V. (1988), 'Environments and Organizations', in Smelser, N. J. (ed.): *Handbook of Sociology*. Beverly Hills: Sage.

Brandal, T. and Selle, P. (1983), 'Endringar i organisasjonsmønsteret i Hordaland 1940-1980', *Heimen*, 4:259-270.

Bregnballe, A. (1987), *Sluttrapport. Undersøkelse om deltaking i frivillige organisasjoner. SSB,* Interne Notater 1987:13.

Freeman, J, Carroll, G. R. and Hannan, M. T. (1983), 'The Liability of Newness: Age Dependence in Organizational Death Rates', *Sociological Review*, 48:692-710.

Hannan, M. T. and Freeman, J. (1984), 'Structural Inertia and Organizational Change', *American Sociological Review*, 49:149-164.

Kanter, R. Moss (1977), *Men and Women in the Corporation.* New York: Basic Books.

Leipart, J. and Sande, T. (1981), *Valgundersøkelsen 1957.* Rapport nr. 47. Bergen: NSD.

Leipart, J. and Selle, P. (1984), *Data og metode - ei vurdering av representativitet, svarprosent og spørjeskjema.* Rapport nr. 3. Bergen: Hordaland Fylkeskommune.

NOU 1988:17. Frivillige organisasjoner.

Selle, P. and Øymyr, B. (1989), *Frivillige organisasjonar i Hordaland 1987/88.* Rapport 89/1. Bergen: LOS-senteret.

Selle, P. and Øymyr, B. (1990), *Frivillige organisasjonar i Finnmark, Buskerud og Bergen, 1941.* Rapport 90/1. Bergen: LOS-senteret.

Selle, P, and Øymyr, B. (1992), Explaining changes in the population of voluntary organizations: aggregate or individual level data? *Nonprofit and Voluntary Quarterly*, No. 2:147-179.

Selle, P, and Øymyr, B. (1994), *Frå verdiorientering til tilbodsorientering: Det lokale organisasjonssamfunnet i endring 1940-1990.* Oslo: Samlaget (forthcoming).

Selle, P. and Svåsand, L. (1987), 'Cultural Policy, Leisure and Voluntary Organizations in Norway', *Leisure Studies*, 6:347-364.

Stinchcombe, A. L. (1965) 'Social structure and organizations', in March, J. G. (ed.): *Handbook of Organizations.* Chicago: Rand McNally.

St. meld. nr. 83, 1984-85.

APPENDIX A: Typology

Main Categories	Typology used in most of this paper	Sub Groups
ECONOMIC	Unions	Unions
	Other	Cooperative org. Farmers assoc. Landowners assoc. Fishermens assoc. Breeding assoc. Other
POLITICAL	Political	All political parties
SPORTS	Sports	Sports Workers assoc. Shooters assoc. Other
LANGUAGE	Language	New Norwegian org. [Mållag] Other
TEETOTAL	Teetotal	All teetotal organizations
MISSIONARY	Missionary	All missionary org. except Christian org. for children and youth
CHILDREN/YOUTH	Christian Children/Youth	Sunday schools Christian youth org.
	Youth assoc. [Frilynde UL]	Youth assoc.
	Other	Scouts Youth clubs 4-H Other
SONG, MUSIC, THEATRE	Song, Music, Theatre	Music assoc. School orchestra (janitsjar) Choirs Dance/Theatre Jazz/Pop Folk dance [Leikarring] Other
SOCIAL & HUMANITARIAN	Social & Humanitarian	Housewives orgs. [Helselag] [Sanitetslag] [NSSR] [Fisker/Bondekvinnelag]
	Red Cross	Red Cross /[N.Folkehjelp]
	Handicap/Self help	Handicap/Self help
	Other	Other
CULTURE AND LEISURE	Culture/Neighbourhood	Culture/Education Neighbourhood assoc
	Pensioners assoc.	Pensioners assoc.
	Leisure	Leisure
	Other	[Nærradio/TV] [Innvandrerlag] [Forsamlingshus] Other

An alternative movement in a 'state-friendly' society: the women's shelter movement[1]

Kristin Morken and Per Selle

Introduction

The women's shelter movement is typical of an alternative social welfare organization in Norway. The movement has played an important role in bringing the abuse of women to the public's attention and subsequently in lending legitimacy to the idea that abuse of women is a serious social problem which requires comprehensive government action. The movement emerged primarily out of the feminist women's movement and is, in fact, the most important *institutional* expression of the modern women's movement.

Understanding the women's shelter movement's *special* relationship to the *welfare state* is the key to understanding the character of both the movement and the welfare state. This relationship demonstrates the most *typical* aspects of the Norwegian welfare state and also illustrates what it *means* to be an alternative movement in a 'state-friendly' society (Hernes 1987, Lafferty 1986, Kuhnle and Selle 1990, 1992a).

The Norwegian welfare state presently regards abuse of women as a 'public' problem and attempts to solve or reduce the problem through an organization which is relatively removed from the welfare state both ideologically and organizationally. This organization, as most alternative organizations in Scandinavia, turns *towards* rather than away from the welfare state. This is a very important feature, and it is necessary to understand its significance. Public financing is considered a *right*, an indication from the state that one's work is important and consequently the autonomy of the organization is not an issue.

[1] We thank Lauri Karvonen, Stein Kuhnle, Anne-Hilde Nagel, Johan P. Olsen, Felice Perlmütter, Nina Raaum and Aaron Wildavsky for comments. An earlier version of this article was published in Felice Perlmutter (ed.): *Case Studies of Nonprofit Organizations*. Washington, D.C.: NASW Press, 1994.

177

A central thesis of this chapter is that the development of the women's shelter movement, both the internal structure and the relationship to its surroundings, is *not* primarily a result of government financing but more closely related to the internal processes and conflicts which are inherent in the organization, processes which were put in motion by the decline of the women's movement.

Wife-battering: from private to public problem

From a historical point of view, Western culture has a long tradition of subordinating women to men. A woman is seen as a man's chattel; for example in old Norse law the woman is not a party in the marriage contract (Ahnfelt 1987), she is the subject-matter of the contract. The violence of husbands against their wives has in many legal systems been expressed as a husband's right. Roman law allowed the husband to punish or kill his wife if she committed adultery (Araldsen and Clasen 1983). With the introduction of Christianity to Norway, women lost the right to a divorce if their husbands beat them in the presence of others. Even so, Norwegian law has not legitimized wife-battering to the same extent as for example British law (Dobash and Dobash 1980).

Even though it was the women's movement in the 1970s which brought abuse of women to the public's attention and put the problem on the political agenda, there were attempts to do the same 100 years previously. At that time feminists and suffragettes tried to achieve similar goals. These efforts were on a very small scale in Norway and were primarily expressed by contemporary women authors. However, Frances Power Cobbe's article, 'Wife Torture in England', and the opening of women's shelters in a few American cities indicate that the first wave of feminism also tried to expose and stop violence against women (Dobash and Dobash 1980).

In contrast to their sisters 100 years earlier, the feminist renaissance represented a much more radical view of abuse of women and its causes. They saw such abuse as a combination of direct and structural violence (Alsaksen 1979, Freeman 1987).

When violence against women again became *visible* and was put on the political agenda at the end of the '70s, there were many who doubted the gravity or extent of the problem. But the rush to the newly established shelters indicated that violence against women was not a thing of the past. The Norwegian health care services alone are in contact with approximately 10,000 cases of abuse per year (Skjørten 1988). Many were even more shocked by the fact that the shelters and independent follow-up reports abolished the myth that abuse of women was of a basically psychopathological or sociostructural nature. There was no overrepresentation of women whose husbands did not behave quite 'normal' socially or in their jobs, i.e. psychologically, among those who sought out the shelters (Moxnes 1981). Nor was there any overrepresentation of women from lower levels of society (Malterud 1981). The myth of violence as a result of the influence of alcohol was also proven to be highly exaggerated (Nisja 1982).

There were undoubtedly many in health care, psychiatry and the police who nodded in agreement when the women activists of the '70s claimed that there was much more abuse of women than was generally believed. Until that time episodes of violence had been recorded in police statistics as 'domestic disturbance', in hospital statistics as 'fell down the stairs', and in the psychologist's journal as 'anxiety and depression' (Morken 1993).

Norwegian studies show that battered women often meet with very little understanding when they look to the established social services for help; everything from complete indifference to attempts to find fault with the woman as a means of explaining the violence. Furthermore, the same studies also indicate that the penal code is not as strictly applied in cases of domestic violence as in cases involving physical assault elsewhere in society (Nisja & Alsaksen 1980).

According to the 'Norwegian Social Services Act' of 1964, municipal social services offices in Norway are required to provide both counseling and practical and financial assistance to those in social need or crisis. That is still the law. However, social services offices have been criticized for having limited their assistance to the purely financial (Øyen 1975) and for being unsuitable in cases involving those with multiple problems (Bleiklie 1980). A battered woman may often be in the latter category; she may need financial, legal, personal, and housing assistance. The social welfare offices' waiting lists, regulated opening hours, and registration requirements create a situation requiring decisive and planned action on the woman's part, a situation which is highly unsuitable for a woman in an acute crisis.

Gradually it became quite clear that traditional welfare institutions could not meet the needs of battered women. How come there was an opening for an alternative and non-public institutional solution?

The women's shelter movement: volunteer work in a social movement

How the organization came about

The women's shelter movement in Norway began when five women from Oslo participated at a tribunal on violence against women in Brussels in 1976. The participants were associated with the women's movement, and upon returning home to Norway they began the process of setting up the first shelter group. The aim was completely clear from the start: they were going to bring domestic abuse of women *to the public's attention* and they were going to run their own shelter. These women considered domestic violence to be a public problem for which *the government was therefore obligated to provide funding.*

To start out with, applications for financial assistance to both central and local authorities were unsuccessful. Nevertheless, the group was able to open a helpline on 2 February 1977, using private funds. After one year's operation the group was able to prove the need for measures to help battered women: they had received an average of two genuine calls per night. They were thus given governmental funding for a trial period of two years.

Such was the birth of a nation-wide women's shelter movement which in the course of a few years managed to set up and take responsibility for shelters and helplines throughout the country. At the same time, the members of the movement managed to make both the media, politicians and the public at large aware of the extent and gravity of the problem. Violence against women was gradually *redefined*; it changed from a private and almost nonexistent phenomenon to what the public generally considered a serious social problem.

By the end of 1991 there were a total of 53 women's shelters and helplines. Approximately 3000 volunteers were active participants in the work. Ca. 2900 women and 2000 children stayed at the shelters that year, altogether approximately 73.000 nights. In the same period the shelters and helplines received 34.000 genuine calls of which about 2000 were from children (Barne- og familiedepartementet: Statistikk-Krisetiltak, 1991).

Welfare ideology

Women's shelters are an alternative source of help for women who have been raped or subjected to psychological or physical abuse. Almost all of the shelters are run by voluntary interest groups, ie the women's shelter groups, on a non-profit basis.. The members of the groups work shifts and one or more daytime staff are employed to take care of office work and other miscellaneous chores. Only women are allowed to participate in this work.

At the same time as the shelters represent a *non-professional source of help*, they may also be characterized as a *form of political action*, a means of achieving the fundamental social changes implied by a society completely without oppression of women. Thus the shelters also have an important function as *an arena for consciousness-raising* both for those who work at the shelters and those who seek help there.

As a source of help, the shelters provide temporary housing for women who wish to get out of a relationship in which they are abused. Unlike the government social services offices, there are no regular opening hours, no waiting lists, no application forms or registration requirements. Here a woman is able to get help and counseling in gaining legal assistance, contacting the proper social services, and making any necessary visits to her residence. It is also important that she may bring her children.

Women's shelters consider themselves a *supplement* to government social services, and *do not aim to replace them*. They view themselves as an *easily available* special institution which serves as a sort of transit station between the social network and the formal social services apparatus. One of the goals has been to recruit women with experience of abuse to work at the shelters, though this has not been achieved to the degree that was expected. Much emphasis is placed on establishing as *equal a relationship as possible between users and staff*. This is evident in the use of the term 'user' instead of 'client' (which is used otherwise in governmental social services). It is equally important that the woman herself defines her situation and possible alternative solutions, something which is regarded as impossible within a system with professional staff as this would imply an *asymmetrical* relation which would deprive the woman of her independence and passify her.

Organizational form and political ideology

Norwegian women's shelters are a 'child' of the women's movement, and what is more important, it was neo-feminists who founded the first shelter in Oslo. This is very significant as there have been two main groupings within the Norwegian women's movement. These two groupings have been characterized by their particular strategy for change, and these different strategies have influenced their choice of organizational form (Haukaa 1982).

The Women's Front (Kvinnefronten) emphasized the *instrumental* in an organization: a strongly centralized and hierarchical organizational structure would create unity and strength, which were considered necessary prerequisites for the achievement of political goals. At the same time, increased consciousness was considered possible only in the battle against the *external* enemy. Politically this group was far to the left.

The Neo-feminists (also including the organization called Bread and Roses), on the other hand, not being that far to the left, opted for a decentralized organization model and a *'flat'* organizational structure. This organizational structure was to contribute to personal consciousness-raising and private politicizing, ie these organizations were more inward looking. Thus the neo-feminists placed greater emphasis on *expressive* values: the means were just as important as the end. Important features of the 'flat' organizational model are the division into small groups, the absence of elected leaders, the rotation of functions, and the general assembly as the supreme authority. This organizational model, in other words, represents a negation of the traditional bureaucratic form of organization with a hierarchy and functional division of labour.

The principal of a 'flat' structure has been an important part of the women's shelter movement's ideological foundation. This explains why the resistance to a central organization has been so great, there has been a fear that the oligarchical monster would materialize. In other words, a grouping of all shelter groups under one organizational unit would, according to its opponents, lead to a shift of responsibility, authority, knowledge and activity from the *local to the central* level. A central organization would quite simply not be consistent with the democratic model on which the women's shelter movement is founded.

Even though the women's shelter movement gained support from the Women's Front and from women with relatively little political awareness, the movement was from the very start mainly influenced by the neo-feminist school within the women's movement. Their value system was later reflected in both the daily work and external strategy of the women's shelter movement. However, as we shall see later, a considerable difference between theory and practice has developed at many shelters. In order to understand this development, it is important to keep in mind the multiplicity within the movement; it may be regarded as a *coalition* of different groups of women. In order to explain changes in the power relationships between these groups it is necessary to consider external as well as internal factors (see Chapter 7).

In the Autumn of 1980 the Women's Shelter Group (Krisesentergruppa) in Oslo held the first national conference for the country's women's shelter groups. Representatives of 26 groups participated, and the aim of the conference was to promote contact among the groups and to agree on a common platform. From that time on, the annual conferences have been the most important forum for the discussion of goals and strategies for Norway's women's shelter groups.

At the national conference in 1980 a common platform was passed. In this platform it is evident that the groups' objective is a two-part one. The shelter groups shall:

- make the public more aware of violence against women and
- be responsible for providing a service for battered women.

Other important resolutions which have been passed at national conferences deal with the recognition of the 'flat' structure as the ideal organizational structure, the principle that *there shall be compensation* for all work done at the shelters, that there shall be *no external involvement in organization or operation of the shelters*, and not least, that the establishment and operation of the shelters shall *be funded by the state*. To put it briefly, the women's shelter movement has allocated considerable responsibility for health and social services to the state, however, in this particular case the government shall neither govern nor regulate, merely finance.

Though national conference resolutions are not binding for the individual shelter, the criterion for full membership in the women's shelter movement is that the individual group adopt the common platform. During the 1980s there were four groups which remained outside the movement. Either these are fundamentally opposed to parts of the platform, particularly the principle of *compensation for all work*, or they do not fulfill the *independence requirement, as they are run by other organizations*.

Even in a Norwegian context it is rare that a pressure group without a highly formalized structure is given public funds in order to operate. The fact that the women's shelter movement is publicly funded is indicative of the lucky timing of the movement's entrance into the political arena. The movement made its presence felt at a time when the welfare state was strongest institutionally speaking, at the same time as there was a growing awareness of the weaknesses and limitations of public solutions to social problems.

The women's shelter movement not only exposed abuse, it also managed to legitimize itself by proving that battered women had a *right* to help, help which the shelters, in contrast to the public social services, had the competence to provide. Other groups have followed in its footsteps, (like the center for incest victims) as the women's shelter movement *paved the way* in both establishing a need · and representing a qualitatively different service. However, as time goes by adaption to both external and internal pressure results in comprehensive organizational and ideological change. It is to these changes we shall now turn.

From theory to reality: from movement to organization

The organizational model under pressure

In spite of the lack of a central organization, the Oslo group has always served as a natural center for the movement. Their leading role at the start of the movement made them the ideological trend setters and the group functioned as a source of both inspiration and practical advice for the other groups that gradually formed. Furthermore, the group found itself physically closest to the various national media institutions, governmental departments and members of Parliament.

With the exception of the development of the last few years, which will be discussed later, the Oslo group has also been the most 'political' of the women's shelter groups. This political orientation was expressed, among other things, in the struggle for full compensation for all volunteer work at the shelter. If there was no money left in the budget for wages, the shelter was closed until additional funds were found.

However, even if the ideal organizational structure in the women's shelter movement is a 'flat' structure, there were in 1988 only three groups which were organized along these lines. After the 'coup' at the Oslo shelter in the Autumn of 1989 (see part VI) this number has been reduced to two. The great majority of the country's shelter groups are thus of a hierarchical or semihierarchical nature. Even so, most of the groups have incorporated elements of the 'flat' model in their organizations. In 1986 there were only six clearly hierarchical groups (Jonassen 1987). The remainder have kept the general assembly as the supreme authoritative body. The general assembly may try resolutions passed by executive committees or the executive board itself, either in all matters or in matters pertaining to internal affairs.

A successful 'flat' organizational structure which works requires not only a high level of activity, but also competence in this form of management. It requires a relatively even distribution of political resources among its members, or if this is lacking, a strong will to work against an uneven distribution. It is easy to imagine an uneven distribution of such resouces between women of different backgrounds. Women who have a long history of involvement in women's political organizations or other political activity are better equipped to deal with meeting procedure, better able to articulate their beliefs and to form alliances, than are women without such a background. The membership of the women's shelter movement consists of just such a mixed group, and there is reason to believe that in the early years the activists tended to be most influential in deciding terms, etc.

There is also reason to believe that in several places this domination was the direct cause of the change in organizational form, ie the majority felt themselves at the mercy of the more ideologically aware, and therefore preferred formalized power to informal power structures. Furthermore, it must not be forgotten that this type of organizational structure also places considerable demands on time and energy, which may be felt to be problematic as the practical work at the shelters is also quite resource-consuming. This fact, together with a certain degree of external pressure toward a more hierarchical organizational structure make it understandable that at present, the majority of shelters have moved away from the ideal type of organizational structure. It remains to be seen whether this is just a step in the direction of a more hierarchical organizational structure as we know it from most other voluntary welfare organizations, or whether the shelter groups will manage to maintain elements of their organizational uniqueness.

A recurring topic of discussion at shelter movement national conferences is the question of gathering all shelter groups under a national organization. The debate concerning the setting up of an umbrella organization has continued throughout the 1980s without ever attaining the support of a majority. The possibility of setting up an information office was at the latest discussed at the national conference of 1992, but no final decision was taken. There are several factors which explain why many in the movement favor a national organization. First, the membership is more heterogenous in interest and background than the common ideological platform would imply. Both the initial starting up phase and later activity have been characterized by the broad spectrum of types of woman and women's organization involved (Jonassen 1987). Thus it is likely that many members have never considered a decentralized organization the alpha and omega of the women's shelter movement.

Furthermore, the daily running of the shelters and the constant shortage of funds have taken most of the groups' time and energy, and as a result the level of political consciousness has declined, both in general and in the context of the schooling of new members. Many shelters feel that they lack the resources to look after their interests and responsibilities adequately outside the shelter itself. This is probably most characteristic of the smaller shelters in less central locations. Additionally, the public funding program consists partly of direct transfers from the central government, and this means that the shelters have a common relationship to the central government (See part V).

These features point in the direction of a need for an umbrella organization. It must not be forgotten that most of the shelters have already developed an organizational structure which is of a hierarchical or semihierarchical nature. The step toward a more permanent national organization is not such a large one for these shelters to take.

'Problems' with 'users' and staff

In theory, shelter users are to be involved in shelter activities both by involving long-term residents in the daily work and by recruiting earlier users to staff positions. This has not been as successful as had been expected (Jonassen 1987). In this respect Oslo stands apart, here approximately 30 percent of staff members were at one time shelter users. Residents were also admitted to the general assembly here, though they seldom attended. It is, however, difficult to decide whether the low level of user involvement is due to a lack of effort on the part of the shelter group, or whether battered women in general do not have the energy to become involved. Nevertheless, studies show that an overwhelming majority of shelter users are satisfied with the help they receive at the shelters, while far fewer say the same of government social services (Jonassen 1989, Skjørten 1988).

The day staff find themselves in a peculiar 'in-between' position as they often identify with the group members at the same time as they are employed either full or part-time. They are often their own employer in that they are also ordinary members of the group. These staff members gain an insight into the shelter's daily operation and its relation to its surroundings that is completely different from that of the regular members who work one or two shifts per week or per month. Members of the day staff are thus in a central position. Research (Jonassen 1987) indicates that approximately half of the day staff members are able to influence the decision making process either through regular participation in meetings or through their function as secretary of the shelter's executive board. Generally speaking, the functioning of the shelters are fully dependent upon them, and the staff members have probably strengthened their position over time, not the least since the contact with local and/or central government has become more time consuming and important.

An important consequence of this increased contact is the fact that during the 1980s several shelters were required by their municipal governments to establish an executive committee to be responsible for finances and to have a municipal representative on that committee. Many shelters were opposed to this requirement. Jonassen's studies (1987; 1989) showed that shelters with a formal tie to the municipal government were in better financial condition that those which had no such formal connection. In 1988, 16 of 48 shelters had external representatives on their executive boards, and the majority have subsequently expressed satisfaction with this arrangement. In most cases, this involvement is limited to issues of a financial nature, and several external representatives have only observer status on the boards.

Nevertheless, this form of tie to local government is still a controversial issue within the women's shelter movement (Jonassen 1989). Even the radical Oslo group had to relent at an early stage to the city's demand for representation in the group's finance committee. It was obvious that the public representatives in Oslo found that there was little necessity for supervision; attendence declined and finally stopped. The women's shelter movement still does not accept shelters with external representatives who have voting rights in all matters pertaining to operation of the shelter.

The women's shelter movement is thus in the midst of a process of change. The majority of the groups have ended up with a hierarchical or semihierarchical organizational structure, and it is also more legitimate to advocate a national organization. These developments must be considered in light of the absolute number one problem; *funds*. In the women's shelter movement in particular, the muffled ideological overtones are accounted for by the eternal struggle to make ends meet. This is extremely problematic for this type of organization: how does one find the time to reproduce oneself ideologically when service production is the major activity? It is noteworthy that this developmental feature is not characteristic of this particular movement alone. The entire women's movement has lost much of its force and ideological essence during the same period. Let us therefore look more in details into these relationships.

Women's shelters: autonomous work, public money

Public funding means legitimacy

With the arrangement of a program for public funding in 1982, the women's shelter movement won the battle for public financing of the shelters. To start out, the program was to be in force in a trial period lasting until 1989. It now seems that funding will continue to be provided indefinitely, even though the matter has not been officially decided. As funds are not provided in accordance with any resolution, the question of continued funding is raised in the consideration of each budget. However, there have not been any signals of change in or elimination of the funding program thus far. Even if this leaves the shelter movement in a somewhat vulnerable and precarious situation, to eliminate such funding programs would have been very controversial and can almost be ruled out now that reducing or eliminate wife-battering has become a public responsibility.

The public funding program is not explicitly designed for any group within the women's shelter movement. On the contrary, it is open for any voluntary group which is involved in help for battered women. But as we have seen, there are actually only a few shelters which are run by voluntary organizations outside the women's shelter movement, or by local government and as long as the women's shelter movement are doing a good job, they will continue to get the funds.

The main component of the official funding program of 1982 is that up to 50 percent of the costs of setting up and operation will be covered by the central government if the local municipality or county municipality will cover the rest. Thus expansion has followed a decentralized model in which the establishment and operation of the individual shelter have been primarily dependent on the good will of the local authorities, and not central government direction. The municipal governments may thus decide the extent of their funding of shelters within their jurisdiction, and there is no regulation of the number of shelters per resident or geographic density. The exception is the county of Finnmark, which is very sparsely populated. In this area the government has taken the initiative to set up two shelters. The Norwegian Ministry of Health and Social Affairs submitted a proposal for hearing in 1988 which suggested a change in the public funding program to a system of distribution of funds to the county governments on the basis of population, with a provision for the compensation of sparsely populated areas. The shelters were opposed to the proposal, and contacted the Minister of Health and Social Affairs in person to express their disagreement. The shelter groups viewed the proposal as an unfortunate attempt to increase government control over the shelters. Furthermore, they were not in favor of the attempt to develop a better geographical spread within the limitations of the department's budget. The proposed program would necessarily have had a negative affect on the existing shelters in certain counties. The proposal was not passed and this shows the extent to which the women's shelter movement is legitimized within the political system.

Public financing: tight budgets, weak control

In contrast to the general program for the transfer of funds from central to local government authorities, the funds for the women's shelters are earmarked. The usual practice in such transfers involves so-called 'blanket allocations', from which the municipal government may allocate funds as it sees fit within the given limitations. Shelters have thus avoided having to compete with other sectors for the central government funds. The fact that the Ministry has guaranteed for up to 50 percent of the approved budget has made it easier for municipal governments to commit themselves to financial involvment in the operation of the shelters.

Even so, the greatest limitation for the women's shelters has been their tight budgets. This has particularly affected the principle of full compensation for all volunteer work. There are many shelters which either continually or periodically have had to resort to little or no compensation in order to maintain a balanced budget. The alternative has been periodic closing while waiting for extra funds to be granted or for the next budget year to begin. The majority of shelters have, in such a situation, chosen to remain open, but it seems evident now that more and more shelters opt for closing part of the year because their funds are inadequate (Jonassen 1989). This may be an indication that the 'pioneer phase' is now over for many women's shelters: they have documented the need for their existence and are no longer willing to give in so easily.

The financial model means that the municipal governments have decided the total amount of money given to the shelters since central government covers up to 50 percent of what is given by municipal governments. At the central level decisions of the early 1990s have been very positive for the women's shelters. The budget almost doubled from 1990 to 1991; from 21.571 million n.kr. to 41.178 million n.kr. (including money to the shelters helping incest victims). Furthermore, in 1992 the Norwegian Storting changed the original budget proposal in important ways. Money from central government shall now cover 50 percent of the total budget, not up to 50 percent. Central government does now cover the same amount of money as coming from municipal governments *plus from other givers*. This really opens up for private 'fundraising' if the women's shelters in the future wish to become more independent of local public financing.

The local variations in the presence of external representatives on the shelters' executive board or other committees represents an adjustment that each shelter has had to make based on local conditions, particularly the need to secure the financial side of operations. Even though this has been relatively unproblematic for most (Jonassen 1989), it serves as a good example of the fact that having a good relationship with a source of funds has required structural adjustments which conflict with original principles. The design of the program for government funding, on the other hand, makes no stipulation for the recipients' daily operations or management. This absence of rules, regulations and other attempts by the central government to standardize and structure the centers is extremely atypical for programs in which the government provides financial assistance to voluntary organizations (Kuhnle and Selle 1992a).

It must therefore be said that the women's shelter movement has been successful in winning public funds for the shelters on its own terms. In a Norwegian context, publically funded, voluntary-run and controlled help organizations with such a degree of independence are very rare. Even more extraordinary is the fact that the movement grew at a time when 'the public sector view' in health and social services was at its strongest. Other social service/help organizations of a partly voluntary, partly public nature are run by older humanitarian organizations which began their work at a time when government involvment was not as extensive. Even though these organizations are closer to the public sector in terms of ideology and service production, government control is in general much greater (Kuhnle and Selle 1992a).

No charity at all

It has been important for the women's shelter movement to emphasize that it does not run any form of charity work. This would be the implication if continued operation was based on collection of funds. The movement is of the view that the government has an obligation to provide financing for a service for battered women, which is understandable considering the rights-based principles on which the Norwegian welfare state is built. In other words, public funding is a source for making both the problem and the problem-solvers legitimate. The problem of autonomy vs complete dependence on government funds has never been an important topic of discussion. This feature has to be explained by the rather strong legitimacy of and the 'openness' of the public sector (Kuhnle and Selle 1992a).

In a Norwegian context, the unusual element is that the women's shelter movement chooses to run the shelters itself rather than leave operation to the public sector as well. It is only when we look at the basic values of the movement that this becomes significant. The operation of the shelters has meant much more than 'just helping', it represents the women's rights battle in practice. The shelter movement became one of the first specific expressions of the concept of self-help: peers can provide help which is qualitatively different and better that public 'therapist help'.

To be able to understand the success of this politicised alternative movement we have to empasize a main difference between the situation in Norway and in Britain or the US. Pahl (1985) for instance describes the problem in Britain of being both a charitable organization and a pressure group. In order to achieve charitable status, a prerequisite for fundraising, an organization may not be political, which is precisely what shelters are in that they relate violence against women to deeper structures in the society at large. This is a totally *unknown* problem in Norway. First of all, we have no strong tradition of fundraising for voluntary or charity organizations. We do not even talk about 'charity organizations'. Secondly, private contributors are not allowed tax deductions. Nor is public support linked to any specific criteria which the organizations must meet.

How the women's shelter movement won the battle with government, or how public responsibility was redefined

In spite of the dependence on municipal goodwill and the eternal struggle against tight budgets, the women's shelter movement must be said to have won its struggle for public funding without further public involvement. It is however, necessary to take a closer look at the background for the establishment of the program for public funding, in order to understand why the central government relented to such a degree to the demands of the movement. First, the demand for publicly funded, privately run and controlled shelters was controversial because it represented a *new form* for the organization of welfare services. Second, one might speculate that the fundamental beliefs of the movement made it problematic for some people to accept its demands.

Three public initiatives distinguish themselves in connection with the gradual acceptance of the abuse of women as a political issue and the gradual acceptance of the demands made by the women's shelter movement. The first was the support granted by the Ministry of Health and Social Affairs to the two-year trial running of the women's shelter in Oslo in 1978. The second was the formation of the program for government funding in 1982. When the Government's 'Program for action against the abuse of women' was presented in 1983, it was the final affirmation of the fact that abuse of women is a serious social problem for which the government has a particular responsiblity, and that efforts in this area should be channeled through the shelters in their existing form.

Behind these initiatives was a tug-of-war between the Ministry of Health and Social Affairs on the one hand, and the Ministry of Consumer Affairs and Government Administration and the Directorate of Health on the other. The Ministry of Health and Social Affairs considered the abuse of women its jurisdiction, but was negative toward the demands of the women's shelter movement. In spite of this attitude, the Ministry was surprisingly passive; they made no attempt to prepare proposals for the integration of new programs for battered women with the existing system.

The Directorate of Health and the Ministry of Consumer Affairs and Government Administration periodically defined abuse of women as a health and family-related matter, in order that they could transfer funds from their budgets for the establishment and operation of shelters whose applications had been rejected by the Ministry of Health and Social Affairs. In this manner the Ministry of Health and Social Affiars was pressured into granting funds in order to maintain control of the area. It was in this fashion the government program for the funding of the shelters came into being in 1982.

At the same time, there was considerable focus on the issue in the media, and broad political support in Parliament. As early as 1980, a unanimous Parliamentary Standing Committee on Health and Social Affairs supported the applications for funds which had been submitted by 13 shelters. Even so, at this time the Ministry rejected the applications.

Norway had a Labour Government until 1981. In light of the party's great emphasis on the responsiblity of the state for national welfare, it is understandable that its members were sceptical towards the voluntary women's shelters. This is probably the cause of the Ministry's opposition. The political leaders in the Ministry of Consumer Affairs and Government Administration were, in spite of their Labour party membership, more positively inclined. Whether this is a function of the Ministry's having a female leader is difficult to say. In 1981 a Conservative Government took over, and it is likely that this Government had fewer problems in accepting women's shelters as a voluntary-run and controlled project, even if the ideological distance was comprehensive.

In order to understand the broad support which the women's shelter movement enjoyed, it is necessary to consider the considerable potential for interpretation of the issue. For the Conservatives, the movement represented an admirable example of an attempt by volunteers to take the initiative and assume responsiblity. The value-conservative Christian Peoples Party considered the movement an important step in the work to protect mother and child. Leftists' concern with the question of private versus public responsiblity gradually surrendered to the desire to support a specific expression of the women's movement's work. Furthermore, it was the women's shelter movement which exposed the problem, and its members were the only ones offering a definite form of help. It was therefore very easy for many to go along with their continuing to be the 'problem-solvers' on their own terms.

The women's shelter movement does not seem to have had centrally-placed supporters within the bureaucracy itself to the same extent as within the broad spectrum of women's organizations and political parties. The weaker support within the administrative system may be a disadvantage in the future. If issues involving any changes in programs for battered women are not raised to the political level, but left to the Ministry's administration, the women's shelter movement's chances of being influential will be reduced. Similarly, there is a danger in the decentralized model represented by the funding program. The shelters' existence is determined by the individual municipality. All the goodwill in the world on the part of the central authorities will not be any use if the question of continued operation of the shelters is out of the Ministry's hands.

To the degree that public funding has been a limitation for the activities of the shelter groups, these limitations have taken the form of municipal representatives on executive boards or finance committees and tight budgets which do not allow for the compensation of the volunteers. Certain groups also claim that the never-ending financial/practical side of operation has overshadowed the more political side. Nevertheless, the main conclusion must be that the women's shelter groups, in spite of their complete dependence on the public sector for funding, have to a large degree been able to maintain their autonomy and control over their product thus far. Will that also be the situation in the nearby future? Does the movement still have the ideological strength and the service potential to meet the challenges of the 1990's?

Will the '90s be a period of consolidation?

The collapse of the 'center': an indication of more profound organizational and ideological change?

In October 1989 there was nearly a revolution at the Oslo shelter, the natural 'center' and trend-setter within the women's shelter movement. Events there provide us with a good picture both of the women's shelters' dependence on the goodwill of the municipal government and how conflict can be problematic within a 'flat' organizational structure.

Until Autumn 1989 the Oslo shelter represented, with its 'flat' structure, the typical organizational ideal within the movement. Members of this shelter were among the most outspoken opponents of a common organization for women's shelters and it was this group which most often chose to close its shelters when the allotted funds were not adequate.

The above was the situation prior to the 'coup' at the Oslo shelter in 1989. The shelter had been closed for 4-5 weeks in protest against the proposed budget for 1990. The group had, however, agreed to a new proposal and the shelter had reopened when the 'bomb' was dropped. A small splinter group had secretly negotiated a takeover of the shelter with Oslo's Municipal Executive Board.

The shock was considerable in many different circles. The 'model' shelter in the movement had collapsed. The media covered the event quite extensively and it was evident that the conflict ran deep. Those with some knowledge of the shelter knew that there had been disagreements in certain areas for quite some time. Differences were evident particularly in such issues as the amount of time and resources which should be spent on incest victims with aftereffects and immigrant women. The splinter group was of the opinion that incest victims with aftereffects were not in an 'acute crisis' and therefore should not have access to the shelter. The same group had aired the idea of creating a separate unit for immigrant women instead of having all women under the same roof. These proposals must be viewed in light of the capacity problems at the shelter, which at times could be extreme.

The splinter group also claimed that in spite of the general assembly, there was no democracy within the organization and that they felt overridden and manipulated. The original group, on the other hand, was nearly in shock: the new group had up till the last general assembly supported the shelter's program and the group consisted of many of the original group's most central members.

The Municipal Executive Board consisted of a coalition of the Conservative Party and the Progress Party, and it gradually became clear that this issue was a matter of prestige for the Board's Conservative Chairman. The original shelter group had broad support: the Oslo Chief of Police and a group of 90 prominent researchers in women's studies and politicians delivered a protest to the Board against its treatment of the matter. Many leading woman politicians in the Conservative party were included in this group. The original shelter group also interpreted the signals from the Labour Party Minister of Health and Social Affairs as positive, however she had no authority to intervene in a municipal government matter. The final result was that the splinter group was allowed to assume operation of the shelter.

The women's shelter in Oslo is still run by the new group. The organizational structure is no longer completely 'flat', but is what the group calls, 'flat internally and hierarchical externally'. This means, among other things, that external contact is channeled through selected representatives. The original shelter group continued to operate a helpline until the Spring of 1991, when it was closed. The group's only hope of resuming control of the Oslo shelter was based on the municipal elections in the Autumn of 1991. They regard a 'socialist' majority in the City Council as their last chance. Oslo did get a 'socialist' majority, but the original group has by now given up the hope of taking 'back' the shelter.

Looking back we can see that if there had existed a national umbrella organization with power, the space open to the split group would have been far more limited. Similary, the takeover expresses disadvantages of being total dependent on public funding. Local government became part of a political play caused by internal conflict within the shelter movement and had a strong influence upon the outcome. However, it is important to emphasize that government could not have intervened (or been used) without deep conflict within the movement.

Will the future be very different?
The women's shelter movement is characterized by greater heterogeneity than the common platform might imply. The percentage of politically active women has probably declined while the percentage of women who are primarily motivated by a general desire to help has increased. Nevertheless, there have been developments during the last years which might indicate that the movement has still not lost all of its original fire. At the national conference in 1990 the 'old' shelter group from Oslo received unconditional backing through the passage of a declaration of support, and that was without any form of prior lobbying. The present shelter group, on the other hand, was the subject of considerable criticism.

Within the women's shelter movement there has been considerable fear that the Ministry will decide that the shelters should be run by municipal governments. There are at present two such shelters. All staff are permanently employed at these shelters, and they are either trained in health care and social services or in other therapist-related subjects. These shelters are run much the same as other municipal institutions. One of these shelters in particular has been critical of the fact that it has not been allowed to join the women's shelter movement, and it is feared that these two shelters are in the process of lobbying the Ministry for the introduction of their model on a national basis.

In the Spring of 1991 these two shelters formed the organization, 'Norwegian Women's Shelter Movement' ('Norsk Krisesenterbevegelse'), which was to be a national organization for all shelters. Helplines were not to be included, and thus the old shelter group from Oslo would be excluded from this organization. By-laws and organizational guidelines were already prepared when the membership invitations were sent out. Two of the shelters within the original movement reacted immediately and called an extraordinary national conference to discuss the development. The unanimous conclusion was that the offer should be refused. Thus the new organization consists of only those few organizations which were already outside the women's shelter movement. Later on a few other shelters have become members of the new organization, but the great majority are still members of the original one. The 'new' women's shelter in Oslo is not part of any of the two, but is autonomous. What we do see here is extensive organizational uncertainty, that may develop into comprehensive organizational change in the near future.

Even if we do see the contour of important organizational and ideological change, the women's shelter movement must be said to have succeeded in its work thus far. They managed to put abuse of women on the public agenda and they won the battle to run the shelters on their own terms with public funds. The principle of full compensation has been deviated from in practice due to tight budgets, but there is no reason to believe that the movement has become more 'charity-oriented' over the years. The shelters have, with few exceptions, moved away from the purely 'flat' organizational structure. The current hierarchical or semihierarchical organizational structures may partly be seen as a result of the necessity of adjusting to financial contributors, but they also reflect the heterogeneous membership's varying views on the significance of organizational structure.

In spite of the fact that the ideological overtones are not as noticeable as they were in the early '80s, the women's shelter movement still seems to be capable of both survival and action. Along the way the members have become less expressive and more instrumentally oriented, however the political features are still present. The movement has a long way to go before it becomes like any other social service. In addition to the operation of the shelters, the members also work with the spread of information regarding their activities and abuse of women in general. It is in this specific area that everyone agrees that some form for national organization would be an advantage. However, there is a growing majority who consider the time ripe for a more permanent national organization in order to secure the shelters in their existing form so that they will be better able to withstand pressure from both within and without.

The women's shelter movement seems to be heading toward an existence as an interest and self-help organization. If the movement survives this transition without splitting it will probably be in a better position to protect its financial interests vis a vis central and local government. At the same time, it will have moved even further from its original value foundation.

Discussion and conclusion: what does the women's shelter movement express?

The women's shelter movement provides us with almost *ideal-type* insight into the essence of being an alternative movement in a 'state-friendly' society. In our type of system it is unusual that alternative movements turn away from the state, it is more common that they turn towards it. This is generally true, and particularly so in service production. The consequence is that most of what is not as it should be ends up being a public responsibility. People are of the opinion that they have a *right* to public funds in order to straighten things out. The state should finance, the organization should produce, as long as that is possible, with state guarantees if anything should go wrong. At the same time, state control should not be too great. It may be that what is typical of the relationship between the women's shelter movement and the public sector is in the process of becoming a more common form of mixing the public and private sectors. It appears that the public sector is to an ever increasing degree opening for public financing in combination with private production and control, a result of that neo-liberal ideas have influenced even the most state-oriented welfare states (Selle 1993).

In the ideological climate which grew forth after the breakdown of the hierarchical and rather centralized management model in the 1980s, we have seen the introduction of comprehensive modernization plans for the public sector in all Scandinavian countries (Olsen 1988). These programs emphasize decentralized and user-oriented solutions which also aim at giving the market and the voluntary sector a larger role than they previously had. The increasing legitimacy of the voluntary sector (and the market) means that one might imagine increasing use of this form of public funding implying an increased service role and a more comprehensive ideological space for the voluntary sector, ie the new welfare pluralism (Kuhnle and Selle 1990; 1992a; Selle 1993). What is of great interest is that the women's shelter movement pressed through such a model before the new-liberal ideas really started to influence public policy.

In a study of how the relationship between the public sector and voluntary organizations has developed historically, it was evident that even though it was not actually uncommon that the public sector took over former voluntary organizations' service production, this did not always happen. Such 'takeovers' did not make voluntary organizations superfluous. The analysis showed, in other words, that there is no empirical support for the suggestion that voluntary organizations which initiated the production of new services were later taken over by force. Thus there was no golden age of the voluntary sector which was later ruined through government intervention. The voluntary organizations, and particularly those in service production, were integrated into public policy quite early and the organizations themselves often served as the *impetus* to public takeover. The organizations looked for *public* rather than private alternatives as early as the turn of the century (Kuhnle and Selle 1990; 1992a).

On the basis of this general historical view, the probability of the public sector assuming the responsiblity for the shelters' work by force, in the current ideological climate, must be considered minimal. However, and this is important, if the shelter movement should dissolve, ie be unable to continue its extensive service production in this very important problem area, the public sector *would have to* build public institutions of one form or another. The public sector would be forced to do so because the women's shelter movement has made abuse of women an accepted social problem. Abuse of women has become a public problem.

One of the reasons that it is so difficult in 'state-friendly societies' to argue against public grants to movements which originally may be quite removed from the ideology and organizational form of the welfare state is connected with the *question of rights*. This is true in general, but particularly true in service production. After abuse of women was accepted as a public matter it was no longer mainly a question of the rights of the members of the movement, but of the rights of the *battered women*. It becomes difficult, if not impossible, to argue that these women do not have a right to help. When service producers are found who take such groups seriously, it is no longer legitimate to argue against grants to these organizations even if one does not agree with their ideology. This is particularly the case if the groups do a good job, indeed, a better job than one believes a new public sector service would do.

What, in addition to the structure of the relationship between the women's shelter movement and the public sector, is it that makes the movement deviant, but at the same time also 'modern'? The movement's emphasis on decentralization and user-orientation corresponds to developmental features in public policy in general. The movement can thus be seen as a part of a growing pluralistic culture resulting from a gradual breakdown in the belief in hierarchy, a culture in which all paternalistic structures shall be broken. Both ideologically and organizationally, more egalitarian values are developed, involving a deemphasizing of the professional orientation of the modern welfare state (Inglehart 1989, Thompson et. al. 1990).

Nevertheless, we have shown that the women's shelter movement has problems today, both concerning objectives, ideology, and organizational form. We have also shown that there are somewhat sizeable differences of opinion inherent in the organization. We seem to see a relatively strong *shift* in the direction of an increasing emphasis on being a source of help and away from being a form of political action. We feel that this is more a result of internal processes within the feminist movement in general and in the women's shelter movement in particular, than of public influence resulting from the program for public funding. The shift is primarily a result of the fact that *the women's movement*, of which the women's shelter movement is an important part, has lost much of its force in the 1980s. This development has strengthened the more service-oriented in the organization and probably altered the frame of reference for the ideology-oriented political activists. A weakened women's movement makes it far more difficult to legitimize the considerable emphasis on women's policy and ideology as integrated parts of service production.

Public funding may be said to have influenced the internal relationships in the movement, ie it has strengthened the position of the most service-oriented. Nevertheless, it is our opinion that this must not be overdramatized. It was during the period in which the ideology-oriented members dominated that the special relationship with the public sector was developed. At that time the women's shelter movement was a highly politicized alternative movement, indeed a form of political action. The fact that the movement was able to negotiate public funding was a result of the fact that as a voluntary organization it was able to make the social problem with which it was concerned *visible to the public*. In other words, movement members made their problem a public problem. The movement succeeded in this goal without reducing the ideological distance between itself and the public sector.

The most important difference from the past is thus that the public sector now increasingly accepts more 'private' control of public problems, also where the ideological distance is considerable at the same time as the women's shelter movement has become less distant ideologically. Comprehensive change in public policy and goal displacement within the women's shelter movement imply that the relationship between the women's shelter movement and government increasingly grows 'normal'.

It has never been easy to continue to be an alternative movement in a 'state-friendly' society. What seems to be rather easy, and probably much easier than in less 'state-friendly' societies, is to influence public policies. However, in doing so one does not stay the same. That is so whether one is part of the women's movement or any other mass movement.

References

Ahnfelt, E. (1987), *Kvinnemishandling - fra privat problem til offentlig ansvar. En dagordningsprosess.* Dissertation. Department of Political Science, University of Oslo.

Alsaksen, I. (1979), 'Camilla', Krisesenteret for voldtatte og mishandlede kvinner. *Hefte for kritisk juss,* 3/4:19-25.

Araldsen, T. and Clasen, A-K (1983): *Kvinnemishandling - om innsnevring av handlingsalternativer.* Dissertation. Department of Psychology, University of Oslo.

Barne- og familiedepartementet (1991),' Statistikk - Krisetiltak'.

Bleiklie, I. et.al. (1980),'Forskning for svaktstiltes forhold til forvaltningen'. Arbeids-rapport, *Forvaltningen og svaktstilte brukere,* 80:1. University of Bergen.

Dobash, R. E. and Dobash, R. P. (1980), *Violence against Wives; a Case against the Patriachy.* London: Shepton Mallet, Open Books.

Freeman, M. D. A. (1987), 'Violence against women, does the legal sytem provide solutions, or does itself constitute the problem?', *British Journal of Law and Society,* No. 7:215-241.

Haukaa, R. (1982), *Bak slagordene.* Oslo: Pax Forlag.

Hernes, H. (1987), *Welfare State and Woman Power. Essays in State Feminism.* London: Norwegian University Press.

Inglehart, R. (1989), *Cultural Change in Advanced Industrial Society.* Princeton: Princeton University Press.

Jonassen, W. (1987), 'Vennetjeneste eller offentlig tiltak? En analyse av organisering og drift av krisesentrene'. Oslo: *NIBR-rapport,* 87/10.

Jonassen, W. (1989), 'Kvinner hjelper kvinner'. Oslo: *NIBR-rapport,* 89/4.

Kuhnle, S. and Selle, P. (1990), 'Meeting Needs in a Welfare State: Relations between Government and Voluntary Organizations in Norway', in Ware, A. and Goodin, R. E. (eds): *Needs and Welfare.* London: Sage.

Kuhnle, S. and Selle, P. (1992): 'Government and Voluntary Organizations: a Relational Perspective', in Kuhnle, S. and Selle, P. (eds): *Government and Voluntary Organizations.* Aldershot: Avebury.

Kuhnle, S. and Selle, P. (1992a), 'The Historical Precedent for Government - Nonprofit Cooperation in Norway', in Gidron, B., Kramer R. M. and Salamon, L. M. (eds): *Government and the Third Sector.* San Francisco: Jossey-Bass.

Lafferty, W. M (1986), 'Den sosialdemokratiske stat', *Nytt Norsk Tidsskrift,* 3:23-37.

Malterud, K. (1981), *Kvinnemishandling: et helseproblem. En utreding om hjelpe-apparatets ansvar og funksjon i Oslo.* Oslo: Oslo Helseråd.

Morken, K. A. (1993), *Fra politisk kamp til altuisme? En ny velferdsordning får fotfeste: De norske krisesentrene*. Dissertation, Department of Comparative Politics, University of Bergen.

Moxnes, K. (1981), *Når kvinner vil skilles*. Oslo: Pax.

Nisja, R. and Alsaksen, I. (1980), 'Krisesenteret for voldtatte mishandlede kvinner'. Oslo: *INAS-rapport*, 80/2.

Nisja, R. (1982), Oppsummering av en del eksisterende kunnskap om kvinnemishandling, spesielt i Norden, og behov for forskning/utredning. Manuscript.

Olsen, J. P. (1988), 'The modernization of public administration in the Nordic countries: Some research questions'. *Administrative Studies*, 7:2-17.

Pahl, J. (1985), *Private Violence and Public Policy*. London: Routledge and Kegan Paul.

Selle, P. (1993), 'Voluntary Organizations and the Welfare State: The Case of Norway', *Voluntas*, Vol. 4, 1:1-15.

Skjørten, K. (1988), 'Når makt blir vold', *KS-serien*, No. 4-88. University of Oslo.

Thompson, M., Ellis, R. and Wildavsky, A. (1990), *Cultural Theory*. Boulder: Westview Press.

Øyen, E. (1975), 'En beskrivelse og sammenligning av to sosialpolitiske systemer', *Tidsskrift for Samfunnsforskning*, Vol. 16:27-46.

Part IV

Public institutions

The declining corporatist state and the political gender dimension

Christina Bergqvist

Introduction

Sweden has been among the countries ranking highest on corporatism. This means that especially a few highly centralised organisations on the labour market and in agriculture have had access to the political decision-making process. These strong organisations together with some other organised interests in society have been able to participate in preparing and implementing political decisions. The corporatist arena can be seen as a meeting-place for élite representation from interest organisations, public administration and political parties. The representation takes place in a number of councils, boards and committees. It is a well-known fact that the corporatist channel, in contrast to the electoral channel, has been more exclusive towards women (Hernes 1987:73-99). However, during recent years Sweden has seen some changes in the possibilities and, in some cases even the willingness, of the large interest organisations to participate in public decision-making. The corporatist mode of representation has been reconsidered from different angles.[1] At the same time women's representation in public bodies has risen. In this chapter I will describe and further explore the reasons for the development of women's representation.

The literature on gender and corporatism paints a rather dark picture of women's position in this system. Most feminist studies on corporatism have shown that mainly men and male-dominated interests have been included. The organisations and institutions included only have a few women at the élite-level where the representatives are recruited from. Women's organisations have rarely been invited into the corporatist circles. Corporatist representation is also problematic from a democratic point of view, as some not very democratic, but powerful, interests are given a semi-official status. The principles of corporatist representation are more

---

[1] For the recent developement see Lewin 1992; Rothstein 1992 and Hermansson 1993.

205

vague and not constitutionally based as in the case of parliamentary representation (Hernes & Hänninen-Salmelin 1983:155-187; Hernes 1987:73-99; Bergqvist 1991).

Corporatist arrangements have a long historical tradition in Sweden and grew in importance after the Second World War until around the 1970s. Women's representation remained on a very low level in the corporatist system at the same time as women to a certain extent were included in the electoral channel. This has given rise to a feminist debate on whether power has moved from the parliamentary system to the corporatist system, which would mean that women have been integrated into 'shrinking institutions'. A recent book from the *Swedish Commission of Inquiry into Democracy and Power* provides the picture of a strong corporatist system and a weak parliamentary system. The author, Ylva Waldemarson, argues that: '(a) corporatist system which grows in influence at the cost of a parliamentary system reduces thereby women's political influence' (Waldemarson 1992:104, translation from Swedish), thus implying that there is a causal relationship between the degree of corporatism and women's political influence. Waldemarson's analysis is not very extensive and she seems to have misunderstood some of the discussion about corporatism. Nor does she supply any empirical evidence to support her argument. However, her argument still appears to be representative of some of the ideas about women and corporatism and thus it is important to refute it.

Waldemarson is, in fact, rendering her interpretation of Helga Hernes and Eva Hänninen-Salmelin's contribution to the corporatist debate from the early 1980s. Waldemarson appears to misunderstand their argument: they do not claim that women's political influence has diminished, nor do they suggest a causal relationship between corporatism and women's power. They describe the situation as problematic from a democratic perspective as corporatist representation is less democratic and more exclusive than parliamentary representation. They also show that women's corporatist representation is much lower than their representation in parliament (Hernes & Hänninen-Salmelin 1983:155-187). This does not automatically imply that women's political influence has diminished (Skjeie 1992:75). Waldemarson's analysis is a bit peculiar and out of date bearing in mind some of the recent developments described in other reports from the *Swedish Commission of Inquiry into Democracy and Power* as well as in other recent studies on corporatism. These studies show that traditional interest organisations and the corporatist mode of representation are losing some of their former power (Chapter 5 in SOU 1990:44; Lewin 1992, Rothstein 1992 and Hermansson 1993). Actually, when the scholarly debate on corporatism intensified in the 1980s, the participation of organised interests in the political decision-making process was declining. The share of representatives from organised interests declined while the share of politicians increased (Hermansson 1993:448).

Related to the argument that women are integrated into 'shrinking institutions' is an assumption of a decline in western parliaments in favour of strong governments, which means that parliament has become increasingly powerless while the 'real' power is in the hands of the government. But recent research has shown a development in Sweden towards weaker minority governments more dependent on the parliament. It is more accurate to describe the power relationship between government and parliament as one shifting from time to time depending on the parliamentary composition (Birgersson & Westerståhl 1992:120-127).[2] There is little evidence that women are integrated into 'shrinking' institutions of less relevance for public decision-making.

The significance of the fact that women's representation has increased in parliament (with one major exception in 1991), in government and, as we will see, in corporatist arrangements during the last two decades has not been much explored in Swedish research. Today all the popularly *elected* bodies at local, regional and national levels consist of about 30 to 40 percent women. In the election, in 1991, the percentage of women in the municipal councils remained at 34 percent, while in the county councils it rose from 41 to 43 percent. But in the Riksdag, the proportion of women fell from 38 to 33 percent.[3] The new right-wing government which took over after the Social Democratic loss appointed 8 female ministers out of a total of 21 ministers. This is a new record in Sweden: the retiring Social Democratic government had seven female ministers out of 21. Many observers have pointed to the fact that several of the women ministers head departments which are not 'typically female', such as finance, foreign affairs and justice. Also in the public bodies chosen by *indirect* means the representation of women has increased, as will be further explored in this chapter. All of this empirical evidence implies that the picture of women's integration is multicoloured and that the relevance of women in political decision-making must be reconsidered. Instead of an analysis in terms of 'shrinking institutions' and women's marginalisation, my argument here is that we must look closer at the processes and mechanisms which *enhance* the possibilities for women's participation and representation.

---

[2] See also Damgaard 1990. For a feminist discussion on a similar development in Norway, see Skjeie 1992.

[3] *Nominerade och valda kandidater vid allmänna valen 1991.* SCB.

208 Women in Nordic Politics

208 *Women in Nordic Politics*

Before going on with the analysis of some empirical facts about gender and corporatism I will discuss the concept of the state-feminist or femocrat. This discussion is relevant for the later analysis concerning women's possibilities to act in favour of their interests through the state. I will then explore a case where a public commission on women's representation actually managed to change the rules in favour of women.

The term femocrat seems to originate in New Zealand or Australia. Australian feminists have sought integration in the state since the 1970s. This resulted in the establishment of new commissions and committees of enquiry, policy advisers in women's affairs etc. These feminist bureaucrats - or femocrats - had often been engaged in the women's movement and continued to maintain contacts with feminist groups outside the bureaucracy. This integration strategy can be contrasted with a strategy which mainly tries to influence the political decisions from outside (Levi & Edwards 1990:142; Watson 1990:120-130).

Sweden has seen a similar development of several public bodies concerned with the question of equality between women and men.[4] (In Swedish there is a special word for equality between the sexes, namely *jämställdhet*.) Since the 1970s new legislation has been approved. New positions were set up both in the public administration and in the powerful organisations on the labour market. The number of femocrats is now rather extensive. An association for persons working with equality between the sexes was set up (*Jämställdhetsarbetarnas förening*). It has about 800 members, mainly working in public administration.

Lately some researchers have studied the significance of femocratic actors in state institutions. Margaret Levi and Meredith Edwards discuss the conditions necessary for femocrats to be able to initiate and implement feminist reforms. A feminist reform is defined as 'any governmental policy change that promotes the interests of women' (Levi & Edwards 1990:143-146). However, the definition of a feminist reform as all policy changes in favour of women's interests seems a bit vague. Different groups of women might have different opinions about their interests. The point with such an open definition must be to define the question of interests from case to case. Women might have a lot of different subjective interests, but in the case of representation in public bodies my point of departure is that women as a group have an objective interest in being represented. As Anna Jónasdóttir puts it:

---

[4] These are the public bodies appointed by the government: *jämställdhetsrådet, jämställdhets-beredningen, jämställdhetssekretariatet, jämställdhetsombudsmannen, jämställdhets-nämnden, delegationen för jämställdhetsforskning* (now cancelled). See Kvinno- och mansvärlden 1986, 15.

'Women's objective political interests today concern building up and controlling *as sex/gender* a concrete presence or attendance in this system' (Jónasdóttir 1991:171).

Levi and Edwards reject the rather common assumption that femocrats will become coopted. In the Michelian formulation of cooptation this would mean that femocrats give up their initial feminist values in exchange for institutional power. Another way to comprehend cooptation was developed by Selznick. Here cooptation is seen as 'a mechanism by which the coopting organization undermines the ability of external militants to set the agenda or have an effective say in decision-making. The prior activists trade the potential for disruptive power for formal--but illusory-- power' (Levi & Edwards 1990:144). According to Levi & Edwards this second perspective in some of their cases comes closer to the truth, although there were also cases were femocrats had been successful.

However, the authors dismiss the concept of cooptation. They do not see it as very useful for understanding the restrictions to act in favour of women's interests. They point to the fact that femocrats, like other actors, are involved in *negotiations* with others whose goals and preferences can be different from their own. Those negotiations take place inside certain restricting *institutional arrangements*.

The constraints on femocratic bargaining are, several, however. First, femocrats vary, among themselves and in comparison with other bureaucrats, in the bargaining resources and, therefore, the bargaining power they possess. Second, they operate within institutional arrangements that create incentives for certain kinds of proposals and disincentives for others (Ibid, 147).

They, thus, define two main factors restricting the possibilities for femocrats to act. First the relative bargaining power, second the institutional arrangements. Restrictions on bargaining power can be things like the femocrats' minority situation or their lack of allies inside the bureaucracy. 'Seldom do femocrats have enough votes or clout to get a policy through themselves. In many cases a particularly powerful ally, such as a minister or department head, is in fact the key to success' (Ibid, 151). Levi & Edwards consider the institutional arrangements as even more problematic. The institutional context can include both restricting and enhancing mechanisms for the possibility to implement reforms or changes in the interest of women. They find it most plausible that the context is more restrictive than promotive.

In the following section I will first outline the development of the relationship between women and men in corporatist arrangements. I will describe the distribution of women and men in different public bodies and along different political sectors during the last 20 - 30 years. Second, I will discuss in more detail the rules, thus the institutional context, for admittance to these bodies. In the third part I study the attempts of women actors, femocrats and politicians, to change the prevailing circumstances.

The challenge against the male-dominated state

In autumn 1985 the cabinet minister Anita Gradin suggested that the government appoint a Commission of Inquiry into women's representation in public bodies. The directives proposed an investigation of the prevailing situation and a mandate for the commissioners to suggest measures to improve it. The government appointed a commission headed by the Social Democratic MP Gerd Engman and the researcher Ann Boman as secretary. The commission thus came about on the initiative of a woman minister and women sympathising with feminist values were appointed to lead the investigation. At an early stage criticism of the status quo was evident; in the directives there is implied disapproval of the prevailing situation in which women's representation had increased in elected political institutions but not in the commissions and boards of public bodies (SOU 1987:19, *Varannan damernas:*193-199).

The first report from the commission was called: *Ska även morgondagens samhälle formas enbart av män? (Is the future society also going to be designed solely by men?) (Ds A 1986:4).*

In the report the question of women's underrepresentation is connected to a discussion of power and democracy. The documents from the commission are very interesting because they are explicitly grounded in a feminist perspective. The language differs from the more gender neutral language normally occurring in public documents on equality (Bergqvist 1990:232; Eduards 1991:695). Here the commissioners declare that equality between the sexes is far from achieved and that women as a group have far less influence than men as a group. They talk about a male-dominated society where men's experiences and values are considered a norm. They also claim that women are systematically discriminated against. The final report from the commission is called *Varannan damernas (Every Other Seat for a Woman).*

The commission mapped out the gender patterns in other Commissions of Inquiry and in the lay boards of state administration during 1986. These institutions are of great significance for the political decision-making process in Sweden, the commissions in preparing political decisions and the administration in implementing them. Modern implementation research sees the organisation of public administration as politically important. The administration is not apolitical and neutral, but as Bo Rothstein puts it 'its organisation and decisions are about politics, i.e. have significance for the distribution of values in society, of who gets what, when and how' (Bergqvist 1990:232; Eduards 1991:695). In both commissions and in lay boards corporatist arrangements are common, which means that among others, representatives of organised interests also participate.

Women's representation in Commissions of Inquiry

As mentioned previously, participation in the work of the commissions is an important means to achieve political influence. Commissions of Inquiry traditionally have a strong position in the political decision-making process in Sweden. A commission consists of a chairperson, members, and usually a group of experts. Recently it has become more common to appoint commissions with only one or a few members. Another feature of the commissions has been the under-representation of women. Between 1925 and 1975 women's representation increased from one percent to eleven percent. During this period of time the number of commissions increased enormously, which means that the total number of women also increased considerably. In 1925 there were a total of four women and in 1975 there were 602 (Eduards 1980:22-23).[5] The figures refer to all categories of representatives. The expansion of commissions can be connected to the growth of welfare programs following the second world war and in the 1960s. The typical procedure in the Swedish parliamentary process is to start with government appointing a Commission of Inquiry.

In Table 1 the distribution between women and men is given for different functions in the commissions between 1981 and 1992. It is clear that women's representation increased relatively strongly during this period, from 16 percent in 1981 to 28 percent in 1992.

It is obvious that women's share in the commissions increased a lot more after the *Commission on Women's Representation* reported their results in 1986 than before. There is an increase in all categories, although there still are very few chairwomen. It is worth noting that during the 1980s the number of commissions, and thus representatives in commissions, decreased considerably. In 1981 the commissions involved 4 777 men and 919 women, in 1992 the corresponding figures were

Table 1
Women and men in inquiry commissions. Percentage of women and total
number of representatives (N).

Category	1981		1986		1989		1992	
	%	N	%	N	%	N	%	N
Chairperson	10	368	8	205	10	201	15	262
Member	21	1 494	21	601	30	623	34	776
Expert	13	2 921	17	1 793	23	1 606	26	1 696
Secretary	22	913	26	395	30	367	34	469
Total percentage	16	5 696	*18*	2 994	24	2 797	28	3 203

Source: Kommittéberättelser, Skr 103.

2 296 men and 907 women. The number of men had thus been reduced by more than half, while the number of women remained the same. The decrease in the number of commissions is due to a new policy and the financial situation (Riksdagens Kommittéberättelser, skr 103 1981-1989; Petersson 1989:89). It is rather remarkable that the decrease in the number of representatives did not affect women more negatively, as other studies have shown that women's positions are more vulnerable in situations when the number of representatives is cut down.[6] The fact that the proportion of women's representation increased a great deal rather implies that there are some mechanisms working towards a more equal relationship between the sexes. During the time of increase in women's representation the system of commissions has been reconsidered and the inequality in representation has been criticised. It seems plausible that these factors contributed to the increase.

Another interpretation is that the system of commissions is a 'shrinking institution' and thus includes women. It might be true that the commissions of inquiry have lost some of their traditional weight in the political process, but there are not yet enough studies to verify that. At any rate, it is difficult to prove that this would be the main reason for the increase in women's representation. Women have strengthened their

---

[6] See Bergqvist 1991, where I describe how women lost in representation in LO and TCO due to centralisation, thus causing a decrease in the number of representatives taking part in the decision-making process.

position in all kinds of political and public decision-making, also in the governmental bodies deciding about appointments of new commissions. Even if the system of commissions can be seen as a shrinking institution, this does not explain why women's share of the representatives grew. It seems more reasonable to examine the dynamics between institutional factors and the relevant political actors.

The question of who is going to be appointed to a commission is addressed from time to time, it is not regulated in detail. The composition has varied. During the 19th century mostly bureaucrats were involved. Later, parliamentarians and representatives of interest organisations were included. The Commission on Women's Representation found that today 68 percent of the representatives are politicians, 17 percent come from the state administration, and only 6 percent from labour-market organisations, like the Confederation of Swedish Trade Unions (LO), the Central Organisation of Salaried Employees (TCO), the Association of Professional Employees and Civil Servants (SACO) and the Swedish Employers' Association (SAF). Here it is worth mentioning that a large majority of all employees in Sweden belong to a union and that there are rather small differences in women's and men's membership rates. Among the different groups included in commissions most women come from the political parties. That is the biggest group and it has also included women at the top in their own party organisations. The other groups are rarely represented by a woman as can be illustrated in Table 2.

Studies on women's representation in political decision-making usually find women clustered in certain policy areas such as social, cultural and educational policies. As Helga Hernes puts it, 'Women are most densely represented in tasks that can be unequivocally defined as 'women's areas'' (Hernes 1987:79). This has often been seen as a sign of women's marginal position. Those areas where women are participating are sometimes defined as politically less relevant.

Also in the final report from the Swedish Commission of Inquiry into democracy and *power* Yvonne Hirdman argues that women have been marginalised into political positions with low status (Skard & Haavio-Mannila 1983:95; Hirdman in SOU 1990:44). This has been questioned in a recent study by Hege Skjeie. She argues that the so-called women's areas do not always rank as less important or less attractive than other 'harder' areas by the participants. She also found that women often preferred the 'soft' areas (Skjeie 1992:24-28). Considering the development of a very extensive Swedish welfare state, my argument here is that it would be wrong to categorise educational, cultural and social politics as low ranking areas in Swedish politics. Especially social welfare and education together with labour market policy have been at the core of the Swedish welfare model. These areas can hardly be dismissed as being less important than many other policy sectors.

Table 2
The distribution of women and men among representatives of different groups
participating in Commissions of Inquiry. 1986

Interest group	Women	Men	% women
Political party	56	145	28
State administration	9	42	18
Trade union	2	8	20
Employers' organisation	0	8	0
Other interests in society	2	24	8
All	69	227	23

Source: Ds A 1986:4.

Table 3 illustrates the percentage of women in the commissions distributed among the different ministries. The ministries have been categorised into three different dimensions suggested by Olof Petersson (Petersson 1989). The categories are named the *basic functions of the state*, the *infrastructure* and *social welfare*. These three categories roughly correspond to three historical phases. In the first category called *basic functions* are such activities as defending the territory (diplomacy and military defence), upholding order (the judicial system) and securing resources (finance, tax and monetary systems). In the first stage, the state worked to secure its survival. Ministries like Justice, Foreign Affairs, Defence and Internal Affairs today belong to this category.

In the second stage the *infrastructure* was developed. The state apparatus participated in the building of roads, channels and railways, as well as in the development of agriculture and post and telegraphic systems. Here we find the ministries of Agriculture, Communication and Industry.

The activities of the state in the third stage concern the *social welfare* of the citizens. This phase usually starts at the same time as universal suffrage is introduced. The ministries of Education, Social Affairs, Cultural Affairs and Labour belong to this category.

In the commissions belonging to the dimension of social welfare women's share is above the average of 28 percent, but women are still far from constituting half of the policy-makers in this area, which is sometimes called women-dominated.

Women's representation in this category is now higher and on a par with their representation in parliament and government. Certainly women are still under-represented in basic functions and infrastructure, but the increase in their representation is nevertheless quite remarkable. Since 1986 women's representation has increased a lot in such 'hard' sectors as for example, the Ministry of Foreign Affairs, the Ministry of Finance, the Ministry of Defence, the Ministry of Industry and the Ministry of Agriculture.

Women's integration into the dimension of social welfare, on the other hand, reflects women's profile in the labour market and in organisations. Certainly this area is closer to women's traditional concern with reproduction and welfare, and being integrated into the political decision-making thus gives women a possibility to have influence over important policy-decisions. The Swedish welfare state has, to a certain extent, included women as policy-makers and decision-makers, not only policy-takers.

For an explanation of the improvement in women's representation in the dimensions of the basic functions and infrastructure it seems more relevant to consider the effects of a new policy of conscious recruitment of women. This policy was activated by the *Commission on Women's Representation*. Before I continue to discuss the impact this commission probably had, I will explore the development of women's representation in the state administration.

Women's representation in public lay boards

The central administration in Sweden today is to a large extent led by lay boards. Both the members and the head of the board are appointed by the government. The idea behind the system of lay boards is to supply the administration with knowledge from outside the administration and to give certain affected interests in society a possibility to participate. The aim has been to broaden democracy (Söderlind & Petersson 1988:58).

The *Commission on Women's Representation* found that while 68 percent of the participants in commissions came from political parties, in lay boards only 19 percent of the participants represented political parties. The largest groups in lay boards are those representing other parts of the central administration and the personnel employed in the administration under the lay board in question. They constitute 24 and 21 percent of the participants, respectively. Another 18 percent represents organisations on the labour market and the last 18 percent represents so called

Table 3
Women's representation in Commissions of Inquiry distributed among the ministries

Basic functions	1986 % (N)	1989 % (N)	1992 % (N)
The Ministry of Foreign Affairs	14 (79)	23 (163)	24 (108)
The Ministry of Internal Affairs	19 (272)	26 (403)	29 (260)
The Ministry of Justice	18 (509)	21 (263)	30 (519)
The Ministry of Finance	14 (552)	17 (445)	21 (497)
The Ministry of Defence	10 (214)	22 (151)	19 (96)
The Ministry of Ministerial Affairs		37 (30)	9 (11)
The Ministry of Industry and Commerce			19 (160)
Infrastructure			
The Ministry of Agriculture	16 (152)	13 (15)	23 (195)
The Ministry of Housing and Physical Planning	21 (103)	19 (74)	
The Ministry of Transport and Communications	12 (66)	17 (100)	15 (102)
The Ministry of Industry	13 (253)	17 (127)	
The Ministry of Environment and Natural Resources		21 (246)	20 (208)
Social Welfare			
The Ministry of Social Affairs	28 (345)	35 (265)	39 (492)
The Ministry of Education	19 (242)	36 (309)	39 (254)
The Ministry of Labour Market Affairs	27 (207)	27 (206)	32 (173)
The Ministry of Culture			38 (128)
Total	18	24	28

Source: Riksdagens kommittéberättelser, Skr 103

other interests in society. As the following table illustrates, women only had 17 percent of the positions on the boards of the central administration, and here as well most women were recruited from the political parties. Women only constituted 10 percent of the representatives from other interests in society. This group mainly represent organisations of trade and industry, the university and national movements.

As illustrated in Table 5, women's representation in boards of central administration has doubled since 1986, from 18 to 36 percent. When it comes to women's representation in the different policy areas, we find a similar pattern to the commissions for 1986, with the highest percentage of women in the dimension of social welfare. In 1992 a new and interesting pattern has emerged: women's average participation in basic functions, infrastructure as well as social welfare is between 30 and 40 percent, which means that women's share, since 1986, has increased in all boards although there have been a few ups and downs.

In some of the traditionally male-dominated policy areas, such as defence, women's participation has risen from four to 25 percent in five years. A closer look at the figures implies that this increase has been made possible by adding more women to the boards; there is now a total of 113 members, while in 1986 there were 77. In the case of the Ministry of Social Affairs the picture is reversed, there was a decline in 1989 both in the total number of representatives and in women's share. But it is not possible to draw any certain conclusions because there are also cases

Table 4
The distribution of women and men in different groups of representatives in boards of central administration. 1986

Interest group	Women	Men	% women
Political party	60	125	32
Employers organisation	12	46	21
Trade union	14	80	15
Central administration	25	225	10
Other interests in society	19	163	10
All	130	639	17

Source: Ds A 1986:4

where the number of members has declined, but women's share has increased. That is for example the case in the Ministry of Finance, which in 1986 had 65 members on its boards and in 1991 had 44. The general picture is that women's representation has increased irrespective of shrinking or expanding activities, which again disqualifies the thesis about women's integration into shrinking institutions.

The hidden side of the recruitment process

When the government appoints the administrative boards or inquiry commissions, it usually gives the party or the organisation which has been invited the possibility of nominating candidates. The commissioners interviewed Under-Secretaries of State or other Heads of the Civil Service, and all the party secretaries and representatives of LO, TCO, SACO and SAF, about their nominating routines. They asked about which criteria were used. I will call these criteria the working rules, which can be described as 'the set of rules to which participants would make reference if asked to explain and justify their actions' (Ostrom 1986:466). The working rules can be contrasted with the formal rules described earlier. In this part I will analyse the interviews to find out which working rules were used.

The interviews illustrate the indistinct nature of the criteria used. The unclear rules seem to have obscured the fact that men were promoted.

In 1981, a new policy was introduced which recommended that the nominating organisation suggest two names for each position it had been offered - one woman and one man. Then it was up to the government, in consultation with the nominating organisation or party, to decide who to choose (Budgetprop. 1980/81:100, bil 3). The *Commission on Women's Representation* found that this recommendation was rarely followed. Most ministries, organisations and parties did not care or even know about the recommendation. In some cases where they knew about it, they did not consider it to be very effective. From the ministries' point of view the organisations did not seem willing enough to suggest two names. One Under-Secretary of State expressed this:[7]

---

[7] All the citations come from interview-notes given to me by, Ann Bohman, the secretary in the commission of women's representation. The quotations are translated from Swedish.

Table 5
Women's representation in the lay boards of the central administration distributed among the ministries

Basic functions	1986 % W (N)	1989 % W (N)	1992 % W (N)
The Ministry of Foreign Affairs	22 (51)	40 (70)	37 (75)
The Ministry of Internal Affairs	12 (67)	31 (106)	41 (17)
The Ministry of Justice	20 (60)	42 (33)	32 (41)
The Ministry of Finance	18 (65)	30 (47)	31 (106)
The Ministry of Defence	4 (77)	20 (117)	25 (118)
The Ministry of Industry and Commerce			29 (96)
Infrastructure			
The Ministry of Agriculture	17 (75)	22 (68)	33 (57)
The Ministry of Housing and Physical Planning	16 (56)	34 (44)	
The Ministry of Transport and Communications	12 (110)	26 (105)	39 (109)
The Ministry of Industry	9 (117)	21 (95)	
The Ministry of Environment and Natural Resources		23 (94)	27 (52)
Social welfare			
The Ministry of Social Affairs	42 (78)	29 (41)	43 (115)
The Ministry of Education	27 (108)	37 (185)	28 (47)
The Ministry of Labour Market Affairs	24 (46)	29 (72)	39 (88)
The Ministry of Culture			49 (130)
Total	18 (910)	29 (1077)	36 (1051)

Source: Ds A 1986:4; Prop. 1989/90:100; Prop. 1992/93:100

When I came here this spring I used the recommendation when we were going to appoint the research councils, I thought you had to. After a lot of complaints I got two names from some, but supplemented with a phone call about how to rank them.

Most ministries did not use the recommendation, but there were a few exceptions. Usually the exceptions were those ministries with a female cabinet minister. One of the Under-secretaries of State said that it was not a problem to inform about the recommendation, but sometimes the nominating organisation got angry and answered that they only had one person for the task.

The most common argument against the recommendation from the organisational point of view was this one put forward by a representative from TCO:

We are in principle opponents of nominating two names because that is an interference in organisational rights...Sometimes the ministries have picked persons without asking us - we really do not like that.

Another common argument was about a lack of women among the relevant groups. LO called attention to this argument:

Our greatest problem is that we do not have any women in the top of the hierarchy - where the representatives are picked.

SAF and SACO also called attention to the lack of women, and the fact that the organisation wanted to decide without the interference of the administration. The political parties were not as negative to the recommendation. The representatives of the parties usually agreed to the ambition to find means to improve the equality between the sexes. Both organisations and parties claimed that the ministries rarely mentioned anything about two names. They were requested to follow the recommendation, but nothing happened if they did not. Thus there were no sanctions associated with the rule.

It is of interest here to find out why the actors thought it hard to find women. A common argument is that there are no women with the right qualifications. What informal rules were thus used in the nomination process? Which were the rules and what qualifications were asked for? Only a few of the ministries demanded very special qualifications; as we will soon see, other criteria were more important. But in some ministries there was a distinct opinion that women usually did not have the qualifications required. The Ministry of Transport and Communications needed persons with 'qualifications in technique and economy. But there are few women who really can provide anything in these questions'.

Most of the time the references to qualifications were rather vague, and it was usually implied that right now women lacked the relevant qualifications, but in time they would have acquired the necessary competence. The references to qualifications and expert knowledge seemed to legitimate the prevailing order. In reality other working rules were followed, a fact which the nominating groups were quite aware of. From the interviews it is possible to categorise the 'real' criteria into five groups. These are: *rewards, status, monopoly, representativity* and *seniority*.

Status

The representatives are often persons with high positions in the organisation, such as persons from the executive boards in unions, chairpersons and researchers. The political parties usually nominate MPs. When answering a question about whether the representatives really had to come from the top level, the interviewed person from TCO said:

> *Competence and qualifications - that is another question. We cannot attack that from the viewpoint of gender equality. I believe that these kinds of bodies would not exist if the representation was on a lower level. But in the lay boards we have loosened the prestige somewhat and have let people in who really know the area - but sometimes when the government appoints expert groups of some kind then it just has to be on the top level.*

A person from SAF said that this was something they could not decide themselves. They just followed the norms given by the government.

> *Often it is the ministries who decide the level. They tell us who will represent the governments office and by that they have implied who we ought to take. It will be persons with titles.*

Rewards

As it gives status and prestige to sit on the boards and in commissions it can be used as a reward. Again we see that the talk about qualifications is often used to hide the real considerations. As the under-secretary at the Ministry of Finance said:

> *This thing about competence is just talk - it is not the world's most qualified people who sit on those boards today... The boards are chosen on other bases, you do not get there because of your competence... Today it is rarely about*

competence, but rather reward. It is usually men who are appointed in gratitude for long and faithful duty.

Monopoly

On some boards, certain trade unions had a monopoly. This was the case in LO, where two highly male-dominated affiliated unions traditionally had been offered important positions on the boards.

Due to the conditions on the labour-market the Construction Workers, Union and the Metal Workers, Union have a monopoly on some of the positions.

The Construction Workers, Union has about one percent of female members and in the Metal Workers, Union about 19 percent of the members are women. Both unions have a strong position in LO.

Representativity

The organisations and the parties often claimed that their candidates had to be representative of the organisation, and therefore had to be from the 'right' groups

For example in LO you just pick the one who handles the question of current interest from the office. You have to have someone fairly representative for LO, means someone who will carry on standpoints deeply rooted in LO. If you, for example, take someone from a section in the Municipal Workers, Union it is doubtful what that person represents. (Under-secretary of State in the Ministry of Labour Market Affairs).

Here representativity seems to stand for expert knowledge, as those employed at the union office hardly have a representative function. On the other hand, a representative from LOs largest union, the Swedish Municipal Workers, Union, whose membership is 80 percent female, should be representative of LO.

Seniority

Seniority might be the most common criterion: a person who has sat on a board usually stays there for a long time. The rule is to renominate the same persons. In the interviews, a person who has sat on a board for 18 years is mentioned. 'The principle is that the one who sits on any boards... often stays on'.

My conclusion is that before the *Commission on Women's Representation* the working rules used in the process to nominate candidates to public boards and commissions favoured men. The working rules had been institutionalised during a time when the male dominance in politics and work life was more widespread than today. The quotations above illustrate that the principle of representation in corporatist arrangements had evolved its own practice. The old routines were followed and consciousness of the need to recruit women was low. Policy formulations regarding gender equality were not followed. The quotations also illustrate that corporatist arrangements are based on representation of organised interests, and the nomination of representatives has often been dominated by pragmatic considerations. Considering the way the corporatist arrangements have been practised, I would argue that the corporatist sector of the political decision-making process has mainly been based on a policy giving priority to men. Every single time a corporatist institution has been constituted according to the established practice, women have systematically and more or less automatically been under-represented. However, after 1987 women's representation increased considerably. In the next section we will look more closely at the political actors and their strategies to change the prevailing situation.

Conclusion: the relevance of gender in the corporatist state

As illustrated in the above sections, women's representation has increased a great deal since the *Commission on Women's Representation* did the interviews in 1986. In this section I will analyse the mechanisms behind this increase. The aim is to investigate the policy suggested by the commission, as well as how the commissioners actively participated in the process to change the institutionalised norms. According to Levi and Meredith the key to success for a femocrat is to have allies at the top of the hierarchy. The work of the commission can be seen as an example of the significance femocrats in co-operation with female politicians can have for changes in favour of women's interests.

Thus the strategic actors in this case are some crucial female politicians and the commissioners (the femocrats). During the time for the appointment of the *Commission on Women's Representation*, the Social Democratic government consisted of six women and 15 men. Female cabinet ministers were in charge of such vital portfolios as equality, labour market affairs and justice. As mentioned, equality minister Anita Gradin appointed the commission. She had been strongly engaged in women's questions since the 1960s. Responsible for the governmental proposition which followed the commission was the minister of labour market affairs, Ingela Thalén. Thalén had succeeded Anna-Greta Leijon who had taken over the portfolio for justice. Both had been active in working for women's representation in politics.

During the work of the commission the interviews seemed to be a vital instrument in making the groups involved conscious of the problems. They had to explain their working-rules and answer questions about why they did not follow the recommendation. The under-representation of women was made visible. They also had to answer as to why they did not use the recommendation of two names. It was then shown that the recommendation was not part of the working-rules used. In the final report the commissioners write:

> *In our interviews with those in power we got the same answer again and again to the question of how to improve women's representation: make us stand in the dunces corner. Almost all of them testified to the opinion-making effect of our investigation. The risk of being pointed out as the villain of the piece contributes to raising consciousness and to applying existing rules* (SOU 1987:19, 164-165).

This led government to accentuate the demands to use the recommendation even before the commission had finished its work. The new order requested the departments to be more active in making the nominating parts suggest both a woman and a man. The government also decided on better co-ordination between the ministries.

The commissioners (the femocrats) were thus included in a process with a distinct goal: to increase women's representation. The quick reaction of government to accentuate the recommendation can be seen as a strong support of the commissioners, who were now involved in a situation of negotiations with the involved groups. The support from government certainly facilitated the position of the femocrats and their possibilities to have an effect on the behaviour of the responsible groups. It also has to be added that the *Commission on Women's Representation* received a lot of attention in mass media all over the country. This contributed to visualise the until now invisible indirectly elected boards.

In the final report from the commission there are no signs that the commissioners have been coopted, thus giving up their original feminist values. But in some ways they have been forced to adjust to the prevailing institutional conditions, which they openly declare in the report. The adjustment can be seen in their suggestions of measures to be undertaken. They wanted to propose legislation to assure that the balance between women and men improved. The commissioners referred to the other Nordic countries where legislation had been an effective instrument in increasing women's representation. At the time of the commission, Sweden had only 16 percent women in public bodies, compared to Denmark and Norway where around 30 percent of the representatives were women. However, legislation was not proposed because of strong resistance to this from organised interests and parties.

Instead of legislation, the members of the commission suggested that the government finance a three-year project aimed at increasing women's representation in public bodies. If the project did not succeed legislation would be necessary. The goal of the project was divided into different stages. In a first stage, women's representation would have to increase to at least 30 percent by 1992; otherwise the government ought to suggest legislation. The next stage is a representation of 40 percent by 1995 and then 50 percent by 1998. In the new government proposition on gender equality from 1990, the same goals as before were repeated (Regeringens proposition 1990/91:113).

The government thus did approve the suggested measures. The project has involved a wide range of women's organisations and networks, unions, political parties, work-places in local and central administration etc. At the suggestion of the commission, the government also decided that the distribution of women and men in public bodies every year had to be reported to the parliament and thus published in the public documents from parliament. Such a yearly report had been suggested by several of the involved groups to make women's underrepresentation more visible.[8]

The development of women's representation shows that the goal of 30 percent has been reached in the boards of public administration at central level where the proportion of women was 36 percent in 1992. The boards at regional level showed 27 percent female representation and the commissions 28 percent. Altogether the average was 30 percent. Taken together, it is thus possible to conclude that the goal has been reached.

To conclude, this study illustrates how femocrats together with sympathising politicians at governmental level acted to carry through a policy in women's interest. First, there was an *alliance* between the commissioners and the responsible ministers, both parts strove towards the same goal: to increase women's representation. It is almost astonishing to see how quickly and efficiently the suggested measures were decided and implemented. In just a few years, women's representation almost doubled in public commissions and boards. The women politicians from all different parties, as well as the women representatives from the organised interest groups were in complete *agreement* over this goal. Was there no resistance? A substantial increase

---

[8] An evaluation of projects has been undertaken by Eduards & Åström 1993.

in the proportion of women means that the recruitment of men almost has to stop and that many men must leave their places earlier than expected. The resistance was shown in the protests against legislation. The increase in women's representation had to be voluntary, it was said. The goal of equal distribution between women and men can hardly be questioned anymore in Swedish political culture. In the prevailing state of opinion all involved groups had to show that they were trying to live up to the goal of equality.

The *Commission on Women's Representation* made the *gender dimension* in corporatist arrangements visible. In the 1970s this had been done in political parties and elected bodies, which had led to a strong expansion of women in especially the more visible positions of political office. In the 1980s and 1990s many of these women have been involved in alliances to find strategies to change and enhance the conditions to allow women to be fully integrated in all parts of political decision-making.

References

Bergqvist, C. (1990), 'Myten om den universella svenska välfärdsstaten', *Statsvetenskaplig tidsskrift*, 3:223-233.

Bergqvist, C. (1991), 'Corporatism and gender equality. A comparative study of two Swedish labour market organisations', *European Journal of Political Research*, 20:107-125.

Birgersson, B.O. and Westerståhl, J. (1992), *Den svenska folkstyrelsen*. Stockholm: Publica.

Damgaard, E. (1990), 'The strong parliaments of Scandinavia', paper prepared for the Carl Albert Center Conference, University of Oklahoma at Norman, April 11-13.

Ds A 1986:4. 'Ska även morgondagens samhälle formas enbart av män?'. Report from the commission on women's representation. Stockholm: Ministry of Labour.

Eduards, M. L. (1980), *Kvinnorepresentation och kvinnomakt*. Stockholm: Statsvetenskapliga institutionen.

Eduards, M. L. (1991), 'Toward a Third Way: Women's Politics and Welfare Policies in Sweden', *Social Research*, Vol. 58, 3:677-705.

Eduards, M. L. (1992), 'Against the Rules of the Game. On the Importance of Women's Collective Actions', in: *Rethinking Change. Current Swedish Feminist Research.* Stockholm: HSFR.

Eduards, M. L. and Åström, G. (1993), *Många kände sig manade, men få blevo kallade.* Stockholm: Socialdepartementet.

Hermansson, J. (1993), *Politik som intressekamp.* Stockholm: Norstedts juridik.

Hernes, H. M. (1987), *Welfare State and Woman Power: Essays in State Feminism.* Oslo: Norwegian University Press.

Hernes, H. M and Hänninen-Salmelin, E. (1983), 'Kvinners representasjon i det korporative system', in Haavio-Mannila, E. et al. (eds): *Det uferdige demokratiet. Kvinner i nordisk politikk.* Oslo: Nordisk Ministerråd.

Jónasdóttir, A. (1991): 'Love Power and Political Interests', *Örebro Studies*, 7.

Kvinno- och mansvär(l)den (1986): Stockholm: National Bureau of Statistics.

Levi, M. and Edwards, M. (1990), 'The dilemmas of Femocratic Reform', in Katzenstein, M. F. and Skjeie, H. (eds): *Going Public. National Histories of Women's Enfranchisement and Women's Participation within State Institutions.* Oslo: Institute for Social Research.

Lewin, L. (1992), *Samhället och de organiserade intressena.* Stockholm: Norstedts.

Nominerade och valda kandidater vid allmänna valen 1991. Stockholm: National bureau of Statistics.

Ostrom, E. (1986), 'A Method of Institutional Analysis', in Kaufmann, F. X., Majone, G. and Ostrom, E. (eds): *Guidance, Control, and Evaluation in the Public Sector.* Berlin: de Gruyter.

Petersson, O. (1989), *Maktens nätverk.* Stockholm: Carlssons.

Proposition 1980/81:100, bil. 3.

Proposition 1990/91:113 om en ny jämställdhetslag, m.m.

Riksdagens kommittéberättelser 1981-1989, skr 103.

Rothstein, B. (ed.) (1991), *Politik som organisation. Förvaltningspolitikens grundproblem.* Stockholm: SNS.

Rothstein, B. (1992), *Den korporativa staten.* Stockholm: Norstedts.

Skard, T. and Haavio-Mannila, E. (1983), 'Kvinner i parlamentene', in Haavio-Mannila, E. et al. (eds): *Det uferdige demokratiet. Kvinner i nordisk politikk.* Oslo: Nordisk Ministerråd.

Skjeie, H. (1992), *Den politiske betydningen av kjønn. En studie av norsk topp-politikk.* Oslo: Institutt for samfunnsforskning.

SOU 1987:19, *Varannan damernas.* Final report of the commission on women's representation. Stockholm: Ministry of Labour.

SOU 1990:44, *Demokrati och makt i Sverige*. Final report of the commission on democracy and power in Sweden. Stockholm.

Söderlind, D. and Petersson, O. (1988), *Svensk förvaltningspolitik*. Uppsala: Diskurs.

Waldemarson, Y. (1992), 'Kontrakt under förhandling - LO, kvinnorna och makten', in Åström, G. and Hirdman, Y. (eds): *Kontrakt i kris*. Stockholm: Carlssons.

Watson, S. (1990), 'Unpacking the State', in Katzenstein, M.F. and Skjeie, H. (eds): *Going Public. Enfranchisement and Women's Participation within State Institutions*. Oslo: Institute for Social Research.

Feminization of the central
public administration

Per Lægreid

Introduction[1]

In this chapter, we will direct our attention towards women in central government administration. Three issues will be considered. First of all, what is the ratio between the genders within public administration, and what changes have taken place in the last decades? Secondly, how can we explain the changes in the proportion of women in the civil service? And thirdly, what effect does gender have on decision-making?

While focussing mainly on the first question, we will also discuss the two other aspects on the basis of existing studies.

Women's research in the field of political science has focussed strongly on the political powerlessness of women. It has been claimed that women have been under-represented, subordinated or excluded from political/administrative institutions (Hernes 1982). However, women have gradually become integrated into party politics, and in this chapter we will show that this is also the case when it comes to central public administration. This development means that earlier pessimistic views on the participation and representation of women in politics have to be moderated, and to a certain extent, this has already been done in studies of other political institutions (Hernes 1987, Skjeie 1992).

A central hypothesis in women's research has been that increases in women's participation have taken place in 'shrinking' institutions (Holter 1981). It is maintained that women have succeeded first and foremost in traditional political institutions whose power and influence are on the decline, for instance in political parties and the Storting. We question this view by directing our attention towards institutions whose political influence it is alleged has increased over time, i.e. the central civil service. Based on a hypothesis of marginalisation (Skard and Haavio-Mannila 1986), it was claimed that the proportion of women was small and not

---

[1] I would like to thank Morten Egeberg, Hanne Nexø Jensen, Lauri Karvonen, Stefan Sjøblom and Mariann Vågenes for their help in the work on this chapter.

230 Women in Nordic Politics

increasing in these institutions. Moreover, from this point of view, we would expect to find a hierarchical structure in which women are to be found primarily in subordinate positions and in subsidiary institutions and institutions with low status.

It has also been maintained that the integration of women into politics leads to segregation, as women's representation and participation increases primarily in the so-called 'soft' areas of politics, for instance in the fields of social welfare, education, and in cultural, child and family policies, while fewer are found in such 'harder' spheres as defence, industry and agriculture (Karento 1990).

In this chapter, we will examine whether in fact there is such a trend towards marginalisation, hierarchisation and segregation, or whether there is a change towards increased state feminization and a more positive interpretation of women's integration in the civil service (Hernes 1987, Dahlerup 1993), with women on their way into the more powerful institutions, central positions and 'hard' political areas.

Research on the organisational demography of political/administrative institutions has been characterised by descriptive recruitment studies. These studies have been concerned with the composition of the staff at a given time and how this has changed over time. Interest has been linked to the distribution of characters related to social background, with particular emphasis in recent years on the distribution between the sexes.

In addition to describing the distribution between the sexes in the public administration apparatus and how this is changing, it is important to raise two other issues (Lægreid 1989). The first is the ability to steer or socially control gender distribution through planned measures and an active recruitment policy. We need to know why gender composition in public administration changes. We will expect that the distribution of gender is not solely a result of an active recruitment policy, but that it also to some degree depends on changes in the labour market and in 'driving forces' beyond political control. Changes in the degree to which women seek higher education in particular will influence the recruitment of women to positions in public administration.

The second important issue is the ability to calculate the consequences and effects of various gender distribution ratios in a rational way (Pfeffer 1983, Egeberg 1989). What effects do various personnel compositions have on the content of politics and on the decision-making prosess itself? The effect of gender composition must be assessed in relation to the control the organisations exert over their members through socialisation and discipline (Lægreid and Olsen 1978).

One question that arises is to what extent women are recruited to various positions and institutions in public administration. Another question is what importance such background features as gender have in relation to the decisions made. A widely held opinion is that minority groups in formal institutions have a tendency to be stigmatised, thus subjecting themselves to pressure to conform. When the proportion of women is small, strong socialising mechanisms will cause those in a minority to conform to the dominant culture of that organisation. It has been claimed that women in 'token' positions are particularly exposed to such pressure (Kanter 1976, 1977). On the same basis, it must be assumed that when the proportion of women rises to what may be said to constitute a 'critical mass' (Dahlerup 1988), this pressure will decrease and the women will be in a better position to shape and alter the organisational culture of the institution. Kanter indicates that when the number of women on the staff of an organisation rises to more than 35 percent, they can no longer be characterised as 'tokens' (Kanter 1977:965). On this assumption, it becomes important to assess how much this relative proportion of women in central public administration has increased over the past ten years, and to discuss the degree to which this may have affected the contents of decisions made.

We would expect civil servants, like other decision makers, to act on the basis of a simplified model of the world. Their rationality is bounded in that they cannot deal with all the problems, all the alternative actions, all the consequences or all the values (March and Simon 1958). It is thus important to ask what circumstances affect selection. We would expect the selection that takes place to be in part a result of the organisational structure within which personnel function, in part a result of special characteristics of such personnel, and partly a result of external circumstances outside the control of the organisation. It is this interplay between individual factors and the organisation that must be studied.

The empirical focus of this chapter will be on Norwegian central public administration, with emphasis on civil servants in the ministries at executive officer level and above, in other words, the central core of public administration. Moreover, comparisons will be made with other Nordic countries and directorates as far as gender composition is concerned.

Feminization of public administration

Over the past 20 years, there has been a marked increase in the proportion of women in public administration. For a long time, women dominated the lower ranks. In 1980, 91 percent of the employees under executive officer level in Norwegian ministeries were women. The corresponding figure for the directorates was 67 percent (Lægreid and Roness 1983). During the 1980s, women entered the higher grades in increasing numbers, first at executive officer level and later at senior management level.

Table 1

Percentage of women among civil servants in Norwegian ministries. Selected years

	1976	1986	1993
Secretary General	0	0	21
Director General	0	9	12
Assistant Director General/ Deputy Assistant Director General	8	13	25
Head of Division	14	18	35
Executive Officer/ Senior Executive Officer	19	37	56
Total	15	26	44

The number of women at executive officer level and above in Norwegian ministries has increased from 15 percent in 1976 to 44 percent in 1993. There has been a gradual revolution in Norwegian ministries over the past 17 years as far as feminization is concerned. In 1993, more than half the executive officers were women. There has also been an increase in the number of women departmental heads. In 1976, no women were employed at the two highest levels in the Norwegian ministerial hierarchy. In 1994, 4 Secretaries General and 14 Directors General were women. Only the Ministry of Finance and the Ministry of Environment did not have at least one woman Secretary General or Director General.

Of 377 top management salary contracts in government service at the end of 1993, beginning of 1994, 35, or 9.3 percent, were with women (Lægreid and Mjør 1993). The proportion of women in top management is highest in the ministries and lowest in the defence forces and the foreign service, where there are virtually no women at the top level. There are also few women in top positions in public administration enterprises.

One study of senior management in government organisations outside the ministries in 1988 shows that 12 percent of the top positions are held by women (Helgesen, Lægreid and Matland 1988). Women civil servants at top level are younger than their male counterparts and have less time in service. Women in senior management are most plentiful in education and the health services (22 percent), and least plentiful in the police and prison services (3 percent). The number of women in senior management decreases in inverse proportion to the size of the government bodies measured by the number of employees (Helgesen 1990).

This survey shows that although women remain clearly in the minority in senior management, they have gained ground particularly in the ministries and in schools and health institutions. The number of women in middle management is sizeable. In 1993, 23 percent of the divisional heads in the directorates were women, as were 35 percent of those in the same positions in the ministries.[2]

In the ministries, we no longer find women in the typically 'soft', traditionally women-dominated ministries. The proportion of women at executive officer level and above in the Directorate of Fisheries has increased from 6 percent in 1976 to 50 percent in 1993. The corresponding increases in the Ministry of Labour and Local Government are 15 percent and 51 percent, in the Ministry of Agriculture 8 percent and 36 percent, in the Ministry of Defence 2 percent and 30 percent and in the Ministry of Commerce and Energy 2 percent and 37 percent. In 1993, women account for half or more of the civil servants in seven of the ministries. Only two ministries have less than 35 percent women employees at executive officer level and above in 1993.

The trend towards an increasing number of women is also being registered in the directorates. A study carried out in 1987 shows that the proportion of women at executive officer level and above was 16 percent (Egeberg et al. 1989). In 1993, 33 percent of all full-time employees at executive officer level and above in central public administration outside the ministries were women.[3] In the 1987 study, there were no women in top management, as opposed to 8 percent in 1993.

This tendency towards increasing numbers of women at executive officer level and above is not a purely Norwegian phenomenon, but one that is also being observed in other Nordic countries. In *Finland*, the proportion of women at this level has increased from 18 percent in 1976 to 38 percent in 1993. Though this increase is regisered for all civil servants, the trend towards a rise in the number of women has

---

[2] In comparison, in 1989, 13 percent of the two highest grades of managers in Swedish ministries and 18 percent of the middle managers were women (SOU 1990:44, p. 332).

[3] Source: Salary statistics. Public administration, 1 October 1993, table 3.0. Oslo: Department of Administration.

Table 2
Percentage of women at executive officer level and above in Norwegian
ministries.[4] Selected years

	1976	1986	1993
Ministry of Consumer Affairs and Administration	18	35	
Ministry of Administration			44
Ministry of Child and Family Affairs			62
Ministry of Health and Social Welfare	31	36	58
Ministry of Justice	23	35	52
Ministry of Labour and Local Government	15	29	51
Ministry of Church, Education and Research	20	31	50
Ministry of Cultural Affairs		30	50
Ministry of Fisheries	6	17	50
Ministry of the Environment	7	25	44
Ministry of Trade	6	22	
Ministry of Foreign Affairs	15	22	39
Department of Overseas Aid		46	
Ministry of Industry	2	17	
Ministry of Commerce and Energy			37
Ministry of Petroleum and Energy		21	
Ministry of Agriculture	8	13	36
Ministry of Finance	19	20	35
Ministry of Transport and Communications	12	15	32
Ministry of Defence	2	19	30
Office of the Prime Minister	0	40	27
Total	15	26	44

[4] - indicates that the ministry did not exist at that time.

been somewhat weaker than in Norway. This difference between countries has intensified over time and is registered both at senior management and executive officer level.

The differences in gender profiles between Finland and Norway are minor when it comes to directorates compared to ministries. In central civil service jobs, there was no clear growth in the number of women employed between 1986 and 1993, but then the number was relatively high even in 1986. However, growth from 1976 to 1986 was stronger, rising from 20 percent women employees at executive officer level and above to 32 percent. In five of the central civil service establishments in Finland, more than 50 percent of the employees at executive officer level and above in 1993 were women, and most of these worked in the field of education, social welfare and health services, but also in such institutions as the Agricultural Board and the Board of Industry.[5]

When it comes to the distribution of women employees in Finnish ministries, the growth in the number of most of these institutions, too, has been strong. The number of women at executive officer level and above in the Ministry of Justice rose from 12 percent in 1976 to 46 percent in 1993. The corresponding figures in the Ministry of Foreign Affairs are 19 percent and 41 percent, and in the Ministry of Agriculture and Forestry the figures are 5 percent and 29 percent. One exception is the Finnish Ministry of Defence, where women have not succeeded in gaining a foothold. Six of the Finnish ministries had 35 percent or less women at executive officer level and above in 1993, while just one ministry had more than 50 percent women employees at these levels.

In *Denmark,* too, some growth has been registered in the number of women civil servants (Maegaard 1986, 1993). The figures indicate that at the beginning of 1990, this country was lagging slightly behind Finland, but was clearly behind Norway. In 1991, the number of women civil servants in the ministries amounted to 34 percent compared to 44 percent in Norway in 1993. The number of women managers in Denmark has also remained fairly constant between 1981 and 1991. If we look at developments within the individual ministries, the number of women has increased by 10 percent or more in the Ministries of Energy, Defence, Industry, Justice,

---

[5] The figures for the Board of Industry are from 1986. This institution was closed down in 1993.

Table 3
Percentage of women in ministries according to job levels and countries.[6]
Selected years

	Executive officers			Senior managers			Total		
	1976	*1986*	*1993*	*1976*	*1986*	*1993*	*1976*	*1986*	*1993*
Finland	22	35	43	6	10	17	18	29	38
Norway	19	37	56	10	15	27	15	26	44
	1981	*1988*	*1991*	*1981*	*1988*	*1991*	*1981*	*1988*	*1991*
Denmark	27	32	40	10	12	14	24	28	34

Table 4
Percentage of women at executive officer level and above in directorates in Finland and Norway.[7] 1986 and 1993

	Senior management		Executive officers		Total	
	1986	*1993*	*1986*	*1993*	*1986*	*1993*
Finland	16	19	38	40	32	36
Norway	10	19	21	41	16	33

[6] Sources: Norway: Lægreid and Olsen 1978, Egeberg et al. 1989. Official government yearbook 1994; Finland: Official government yearbook, systematised and made available by Lauri Karvonen; Denmark: Maregaard 1986, 1993.

[7] The figures for Norway are not directly comparable for 1987 and 1993. The 1987 figures are based on a somewhat more limited population (Egeberg's (1989) study of the directorates) than are the 1993 figures (Wage statistics. Public Administration).

Table 5
Percentage of women at executive officer level and above in Finnish ministries in three selected years

	1976	1986	1993
Cabinet Chancellery	34	61	64
Ministry of Foreign Affairs	19	32	41
Ministry of Justice	12	26	46
Ministry of the Interior	17	21	29
Ministry of Defence	4	7	7
Ministry of Finance	12	23	32
Ministry of Education	31	38	45
Ministry of Agriculture and Forestry	5	23	29
Ministry of Transport	3	13	24
Ministry of Trade and Industry	20	24	32
Ministry of Health and Social Welfare	25	37	55
Ministry of Labour	30	42	35
Ministry of the Environment		37	44

Agriculture, Social Welfare, Education and Taxation. There has been little change in the other ten ministries between 1981 and 1991. Compared to Finland, the gender composition of the Ministry of Defence is particularly interesting. In 1991, 45 percent of the civil servants in the Danish Ministry of Defence were women, compared to 7 percent in Finland. In Denmark, 12 of the ministries had fewer than 35 percent women employees at executive officer level and above, and only one ministry had more than 50 percent women. However, in five of the ministries, more than 50 percent of the employees at executive officer level in 1993 were women (Maegaard 1993).

Table 6
Percentage of women at executive officer level and above in Danish ministries in three selected years

	1981	1986	1991
Ministry of Labour	41	38	48
Ministry of Housing	26	33	28
Ministry of Energy	10	22	30
Ministry of Finance	21	20	25
Ministry of Fisheries	13	17	11
Ministry of Defence	23	20	45
Ministry of the Interior	31	34	30
Ministry of Industry	24	35	46
Ministry of Justice	23	33	41
Ministry of Church Affairs	24	30	30
Ministry of Agriculture	20	25	32
Ministry of the Environment	40	43	31
Ministry of Cultural Affairs	40	44	40
Ministry of Social Welfare	38	39	49
Prime Minister's Office	21	19	20
Ministry of Foreign Affairs	13	17	18
Ministry of Education	32	47	46
Ministry of Economy	19	21	21
Ministry of Taxation	21	29	33
Ministry of Health			53
Ministry of Transport			37

Summing up

This survey shows that the trend towards feminization of the central public administration is most advanced in Norway, but also in the other Nordic countries, the proportion of women employees is rising. The position of women is strongest in the ministries, at executive officer level and in sectors traditionally dominated by women. However, the trend for women to assert themselves in central public administration is clear also outside the ministries, at senior management level and in typically male-dominated sectors. In the ministries in particular, women are in the process of taking over areas and senior management positions not directly related to labour market, educational and welfare policy.

Explaining the feminization of central public adminstration

There may be many reasons for the increasing number of women in the ministries. One possible explanation can be traced back to distinct personnel policy measures. Partly as a result of the Equal Opportunities Act of 1978, policy guidelines were introduced in the Basic Labour Agreement of 1981 opening for a moderate equal opportunity policy in appointments to vacant positions in the civil service. Equal opportunity policies can be linked to arguments based on the utilisation of resources, the introduction of new experience and knowledge, improved justice, equal rights to employment, and to arguments regarding interests and the fact that men and women have contradictory interests (Hernes 1982). However, such a principle of quota systems for civil service positions combined with a representative bureaucracy is not firmly founded in Norwegian civil service traditions (Lægreid and Olsen 1978).

The recruitment process takes place within well established norms, routines and rules of standards which do not change quickly in response to changing political signals or changes in the labour market situation. The principle of recruitment based on merit holds a strong position in civil service appointments. At the same time, responsibility for recruitment has been decentralised and left to the individual institution, with the immediate superior playing a central role in these appointments. The traditional autonomy of civil service institutions in personnel matters suggests that they would not be receptive to centrally introduced reforms. These factors, together with little activity from central agencies and few measures allowing central authorities to follow up agreements on equal rights in public administration, mean that these arrangements are not automatically implemented in the individual civil service institution (Lægreid 1987). When the framework agreement on personnel policy guidelines was adopted in 1981, it was a clear presupposition that the individual civil service institution would enter into local agreements before the end of 1982. By 1987, however, only 20 percent had such a local agreement in place (Klokkeide 1988).

The issue of equal rights was central to the political debate at the end of the 1970s and the first half of the 1980s, and gender quotas were presented as an important tool. However, much seems to suggest that it was difficult to gain support for this principle in an administration where recruitment principles based on merit had traditionally been very strong. Moreover, the efficiency perspective gradually came more into the forefront in public administration policy, with increasing focus on market and management. In addition, then, attention was focussed on the need to expand the basis for recruitment and to change appointment procedures to comply with those in the private sector, with increased use of 'head hunting' and the external recruitment of managers with experience from private industry. Special programmes for 'women in management' were introduced, but these were limited (Grandaunet 1989). The representativeness perspective, with emphasis on gender quotas, was displaced slightly by the efficiency-oriented perspective towards the end of the 1980s. In 1988, only 3 percent of the senior managers in the civil service expressed the view that more use should be made of gender quotas (Lægreid 1993).

In all probability, the changes in the composition of the gender of ministry employees are more a reflection of changes in the recruitment of women to higher education than of active application of a gender preference policy (Lægreid 1989b). Quota arguments were clearly rejected in Norwegian ministries at the end of the 1970s. Of six given criteria, members of the appointments committees in the ministries clearly ranked the applicant's sex as the least important factor. Even though the Ministry of Petroleum and Energy had encouraged women to apply for vacant positions since 1981 and since 1983 had introduced an equal opportunities agreement determining moderate gender preference, by the middle of the 1980s, it was virtually impossible to show that gender preference arguments prevailed in appointments (Jensen 1984, Skjeie 1986). This conclusion is supported by studies of recruitment to the Ministry of Industry (Røberg 1991), to municipal councils (Heggholmen 1988) and studies on the introduction and practice of equal opportunity agreements (Klokkeide 1987, 1988). Nor is gender preference prominent among recruitment principles applied when appointing senior managers to Norwegian state institutions (Helgesen 1990). Introduction of quotas in the civil service has not been a 'critical act', which is supposed to be the case when it comes to quota rules in political parties (Dahlerup 1988).

Explanations of changes in recruitment patterns can probably not be found in any single factor. Alterations in the gender composition of the relevant groups completing higher education programmes are probably important to our understanding of the strong growth in the number of women employees in the civil service. The fact that women more frequently seek higher training in the professions from which the civil service recruits candidates for central management positions leads naturally to more women applicants for these jobs. At the same time, the rate of retirement among ministry personnel has been rising, particularly among men. The proportion of women managers is larger in the civil service than in the private sector (Strand 1993). This suggests that the civil service might be a friendlier employer for women than is the private sector, and this is expressed in - among other things - more liberal arrangements when it comes to leaves of absence. In addition, attitudes among those managers responsible for recruitment are changing, thanks to their experience of women employees and compliance with formal regulations and agreements.

The main conclusion, therefore, is that the explanation for the changes in recruitment patterns is multi-faceted, but that an incremental adjustment in the figures on gender distribution among those with higher education, resulting in improved availability of more qualified women applicants, is probably more important that conscious and active recruitment policy. We interpret this to mean that altered gender composition in public administration is a result of changes in self-selection processes rather than in selection processes.

The effects of increased female representation

We may differentiate between the symbolic and the substantive effects of increased representation of women in public administration. The symbolic aspects refer to the fact that women in public administration symbolise the identity of women in society. Increased representation in public administration may be regarded as a sign of equality, status and acceptance. It may be seen as democratisation of public administration, increasing its legitimacy, and thus seen as an advantage in itself. The symbolic aspect is a distinctly separate reason for the desire to seek a more representative public administration, irrespective of the effects gender composition may have on the decisions made or the content of public policies. This type of effect will not be pursued here; instead we will concentrate on the possible relationship between the gender of civil servants and the contents of decisions made in public administration.

The discussion is based on the fact that certain characteristics in the social background of the civil servants, for instance gender, affect the decisions they make. But at the same time, these are not the only factors that are important. The formal organizational structure within the institutions in which the civil servants work also exerts considerable influence on their actions (Lægreid and Olsen 1984). The values, perceptions and social identifications, and the strength of these, that women bring with them to their work in public administration are also important. Women recruited to public administration bring with them a number of affiliations which to a varying degree will influence them and the decisions they make.

Studies of central Norwegian public administration suggest that factors such as education are more important than attributes such as gender. Traditionally, gender has not been considered important when recruiting personnel or for the way in which the work of public administration is effectuated. A study of Norwegian ministries in the middle of the 1970s concluded that the opinions and attitudes of women employed in these ministries only to a limited extent differed from those of the men (Lægreid and Olsen 1978). At that time, the percentage of women at executive officer level and above was 15 percent. A substantial increase in the number of women was presented as an important condition for achieving greater gender impact on the content of public policies. This increase must be said to have been achieved in as much as women now account for 44 percent of the civil servants in ministries.

However, this sharp increase in the relative proportion of women employees is not sufficient to cause the decision-making conduct of women bureaucrats to deviate systematically from that of men. In addition, women first have to develop attitudes and opinions that are more unanimous and that differ more from those of men than they did in 1975. This does not appear to be the case yet. The major changes in the educational level and professional participation of women have contributed towards increasing differences between women themselves, making it less relevant to study women as a homogenous group (Raaum and Skogerbø 1993). Secondly, it must be possible to link women's gender-related attitudes and opinions more closely to their activities in public administration. This will probably be more difficult now that women are recruited not only to areas traditionally associated with women, such as health, family, children, and education, but are also gaining a firmer foothold in other branches of public administration. Thirdly, the importance of gender will increase if women in public administration put together formal organisations and construct informal networks between themselves. We do not yet have systematic data on the degree to which this has already taken place.[8] Fourthly, the importance of background factors such as gender will increase if the socialising and disciplinary potential of the ministries is reduced substantially from the position at the end of the 1970s.

Studies carried out at the end of the 1980s do not suggest that more systematic differences in attitudes and decision-making conduct have developed between women and men employees (Egeberg 1990, 1994). A study of managers in the public and private sectors reaches the same conclusion (Strand 1993). Decision-making conduct is affected first and foremost by formal organizational structure, while background features such as gender seem to have little impact. The gender of employees in the ministries, for instance, has little influence on their innovatory conduct (Christensen 1989). Even in organisations with relatively short service and with high personnel turnover (Lægreid 1988) and in institutions without a hierarchical organisational structure (Stigen 1989), background characteristics such as gender mean less than position within the public administration apparatus. Nor have studies of Scandinavian institutions given clear support to Kanter's hypothesis on the importance of relative numbers of women when it comes to decision-making conduct (Dahlerup 1988, Christensen 1989, Skjeie 1992).[9] The fact that women's representation is increasing to more than 35 percent in many ministries does not necessarily lead to marked changes in the attitudes, opinions and patterns of action that characterise public adminstration personnel.

One interpretation of these relationships is that formal organisational structure places strong restrictions on the opportunities for decision-making conduct to vary with the gender of the personnel. The numeric skewness of women in a civil service agency is only one of several factors affecting women's behavior in the organization. Reliance on numbers as the cause of, and the solution to, gender differences in public bureaucracies neglects the complexities of gender integration in formal organizations (Yoder 1991). Norms, rules and routines for what are standard, fair, reasonable and acceptable actions place clear restrictions on the degree to which the demographic characteristics of personnel, for instance gender, may influence the power of judgement delegated to the individual civil servant. Position, speciality and

---

[8] A study of other institutions, such as the Storting, does not suggest that increased representation of women *per se* leads to the development of strong networks among women across formal organisational barriers (Skjeie 1992).

[9] This conclusion is also supported by a study of female civil servants in a large federal bureaucracy in USA, where contrary to Kanters theory, token women are not found to face more severe organizational pressure than non-tokens (South et al. 1982)

professional integrity, and loyalty to the institution in which the civil servant is employed at any time, seem to be more important to the understanding of variations in decision-making conduct than gender.

Conclusion: from movement to management

Fairly good empirical data is available showing the gender profile among public adminstration employees and how this has changed over time in the Nordic countries. However, knowledge is more limited when it comes to explaining stability and changes in gender composition or disclosing effects of various gender distributions. However, this does not mean that we do not know anything about these factors.

Our data do not support the idea that women have first and foremost gained a foothold in shrinking institutions. Over recent decades, women have secured central positions within the ministries, where they are found not only at subordinate, clerical levels and in ministries responsible for what traditionally have been considered women's affairs. There has been a gradual feminization of the ministries. Women have become integrated into central public adminstration to the extent that they have gained firmer footholds in formerly male-dominated institutions and positions. Nevertheless, the proportion of women is still greatest in the traditionally 'soft', women-dominated sectors and declines as the level of positions rises. With the sharp growth of women executive officers in general in central public adminstration, however, it is probably a question of time before they take over an even stronger share of the positions at senior management level and in the more male-dominated sectors.

However, it is not certain to what degree this change in gender composition can be traced back to active and controlled personnel policies using gender quotas as a central tool to implement these policies. Political management is not free to select the recruitment pattern it would like to use, but it is not without choice when it comes to influencing the composition of the staff employed in public administration. It is our interpretation that changed gender distribution in public administration management is more an adjustment to more wide-ranging changes in the gender composition of the relevant groups in higher education and in women's choice of occupations.

The integration of women into senior management positions within the bureaucracy has an important symbolic aspect. An evening out of gender differences in public administration may be seen as a step in a general democratisation process, increasing the legitimacy of public administration and the chances that public measures will be accepted by the community. But it is also important to compare various forms of representativeness, e.g. gender, geography and class. Studies of ministries in the middle of the 1970s show that women civil servants to a greater extent than men grew up in the nation's capital and in social environments dominated by academics or self-employed businessmen (Lægreid and Olsen 1978). If this trend is sustained, an evening out of gender differences in the civil service could contribute towards increasing the distortions in relation to geographic areas and between social classes.

There is less uncertainty surrounding the extent to which the increased number of women has led to changes in decision-making or policy contents. The studies referred to in this chapter point towards more importance being attached to where people are rather than where they come from when it comes to understanding the way in which they make their decisions. It is the position of the employee within the organisation rather than his or her gender that decides his or her conduct on the job. However, these studies have their limitations. They are largely based on indirect measurements of decision-making conduct and the contents of these decisions. Attention is focussed on the attitudes, opinions and contact patterns of the employees. But it is well-known in organisational research that attitudes are not necessarily closely linked to actions (March and Olsen 1976). A priority task should therefore be to supplement studies of the statements and opinions of the civil servants with studies of what actually happens. This will require analyses of concrete results, something not easily registered by surveys. The finding so far, made first and foremost through quantitative survey studies in which the biological category sex is used as a background or explanatory factor, show that there is little difference between the decision-making conduct of men and women civil servants. One important challenge will be to investigate whether such a conclusion is also valid when using a more dynamic and procedural approach based to a greater extent on more explicit theories concerning gender and gender differences.

In order to expand our background of knowledge on how the gender composition of personnel in public administration is changing, what factors affect these processes of change and what effects a rising proportion of women employees have, it is also necessary to carry out more systematic comparative studies. Comparative studies across national borders in particular should provide new insight. Many of the changes taking place seem to appear virtually simultaneously, but with varying strength, in several countries, and it is therefore difficult to see these change processes as purely internal national phenomena. We are faced with an internationalisation of public administration, making it necessary to analyse how various civil service institutions are affected by and relate to changes also outside the nation's borders. Central public administration institutions in particular will face a challenge when it comes to expanding competence, and an important issue in this connection will be the extent to which Europeanisation of the public administration will affect women's integration into this public administration.

References

Christensen, T. (1989), 'Innovasjonsatferd i sentralforvaltningen: Strukturelle og demografiske forklaringer på variasjon', in Egeberg, M. (ed.): *Institusjonspolitikk og forvaltningsutforming*. Oslo: Tano.

Dahlerup, D. (1988), 'From a Small to a Large Minority: Women in Scandinavian Politics', *Scandinavian Political Studies*, Vol. 11, 4:275-298.

Dahlerup, D. (1993), 'From movement protest to state feminism: The Women's Liberation Movement and unemployment policy in Denmark' NORA, Vol. 1, 1:4-20

Egeberg, M. (1989), 'Mot instrumentelle modeller i statsvitenskapen', in Egeberg, M. (ed.): *Institusjonspolitikk og forvaltningsutvikling*. Oslo: Tano.

Egeberg, M. et al. (1989), 'Departementene og andre sentraladministrative organer: En sammenlikning av enkelte trekk ved formell struktur, personell og beslutningsatferd', in Egeberg, M. (ed.): *Institusjonspolitikk og forvaltningsutvikling*. Oslo: Tano.

Egeberg, M. (1990), 'Forvaltningspolitikkens kunnskapsgrunnlag', *Norsk Statsvitenskapelig Tidsskrift*, Vol. 6, 2:121-126.

Egeberg, M. (1994), 'Bridging the Gap Between Theory and Practice: The Case of Administrative Theory', *Governance*, Vol. 7, 1:83-98.

Grandaunet, A. (1989), *Likestilling og ledelsesutvikling i prosjektet 'Kvinner til ledelse'*. Evalueringsrapport. Oslo: NOSAS/Statens personaldirektorat.

Heggholmen, K. (1988), Rekruttering - prosess og prinsipper. Bergen: Institutt for administrasjon og organisasjonsvitenskap. Hovedoppgave.

Helgesen, K. (1990), *Ledere i statlige etater*. Notat 90/12. Bergen: LOS-senteret.

Helgesen, K., Lægreid, P. and Matland, R. (1988), *Tilknytningsformer i staten*. Rapport 3/88. Bergen: LOS-senteret.

Hernes, H. (1982), *Staten, kvinner ingen adgang?* Oslo: Universitetsforlaget.

Hernes, H. (1987), *Welfare State and Woman Power. Essays in State Feminism*. Oslo: Universitetsforlaget

Holter, H. (1981), 'Om kvinneundertrykkelse, mannsundertrykkelse og herskerteknikker', in Andenæs, K. et al. (ed.): *Maktens ansikter*. Oslo: Gyldendal.

Jensen, A.G. (1984), *Personellstrømmer i oljesektoren*. Bergen: Department of administration and organization theory, University of Bergen. Dissertation.

Kanter, R.M. (1976), 'Some Effects of Proportions on Gender Life: Skewed Sex Ratios and Responses to Token Women', *American Journal of Sociology*, Vol. 82, 5:965-990.

Kanter, R.M. (1977), *Men and Women of the Corporation*. New York: Basic Books.

Karento, H. (1990), 'Behind the Formal Equality: Finnish Women in State Administration', in Keränen, M. (ed.): *Finnish 'Undemocracy'*. Helsinki: The Finnish Political Science Association.

Klokkeide, L. (1987), 'Likestillingsavtaler i arbeidslivet - sentralstyring og lokal iverksetting', *Norsk Statsvitenskapelig Tidsskrift*, Vol. 5:17-36.

Klokkeide, L. (1988), *Reformer av statlig personalpolitikk - styring og effekter*. Rapport 88/9. Bergen: LOS-senteret.

Lægreid, P. (1987), 'Styring av personalressurser i statsforvaltningen', *Politica*, Vol. 19, 4:403-419.

Lægreid, P. (1988), *Oljebyråkratiet*. Oslo: Tano.

Lægreid, P. (1989), *Organisasjonsdemografi som personalpolitisk studiefelt*. Notat 89/37. Bergen: LOS-senteret.

Lægreid, P. (1989a), 'Reformer i statens personalpolitikk - sentralstyring og fristilling', in Baldersheim, H. et al. (ed.): *Sentral styring og institusjonell autonomi*. Bergen: Alma Mater.

Lægreid, P. (1989b), *Rekrutteringspolitikk i sentraladministrasjonen*. Notat 89/31. Bergen: LOS-senteret.

Lægreid, P. (1993), 'Lønns- og personalreformer', in Lægreid, P. and Olsen, J. P. (eds): *Organisering av offentlig sektor*. Oslo: Tano.

Lægreid, P. and Mjør, M. (1993), *Toppsjefar og leiarlønsreformer i staten*. Rapport 93/3. Bergen: LOS-senteret.

Lægreid, P. and Olsen, J. P. (1978), *Byråkrati og beslutninger*. Bergen: Universitetsforlaget.

Lægreid, P. and Olsen, J. P. (1984), 'Top Civil Servants in Norway: Key Players - On Different Teams', in Suleiman, E.N. (ed.): *Bureaucrats and Policy Making*. New York: Holmes and Meier.

Lægreid, P. and Roness, P .G. (1983), *Statsadministrasjonen*. Oslo: Tano.

March, J.G. and Olsen, J. P. (1976), *Ambiguity and Choice*. Oslo: Universitetsforlaget.

March, J. G. and Simon, H. (1958), *Organizations*. New York: Wiley.

Maregaard, B. (1986), 'Kvinder i departementerne', *Djøf-bladet*, No. 17:10-14.

Maregaard, B. (1993), 'Kvindernes lange march', *Djøf-bladet*, No. 7:22-25.

Pfeffer, J. (1983), 'Organization Demography', in Cumming, L. L. and Staw, B. M. (eds): *Research in Organizational Behavior*. Greenwich CT: JAI Press.

Raaum, N. and Skogerbø, E. (1993), 'Statsvitenskap og politisk (s)kjønn', *Norsk Statsvitenskapelig Tidsskrift*, Vol. 9, 3:201-218.

Røberg, V. (1991), Politikkutforming gjennom personellrekruttering? Oslo: Department of political science, University of Oslo. Dissertation.

Skard, T. and Haavio-Mannila, E. (1986), 'Equality between the Sexes - Myth or Reality in Norden?', in Graubard, S. R. (ed.): *Norden - The Passion for Equality*. Oslo: Norwegian University Press.

Skjeie, H. (1986), 'Likestillingspolitikk som personalpolitikk - om kvotering ved ansettelser i staten', *Tidsskrift for samfunnsforskning*, Vol. 27:52-76.

Skjeie, H. (1992), *Den politiske betydningen av kjønn*. Rapport nr. 11. Oslo: Institutt for samfunnsforskning.

SOU 1990:44. Demokrati och makt i Sverige.

South, J. S et al. (1982), 'Social structure and intergroup interaction: Men and women of the federal bureaucracy', *American Sociological Review*, Vol. 47:587-599

Stigen, I. M. (1989), 'Demografisk profil og mulige effekter av denne - En analyse av kollegiale organer knyttet til etatenes sentralledelse', in Egeberg, M. (ed.): *Institusjonspolitikk og forvaltningsutforming*. Oslo: Tano.

Strand, T. (1993), 'Bureaucrats and other managers: roles in transition', in Eliassen, K. A. and Kooiman, J. (eds): *Managing Public Organizations*. London: Sage.

Yoder, J. D. (1991), 'Rethinking Tokenism: Looking Beyond Numbers', *Gender & Society*, Vol. 5, 2:178-192.

Women in local democracy[1]

Nina Cecilie Raaum

From state feminism to local democracy?

Through rapid and extensive mobilization during the 1970s and 1980s Nordic women increased their numbers in political bodies and brought new issues to the political agenda (Dahlerup 1993, Hernes 1987, Raaum 1994, Skjeie 1991). The gender gap of political power is definitely not closed yet, but it has been continuously declining since the 1960s. A similar transition is not evident in any other part of the world, and while international literature on women and politics most often stresses patriarchal traits of state and society, some Scandinavian feminists have lately developed more positive perspectives. The Nordic democracies are considered as a state form that may transform into woman-friendly societies and polities (Hernes 1987, Siim 1988). This development is a result of an alliance between the state and women. Agitation from *below*, ie the political mobilization of women, and state feminism from *above*, ie policy designed to solve social and economic problems particularly to enhance gender equality, characterizes these systems (Hernes 1987:135,162).[2]

The political position of Nordic women is most often examined at macro level, using national statistics and survey data. The aim of this article is to go beyond the national average figures, and explore the position of women at the *local* level. Do most local governments promote a gender equal citizenship, or do they to varying

---

1. I would like to thank Ottar Hellevik and Per Selle for comments on earlier versions of the paper, and Ole Johan Eikeland and Tor Midtbø for methodological advice.

2. The assertion that the welfare policies empower women is controversial. Scandinavian experiences have shown that the feminization of the welfare state has two contradictory aspects concerning women; the oppresssive side, and the supportive side (Hernes 1984, Siim 1988). Firstly, women have been subsumed to a new form of public hierarchies and dependence (Siim 1988). There has been a transition from private to public dependence (Hernes 1987). On the other hand, women have gained power as mothers, workers and citizens to an extent which makes it appropriate to label the Norwegian state form as 'state feminism' (Hernes 1987).

degrees engender local democracy? In exploring this question, the mobilization from below is of primary interest. Why?

Up to the 1980s local welfare policies were strongly regulated by central government. The Nordic countries have taken an interventionist role in regulating tasks that in many other countries have been regarded as predominately private affairs. State legislation has to a large extent defined national goals and standards, while regional and local governments primarily have been responsible for their implementation. The degree of state regulation has varied sectorwise, and important matters for women, such as policies concerning care for children and the elderly, have mainly been a local responsibility. Local authorities have been free to regulate matters that are not explicitly the responsibility of the state, but due to economic reasons most local governments have taken few measures beyond state orders. However, the responsibility of local authorities implies that the expansion of the welfare state is primarily through the local level, and the concept welfare municipalities is in many ways more appropriate than 'welfare state' (Nagel 1992). Accordingly, the significance of the public sector to women, and vice versa, mainly finds expression at the local level. In 1990 local governmental spending amounted to about 20 percent of the gross national product, and about 70 percent of public expenditure. Local authorities employed 74 percent of the public employees, and about 70 percent of these were women (Central Bureau of Statistics, 1992).

Measuring the impact of public welfare provisions on the position of women in local democracy is an extremely complicated matter. A standard level of living certainly depends on both public and private welfare, and increasing public expenditure does not necessarily mean increasing welfare. Besides, and *more important*, even if we could stipulate to what extent local policy empowers women, we would not grasp what democracy is all about, namely *participation* in public *decision-making*. A woman-friendly policy may be a necessary, but never a sufficient condition for realizing an equal citizenship. Woman-friendly policies combined with low female participation can - at best - be characterized as woman-friendly paternalism, at least as long as the non-participation of women does not follow from deliberate choice. The fundamental question concerning the position of women in local democracy is therefore women's *involvement in local politics*.

Data on women's political participation in local decision-making is only available concerning representation in elected bodies. The discussion is thus concentrated on the recruitment of women to *local councils*. This approach will only expose formal aspects of local democracy. Nonetheless, representation in local councils is a most important channel in local decision-making. The councillors are elected every fourth year, and the councils are the superior political bodies of the municipalities. Furthermore, members of various local political bodies, such as executive committees of local councils and various sector-committees,[3] are indirectly elected by the councilors, who themselves often hold central positions in these committees.

The rosy picture of Nordic gender equality is challenged by data on female representation in local councils. On average women hold a lower percentage of positions in elected bodies at the local as compared to the national level. Contrary to most countries, where female representation is often more extensive in local politics, the pyramid in many of the Nordic countries is inverted (Raaum 1995). Besides, aggregate national figures conceal wide *territorial discrepancies*. At the end of the 1970s women captured almost 60 percent of the council seats in some local governments, while in others they were totally absent. A similar picture has existed in all Nordic countries (Sinkkonen 1985). This indicates that the activation of women can not be explained solely by different individual resources or by patriarchal traits of the state and society at large. We have to distinguish between different types of local contexts too.

My approach is basically ecological. By letting municipalities ('kommune')[4] constitute the unit of analysis, I explore the varying female representation in time and space. I concentrate on Norway for two main reasons. Firstly, Norway is an especially interesting case. Norwegian women constitute nearly 40 percent of the members in parliament, and since 1985 they have occupied between 42 and 45 percent of the cabinet positions. At the same time, and in spite of the fact that four out of the seven largest parties have introduced gender quotas to secure 40 percent women members, Norway still has a local council without a single woman councillor. Secondly, the Norwegian Commune Data Base offers a unique quantity

---

3. The sector committees are subordinated to the local councils, and responsible for distinct policy areas, such as public health and social services, education, culture, environmental and technical matters, economy and personnel management.

4. The Norwegian system of government consists of three district levels: the national (statlig), regional (fylkesskommunale), and local (kommunale). The regional level consists of 18 regional administrative entities. The local level includes 439 'kommune'. I use the concept 'municipality' as a synonym for 'kommune'.

of local statistics that makes possible empirical analysis of *all* Norwegian municipalities.[5]

I shall address two main questions. First, how does the political mobilization of women vary through time and space? *When* did women enter local councils, and how is the variation in the number of female councillors affected by the extensive mobilization of women in the 1970s and 1980s? Furthermore, *where* geographically do we find the various degrees of female representation today? Second, *why* does female mobilization, within the same 'woman-friendly' state, vary across municipalities? Do we find clear *structural, cultural or political* differences between municipalities with varying female representation, and what is the *relative impact* of these factors? To answer this question I first carry out a multivariate regression analysis of all municipalities, and then examine the most extreme cases.

Lags in time and space

The political mobilization of Norwegian women occurs in different *stages*. Up to World War II, following the introduction of universal suffrage in 1913, it took approximately 20-30 years before the difference in voter turnout between male and female was reduced to less than 10 percent. The debate on prohibition in the 1920s and the referenda on the sale of alcohol mobilized women to vote, but it was not until the parliamentary election of 1936 and the local election of 1947 that the turnout was less than 10 percent in men's favor (Means 1973). Because of the extremely small number of women elected before 1945, a comparative analysis of the percentage of women in local councils before the second world war is of little interest (Rokkan 1970).

The second stage, up to 1970, is characterized by equal voting turnout, and a decreasing number of local councils with men only. However, in the early post-war years, relatively few women were elected. The national average of female representation increased by only about 1 percent in each election up to the 1970s. However, as shown in Table 1, there has been a steady decline in the number of

---

5. The Commune Data Base is built up by the Norwegian Social Science Data Services (NSD) in Bergen, and contains statistics for all municipal units of administration in Norway since 1976. Almost 108,000 variables are available on each unit, covering areas such as demographic and occupational information, electoral statistics, public economy and welfare state related statistics. The empirical analysis is solely my responsibility.

purely male councils in the entire period. Nevertheless, up until the local election of 1955, the majority of local councils in Norway lacked female members. The number of purely 'male councils' showed a particularly sharp decrease in the 1960s, though the number of female representatives was still so low that it almost did not show up in the national average.

Table 1

Number of municipalities (communes), percentage of local councils without female representation, and national averages of female councillors on local municipal councils

Year	Number of communes	Local councils without women		% women of councillors (national average)
		N	%	
1945	744	501	67	3,4
1947	744	434	58	4,8
1951	744	369	50	5,8
1955	744	298	40	6,4
1959	732	281	38	6,0
1963	525	177	34	6,3
1967	451	78	17	9,5
1971	444	22	5	14,8
1975	445	16	4	15,4
1979	454	4	1	22,8
1983	454	3	1	23,8
1987	448	0	0	31,2
1991	439	1	0	28,5

Source: Central Bureau of Statistics of Norway (1993): Local Municipal Elections 1991

What was the background for the change in the 1960s? As we see in Table 1, the number of municipalities was drastically reduced in this period. Structural reforms cut the number of municipalities from 732 in 1959 to 451 in 1967. During the course of a mere eight years, more than 280 small municipalities were incorporated into existing larger ones, or joined together to form new, larger entities. Thus the merging of municipalities served as a *catalyst* for the mobilization of women. This implied that the smaller and more peripheral municipalities, in which men, and women even more so, were politically activated at a late stage were incorporated into the larger, more central ones. In the 1955 election, 116 municipalities still had no, or only one party list (Rokkan 1970:195). After the merging of the municipalities, several political parties were able to enter in the majority of municipalities. The merging thus *politicized the municipalities*, and the mobilization of women picked up speed with the increasing party competition. This phenomenon is well-known from comparative studies of national electoral systems, which show that the representation of women is higher in proportional systems as compared to single member district systems (Matland 1993, Lovenduski and Norris 1993).

The merging of the municipalities, and a subsequent simplification of the sector-committee system during the 1980s, in which the total number of representatives was cut by more than 50000, implied that the number of positions being competed for was drastically reduced (Raaum 1995). If the system was characterized by patriarchal structures and norms, we might expect that the reforms would cause a stagnation in the political mobilization of women. In reality, however, the effect was the opposite. The elimination of municipalities and committees also represented an elimination of men: a large number of men dropped out of politics at the same time as women were called in.

The politicization of the municipalities was soon followed by a general radicalization and *politicization of women* at the end of the 1960s. During the third stage of women's mobilization, in the 1970s, women increased their relative number as ordinary representatives, but they remained highly underrepresented as political leaders. During the next decade, the last stage of the mobilization process, there was a relatively more comprehensive mobilization of women to elite positions (Raaum 1995). We recognize this gradual development from Stein Rokkan's comprehensive studies of the mobilization of new groups, ie workers and women, from the end of the 19th century. Rokkan shows how mobilization and activation concerning participation in general elections, membership in political parties and political representation, is *time-lagged* and shows considerable *geographical variations*.

In 1963 the proportion of women councillors in Norway ranged from 0 to 33 percent. The range increased to 57 and 59 percent respectively in 1971 and 1979 (Sinkkonen 1985). In the present election period the range is still 57 percent. Table 2 illustrates that Norway is not a special case in this regard. Up until the 1980s all Nordic countries had councils without female representation, but the range has grown during the 1970s and the 1980s. In Sweden, which leads as far as the average of female representation is concerned (Dahlerup 1988, Raaum 1995), every municipality has had female councillors since 1982. Today, only Iceland and Norway still have councils without women councillors, but there is still an extensive gap between the minimum and maximum 'kommunes' in all Nordic countries.

However, the range only tells us that *at least one* local government enters into each
extreme category, and gives no information about the distribution between the
extremes. Are these extremes just an indication of a few deviant cases, while most
local governments take a position close to the national average, or is the distribution
really skewed?

Table 2
The proportions of councils without women, and the range of female
representation in Nordic countries

Country and year of election	Total number of munici-palities	No women councillors, % of councils	Proportion of women councillors (Range) Minimum (%)	Maximum (%)
Denmark 1966	1108	42.0	0	43
1981	275	0.0	5	53
1985	275	0.7	0	53
1989[1]	275	0.0	6	60
Finland 1968	536	17.0	0	33
1980	461	0.4	0	48
1984	461	0.2	0	49
1988	461	0.0	5	48
Iceland 1974	224	84.0	0	29
1982	224	50.0	0	43
1986	224	36.0	0	60
Norway 1963	525	33.7	0	33
1971	444	5.0	0	57
1987	448	0.0	0	65
1991[2]	439	0.1	0	57
Sweden 1971	464	2.0	0	[3]
1982	279	0.0	12	38
1986	279	0.0	12	46
1988	279	0.0	15	49

Source: Sinkkonen (1985:90); Dahlerup (1988:19); [1] *Central Statistical Office of Denmark,
Befolkning og valg (Population and elections) 1990:50;* [2] *Central Statistical Office of Norway:
Local elections 1991.* [3] *Data not available (Sinkkonen 1985, Dahlerup 1988).*

Table 3
Proportion of councils with varying female representation, 1963-1991

Year	Min.	Q1	Mean[1]	Q3	Max.	STD
1963[2]	0.0	0.0	5.5	9.5	33.0	5.5
1967	0.0	4.0	8.5	12.9	32.6	6.5
1971	0.0	7.4	13.3	17.7	57.5	8.6
1975	0.0	9.5	14.5	19.1	46.2	7.4
1979	0.0	13.8	21.0	26.8	59.2	9.5
1983	0.0	17.2	22.5	28.6	47.1	8.4
1987	9.5	23.8	30.1	35.9	64.9	8.5
1991	0.0	23.1	27.7	33.3	57.1	8.6

[1] *The mean is slightly lower than the national average figures shown in Table 1. The reason for this is that the national average of female councillors is calculated as the relative number of women of all representatives, while the mean in this table is calculated on the basis of each local council. Because the proportion of women decreases slightly with size of the council (number of representatives), the mean is a little lower here. Since I am concerned with local variations there is no point in weighting the data.*
[2] *Data is only available for 353 out of 525 communes.*

Table 3 presents the distributions in Norway from 1963 to 1991, by displaying extreme scores (minimum and maximum), the 25th and 75th percentiles (Q1 and Q3), mean and standard deviation (STD), for each election. The numbers within the lower and upper quartile have been steadily increasing. The increase seems to be the strongest every second election, but up to the election of 1991 neither Q1 nor Q3 drops in any election. The interquartile range (Q1-Q3) is relatively stable. In 1963 more than 25 percent of the municipalities had councils without female councillors (Q1), while women contributed to at least 9.5 percent of the councillors in 25 percent of the municipalities. The interquartile range is still about 10 percent, but the number has changed quite dramatically. In the low quartile women constitute 23.1 percent or less of the councillors, while in the high quartile they constitute at least 33.3 percent of the council members. However, the relative size of the standard deviation as compared to the mean illustrates that the dispersion decreases during the three decades. In 1963 the value of the mean equalized the standard deviation, while in 1991 the size of the standard deviation is reduced to one third of the mean. The territorial differences in female representation are obviously declining.

Note that the maximum figure rises and falls every second election. The reason for this can probably be traced back to the Norwegian election system of preferential voting. At local elections the voters are allowed to express candidate preferences by altering party lists. By deleting, adding or cumulating candidates, and by changing the order of the candidates, the voter can clearly affect the candidate selection - and thereby the composition of the councils. About 40 percent of the voting slips were changed in 1991. The amount of preferential voting has a great impact on the election result - especially concerning candidates that are not cumulated (candidates that are put up twice on the list) by the political parties. In every election since 1957 preferential voting has affected the recruitment of women councillors negatively; the percentage of women councillors has been reduced by 5-10 percent as compared to the result that would have followed from the party lists themselves (Hellevik and Bjørklund 1991). The voters seem to be more conservative than the parties concerning female candidates.

The election of 1991 brought a decrease in the national average of women councillors, from 31.2 to 28.5 percent (see Table 1). The decrease implied a drop in every distribution score, i.e. it seemed to affect most municipalities. In the public debate following the election many maintained that the declining national average signalled a 'backlash' in the political mobilization of women. This is probably not true, or at least not the entire story. First of all, it should be noted that in spite of the slight decrease in female representation in local councils, the election of 1991 brought relatively more women into political élite positions - as members of executive committees of local councils, as leaders of the sector committees and as mayors (Raaum 1995). Secondly, the time series indicate that the deviant election was that of 1987 rather than that of 1991. Figure 1 shows this quite clearly.[6] For example, after the election of 1979, when the national average of female councillors increased from 15.4 percent to 22.8 percent, the proportion of councils which were

---

6. The figure is based on the following data showing the percentage of councils with the varying percentages of women representatives.

Female councillors	1963	1967	1971	1975	1979	1983	1987	1991
-20%	82.7	95.2	84.2	81.9	50.3	43.1	13.2	20.7
21-30%	16.4	4.6	12.8	16.9	36.0	40.2	38.9	44.9
31-40%	0.6	0.2	1.8	1.8	10.5	14.7	37.3	27.1
41% +	0.3	0.0	1.4	0.2	3.1	2.0	10.6	7.7

Figure 1
Female representation in local councils, 1963-1991. Percentage of councils.
N=439.[6]

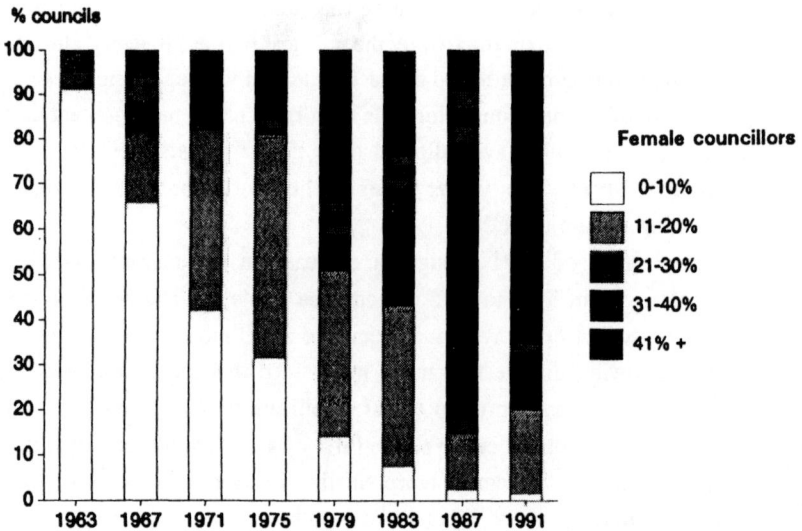

more than 20 percent female increased from 19 percent to 50 percent. As a consequence of the 1983 election, the percentage of councils in which more than 20 percent of the members were women increased to 57 percent, although the national average increased by only 0.6 percent. Nevertheless, in 43 percent of the municipalities, women still accounted for 20 percent of the councillors or less. Setting aside the 'deviant' election of 1987, today only 21 percent of the councils have such a poor representation of women. The election of 1991 may appear as a 'backlash' compared to the election of 1987, but compared to all other elections the figures are high. We need at least one more election before we can start talking about a 'backlash'. However, there are still considerable differences across municipalities with regard to female representation. The next question thus is: what territorial pattern follows as a consequence of the time-lag? In other words, *where* do we find the most and least 'women-friendly' municipalities?

Rokkan (1970) demonstrates that up to the 1960s the timing of female electoral mobilization varies both between central and peripheral regions, as well as between urban and rural municipalities within the same regions. The 'kommune' within the central provinces of the East were the first to reach a high level of politicization, while the peripheral municipalities of the outer provinces, most obviously the fisheries communities along the coast in the West and the North, lagged furthest behind. To be able to compare with Rokkan's findings the municipalities are classified according to his center-periphery cleavage model, by distinguishing between *cities and rural* communes, and *five regions*: The East, the South-West, the North-West, Mid-Norway and the North of Norway,[7] including a total of eighteen counties and 439 municipalities. The impact of the center-periphery dimension within the regions is analyzed using the concept of *centrality*. This variable consists of four categories, ranging from municipalities with no densely populated areas, to the most densely populated areas.[8]

The East region includes the urban municipalities surrounding the capital, as well as more rural municipalities at greater distances from the capital area. The central 'kommune' of the East were the first to be commercialized and industrialized, while the more peripheral ones dominated by primary industry lagged behind. In the Eastern region and in Mid-Norway Rokkan found the great majority of the municipalities completely politicized as regards voting turnout and the spread of party

---

7. This classification differs somewhat from Rokkan's typology. Rokkan split the region of the East into two categories: the inner region around Oslofjorden and the outer East region. However, when controlled for by centrality, the peripheral municipalities in the East region include a high number of the municipalities in the outer East region (see figure 2).

8. Centrality means the geographical position of the municipalities, in relation to one or more centres with main functions and institutions. The variable is recoded from the index of centrality, constructed by the Norwegian Central Bureau of Statistics in 1984. It originally contained 7 categories, recoded in the following way: 1 and 4=1, 2 and 5=2, 3 and 6=3, 7=4. The recoded variable of centrality has the following categories: *Category 1:* the municipality has no densely populated areas; *category 2:* the municipality includes a densely populated area at level 1, or is situated within 45 minutes of travel to such an area, normally between 5 and 10,000 inhabitants; *category 3:* the municipality includes a densely populated area at level 2, or is situated within 60 minutes of travel to such an area, normally between 10,000-50,000 inhabitants; *category 4:* the municipality includes a densely populated areal at level 3 and functions as a regional center, normally minimum 50,000 inhabitants. According to this operationalization, the percentage of the most peripheral municipalities (category 1) is highest in the North (80 percent) and lowest in the East (35 percent). In the South-West 41 percent of the municipalities are classified as peripheral, while the figure for the North-West and Mid-Norway is about 65 percent.

politics. On the contrary, 'kommune' in the South and West and particularly along the coast in the North, showed the lowest level of politicization (Rokkan 1970:196). Rokkan accordingly identified the South-West and the North regions as the most peripheral, though he emphasized important political differences between them. The so-called countercultures, ie the teetotalist movement, the religious layman movement and the vernacular movement - represented a strong tradition of territorial and cultural opposition to the national center in the South. Even the industrializing municipalities in the South-West were characterized by a low level of politicization.

Figure 2
Female councillors in peripheral (P) and central (C) 'kommune' in five regions.
Percent of councils, N=439 municipalities

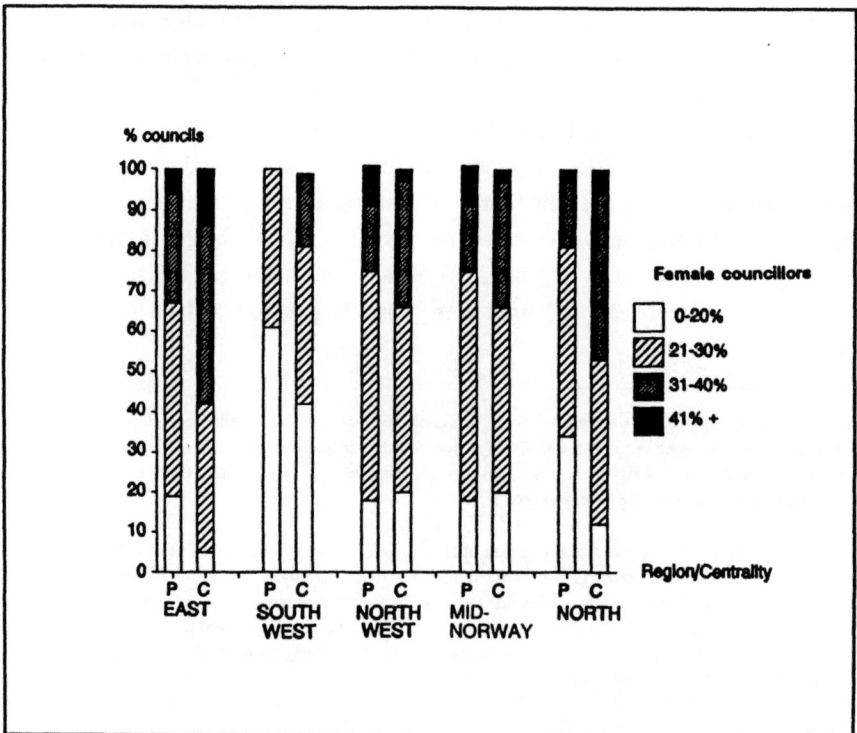

The North region, though, was traditionally marked by class polarization, and tended toward a stronger politicization in industrializing municipalities. The North region is still the most peripheral region in terms of the economy, but, because of the oil economy, the South-West is by no means an economically peripheral region any more. The counterculture is still the strongest in this region, though it has declined also here. However, in spite of that the traditional characteristics of the regions may have changed, the impact of regional differences related to the political cleavage structures are actually characterized by a high degree of continuity (Valen, Aardal and Vogt 1990).

Table 4 indicates the territorial variation of the representation of women in the present election period (1992-1995). It demonstrates a pattern quite similar to Rokkan's findings, but there are interesting differences as well. The range of the percentages of women councillors is lowest in Mid-Norway, and largest in the East and North-West. The figures illustrate that the East and South-West regions are still the most different. On average women constitute 31 percent of the councillors in the East region, compared to only 21 percent in the South-West. Similarly, the highest percentage of female council members occurs in the East region, while the 'kommune' governed by men only occur in the South-West. Nearly 50 percent of the councils in the East, but only 11 percent of the councils in the South-West, have *more* than 30 percent women. Actually, women make up less than one out of five councillors in 50 percent of the South-West municipalities. Corresponding percentages for the East, North-West, Mid-Norway and the North are 10, 18, 27 and 17.

There are two imporant differences compared to Rokkan's findings. Firstly, the representation of women in the North-West region is now far better than in the South-West. Secondly, the North region, where Rokkan found so many 'extreme periphery kommune', now is second highest concerning both average of female councillors and proportion of councils with more than 30 percent women. The South-West seems to hold its position as the most 'backward' region concerning female representation, while the differences between the other regions are actually declining. This is in accordance with Bjørklund and Hellevik (1987) who find that regional variation decreased from 1945 to 1983, and suggest that differences between central and peripherial municipalities within the regions have increased.

Table 4
Percentage of councils with different proportion of women councillors in five regions and in cities and rural municipalities (N=439)

% female councillors	East	South West	North West	Mid-Norway	North	City	Rural
0-10%	0	7	1	2	1	0	2
11-20%	10	43	17	25	16	2	21
21-30%	42	39	53	45	46	39	46
31-40%	38	11	21	25	27	50	24
41-50%	10	0	6	4	10	0	1
51%+	1	0	1	0	0	0	1
Total	101	100	99	101	100	100	101
(N)	(147)	(56)	(98)	(49)	(89)	(46)	(393)
	30	21	27	27	29		
Mean	12	0	10	10	9	31	27
Min.	57	36	54	44	49	18	0
Max.						42	57

East: County 1-8; Østfold, Akershus, Oslo, Hedmark, Oppland, Buskerud, Vestfold, Telemark.
South-West: County 9-11; Rogaland, Aust-Agder and Vest-Agder.
North-West: County 12-15; Hordaland, Sogn- and Fjordande and Møre -and Romsdal.
Mid-Norway: County 16-17; Sør- and Nord-Tøndelag.
North: County 18-20; Nordland, Troms and Finmark.

Our data verify that women councillors are more numerous in cities than in rural areas. In almost 60 percent of the cities women constitute more than 30 percent of the councillors, while in rural municipalities 65 percent of the municipalities have 30 percent or fewer female representatives.[9] Rokkan (1970) demonstrates that up to the 1960s the strongest time-lag concerning peripheral municipalities occured in the North and the two regions of the West. Figure 2 illustrates that the impact of

---

9. The differences between cities and rural municipalities are found in the East, the North-West arid the North regions, but are not significant for the two other regions.

centrality on female mobilization still differs from one region to another. Just like before the 1970s the impact of centrality is strongest in the South-West (r= .40). There is also a clear effect in Mid-Norway and the East (r= .37 and .31 respectively). But, contrary to Rokkan's findings, centrality is of less importance in the North (r= .15), and not significant in the North-West region (r= -.03). Figure 2 illustrates this. In the East, South-West and North we find the traditional pattern; i.e the proportion of female councillors increases with centrality. In the East, where the average of female councillors exceeds the other regions, there are considerable differences between central and peripheral municipalities. Nearly 60 percent of the central municipalities, but only about 30 percent of the peripheral ones, have more than 30 percent female councillors. In the South-West about 60 percent of the municipalities have councils with less than 21 percent women, while in the central municipalities 60 percent of the councils have *more* than 20 percent women.

The impact of centrality differs in the North-West and the Mid-Norway. Compared to the central 'kommune', the peripheral 'kommune' in these regions have a lower percentage of councils with few women (up to 20 percent), and a higher percentage of councils with a high proportion of women (41 percent or more). The varying impact of centrality across regions must be explained by distinctive characteristics of the local contexts. This leads us to our next main question: why does female mobilization, within the same 'woman-friendly state,' vary so considerably in time and space?

The impact of structure, culture and politics

Research on political mobilization indicates that the lags in time and space can be traced back to certain types of structural, cultural and political determinants. I shall briefly discuss the impact of the determinants to be considered in the empirical analysis of the present election period (1992-95).

Structural conditions affecting women's access to local politics are related to both *demographic, territorial and socioeconomic* factors. Demographical variables are the size of the municipality and the age and sex structure. The relative number of women councillors is expected to be higher in large 'kommune' with a relatively young population, than in smaller 'kommune' with an elderly population and a majority of men (Schive 1981, Sinkkonen 1985). The impact of *size* can easily be measured by the number of inhabitants, and population structure by sex is estimated by the number of women pr. 1000 inhabitants. In exploring the effect of age, we could simply measure the impact of increasing average age. However, councillorship demands a relatively long political apprenticeship as compared to other types of political involvement. It thus seems appropriate to define a relevant upper and lower value. By analyzing the impact of the relative number of inhabitants between the age of 30 and 60, ie the 'supply' of those most likely to run for councillorship, rather than the percentage of elderly people only, we get a more adequate measure of the relevant age structure.[10] My expectation is that the relative number of women councillors increases with an increasing number of women per 1000 inhabitants and the share of the population between 30 and 60 years of age.

As for the *territorial* dimension, it has already been demonstrated that female mobilization varies according to both region and centrality within such regions. The reasons for this are probably related to both structural and cultural characteristics. However, in order to understand *why* these differences appear, and to explore the geographical variance in relation to other structural determinants, we need to include both region and centrality in a multivariate analysis. *Region* - which is a discrete variable, is computed as a dummy variable, measuring the differences between the South-West and the other regions, while *centrality* is operationalized in the same way as earlier (see note 9), ranging from municipalities with no densely populated areas to municipalities with the most densely populated areas.

The center-periphery cleavage is closely related to *socioeconomic* structures. Rokkan (1970) found that the mobilization of women was markedly higher in urbanized and industrialized municipalities as compared to agricultural and primary-sector areas. Later studies confirm that women councillors are most numerous in urban and industrialized regions (Bjørklund and Hellevik 1987, Schive 1981, Sinkkonen 1985). The effect of economic structure is measured by *percent of labour employed in the primary sector*. In accordance with previous research I assume that an extensive primary sector hinders the mobilization of women. In addition, I examine the primary impact of standard of living by using an index of *local welfare* constructed by the Central Bureau of Statistics. This index contains 17 different variables, covering general living conditions, such as rate of unemployment and average income of the population, as well as variables measuring local welfare provisions, such as policies concerning care of the elderly and children. On the basis of public statistics the 'kommune' are classified into four categories for each variable, ranging from the 25 percent of the municipalities at the lowest end (value

---

10. Statistically the percentage of the population between 18 and 30 (the rest of the population with the right to vote) has only a weak positive effect on the proportion of female councillors (r .09).

1), to the 25 percent of municipalities at the highest end (value 4). On the basis of these indicators a simple additive index is constructed, with a minimum value at 18 and maximum value at 68.[11] The index reflects both public welfare provisions that may relieve women from responsibility of caring, as well as factors which are commonly acknowledged to enhance political participation. The proportion of women councillors should thus very likely increase with growing level of welfare.

Cultural determinants are hard to define precisely - both theoretically and empirically. Culture serves as a cognitive filter, i.e. as a link between structures and actions, but it neither mirrors structures directly, nor is it the mere aggregate of individual actions. Thus, culture is embedded in the 'climate' of the municipality - like a context of meaning and a way of life - that surrounds human interaction (Berntzen and Selle 1991). With regard to women's access to local decision-making, the decisive aspect of political culture should be the ideological climate concerning gender, i.e. the overall attitude towards women's public and private roles. If the dominant culture is in favor of traditional female roles, it should affect the proportion of women councillors in a negative way. When the political culture reflects a more progressive and friendly attitude toward the new roles of women, the proportion of female councillors should increase.

Political culture can certainly not be fully tested by quantitative data. However, we may get an indication of the cultural dimension by exploring the impact of factors associated with values of gender-equality. Researchers have considered both education and support for the Christian Democratic Party as empirical cultural indicators. Sinkkonen (1985) finds that cultural modernization, measured by level of

---

11. The index consists of the following variables: (1) level of unemployment: percentage of unemployed men, 20-66 years old, first quarter of 1991, (2) level of education: percentage of population with grade school (primary school) only, 1989, (3) percentage of population between 16 and 18 in secondary education, 1989, (4) medical practitioner: number of man-labour year per 1000 inhabitants, 1989 (5) physiotherapy: number of man-labour year pr. 1000 inhabitants, 1989, (6) after-school child care for school children up to about the age of 10, 1989, (7) daycare-facilities, promotion of preschool children enrolled,1989, (8) geographical mobility: net migration per 1000 inhabitants, 1990, (9) social security: number of clients per 1000 inhabitants who receive economic assistance, 1989, (10) number of recipients of disability benefits/pensions, percent of population 1989, (11) number of crimes per 1000 inhabitants, 1987-89, (12) home help: number of hours per inhabitant of 67 years or more, 1989, (13) community nursing: number of man-year per 1000 inhabitants of 67 years or more, 1989, (14) average income, 1989, (15) gross income of the municipality per inhabitants 1989, (16) traffic accidents, number of individuals killed or injured in the 'kommune' per 1000 inhabitants, 1989, (17) deaths per 1000 inhabitants, 60-74 years old, 1989-90.
All variables range from 1 to 4, except geographical mobility and after-school child care which have two values (least and most mobility, and have/do not have after-school child care). In addition, level of unemployment which is given double weight (ie value 2,4,6,8).

education, is among those variables that provide the best explanation of the spread of women councillors in Finland in the 1960s and 1970s. Schive (1981) analyzes the impact of culture in Norway by looking at support for the Christian Democratic Party, a party stressing the maintenance of traditional values and gender roles. The level of education obviously is an adequate indicator of modernizing gender-roles, but the other indicator is in many ways problematic. The Christian Democratic Party certainly defends traditional family-values, but compared to other Norwegian parties women are fairly well represented both in the party organization and in elected bodies. Advocacy of traditional family-values is obviously *not* to be considered equal to the exclusion of women from public decision-making.[12]

An alternative approach, however, is to turn the question around, and look for political parties that stress gender equality. In Norway the Socialist Left Party, the Labour Party and the Liberal Party have been practicing gender quotas for about ten years.[13] In order to measure the impact of *gender-egalitarian culture* it seems reasonable to examine the combined effect of educational level and percentage of votes supporting the gender-quota parties. For this purpose I have constructed an index of 8 categories, ranging from the most traditional cultures, i.e relatively low support in favor of the gender-quotas parties and a low proportion of women with a college- or university-level education, to the most gender-egalitarian culture, i.e. a high proportion of votes supporting gender-quota parties and a high proportion of women with a high education.[14] The assumption is that the number of women councillors rises in municipalities characterized by the most gender-egalitarian culture.

Political determinants of female representation concern both the process of candidate selection and distinctive features of the electoral system. Political parties

12. Women constituted 52 percent of the party members in 1986, and respectively 43, 45, 33 and 50 percent of representatives in the national congress, the national committee, the national executive committee and the working committees. In the 1991 election the Christian Democratic Party got 7.8 percent of the votes. About 60 percent of the votes came from women. On average the party represents 8 percent of local councillors. Women constitute 30 percent of the representatives, ie about the same amount as the national average (28.5 percent). (See Heidar and Raaum 1995).

13. In the present election period the Socialist Left Party, the Labour Party and the Liberal Party have respectively 10, 32 and 4 percent of the local councillors. The percentage of female members is correspondingly 44, 31 and 31. The agrarian Center Party, which has only practiced gender quotas for five years (since 1989), is not included in the analysis.

14. Voter turnout in favor of the gender-quotation is divided into 3 categories:
(1) less than 35 percent, (2) 35-54 percent, (3) 55 percent or more. Concerning the distribution of women's higher education, the 'kommune' are dichotomized as high and low on the basis of the population mean.

have a vital function as a main link between citizens and government by structuring the electoral choice through recruiting council candidates (Lovenduski and Norris 1993). First of all, the relative number of elected women depends on the percentage of women among *nominated* and *cumulated candidates*. As cumulated candidates appear twice on the party list, they thus have a double chance of being elected. The percentage of women among nominated candidates, and even more so of cumulated candidates, should have a strong impact on the election of women councillors.

As regards the impact of cumulations we must also pay attention to the consequences of the voters' candidate preferences, i.e. the *amount of preferential voting*. With reference to the so-called women coups in the 1970s, preferential voting is commonly perceived as an arrangement which enhances female representation. As mentioned earlier, though, it generally results in the opposite. Most probably, we will therefore find the number of female councillors declining when preferential voting increases.

Furthermore, we should also explore the relevance of *district magnitude*, ie the number of seats in the electoral district, ie the 'kommune', and the degree of proportionality in the electoral system. Research on national electoral systems demonstrates that both variables prove to have a significant positive effect on female representation (Matland 1993, Lovendunski and Norris 1993). Analogous effects may occur at the local level. The number of council seats is, of course, closely related to the number of inhabitants, but even in the smallest 'kommune' we find considerable variance in the size of the councils. For example, in municipalities with fewer than 4000 inhabitants the number of councillors varies from 13 up to 29, and even in municipalities with fewer than 2000 inhabitants the range varies between 13 and 21 councillors. With reference to national elections, Matland (1993) suggests that female mobilization may pick up speed with increasing district magnitude, because men do not need to be deposed in order for women to gain slots on the party list. Correspondingly, the exclusion of women from local council may be less legitimate when the number of council members is relatively high. Considering the fractionalization of the party system, Rokkan (1970) found that the time-lag of female mobilization was largest in the least politicized municipalities with only one or no party list. We have also seen that the merging of Norwegian municipalities in the 1960s, which increased the district magnitude and intensified the partisan competition for votes, brought a sharp decrease in the number of purely male councils. It can thus be anticipated that the mobilization of female councillors is positively related to both district magnitude and the fractionalization of the party system. District

Table 5
Percentage of female councillors by structural, cultural and political factors.
Bivariate effect (r), unadjusted (B) and adjusted (beta) effects. N=439.

	r	B	beta	B	beta	B	Beta
Structure:							
REGION	-.29	-7.366	-.28	-5.938	-.23	-2.778	-.10
PRIMARY	-.24	-.115	-.13	-.074	-.08	-.061	-.07
POPAGE	.30	.378	.10	.132	.04	-.056	-.02
SIZE	.17	.00003	.09	.00003	.09	.00002	.07
CENTRAL	.20	.475	.07	.9166	.13	.535	.07
WELFARE	-.13	-.048	-.03	.026	.02	-.012	-.01
POPSEX	.10	-.025	-.03	-.041	-.07	-.083	-.11
Culture:							
EGALIT	.36			.899	.24	.391	.10
Politics:							
PREFVOT	-.43					-.129	-.27
CUMWOM	.33					.147	.20
NOMWOM	.28					.387	.19
MAGNIT	.20					-.004	-.01
EFFPART	-.13					-.576	-.03
		a=30.0 R²= .16		a=38.05R²=.25		a=57.33 R²=.32	

REGION: dummy variable (South-West=1, Other regions=0).
PRIMARY: percentage of labour employed in primary sector.
POPAGE: population structure by age (percentage of population between 30-60).
SIZE: number of inhabitants.
CENTRAL: centrality (densely populated areas).
WELFARE: index of private welfare and public welfare provisions.
POPSEX: population structure by sex (women pr. 1000 inhabitants).
EGALIT: gender-egalitarian culture.
PREFVOT: preferential voting, percent of ballot paper altered by the voters.
CUMWOM: percentage of women of cumulated candidates.
NOMWOM: percentage of women of nominated candidates.
MAGNIT: district magnitude (number of candidates running for election).
EFFPART: effective parties (N), degree of fractionalization of party system.

magnitude is simply measured by the number of seats in the local council. The degree of proportionality, i.e. the fractionalization of the party system, is measured by '*the effective number of components (N)*' (Taagepera and Soberg Shugart 1989). This index is based on the number of party lists, and measures the effect of party fractionalization by taking into account the relative size of the parties.[15]

The empirical analysis is conducted through blockwise regression analysis, by first introducing variables of structure, then culture, and lastly politics.[16] Table 5 displays the bivariate and controlled effects. At the bivariate level all indicators, except for two, affect the percentage of female councillors in the expected direction. Preferential voting has the strongest negative effect, while gender-egalitarian culture has the most positive effect. Local welfare and the degree of fractionalization of the party system, though, unexpectedly affect female representation negatively.

The structural variables account for only 16 percent of the explained variance. The negative effect of region confirms the relative poor representation of women in the South-West region (r -.29). Furthermore, the effect remains as strong when controlled for by the other structural factors (beta -.28). Women in the South-West have in general a smaller chance of being elected than women in the peripheral municipalities of the other regions. The controlled effects of the other structural variables are considerably weaker as compared to the bivariate relations. Municipalities dominated economically by primary sector and an elderly population are lagging behind, as compared to municipalities with a more modern economy. The sex composition and the level of local welfare bear no significant effect on female representation.

When the impact of culture is taken into consideration the explained variance increases to 25 percent. The positive bivariate effect of culture (r .36) remains clear when controlled for by structural characteristics of the municipalities (beta .24). Furthermore, as compared to every indicator concerning structural and political conditions, culture comes out with the strongest positive effect on the election of women councillors. It should also be noted that culture seems to affect the impact of

---

15. The least arbitrary way is to let the votes' shares 'determine their own weights' in the following way. A party with a fractional share of .40 (that is 40 percent of the votes) also receives a weight of .40, so that the weighted value is 40 x 40 = .16. The result of adding up such weighted values for all party votes is called the Herfindahl-Hirschman concentration index (HH). The effective number of components (N) is defined as the inverse of HH (N=1/HH), and indicates the number of hypothetical equal-sized parties that would have the same effect on fractionalization of the party system. The concentration index HH also leads to what is called the Rae fractionalization index (F), F= 1-HH. N and F is connected through the equation N=1(1-F) (Taagepera and Soberg Shugart 1989:77-81).

16. A test of significance is not applied since the data cover every Norwegian 'kommune'; i.e. the whole population.

structural determinants in different ways.[17] The effect of primary sector and age decreases, while the impact of centrality and sex composition increases. Contrary to research concentrating on the national level (Hernes 1987), it is interesting to note that local welfare, which includes indicators of both private welfare and public welfare provision, has no significant effect (beta 0.02) on the mobilization of women into local government. The so-called 'women-friendliness' is seemingly not a matter of the quantity of welfare, but rather dependent on the ideological climate concerning gender equality.

In introducing the political factors, the amount of explained variance increases to 32 percent. The bivariate effect of district magnitude is, as expected positive, but the effect of party fractionalization surprisingly goes in a negative direction. However, when controlled for by the other variables, the effect of district magnitude becomes insignificant (beta -.01), while party fractionalization decreases slightly (beta -.07). Among the political variables, level of preferential voting has the strongest negative effect on female representation (r -0.43), while the percentage of women among nominated and cumulated candidates has the strongest positive impact (r .28 and .33). The effects decrease when controlled for by the other indicators, but next to preferential voting they are still the most successful determinants of female representation.

All in all, preferential voting has the strongest negative impact on the proportion of female councillors (beta -.27), while the percentage of women of nominated and cumulated candidates have the strongest positive effects (beta .20 and .19). Yet, the proportion of women of nominated and cumulated candidates has less impact on the election of women than could be assumed. The explanation for this may be complex.

---

17. The bivariate effect of structural and cultural variables on the various political variables is measured by r. (See abbreviations in table 4.)

Structure/ Culture	% women of candidates	% women of cumulated	District Magnitude	Effective parties	Preferential voting
Size	.02	.08	.66	.15	-.31
Popage	-.07	.12	.32	.12	-.63
Popsex	-.02	.15	.39	.18	-.41
Region	-.31	-.09	.05	.25	.14
Centrality	-.16	.10	.48	.30	.58
Primary	.17	-.15	-.47	-.27	-.58
Welfare	.10	-.08	-.22	-.10	.27
Culture	.17	.14	.12	-.27	-.47

Actually the figures indicate that all structural and cultural variables affect the various political determinants, however, often in opposite directions. In general, their impact on the percentage of women among nominated and cumulated candidates is relatively weak, but we may be faced with intercorrelatedness among the independent variables. An alternative explantion can be related to the amount of preferential voting and women's placement on the party lists. Unfortunately, it is not possible to explore the impact of such 'placement' using the present data, because it does not contain information about the consecutive order of male and female candidates. But a brief look at preferential voting is worthwhile.

Figure 3
The relation between proportion of female councillors and amount of preferential voting

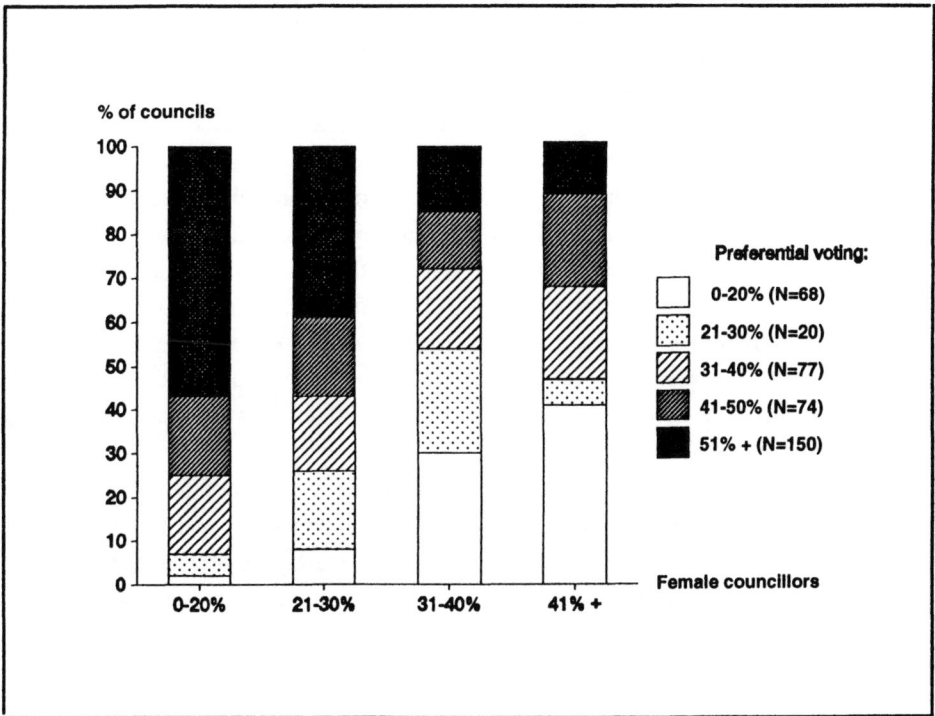

The data contained no information about the sex of the candidates that were exposed to voter preferences, nor about the sex of 'the preferential voters'. I thus examine the amount of preferential voting in relation to varying percentages of female councillors.

Figure 3 demonstrates that women in municipalities with a high level of preferential voting are least likely to be elected as councillors. Generally, the number of women councillors falls with increasing frequency of changing the lists. In nearly 20 percent of the municipalities with less than 21 percent female councillors, more than 51 percent of the ballot papers were altered.

By contrast, in municipalities with more than 40 percent female councillors, only 10 percent of the municipalities have such a high amount of preferential voting. Within the limits of this article it is not possible to explore this phenomenon fully. However, an easy way to get an impression of what this is all about is to change the dependent variable, from the proportion of female councillors to the amount of preferential voting, and introduce the same causal variables as in the former regression model.

Table 6 shows that these variables explain 67 percent of the variance of preferential voting. It is not appropriate to compare this result with the explained variance of female representation, since we examine different phenomena. However, the figures demonstrate two notable differences concerning the contextual variables. Firstly, many of the independent variables that are not significantly related to female representation have a strong impact on the amount of preferential voting. Secondly, the structural variables generally have a stronger impact on the voter's candidate preference than on female councillorship. Furthermore, the effects often go in opposite directions. Preferential voting is most frequent in 'kommune' dominated by traditional gender values, an elderly male-dominated population and low district magnitude. The negative controlled effect of district magnitude on female representation may thus be due to the high level of preferential voting in smaller 'kommunes'. Preferential voting is most prevalent in the less central municipalities, but the negative effect of primary sector is barely significant when controlled for by the other factors.

The controlled effects are weaker than the bivariate ones, but they generally go in the same direction. The only exceptions are 'kommune' size and fractionalization. The fractionalization of the party system is only weakly negatively correlated with preferential voting at the bivariate level, but turns into a positive effect when controlled for by the other indicators (beta .10). By contrast, the number of inhabitants is strongly negatively related to preferential voting at the bivariate level, while the controlled effect is insignificant (beta .04). Last, but not least, 'kommune' with a relatively high percentage of women among cumulated candidates seem to have a low amount of preferential voting, but when controlled for by the other factors this correlation becomes insignificant too.

Table 6
Amount of preferential voting by structural, cultural and political factors. Bivariate
(r) and unadjusted (B) and adjusted (beta) regression coefficients

	r	B	beta
District magnitude	-.60	-.449	-.32
Population structure by age (31-60)	-.63	-2.063	-.27
Gender-egalitarian culture	-.47	-1.639	-.21
Centrality	-.58	-2.765	-.19
Population structure by sex	-.41	-.245	-.15
Effective parties (fractionalization)	-.05	1.772	.10
Size (number of inhabitants)	-.31	.00003	.04
Primary sector	.58	.085	.05
Region (South East)	.14	4.055	.07
% women of cumulated candidates	-.21	-.068	-.04
% women of nominated candidates	.04	.023	-.01
Standard of living	.27	.016	.01
		a=265.2	R^2 = .67

The extreme cases: 'minimum kommune' and 'maximum kommune'

Let us finally examine the most extreme municipalities to see if they may contribute to our understanding. The selected municipalities are those with less than 15 percent female councillors (31 'kommune'), and those with more than 40 percent female councillors (37 'kommune'). I simply call them 'minimum and maximum kommune'. Table 7 describes structural, cultural and political characteristics of the 'minimum and maximum commune' as compared to the national average.

All the 'minimum kommune' are rural, and they are most often situated in the South-West (36 percent) and North (22 percent) regions. On average they have few inhabitants and 81 percent of these municipalities have no densely populated areas. The gender egalitarian culture-score is on average 3.0 (ranging from 1-8), and the standard of living is higher than in the 'maximum kommune' (46 points versus 43).

Table 7

Minimum and maximum 'kommune' as compared to the national average

	Minimum 'kommune'	National figures	Maximum 'kommune'
Number of inhabitants (average)	3.481	9.734	23.518
Region (Percentage of 'kommune'):			
East	19%	34%	49%
South-West	36%	13%	0
North-West	16%	22%	19%
Mid-Norway	6%	11%	5%
North	22%	20%	27%
Standard of living (index: 18-68)	46	43	43
Centrality: no densely populated areas	81%	54%	46%
Labour, primary sector	18%	14%	11%
Gender-egalitarian culture (1-8)	3.0	4.4	5.5
% women of nominated candidates	37%	39%	42%
% women of cumulated candidates	29%	37%	41%
Preferential voting, percent of altered lists	57%	42%	31%
District magnitude (number of candidates)	23	30	32
Effective parties (fractionalization) (0-7.3)	4.5	4.3	3.8
Discrepancy: % nominated - % elected women	-25%	-10%	2%

Women account for nearly 40 percent of the nominated candidates, ie about the same amount as the national average, but only 29 percent of the cumulated candidates, ie 8 percent less than the national average. There is a very high level of preferential voting in these municipalities, and the score on the party fractionalization index is also higher than the national average. As regards district magnitude, the councils of these 'kommunes' have very few seats, on average 7 less than the national average. This demonstrates that the mobilization of women is delayed when the number of elected offices is low. As a consequence, the discrepancy between the percentage of female candidates and female councillors is on the average as high as 25 percent to the disadvantage of women.

The 'maximum kommune' are very different. They are rather big, and are most often situated in the East and, just as the 'minimum kommune', in the North. They are quite densely populated, the standard of living equals the national average, and the political culture reflects gender-egalitarian values. The proportion of women among nominated candidates is quite similar to what we found in the 'minimum kommune', but women constitute a higher share of the cumulated candidates. Contrary to the 'minimum kommune', the 'maximum kommune' have a low score on the party fractionalization index and a high district magnitude. Last, but not least, preferential voting is far less extensive than in the 'minimum kommune'. This implies that the percentage of women among local councillors actually is a little higher, on average 2 percent, than the percentage of women among the candidates on the party lists.

Table 8 displays interesting differences concerning the impact of contextual variables. The correlations go in different directions in 'minimum and maximum kommune'. Concerning the 'minimum kommune', both primary sector, local welfare and preferential voting have a negative impact on the mobilization of women councillors. In the 'maximum kommune', though, these variables are positively related to female councillorship. Contrary to what we have seen so far, preferential voting works in favor of women in the 'maximum kommune'. Similarly, in the 'minimum kommune' both growing number of inhabitants, centrality, egalitarian gender culture, in addition to party magnitude and fractionalization of the party system, bear a positive relationship to the election of women, while in the 'maximum kommune' they are, surprisingly, negatively related to female mobilization. The only variables working in the same direction are percentage of women among nominated and cumulated candidates.

The reasons why women constitute a higher percentage of councillors than candidates in the 'maximum kommune', is probably due to both the positive effect of preferential voting as well as the somewhat higher percentage of women among cumulated candidates. The relatively high district magnitude probably also works in favor of women. Of course, these figures must be taken with a grain of salt, since they do not express the controlled effects, and further analysis of the relationship is necessary to estimate their effect on female representation more precisely.

Table 8
Bivariate effect (r) of structural, cultural and political variables on proportion of women councillors in 'minimum kommune' (less than 15%) and 'maximum kommune' (more than 40%)

Structural, cultural and political factors	Minimum 'kommune'	Maximum 'kommune'
Primary sector	-.32	-.31
Population structure by age	.03	-.31
Size (number of inhabitants)	.39	-.22
Centrality	.12	-.36
Local welfare	-.08	.28
Population structure by sex	-.02	-.13
Gender egalitarian culture	.12	-.06
Amount of preferential voting	-.42	.27
Percent women of nominated candidates	.51	.44
Percent women of cumulated candidates	.14	.44
District magnitude	.37	-.46
Number of effective parties	.32	-.01

In conclusion, the data presents a puzzling picture of the mobilization of women to local councils. Preferential voting is generally most successful in explaining the varying proportion of women in local councils. Except for municipalities with a very high proportion of females, the effect is clearly negative, even when controlled for several structural, cultural and political variables. Furthermore, variables that affect female representation positively often affect preferential voting negatively. All in all, this demonstrates that the effects of structural, cultural and political factors on female mobilization are far more complex than anticipated by previous research. Structure and culture affect the various political factors in different directions, and their impact on female representation seems to depend on combinational effects. To grasp the dynamics of the process of mobilization of women, we obviously need to develop more distinct models concerning different types of municipalities.

Conclusion: structure and culture count, but politics decides

The political mobilization of women varies in time and space. The number of purely 'male councils' declined steadily during the postwar period, though the number of female councillors was so low that it really did not show up in the national average. After the merging of the municipalities in the 1960s, which implied higher district magnitude and intensified party competition, the number of 'male councils' was drastically reduced to only 5 percent in 1971. The 1971 election also represented a take-off in the extensive mobilization of women during the 1970s and 1980s. The time-lagged mobilization is clearly demonstrated by the large variance across municipalities with regard to the percentage of female councillors.

The maximum and minimum figures of female representation increase as a consequence of the extensive mobilization after 1970, and except for one election period (1987-1991), Norway has always had at least one local council without women. Norway is not a special case in this regard. The time-lags of women's mobilization are prevalent are all Nordic countries, and the differences between the minimum and maximum figures are still very high. Norwegian data show that the geographical variation is declining, though. An increasing share of the 'kommune' have a percentage of female councillors closer to the national average.

In 1971, 84 percent of the councils had less than 20 percent women, while, in 1991, only 21 percent of the councils had such poor female representation. Today 50 percent of the Norwegian councils have between 27.6 and 55.1 percent women, but there are considerable differences between regions and across central and peripheral municipalities. The differences between regions have been declining since the 1960s. The South-West region is still lagging behind. In 50 percent of the councils in this region women only represent 0-20 percent of the council members, and the highest rate of female representation is 36 percent. However, the North region, which traditionally was characterized by huge time-lags in the process of mobilization, is now second best, following the East. The impact of centrality varies considerably between regions. In general, women councillors are most numerous in central 'kommune', but it should be noted that the smaller and peripheral municipalities have both the lowest and the highest amount of female councillors.

Structural, cultural and political characteristics of the municipality affect women's access to local decision-making, but the impact of these factors is far more intricate than expected. Surprisingly, the structural variables included in the empirical analysis concerning demographical, territorial and socioeconomic structures, account for only

16 percent of the explained variance in female representation. When controlled for by each other, region and primary sector have the most negative effect on female representation, while female-dominated population and increasing number of inhabitants affect the percentage of women councillors in a positive direction. The political culture concerning gender roles has a clear impact on the presence of women in the councils. An interesting finding is that the standard of local welfare, measured by an index which includes indicators of private welfare as well as public welfare provisions, does not affect the representation of women. A so-called 'women-friendly society' seems to be more dependent on culture than on standard of living.

Political factors have the strongest controlled effects on the recruitment of women. The percentage of women among nominated and cumulated candidates expectedly affects female representation in a positive direction, but the controlled effects are not as strong as one might expect. This is partly due to the effect of preferential voting which in general contributes to a substantial reduction in the percentage of women councillors as compared to the result that would have followed from the party lists. Preferential voting is most prevalent in peripheral municipalities with a low district magnitude, an elderly and male-dominated population, and a traditional culture, ie low voter turnout in favor of the 'gender-quota parties' and relatively few women educated at a high level.

The characteristics of the extreme cases, the municipalities with exceptionally low and high percentages of women councillors in general confirms the general pattern of variance. The 'minimum kommune' are rather small and densely populated, most often situated in the South-West, primary sector is important to the economy, and the culture reflects traditional gender roles. They have a very low district magnitude, and women constitute a relatively small share of the cumulated candidates. In the 'maximum kommune', most often situated in the East region, this pattern is reversed. Women in these municipalities actually have a higher percentage of the councillors than of the candidates, probably due to the relatively high percentage of women among cumulated candidates and the low amount of preferential voting. Actually, preferential voting seems to be conducive to the mobilization of women. Last, but not least, the analysis of the extreme cases demonstrates that the structural, cultural and political factors work in different directions in 'minimum kommune' and 'maximum kommune'.

All in all, the findings demonstrate the importance of a multivariate approach to grasp the complex interplay between structural and cultural characteristics of the local contexts. In order to find our way to an understanding of the political mobilization of women, we need to devise local maps and develop separate causal models concerning different types of municipalities. We should also search for the impact of other factors than those included here.

The easy way to strengthen the integration of women in local councils is obviously to remove the preferential voting system. This means that we would eliminate the citizen's impact on the election of their representatives, though, and it is doubtful whether this is an appropriate strategy with regard to democratic decision-making. Besides, we may expect that the negative effect of preferential voting, which is most frequent among elderly people and in less densely populated areas, will literally die out over time.

Taken together, the data point to one overarching theme in particular: the effects of *centralization*. Women's influx into local councils passed one of the critical thresholds thanks to the amalgamations of municipalities in the late 1950s and early and mid-1960s. Larger municipalities meant more women councillors. Much in the same vein, central control on the part of political parties in the process of candidate selection enhances women's chances to gain office. Where preferential voting prevails - and the rank-ordering of candidates by the party organizations not honoured - the share of women among elected representatives tends to be low.

Those who stress the merits of *both* gender equality and a high degree of local autonomy and governmental decentralization, may therefore find the results of this study to be somewhat disheartening reading.

References

Berntzen, E. and Selle, P. (1991), 'Kvifor politisk kultur?', in Berntzen, E. and Selle, P. (eds): *Politisk kultur. Misjon og revolusjon frå Bremnes til Buenos Aires.* Oslo: Tano.
Bjørklund, T. and Hellevik, O. (1987), *Barrierer mot kvinners deltakelse i lokalpolitikken. Valgordning, motivasjon og periferiens mottrykk.* Rapport nr. 11. Oslo: Institutt for samfunnsforskning.
Central Bureau of Statistics (1992), *Arbeidmarkedsstatistikk.* Oslo.
Central Bureau of Statistics (1993), *Municipal council elections 1991.* Oslo.
Dahlerup, D. (1988), 'From a Small to a Large Minority: Women in Scandinavian Politics', *Scandinavian Political Studies*, Vol. 11, 4:275-298.
Dahlerup, D. (1993), 'From movement protest to state feminism: the Women's Liberation Movement and unemployment policy in Denmark', *NORA*, No. 1:4-20.

Heidar, K. and Raaum, N. (1995), 'Kvinner i partidemokratiet', in Raaum, N. (ed.): *Kvinner i norsk politikk. Medborgerskap i endring.* Oslo: Tano (forthcoming).

Hellevik, O. and Bjørklund, T. (1991), *Retting på stemmeseddelen ved kommunevalg og rettingens effekt på rekrutteringen av kvinner.* Arbeidsnotat nr. 10. Oslo: Institutt for samfunnsforskning.

Hellevik, O. and Skard, T. (1985), *Norske kommunestyrer - plass for kvinner?* Oslo: Universitetsforlaget.

Hernes, H. (1984), 'Women and the Welfare state. The transition from Private to Public Dependence', in Holter, H. (ed.): *Patriarchy in a Welfare Society.* Oslo: Universitetsforlaget.

Hernes, H. (1987), *Welfare State and Woman Power. Essays in State Feminism.* Oslo: Norwegian University Press.

Lovenduski, J. and Norris, P. (eds) (1993), *Gender and Party Politics.* London: Sage Publications.

Matland, R. (1993), 'Institutional Variables Affecting Female Representation in National Legislatures: The Case of Norway', *Journal of Politics*, Vol. 55, 3:737-755.

Means, I. Norderval (1973), *Kvinner i norsk politikk.* Oslo: Cappelen.

Nagel, A. H. (1992), *Velferdskommunen.* Bergen: Alma Mater.

Raaum, N. C. (1995), 'The Political Representation of Women: A Bird's Eye View', in Karvonen, L. and Selle, P. (eds): *Women in Nordic Politics: Closing the Gap.* Aldershot: Dartmouth.

Rokkan, S. (1970), *Citizens, Elections, Parties.* Oslo: Universitetsforlaget.

Schive, J. van der Ros (1981), 'Kvinners representasjonsvilkår i norske kommuner', *Tidsskrift for samfunnsforskning,* No. 2-3:87-101.

Siim, B. (1988), 'Towards a Feminist Rethinking of the Welfare State', in Jones, K. B. and Jònasdòttir, A. G. (eds): *The Political Interests of Gender.* London: Delhi: Sage Publications.

Sinkkonen, S. (1985), 'Women in local politics', in Haavio-Mannila, et. al (eds): *Unfinished Democracy. Women in Nordic Politics.* Oxford: Pergamon Press.

Skjeie, H. (1991), 'The Uneven Advance of Norwegian Women', *New Left Review*, No. 187:79-102.

Taagepera, R. and Shugart, M. Soberg (1989), *Seats and Votes.* London: Yale University Press.

Valen, H. Aardal, B., and Vogt, G. (1990), *Endring og kontinuitet. Stortingvalget 1989.* Oslo: Central Bureau of Statistics of Norway.

How the election system structure has helped women close the representation gap

Richard E. Matland

Women are greatly underrepresented in national legislatures throughout the world.[1] In 1992, the Inter-Parliamentary Union estimated that only 11 percent of the legislators in its 144 member countries were women. While the overall picture is one of very limited representation, there is substantial variation. The United States at 11 percent and United Kingdom at 9 percent are at or below the international average, while Finland and Norway at 39 percent have the highest levels of representation. Recent research aimed at explaining underrepresentation and variations in representation has concentrated on three basic categories of explanations: cultural, socio-economic, and institutional (Norris 1985).

This chapter concentrates on electoral institutions and argues that the electoral system structure plays a crucial role in women closing the representation gap in Norway. Researchers have increasingly turned to electoral institutions as important determinants of female representation (Darcy, Welch, and Clark 1987, 1994). This has coincided with a general increase in research on the political effects of electoral institutions (Lijphart 1985; Grofman and Lijphart 1986; and Taagepera and Shugart 1989). Emphasis on institutional factors is both a result of these factors' substantive importance in understanding representation processes and their significance from a policy perspective. Institutional arrangements, unlike most cultural and many socio-economic factors, are pliable. Conclusive findings of an institutional arrangement's effect can lead to proposals for changing institutions in order to produce a desired policy outcome.

Most of the early work on electoral institutions' effect on representation of women emphasized the differences between proportional representation (PR) and single member district systems (Duverger 1955; Lakeman 1976; Castles 1981; Rule 1981, 1987; Norris 1985). This research shows conclusively that PR systems provide a

---

[1] Portions of this chapter have appeared earlier in 'Institutional Variables Affecting Female Representation in National Legislatures: The Case of Norway.' *The Journal of Politics*, Vol. 55(3):737-755.

higher level of representation for women. More recently other institutional factors have come under closer scrutiny. This chapter discusses two institutional factors: district magnitude, which is the number of seats per district, and candidate nomination processes. Norway has, comparatively speaking, a high average district magnitude, while the candidate nomination procedure is sufficiently open to allow for cohesive pressure groups to influence nomination procedures. Both are important to understanding why women have been able to increase their representation in Norway so dramatically.

District magnitude

The primary theoretical arguments for why district magnitude should have a positive effect on female representation are closely related to the assumption that as district magnitude increases, strategies change. Contests in single member districts are by definition zero-sum games. Multi-member districts, while fixed-sum games, are not zero-sum games. This can affect party officials, candidates, and voters. Of these three possible effects, the effects on party strategies are expected to be by far the most important.

For party officials, increases in district magnitude should make it easier to slate women candidates (given that party officials have some control over the choosing of candidates) for two reasons. First, as the party searches for different types of candidates to nominate in order to attract different voter groups, the slating of women becomes more and more probable as a way to appeal to new groups of voters. Conversely, as district magnitude increases, the exclusion of women from the party's list of candidates becomes increasingly obvious and increases the danger of a negative reaction from voters. Second, within the party, it is easier to slate women in districts with large magnitudes. If district magnitude is one, there is a zero-sum context within the party; by slating a female candidate all male candidates are shut out. With a larger magnitude, men who represent powerful intra-party constituencies do not need to be deposed in order for a woman to receive a spot on the party's list. Balancing the ticket is possible when district magnitude is large; it is more difficult when district magnitude is small, and impossible when district magnitude is one.

The non-zero sum nature of multi-member district elections allows candidates to concentrate on winning votes for themselves and provides correspondingly less emphasis on attacking one's opponents. To the degree Kirkpatrick's (1974) assertion that women prefer to highlight their own strengths rather than denigrate their opponents' is true, women should be more interested in running in multi-member districts.

Voters may also react to these distinctions. Voters who might be hesitant to vote for a woman if she was their only representative may be more willing to vote for a woman as one of many candidates. While this is unlikely to be the attitude of a large number of voters, even a few percentage points can influence election outcomes.

In addition, district magnitude may have a positive effect on female representation if higher district magnitudes are associated with greater turnover. Districts with many representatives lead to diminished visibility for each individual representative. Multi-member district representatives also tend to do less constituency work than single-member district representatives (Jewell 1982). Both of these factors can diminish incumbency advantages and therefore lead to higher turnover rates. Very low turnover serves as an anchor impeding changes and keeping representation rates unnecessarily low. If social or institutional conditions change so that women who were previously discriminated against are now competing on a level playing field, low turnover rates delay equalization. Both Andersen and Thorson (1984) and Darcy and Choike (1986) have forcefully shown that the extremely low levels of turnover in the U.S. Congress make it unlikely that women will reach an equitable level of representation, even if all other factors are perfectly equal, until well into the next century.

There is an extensive literature which considers the effects of district magnitude on female representation in legislative bodies (Darcy, Welch, and Clark 1985; Engstrom 1987; Rule 1987; Beckwith 1990, Welch and Studlar 1990; Studlar and Welch 1991; Matland and Brown 1992; Moncrief and Thompson 1992; and Matland 1993). While the results of these empirical studies are not uniform,[2] most studies find district magnitude does have a positive effect.

Part of the inconsistency in the research findings on district magnitude occurs because district magnitude does not directly measure the factor which is expected to influence women's chances. District magnitude measures the number of seats in the whole district, while as the previous discussion noted, it is the number of seats a party expects to win that is important. Normally the two are strongly correlated. As district magnitude increases the number of seats won by the largest party increases and the number of parties with multi-member delegations increases. Both should lead to increased opportunities for women. As Darcy, Welch, and Clark (1987) point out, however, large district magnitude may lead to many small parties, rather than a few

---

[2] See Matland (1993) for an extensive review of this literature and a critique.

parties which expect to win several seats. Under these conditions, where a party expects to only win one or two seats, women are likely to face the same difficulties as in single member district systems. Competition for slots at the top of the party list becomes a zero sum game.[3] The empirical work presented here tries to get around this complication by directly studying the effect of party magnitude, the size of a party's district delegation, on the proportion of the party district delegation which is female. The hypothesized relationship is that as the size of a party's district delegation increases, the female proportion of the delegation will increase. This hypothesized relationship will be tested in 11 elections over a 40-year period.

There are strong methodological reasons for taking an intensive look at the relationship between party magnitude and female representation in Norway. By looking at an individual country, political culture is largely controlled.[4] A strong indication that party magnitude has a significant effect in Norway lessens the concern that previous results, based on cross-national studies, may have been spurious. Choosing Norway is particularly appropriate for several other reasons. At 39 percent the Norwegian Storting has the highest level of female representation in the world. It is important to test whether the comparatively large party magnitudes found in Norway may be one of the reasons that Norway has attained its forward position. Finally, because the electoral system has remained stable, it is possible to look at the relationship over a 40-year period; this enables us to see if party magnitude's effect varies across time periods.

Data and methods

Data was collected for each member of parliament and each electoral district (i.e. each county) for a 40-year period (Nordby 1985; Torp 1978, 1982, 1986, 1990, 1994). The period considered, 1953 to 1993, encompasses eleven parliamentary elections. Changes in election laws make it difficult to compare elections prior to 1953.

---

[3] Darcy, Welch, and Clark (1987) point to the Israeli electoral system as a case which fits this scenario.

[4] Obviously there are different political cultures within the country, but the spread in culture is likely to be much less from Kristiansand to Hammerfest, than from Hammerfest to Bonn, Paris, or Rome.

Table 1
Female Representation in the Norwegian Storting, 1953-1993

YEAR	Number of Women MPs	Number of MPs	Female Pct. of Storting	Correlation Between Party Magnitude and Female % of Party District Delegation
1953	7	150	4.7%	.34**
1957	10	150	6.7%	.45**
1961	13	150	8.7%	.52**
1965	12	150	8.0%	.32**
1969	14	150	9.3%	.38**
1973	24	155	15.5%	.25*
1977	37	155	23.9%	.20
1981	40	155	25.8%	.24*
1985	54	157	34.4%	.15
1989	59	165	35.8%	.21
1993	65	165	39.4%	.33**

* = Significant at the .05 level (2-tailed test)
** = Significant at the .01 level (2-tailed test)

Table 1 provides data on the number of women MPs in the Storting, the total number of MPs in the Storting, the percentage of the Storting which was female, and the zero-order correlation between party magnitude and female percent of party district delegation for each of the eleven sessions.[5] The zero-order correlations in column five provide an initial test of the party magnitude hypothesis. The correlation between party magnitude and the female proportion of the delegation is quite strong and

---

[5] In 1973 and 1985 the size of the parliament was increased, first from 150 to 155 members, then to 157 members. Districts which had significantly increased their population were given new seats. In 1989 the parliament was increased to 165 members as a system of 'vote equalization seats' was used for the first time.

statistically significant for the first six elections, but then weakens and is only statistically significant in two of the last five elections considered. Female representation consistently increases over the eleven Stortings, reaching its high point with the 1993 elections when 39.4 percent of the elected representatives were women.

To further test the effect of party magnitude, regressions were run for each of the parliamentary elections. The dependent variable is the female percent of party district delegation. When delegations are counted as district and party specific there are between 69 (1977) and 88 (1989) delegations. In the regressions each case is weighted by delegation size.[6]

The crucial independent variable is party magnitude. If my argument is correct, party magnitude should be positively associated with percent of delegation which is female. In addition, three control variables are included: leftist party delegation, progress party delegation and urban district. In the international political science literature, leftist parties frequently have been found to be more supportive of women candidates than conservative or centrist parties (Duverger 1955; Lakeman 1976; Rasmussen 1983; Norris 1987). The data set provides a chance to test if such an effect exists in Norway. Leftist party delegation is measured as a dummy variable which is one when the district delegation is Communist, Labour, Socialist People's Party, Socialist Left, or Red Electoral Alliance (NKP, DNA, SF/SV, RV). The inclusion of a dummy variable for Progress party delegations is based on an evaluation of the Norwegian political scene. The Progress party is on the far right of Norwegian politics. While over time *all* other parties have at least made some efforts to include women on their party lists, the Progress party has remained adamant in refusing to consider active promotion (they would call it favoritism) of women. It is expected that the Progress party delegation variable will have a significant negative effect on proportion of women in the delegation.[7]   Finally,

---

[6] For example, a one-member delegation gets a weight of one, while a five-member delegation gets a weight of five. Weighting by delegation size provides an *N* equivalent to the number of MPs in parliament. As our ultimate concern is with the number of women in parliament, this is the correct weighting procedure. Weighting will decrease the standard errors of the regression coefficients, but should not affect the regression coefficients themselves.

[7] The Progress party first appeared on the national scene in 1973 as Anders Langes Parti. It won four seats in the 1973 Storting elections, but failed to win any seats in the subsequent 1977 parliamentary elections. The Progess party returned to parliament in 1981 and has been continuously represented in the national assembly since then. Since no Progress party delegations exist before 1973 and none were elected in 1977, this variable is not included in regressions for those years.

Table 2

Regressions Results, Female Percentage of Party District Delegation
as Dependent Variable, 1953-1993

Year	1953	1957	1961	1965	1969	1973	1977	1981	1985	1989	1993
Constant	-.43 (1.68)	-3.28 (1.78)	-3.93* (1.94)	-3.04 (2.14)	-4.31* (2.09)	4.91 (3.31)	15.27** (3.66)	12.62** (3.89)	24.25** (4.11)	25.06** (4.66)	25.16** (4.21)
Party Magnitude	1.34* (.67)	2.39** (.77)	3.23** (.87)	3.23** (1.02)	4.91** (1.02)	2.81* (1.45)	1.38 (1.38)	3.11** (1.24)	1.24 (1.28)	.65 (1.69)	4.83** (1.52)
Left Party	.43 (2.34)	1.82 (2.65)	4.72 (2.70)	2.30 (3.03)	-1.12 (3.27)	3.19 (3.77)	3.58 (4.64)	11.98** (3.54)	14.44** (4.04)	17.81** (4.79)	2.64 (4.45)
Progress Party						-13.49 (10.66)		-11.44 (11.28)	-23.29 (17.20)	-26.76** (6.46)	-23.43** (8.25)
Urban District	2.37 (1.34)	4.79** (1.49)	2.37 (1.59)	3.84* (1.91)	-.03 (1.83)	4.62 (2.83)	4.38 (3.23)	-3.43 (2.88)	-1.47 (3.20)	7.35* (3.47)	3.77 (4.18)
Adjusted R^2	.07	.24	.29	.21	.27	.09	.04	.15	.11	.26	.16
N	74	72	74	80	77	86	69	70	70	88	85
Weighted N	150	150	150	150	150	155	155	155	157	165	165

* = Significant at the .05 level (2-tailed test)
** = Significant at the .01 level (2-tailed test)

urban areas have been found to be more supportive of female candidates in other studies and therefore an urban variable is included here (Moncrief and Thompson 1991; Matland and Brown 1992). Urban district is measured as an ordinal variable equal to 2 for districts with cities over 250,000 (only Oslo meets this criteria), 1 for districts with cities over 75,000 (Bergen/Hordaland; Trondheim/Sør-Trøndelag; Stavanger/Rogaland), and 0 otherwise.

The regression results presented in Table 2 provide strong evidence that all the variables are relevant, but that their effects are distinctly time bound. Urban district has a statistically significant and positive effect for two of the first four elections, but then is not significant in six of the last seven elections. While urbanization is significant in 1989, it has a negative effect in 1985, and does not begin to approach significance in 1993, making it tempting to consider the significant effect in 1989 as simply random noise. The leftist party dummy also shows a clear time bound effect. Not once in the seven elections held in the 1950s, 1960s, and 1970s were leftist delegations more favorable towards women. In the 1980s, however, the effect of leftist parties was both statistically and substantively significant. The effect of being a leftist delgation on the percent of women in the delegation was 12 percent in 1981, 14.5 percent in 1985, and an impressive 17.8 percent in 1989. This variable becomes insignificant, however, for the 1993 election.[8] The one variable that consistently shows the same effect is the Progress party delegation variable. While only statistically significant in the last two elections, the Progress party dummy produces a noticeable and strong impact in every regression it is entered into.[9] In the last two elections the average effect of a delegate representing the Progress party is a tremendous 25 percent decrease in the proportion of women in the delegation.

---

[8] What we see in 1993 is that the center parties have caught up to the leftists in terms of women's representation. The regression includes party dummies for both leftist parties and the Progress party. This means that the level of representation in the centrist parties and the Conservative party are measured by the constant term, and the leftist and Progress party dummies compare the effects of these parties against a base which consists of the centrist parties and the Conservatives. During the 1980s, the leftists surged ahead of these centrist and Conservative party and therefore the leftist dummy has a statistically significant positive effect throughout this time period. By 1993, however, both the Christian People's party and the Center party had markedly increased their proportion of women to the point that the leftist party delegations no longer had significantly higher proportions of women, therefore the leftist party delegation dummy variable ceases to be significant.

[9] The Progress party dummy variable fails to be statistically significant in 1973, 1981, and 1985 because of the paucity of Progress party delegations. There are only four representatives in 1973, four in 1981, and two in 1985. As soon as the number of representatives increases in number, there are 15 delegations with 22 representatives in 1989 and 8 delegations with 10 representatives in 1993, the standard error of the coefficient decreases and the effect becomes statistically significant.

Looking at the crucial party magnitude variable, it has a relatively weak effect in 1953, but increases in strength (as indicated by the increase in the size of the unstandardized coefficients) and remains powerful from 1957 through 1973. Party magnitude has its most powerful effect in 1969 where for each unit increase in party magnitude the delegation's percentage of women went up by 4.9 percent.[10] After 1973, party magnitude weakens in effect and is statistically significant in only two of the last five elections.

Discussion

These regressions provide a couple of interesting findings in terms of the effect of party magnitude. First, party magnitude clearly affects the proportion of a party's delegation which is female, at least for the earlier periods considered. This provides confirmation of the party magnitude hypothesis. For theory building, it is important to tie this behavioral manifestation of parties' strategic action to the institutional framework. It has been proven that parties increase the proportion of women in their delegations when the number of seats they win increases. To tie this finding to the institutional structure it is necessary to consider whether party magnitude increases with district magnitude.

There are two relevant ways that district magnitude, the institutional variable which is part of the electoral system structure, may positively affect party magnitude. First, as district magnitude increases the number of seats won by the largest party may increase. Second, the number of parties with multi-member delegations, and therefore with the possibility to do ticket balancing, may increase with increasing magnitude. Both effects appear to be happening in Norway. The correlation between district magnitude and party magnitude for the largest party in a district averages .81 across the eleven elections and at no time falls below .74. The number of parties with multimember delegations correlates with district magnitude at an average level of .74 across these eleven elections and never falls below .62.[11]

---

[10] Party magnitude varies in size from one (the most common) to seven-member delegations. The units are discrete, not continuous. Obviously a coefficient of 4.90 cannot mean that when a delegation increases from one to two members that it would go from having 0 women to having 1/10th of a woman. What it does mean is that for a large sample of two-member delegations there would be about 5 percent more women than would be found in a sample of single member delegations with the same total number of representatives.

[11] The effect of district magnitude on these two variables can also be tested as simple bivariate regressions. Running bivariate regressions for all 11 elections, the regression coefficient for district magnitude, with size of largest party as the dependent variable, averages .34. The regression coefficient for district magnitude on number of multimember district delegations averages .23. In other words, an

Based on these results it is reasonable to assert that the high average district magnitude, via its effect on party magnitude, has helped women gain access to the Storting, at least initially.

The second finding is that party magnitude's effect on female representation varies across time, and appears to follow a cycle. Initially there is a weak effect which strengthens over time. Once women are well established within the parties, however, party magnitude's effect diminishes and appears to decrease in importance.

As the importance of party magnitude becomes clearer, the need to consider internal party decisions becomes obvious. Specifically, candidate selection procedures loom as a factor of considerable importance. By carefully considering the interaction between candidate selection and party magnitude, conditions can be explicitly defined under which party magnitude has a positive effect on female representation in Norway. In doing so, a more general understanding of how the electoral system affects representation can be developed. In addition, candidate selection processes have become increasingly recognized as a crucial point for women's access (Norris and Lovenduski 1993a; Norris and Lovenduski 1993b). As research has accumulated showing that voters do not discriminate against women candidates (Darcy and Schramm 1977; Hills 1983; Rasmussen 1983; Hunter and Denton 1984; Kelley and McAllister 1984; Welch and Studlar 1986) attention has turned to the role of the party selectorate and how they impede or aid women's attempts to gain access to the halls of power.

Candidate selection processes

Norwegian elections, as most party list proportional representation system elections, are first and foremost competitions between parties and not between individual candidates. Valen (1988) reports that in a national survey, 33 percent of respondents were unable to name a single candidate in their district, 28 percent were able to name one or two, and only 39 percent were able to name three or more. Campaigns focus on national party leaders and policies formulated by the national parties, individual candidates can only to a very limited degree influence their election results. This is

---

increase in district magnitude of 3 will lead to an increase in the size of the largest party delegation of approximately 1, while an increase in district magnitude of 4 will tend to increase the number of multimember district delegations by approximately 1.

not unreasonable since strict party discipline in the Storting insures that representatives vote the party line.

In addition, for much of the post World War II period Norwegian politics has seen only very small vote changes from one election to another. Parties could predict, with a high degree of certainty, how many seats they could win and in what districts. Under these conditions, the party nomination processes become crucial to an individual candidate's likelihood of becoming a member of the Storting.

While election outcomes are largely decided by national trends, the list of candidates running in each district is promulgated by the local party organizations. The national party provides guidelines, but they have no veto power over candidates and cannot force a local party to slate a candidate it finds unacceptable (Valen 1988). The process varies slightly from party to party, but the basic elements are the same and are governed by the Act of Nominations, a law dating back to 1921. A county nominating committee, composed of 5-15 county party leaders, receives suggestions, proposals, and generally a rank ordering of possible candidates from local party organizations. Based on the recommendations made by the local organizations and on their own evaluations, the county nominating committee proposes a slate of candidates and alternates, with rank orderings. This proposal is presented to a county nominating convention where the final decisions are made on the county party's Storting list.

The county conventions are usually all-day sessions. Delegates are elected from local party organizations and must be dues-paying party members. County conventions vote on each position on the list individually. The most common outcome is that the nominating committee's proposal is accepted with only minor changes, but major changes can be made and it is not unusual for a county nominating convention to change the rank ordering of candidates, propose new candidates, or even reject the committee's top candidate.

Valen (1988) describes the Norwegian nomination process as one of decentralized group representation. Decentralization refers to the local county party organizations' control over nominations. Group representation refers to the importance of having a base in interests which a party aspires to represent. Descriptive representation (Pitkin 1967) posits that for effective representation delegates must have the characteristics of the group they are to represent (for example, only a labourer can understand what the workers want). This concept is strongly embedded in Norwegian parties and is taken very seriously as a legitimate principle of representation, as a method of integrating various party factions and thereby maintaining party peace, and as a manner in which to maximize the party's appeal to voters (Valen 1966). A candidate's chances are substantially strengthened if the candidate is associated with and draws support from groups perceived of as having a legitimate demand for representation. The relevant interests varies across parties. Traditionally, geographical considerations and occupational groupings have been central considerations in all parties (Valen 1956, 1966, 1988). In addition, support from various cultural and issue-specific groups tied to a party are important. The rise of women in Norwegian national politics is a story of changes in their position in this ticket balancing puzzle. In forty years they have moved from a position of irrelevance and peripheral status to one of the central considerations in composing a party's slate.

Changing patterns of female representation

While the institutional framework has remained stable, there have been large changes in female representation. These changes are directly tied to changes in the position and legitimacy of women candidates within the county nominating conventions. Female representation in the Norwegian Storting can be split into four time periods: 1909-53, 1957-73, 1977-81, 1985-1993. In each of these time periods there are distinct patterns which are described below.

1909-1953: Giants among men. From the time women gained the right to vote in national elections in 1909 through 1953 there were 16 women who served in the Storting (Means 1973). The first was elected from Oslo in 1921. The most accurate description of these representatives may be that they were very unique women, giants among men if you will. They were able to win positions at a time when politics was completely dominated by men. Their rarity and uniqueness make it quite hard to predict where they were likely to appear, although some patterns do appear.

During this time period party magnitude had some effect, almost all of these women were elected in districts where their party had at least three seats (Aasland 1964). The effect of party magnitude, however, is quite weak. Party magnitude's regression coefficient in 1953 indicates that when party magnitude increases by one the female delegation percentage increases by only 1.3 percent. Large district delegations were effectively a necessary, but not a sufficient condition for female representation in this era. Where there was a woman MP there was a party with a large district delegation. Where there were large party district delegations, however, there was no certainty of finding a female representative. For example, the largest single party county delegation in 1953 was the seven-member Nordland Labour party delegation where all the MPs were male. Another pattern is that the earliest representatives tended to come from the cities. While historically Oslo has been about 10 percent of the country's population, during this first period more than 30 percent of the female representatives came from Oslo. The high proportion from Oslo may be an indication that tolerance for women in traditionally male roles was greater in urban centers than in rural areas.

Women in this earliest period were not only disadvantaged by discrimination, they were also disadvantaged by being very poorly represented in the pool from which candidates were generally chosen. In 1957, Henry Valen (1966) surveyed over 100 party leaders in the seven largest parties in one county regarding the qualifications needed of a good parliamentary candidate. Respondents within the Labour Party emphasized the importance of being active in and loyal to the Labour Party. Within the non-socialist parties emphasis was placed upon having a position of standing within the local community. This usually referred to an important occupational position, previous experience in public office, or activity in social organizations outside the party. As women had substantially lower labour force participation rates and were rarely represented in prominent positions in organizational life, they were at a distinct disadvantage when candidates were chosen. In addition, women were very poorly represented on local councils which were often a required training ground for future parliamentarians. In 1957, 89 percent of the Storting members had served as members of local councils. In 1955, however, only 6.4 percent of local council representatives were female (Statistisk Sentralbyrå 1980).

Throughout this first era and into the second, substantially lower labour force participation rates, lower levels of education, and limited experience in local government and in other social organizations provided women with a distinct disadvantage. Those few women who did make it to the Storting tended to be atypical. They were more likely to have worked outside the home than the average woman, many had substantial schooling, and several had had family members who had served in the national assembly before them.

1957-1973: One is enough. Means (1972) interviewed 15 of the 16 female representatives serving in the Storting in 1970 regarding their recruitment. She quotes extensively from her interviews and one of the most telling conversations is the following,

> *'Oh, the old male attitudes are still with us! We aren't free of them yet. All the parties preach loudly about recruiting more women, but when the actual recruitment begins, it is still the case that they tend to consider only men. And then*

suddenly someone remembers: By Jove, we haven't got a woman! Let's find a woman! But one is enough --- that will suffice.'

One is enough describes this era well. In this time period only one party district delegation had more than one woman, the exception was the Oslo Labour Party. While the pressure exerted to increase female representation resulted in some increase, representation was far from equal. Nevertheless, female representation gradually rose throughout this period from 8 percent in 1957 to 15.5 percent in 1973.

In the previous period, women were elected in spite of their being women. By the 1960s, the women's movement started making significant inroads at the local political level and in public debate. Women's auxiliaries of the parties slowly turned from seeing their interests in terms of party success to also seeing an interest in being represented. In 1967, for example, there was an active multi-party campaign to recruit more women to the local party lists (Bystydzienski 1988). In 1971, there was an active campaign to get women to vote for female candidates at the local level which provided a shock when women suddenly moved from approximately 20 percent of the city council to a majority in several major cities, including the capitol, Oslo.[12] In this second period, women became an organized and legitimate interest; one which parties had to consider in developing their party lists. One indication of this is that by 1973 all party district delegations of four representatives or more included a woman in the delegation.

While women as a group came to be viewed as a legitimate interest, they were not a strong interest. It is exactly under these conditions that party magnitude plays a role. A party will satisfy the more powerful interests first and move on to weaker interests second. If the party has several seats then those legitimate, but weaker, interests will be represented. If the party has few seats, however, viable seats will already be allocated before those weaker interests have made it to parliament. The regressions in Table 2 reinforce this point, party magnitude was statistically and substantively significant precisely during this time period.

The female Storting representatives Means (1973) interviewed strongly believed that women candidates' inability to draw support from the traditional power groups within their parties was their most important handicap. At the same time, several women said that being a woman had been an advantage in their own case. Especially

---

[12] Local elections are also party list elections, but at the local level voters are allowed to strike names, add names, and to cumulate their votes for one candidate on the list. By systematically urging women to strike all the male names from their party's list, the surprising results of the 'women's coup' were created.

among the non-socialist parties, women with relatively little political experience were placed high up on their party's list. While this may seem contradictory, it is easily explained by the words used to describe this period, one is enough. Women could expect to receive some representation under the existing rules, but these women believed if women were to increase their representation significantly they would have to be seen not as female representatives, but as representatives of other more powerful interests within the parties.

1977-1981: Tokenism no more. The Storting representatives Means interviewed believed women needed to become the candidates of the traditionally powerful groups within the parties. An alternative, not foreseen by her respondents, was for women to move from a position of being one of several peripheral interests to being a central interest and finally to institutionalizing demands for gender equality. Moves in this direction occurred in the late 1970s.

The election results from 1977 show several significant trends. First, representation jumped from 15.5 percent to 23.6 percent. Second, for the first time, there were district party delegations, other than the Oslo Labour Party, which had more than one woman. The number of party district delegations with more than one woman jumped from one in 1973 to seven in 1977, striking evidence that the period of 'one is enough' was over. Also note that by 1977 party magnitude is no longer statistically significant in the regression equations.

Women within the parties continued to press for equal status. Arguments for equal representation, rather than merely some representation, were heard with increasing force in this period. Two distinct arguments for equal representation were made (Skjeie 1991a). Both the resource argument and interest argument are consistent with Pitkin's concept of descriptive representation. The resources argument is that women have life experiences which are different from men and they are able to contribute a new perspective on public policy issues which would improve the quality of public decisions. The interest argument is that women have a separate set of issue priorities and to insure that their issue areas receive their fair share of scarce public resources, women must be represented in accordance with their numbers.

In 1977 both the Liberal and Socialist Left Parties endorsed affirmative action plans to insure that at least 40 percent of their candidates were women. The substantive effects of these actions were extremely limited since the Liberal and Socialist Left parties won only four seats in the 155 member Storting in 1977. The symbolic effect was, however, significant. The Socialist Left in particular plays an important role in Norwegian politics in trying to push the Labour party to the left.

The Labour party needs to be conscious of possible defections from its left flank to the Socialist Left party. By taking an aggressive stand for equality on the issue of candidate quotas, along with several other issues being promoted by feminists, the Socialist Left added additional pressure to that already coming from women's groups within the Labour Party.[13]

1985-1993: Quota heaven or second among equals? In this period, representation increased to 34.4 percent in 1985, 35.8 percent in 1989, and up to 39.4 percent in 1993. The 1993 level places Norway at the very top of the list worldwide, no country has a higher proportion of women in their national legislature. In reviewing this period we find clear indications that women have become well established and integrated into the political arena. Nevertheless, complete equality has not been reached and there are several signs that it is unlikely to be reached.

When looking at the impressive gains in this period a crucial turning point can be identified as the Norwegian Labour Party's national convention endorsement of an affirmative action proposal to ensure that at least 40 percent of its parliamentary candidates were female. This rule change, while merely a guideline for county nominating conventions, has had a strong and rapid effect on the composition of the total Labour Party parliamentary delegation. In 1981 women constituted 33 percent of the Labour Party delegation; by 1989 they were in the majority: 51 percent of the Parliamentary delegation was female. Labour's undisputed position as the largest party in Norwegian politics has made this an especially significant event. Labour's adoption of quotas strengthened female activists in all the other parties and one can see a clear increase in female representation in all parties. By the 1993 election the two parties in the center which had not adopted quotas, the Center and Christian People's parties, formally adopted quotas, though the Christian People's party adopted quotas too late to have an effect on their 1993 nomination process (Skjeie 1993). Six of the eight parties represented in the Storting, with 77 percent of the seats, have adopted gender quotas for their candidates. The institutionalization of equal representation, via quota rules, virtually guarantees women significant representation.

While women are effectively guaranteed significant representation they are not guaranteed equal representation. The representation of women at the present time can best be described as second among equals. When the number of positions to be

---

[13] For a general discussion of the spreading of quotas from smaller parties on the political wings to major parties closer to the political center, see Matland and Studlar (1993).

divided between men and women can be divided equally, i.e. the number of representatives elected is an even number, the political parties have shown in the 1980s an increasing trend towards equal representation. When it is not possible to divide the number of positions between men and women equally, however, men consistently come first: hence, women are second among equals.

Figure 1

Female percent of MPs. Odd vs. Even Numbered Delegations

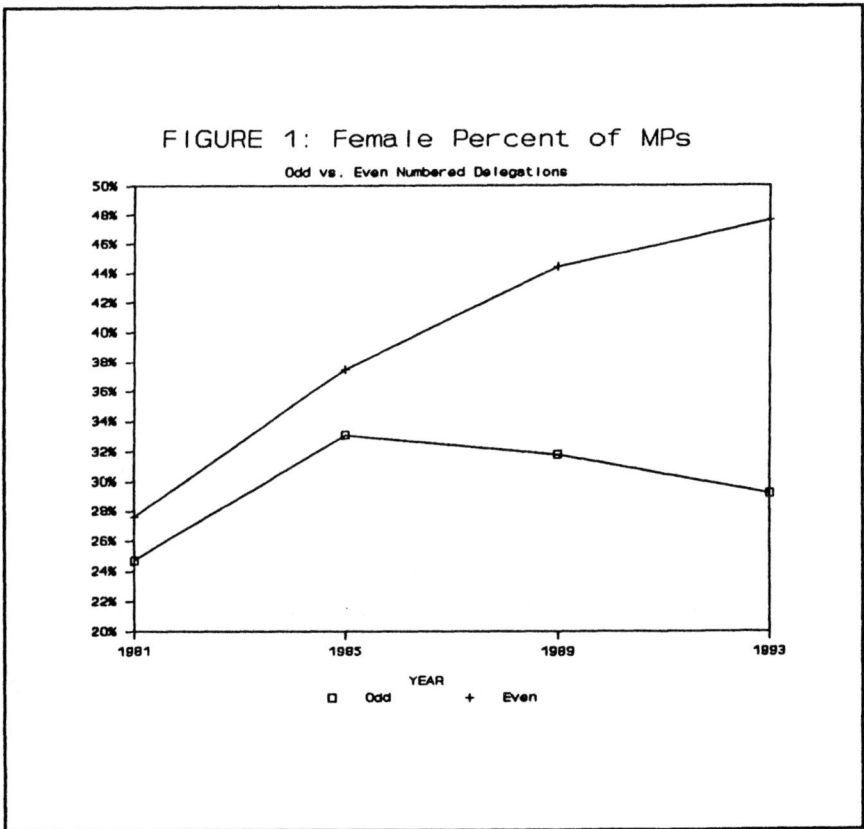

FIGURE 1: Female Percent of MPs
Odd vs. Even Numbered Delegations

Table 3

Female Percentage of Delegations, Odd Numbered vs. Even Numbered Party District Delegations

	1981	1985	1989	1993
ODD	24.7%	33.1%	31.8%	29.2%
EVEN	27.6%	37.5%	44.4%	47.6%

Table 3 and Figure 1 show how the representation of women has changed in even numbered delegations, i.e. where the party district delegation is 2, 4 or 6 MPs, versus odd numbered delegations, i.e. 1, 3, 5 or 7 MPs. Both the table and figure show that women have made significant gains in their percentage of representatives in even number delegations. They have almost doubled from 27.6 percent of the MPs in even numbered delegations in 1981 to just shy of full equality in 1993 at 47.6 percent. Among odd numbered delegations, however, there has been very little gain overall and the trend is actually negative from 1985 to 1993.

What appears to be happening in the 1980s is that in districts where a party has had an even number of seats and there has been a gender imbalance, male incumbents who retire (voluntarily or involuntarily) have been replaced by women. In districts where the party tends to win an odd number of seats, male incumbents have largely been replaced by other men.[14] Such a development would lead to the trend we see in Figure 1 with even delegations getting closer and closer to full equality over time as more incumbents retire and more parties adopt quotas, while in the odd districts there is very little movement.

Another manifestation of this trend towards men first, women second is representation in single member delegations. The strong effect that party magnitude shows in the regression for the 1993 elections is largely a result of the significantly lower level of female representation in single member delegations compared to larger delegations (25 percent of single member delegations are women, while 46.3 percent of multimember delegations are women). Single member delegations are

---

[14] While the discussion here refers to elected representatives, a more general description of what is occurring is that when district parties set up their list of parliamentary candidates, the lists are set up so that the positions alternate between men and women candidates, but the lists start with a man. Therefore, if only one candidate is elected it is generally a man. If two are elected the delegation is balanced, but when three are elected the imbalance is again to men's advantage. This pattern continues as the number of MPs elected alternates between even and odd numbers.

predominately male across all political parties. A striking example of this problem can be seen by looking at the composition of the Socialist Left delegation in 1993. The Socialist Left was the first party to establish quotas and has for many years had a strong feminist profile to its party program. The party did poorly in the 1993 election campaign and ended up electing substantially fewer representatives than they had anticipated. As a result of largely getting only one representative in the counties where they won seats, the Socialist Left's parliamentary delegation barely had a higher proportion of women than the Conservative party (30.8 percent vs. 28.6 percent).

The second factor which kept representation rates from going even higher in this period was the increase in the number of Progress party MPs. The regressions in Table 2 showed that being a Progress party delegation significantly diminishes the female proportion in a delegation. The raw numbers drive this point home. When the Progress party parliamentary delegation jumped from two representatives in 1985 to 22 representatives in 1989 only one of the representatives was a woman. Of the 10 Progress party MPs elected from 1993-1997, only one was female. The Progress party has shown little interest in proactive arrangements to increase the number of women in its parliamentary ranks. In addition its voters are overwhelmingly male, 69 percent in 1985, 65 percent in 1989 (Valen, Aardal, and Vogt 1990) and 68 percent in 1993 (personal calculation). Many of these voters have extremely traditional views of the role of women. While an occasional female representative may be elected by the Progress party there is little reason to expect a substantial female representation in the Progress party delegation and women's representation in the Storting will vary inversely with the success of the Progress party.

It is not going too far to say that the increase in women's representation from 1989 to 1993 can largely be explained by the drop in Progress party representatives. To test this assertion, election simulations were run to see what women's representation would have been in the 1989-1993 Storting had the Progress party support been weaker.[15] Three different simulations of the 1989 election were run. For each simulation, the Progress party level of support was set at 6.5 percent, quite close to their 1993 result of 6.3 percent, but well below their actual 1989 vote percent of 13.0 percent. Each of the simulations result in an all male Progress party delegation of ten representatives. The level of support for the other parties was varied in each simulation. The effects are, however, consistent. Whether the 6.5 percent difference

---

[15] The simulation program CELIUS has been developed by Bernt Aardal and translates vote percentages into representatives at the district level. Aardal was kind enough to provide access to this program. His help is greatly appreciated.

between the hypothesized and real Progress party vote went primarily to the Conservative party, to the Labour party, or to the parties in the center (Center party and Christian People's party) all lead to a significant increase in female representation. The simulation which most closely adheres to the findings in voting studies, i.e. that Progress party voters were primarily former Conservative party voters (Valen, Aardal, and Vogt 1990), gave the Conservative party a 5 percent increase in votes, Labour a 1 percent increase, and 0.25 percent to the Center Party and the Christian People's Party. Had this been the outcome of the 1989 election, 40 percent of the Norwegian Storting would have been women in 1989. This is almost exactly the same as the result from 1993, when the Progress party's Storting delegation declined from 22 to 10 members.

In reviewing this period, we can see that significant gains have been made, but the trend towards equality is quite likely to slow down in the future. There is little reason to expect increased gains in even numbered delegations as these are quite near 50 percent women. If women are to increase their representation even more they will need to win more slots in odd numbered delegations. This would require becoming the number one of their party or having two of the three top slots. The trends for the 1980s and early 1990s show little indication that such a trend is developing. Nevertheless, some gains may occur as male incumbents retire and are perhaps replaced by women who have served as their substitute representatives. It is also possible that the Progress party could further shrink in size as it is racked with serious internal dissension.

Power is clearly shared between the sexes, but not entirely on an equal basis. While it seems unlikely that complete equality will be reached it is important to emphasize that percentages just under 40 percent mean that women are prominently placed in all decision making bodies within the Storting and wield considerable influence. The record of the Norwegian Storting is a precedent setting one, and it is far more appropriate to emphasize how far women have come, than to bemoan the fact that complete equality has not been reached.

Discussion

In reviewing this 40 year advance from limited to broad representation the obvious question is why did it happen here? The answer is partly cultural, but institutions are a critical part of the story. The institutional arrangements, especially the candidate selection system, were ideal for effective change to occur once women become effectively organized. In addition, many Norwegian feminists made a conscious decision to use an inside strategy, working within the existing political parties' and institutional rules.[16] Because Norwegian elections are primarily party - and not candidate-oriented, the real battle for equitable representation occurs at the county nominating conventions. These are limited access affairs dominated by political élites. While 80-85 percent of the Norwegian public votes in parliamentary elections, only 0.6 percent of the voting public participates in county nominating meetings (Valen 1988). It may be easier to establish equal representation principles when only élites need to be convinced, rather than the voting public. In addition, this elite may be more sympathetic to demands for greater representation than the public as a whole.

I believe, however, that more important than an 'enlightened' elite is the electoral structure and candidate selection system, which allows limited access but does not deny access. In such a system, outcomes can come down to pure power politics, where the ability to mobilize women to pack a county convention with pro-women delegates can carry the day. The access threshold is high enough that only highly motivated actors participate, yet it is low enough that concerted actions are a plausible threat. The threat of packing the convention, defecting to another party (especially salient for the Labour Party vis-a-vis the Socialist Left), or simply sitting out an election, can be significant enough that in discussions prior to the county convention, that is the nominating board meetings to establish the initial list proposal, a compromise solution can be reached.

Over time the compromise solution gradually changed. In the 1960s the idea of 'some' representation became a legitimate concern. The 1970s saw a transition as demands for more equal representation were made and, finally, the 1980s saw that demand accepted as quotas institutionalized gender equality. The lynchpin that has made this work is that the decisions controlled by the party organization have *clear* and *immediate* effects on representation.

Just how important party control over candidate selection is can be seen by comparing women's representation at the national and local level in Norway. At the local level voters are presented with candidate lists from the various parties, but are free to strike names, add names, or use bullet voting (all votes for one candidate). The mandates are divided up among the parties based on total votes, and then within the party those candidates with the most votes are elected. This system is one that

---

[16] An example of an outside strategy is the Women's party in Iceland. This party was started due to dissatisfaction with the mainstream parties. It has received substantial publicity and has been represented in the Allting, but in taking an outside strategy the women's movement within other parties may have been weakened. Iceland has the lowest level of female representation in parliament among the Scandinavian countries.

makes it fairly easy for voters to affect the composition of the party's delegation on the local council. At the national level the electoral laws make it effectively impossible for voters to alter the decisions made by the county nominating conventions.[17] The effects of these rule differences are striking. While women's representation in the Storting has climbed ever higher, representation on municipal councils has lagged and even stagnated. The last local election in 1991 saw the proportion of women actually fall from 31.2 percent to 28.5 percent, more than 10 percent lower than the parliamentary proportion. Almost all of this difference can be explained by the difference in electoral rules. Calculations by Hellevik and Bjørklund (1995) show that the expected proportion of women, if the effects of voters' changes in lists had been gender neutral, was 37.2 percent in 1991. In other words voters, through their ability to influence party delegation composition via list corrections, have decreased women's representation on municipal councils by almost 9 percent.

A couple of other interesting contrasts illustrate the importance of institutional arrangements and simultaneously help to explain why a cultural explanation is insufficient. Norwegian women have made substantial progress towards equality in the Storting. In the Norwegian labour movement and in managerial positions in private industry, however, women are in very weak positions (Skjeie 1991b). Barely 10 percent of the top trade union congress officials are women, despite 40 percent of the rank and file being women. The number of women in top managerial positions in private industry is even less.

These facts have led some researchers to suggest a 'shrinking institutions' argument, which holds that women are given access to the political process, because power is being transferred elsewhere (Holter 1981). Men are consciously not entering electoral politics, because real power resides in other spheres, primarily business and the corporatist political channel. The increase in women in politics is effectively occurring by default. This argument has come under considerable attack (Skjeie 1991b, 1992; Raaum 1994). In a country where over 50 percent of GNP flows through the public sector, the idea that the political system has little power seems suspect at the outset. The shrinking institutions proponents have been willing to admit that some power exists in the public sector, but they argue most of this power is in the corporatist channel not the parliamentary/electoral channel.

---

[17] The law requires that 50 percent or more of voters make the *exact same* changes in their election lists for voters to be able to override the decisions made by the county convention. This has never happened.

This argument can be challenged on at least a couple of points. While female representation in the corporatist channel initially lagged behind representation in the electoral channel, that has changed in the past decade to the point where women are equally well represented in both channels (Raaum 1994). In addition, parliamentary power can hardly be described as shrinking. With the complicated parliamentary constellation which has existed over the past eight years parliamentary power has clearly increased, more and more issues have had to be resolved in the Storting rather than in the government. Parliament is probably more powerful today than at any point in the post World War II period. Far more plausible than the assertion that men are leaving politics because there is no power left there, is an explanation that emphasizes a comparative institutions approach.[18]

A comparative institutions approach considers how different institutions process similar demands. The common thread that goes through this approach is that differences in the institution's structures affect how demands are dealt with and result in different outcomes. In this case demands for greater access for women to legislative organs, trade union decision making structures, and business higher echelons have all been made. The structures of these three different institutions differ radically. The selection of candidates for parliament is open to public scrutiny with an access structure which allows influence from outside interests. Parties face a strongly competitive environment where failure to react to requests for action can result in defections to another party. Many of the same interests which have been so successful at changing the face of political representation have tried mightily, but with little success, to influence the advancement of women in private firms and leadership arenas in labour unions. For private firm advancement, attempts at opening this process up to scrutiny have been rebuffed as unacceptable meddling. Access has been denied. While the trade union congress has been somewhat more open, there have been very few concessions offered by union officials. Part of the explanation for this intransigence is that the trade union congress maintains a pre-eminent position as the representative of workers. Unlike political leaders, union officials can afford to alienate some members, because it has little consequence for the trade union congress' position in the corporatist structure (Skjeie 1991b).

---

[18] See Skjeie (1991b; 1992) for a more extensive description of this argument.

Summary

This chapter started by describing the expected effect of district magnitude on female representation. In discussing district magnitude, party magnitude was identified as an intervening variable that was causally closer to the dependent variable, women's representation. The data analysis found that party magnitude did have a statistically significant effect on female proportion of the party district delegation. Further analysis found that party magnitude was strongly affected by district magnitude. Because Norway has a comparatively high average district magnitude, and because party magnitude is causally related to improved representation of women, it is reasonable to claim that the electoral structure has helped women initially gain access in Norway.

While party magnitude influences female representation, there is an important interaction between the electoral institution and the political environment. Party magnitude has its greatest influence in a time period where agitation for greater influence has a base, but is not firmly established. In this time period, roughly 1957-73 in Norway, women's probability of being represented clearly increased as a party increased its seats per district. Prior to the late 1950s, women's representation was not a political issue. In that environment, the institutional mechanism had no effect on women's representation. By 1977, women had become sufficiently well established that party magnitude's effect was weakened and more sporadic. By this period women are a major political force in even the smallest districts.

After establishing that party magnitude was an important factor, attention turned to the role played by the internal party nominating processes. Within the Norwegian context this process is of substantial significance because it is directly linked to who serves in the legislature. The system of county nomination meetings was sufficiently open to allow newly organized interests to enter. At the same time these meetings were sufficiently closed and limited in size that a cohesive and well organized interest would have substantial influence on the choice of candidates, even if they only represented an intense minority within the population as a whole.

Women in Norway have made impressive gains in political representation. Politicians and political scientists in other countries look in amazement at the level of integration of women into the political process. Especially when similar high levels of representation are found in the other Nordic countries it has been very tempting to explain the results as an indication of a unique Nordic culture, where the noted passion for equality also includes gender equality.[19] This perspective often ends up by noting that the Nordic culture cannot be easily transplanted to other countries and therefore provides only limited guidance for those wishing to increase female representation in their own countries. The message of this chapter is that while culture may be part of the explanation it is surely not all of it. The structure of the electoral institutions play a critical role. The existing electoral institutions provided the opportunity to press demands for representation. They insured that a well organized effort was able to pay impressive dividends in terms of increased representation. Political scientists studying representation in other countries would be well advised to consider the structure of electoral institutions when looking for explanations as to why women's representation in other countries has lagged behind the Norwegian case.

References

Aasland, T. (1964), 'Kvinner i Stortinget,' in Kaartvedt, A. (ed.): *Det Norske Stortinget gjennom 150 År*, Vol. 4. Oslo: Gyldendal Forlag.

Andersen, K. and Thorson, S. (1984), 'Congressional Turnover and the Election of Women,' *Western Political Quarterly*, 37:143-156.

Beckwith, K. (1990), 'District Magnitude and the Nomination and Election of Women to Parliament.' College of Wooster, Manuscript.

Bystydzienski, J. (1988), 'Women in Politics in Norway', *Women and Politics*, 8: 73-95.

Castles, F. (1981), 'Female Legislative Representation and the Electoral System', *Politics*, 1: 21-26.

Darcy, R. and Choike, J. R. (1986), 'A Formal Analysis of Legislative Turnover: Women Candidates and Legislative Turnover', *American Journal of Political Science*, 30:237-255.

Darcy, R. and Schramm, S. Slavin (1977), 'When Women Run Against Men', *Public Opinion Quarterly*, 41:1-12.

---

[19] See Matland (1994) for an experimental test showing that the Scandinavian political culture may be considerably less progressive in terms of gender equality than is commonly assumed.

Darcy, R., Welch, S. and Clark, J. (1985), 'Women Candidates in Single and Multi-Member Districts: American State Legislative Races', *Social Science Quarterly*, 66:945-953.

Darcy, R., Welch, S. and Clark, J. (1987), *Women, Elections and Representation*. New York: Longman.

Darcy, R., Welch, S. and Clark, J. (1994), *Women, Elections and Representation*. 2nd edition. Lincoln, Neb.: University of Nebraska Press.

Duverger, M. (1955), *The Political Role of Women*. Paris: UNESCO.

Engstrom, R. (1987), 'District Magnitudes and the Election of Women to the Irish Dail', *Electoral Studies*, 6:123-132.

Grofman, B. and Lijphart, A. (eds) (1986), *Electoral Laws and Their Political Consequences*. New York: Agathon Press.

Hellevik, O., and Bjørkland, T. (1995), 'Nedgangen i kvinneandelen i kommunestyrene etter valget i 1991,' in Raaum, N. (ed.): *Kvinner i Norsk Politikk: Politisk Medborgerskap i Endring*. Oslo: Tano.

Hills, J. (1983), 'Candidates, the Impact of Gender', *Parliamentary Affairs*, 34: 221-228.

Holter, H. (1981), 'Om kvinneundertrykkelse, mannsunderstrykkelse og herskerteknikker', in Andenæs, M. et al. (eds): *Maktens ansikter*. Oslo: Gyldendal.

Hunter, A. A. and Denton, M. A. (1984), 'Do Female Candidates Lose Votes? The Experience of Female Candidates in the 1979 and 1980 Canadian General Elections', *Canadian Review of Sociology and Anthropology*, 21:395-406.

Inter Parliamentary Union (1992), Distribution of Seats Between Men and Women in National Parliaments: Statistical Data from 1945 to June 30, 1992. Geneva: IPU.

Jewell, M. (1982), *Representation in State Legislatures*. Lexington, KY: University Press of Kentucky.

Kirkpatrick, J. (1974), *Political Women*. New York: Basic Books.

Kelley, J. and McAllister, I. (1984), 'Ballot Paper Cues and the Vote in Australia and Britain: Alphabetic Voting, Sex and Title', *Public Opinion Quarterly*, 48: 452-466.

Lakeman, E. (1976), 'Electoral Systems and Women in Parliament', *Parliamentarian*, 56:159-162.

Lijphart, A. (1985), 'The Field of Electoral Systems Research: A Critical Survey', *Electoral Studies*, 4:3-14.

Matland, R. E. (1993), 'Institutional Variables Affecting Female Representation in National Legislatures: The Case of Norway', *The Journal of Politics,* 55: 737-755.

Matland, R. E. (1994), 'Putting Scandinavian Equality to the Test: An Experimental Evaluation of Gender Stereotyping of Political Candidates in a Sample of Norwegian Voters', *British Journal of Political Science,* 24: 66-85.

Matland, R. E. and Brown, D. D. (1992), 'District Magnitude's Effect on Female Representation in State Legislatures', *Legislative Studies Quarterly,* 17:469-492.

Matland, R. E. and Studlar, D. T. (1993), The Contagion of Women Candidates in Single Member and Multimember District Systems: Canada and Norway. Paper presented at the Midwest Political Science Association Meetings, Chicago, Ill.

Means, I. N. (1972), 'Political Recruitment of Women in Norway', *Western Political Quarterly,* 25:491-521.

Means, I. N. (1973), *Kvinner i Norsk Politikk.* Oslo: Cappelens Forlag.

Moncrief, G. F. and Thompson, J. A. (1991), 'Urban and Rural Ridings and Women in Provincial Politics: A Research Note on Female MLAs', *Canadian Journal of Political Science,* 24:831-837.

Moncrief, G. F. and Thompson, J. A. (1992), 'Electoral Structure and State Legislative Representation: A Research Note', *The Journal of Politics,* 54:246-255.

Nordby, T. (1985), *Stortinget og Regjeringen, 1945-1985: Institusjoner og Rekruttering.* Oslo: Kunnskapsforlaget.

Norris, P. (1985), 'Women's Legislative Representation in Western Europe', *Western European Politics,* 8:90-101.

Norris, P. (1987), *Politics and Sexual Equality.* Boulder, CO: Rienner.

Norris, P. and Lovenduski, J. (1993a), 'If Only More Candidates Came Forward: Supply Side Explanations of Candidate Selection in Britain', *British Journal of Political Science,* 23:373-408.

Norris, P. and Lovenduski, J. (1993b), *Gender and Party Politics.* London: Sage.

Pitkin, H. (1967), *The Concept of Representation.* Berkeley, CA: University of California Press.

Raaum, N. (1994), 'Kvinners Politiske Mobilisering: Mannefall og Kvinnekall,' in Nagel, A. H. (ed.): *Kvinner i Velferdsstaten.* Bergen: Alma Mater.

Rasmussen, J. (1983), 'Women's Role in Contemporary British Politics: Impediments to Parliamentary Candidature', *Parliamentary Affairs,* 36:300-315.

Rule, W. (1981), 'Why Women Don't Run: The Critical Contextual Factors in Women's Representation', *Western Political Quarterly,* 34:60-77.

308 *Women in Nordic Politics*

Rule, W. (1987), 'Electoral Systems, Contextual Factors and Women's Opportunity for Election to Parliament in Twenty-Three Democracies', *Western Political Quarterly*, 40:477-498.

Skjeie, H. (1991a), 'The Rhetoric of Difference: On Women's Inclusion into Political Elites', *Politics and Society*, 19:209-232.

Skjeie, H. (1991b), 'The Uneven Advance of Norwegian Women', *New Left Review*, 187:79-102.

Skjeie, H. (1992), *Den Politiske Betydningen av Kjønn: En Studie av Norsk Topp-politikk*. Doktoravhandling. Rapport nr. 11. Oslo: Institutt for Samfunnsforskning.

Skjeie, H. (1993), 'Målrettet og Tilfeldig: Kvoteringspraksis og Kvinnerepresentasjon på Stortinget', *Tidskrift For Samfunnsforskning*, 34:479-486.

Statistisk Sentralbyrå (1980), *Kommunevalget 1979*. Oslo: Statistisk Sentralbyrå Trykkeriet.

Studlar, D. T. and Welch, S. (1991), 'Does District Magnitude Matter? Women Candidates in Local London Elections', *Western Political Quarterly*, 44:457-466.

Taagepera, R., and Shugart, M. Soberg (1989), *Seats and Votes: The Effects and Determinants of Electoral Systems*. New Haven, CT: Yale University Press.

Torp, O. Chr. (1978), *Stortinget: I Navn og Tall, 1977-1981*. Oslo: Universitets-forlaget.

Torp, O. Chr. (1982), *Stortinget: I Navn og Tall, 1981-1985*. Oslo: Universitets-forlaget.

Torp, O. Chr. (1986), *Stortinget: I Navn og Tall, 1985-1989*. Oslo: Universitets-forlaget.

Torp, O. Chr. (1990), *Stortinget: I Navn og Tall, 1989-1993*. Oslo: Universitets-forlaget.

Torp, O. Chr. (1994), *Stortinget: I Navn og Tall, 1993-1997*. Oslo: Universitets-forlaget.

Valen, H. (1956), 'Nominasjoner til Stortingsvalget', *Statsøkonomisk Tidskrift*, 70:115-142.

Valen, H. (1966), 'The Recruitment of Parliamentary Nominees in Norway', *Scandinavian Political Studies*, 1:121-166.

Valen, H. (1988), 'Norway: Decentralization and Group Representation,' in Gallagher, M. and Marshed, M. (eds): *Candidate Selection in Comparative Perspective: The Secret Garden of Politics*. London: Sage.

Valen, H,. Aardal, B. and Vogt, G. (1990), 'Endring og Kontinuitet: Stortingsvalget 1989', *Sosiale og Økonomiske Studier*, 74. Oslo: Statistisk Sentralbyrå.

Welch, S. and Studlar, D. T. (1986), 'British Public Opinion Toward Women in Politics: A Comparative Perspective', *Western Political Quarterly*, 39:138-154.

Welch, S. and Studlar, D. T. (1990), 'Multi-Member Districts and the Representation of Women: Evidence from Britain and the United States', *The Journal of Politics*, 52:391-412.

Part V

Attitudes and Symbols

A gender gap that vanished: tolerance and liberalism[1]

Lise Togeby

Introduction

In addition to conservatism, moralism, and lack of involvement, intolerance belongs to the traditional picture of 'women and politics'. But while this picture has been revised with regard to women's political ideology and involvement, little attention has been paid to their tolerance. Women have become more politically involved and have moved to the left of men on a number of issues. But what about tolerance?

In his famous 1955 study of the American public's attitudes towards communists and other divergent groups, Samuel A. Stouffer found an overall gender difference of seven percentage points in favor of men in the distribution of tolerance. Stouffer devoted an entire chapter of the book to a discussion of this difference, but was, nevertheless, eager to minimize its importance. First of all, the difference was not very large, and it apparently only appeared in connection with questions about communists. Nothing indicated more general gender-based differences in tolerance. Furthermore, it was difficult for Stouffer to explain the difference, because a control for the most obvious factors, such as education, political interest, or religion, did not eliminate the gender gap (Stouffer 1955). Commenting on Stouffer's findings, David Riesman pointed to women's 'cultural role of protecting the young', but he concluded that 'it is not entirely clear why women, who as various studies show are more empathic than men, should register on Stouffer's scales as almost invariably more intolerant' (Riesman 1956:61; cf. Nunn et al. 1978:112).

Later studies have shown that the findings were neither restricted to Stouffer's data nor conditioned by the special political climate at the beginning of the 1950s. An equally large gender gap appeared in the mid-1970s, but also this time only in connection with the communists (Nunn et al. 1978, ch. 7; Jennings and Niemi 1981, ch. 9). During recent years the question has not received much attention, but

[1] An earlier version was published in *Scandinavian Political Studies*, Vol. 17, No. 1:47-68, 1994.

314   *Women in Nordic Politics*

available studies suggest that the differences have diminished during the 1980s and probably do not exist any longer (McClosky and Brill 1983; Bobo and Licari 1989; Golebiowska 1992, Gibson 1992).

In the United States, women's intolerance has apparently been a real, but rather limited, phenomenon, and is, in any case, a phenomenon of the past. American women may, however, be more tolerant than women in most other countries. In general, American women are, and have been for a long time, more integrated in the political system than women elsewhere (Verba, Nie and Kim 1978; Baxter and Lansing 1983; Kaase 1989; Jennings and Farah 1990). Regardless of the much commented gender gap in voting, comparatively, only few and small gender differences in political attitudes and behavior have been found in the United States (Goertzel 1983; Shapiro and Mahajan 1986; Deitch 1986; Gilens 1988; Conover 1988; Carroll 1989; Jennings and Farah 1990; Cook and Wilcox 1991). Until recently, however, the exclusion of women from the political system has been more pronounced in Europe than in the United States. Consequently, gender differences in political tolerance may also be larger in Europe. The picture of women's relations to the political system has perhaps been colored by the fact that most information comes from American studies.

Contrary to the popular image of Nordic women as being politically progressive as well as sexually liberated, evidence from Denmark suggests that as late as the 1970s the gender gap in tolerance was also greater there than in the United States (Table 1).[2] Women's intolerance was most pronounced in connection with the idea of a strong man taking power in times of economic crisis, but also appeared in

---

[2] The election survey of 1971 was conducted in connection with the general election September 21, 1971 by Ole Borre, Erik Damgaard, Hans Jørgen Nielsen, Steen Sauerberg, Ole Tonsgaard and Torben Worre, all from the Universities of Copenhagen and Aarhus. The survey was financed by The Danish Social Science Research Council and the data was collected by The Danish National Institute of Social Research. It was a two wave panel study where 62 percent (or 1302 persons) of the original sample participated in both waves.

The 1979 election study was conducted in connection with the general election October 23, 1979 by Ole Borre, Jørgen Goul Andersen, Ingemar Glans, Hans Jørgen Nielsen, Steen Sauerberg and Torben Worre, all from the Universities of Copenhagen and Aarhus. The survey was financed by The Danish Social Science Research Council and the data was collected by 'Gallup Markedsanalyse A/s'. The response rate is not reported.

The 1990 election study was conducted in connection with the general election December 12, 1990 by Ole Borre, Jørgen Goul Andersen, Steen Sauerberg, Hans Jørgen Nielsen and Torben Worre, all from the Universities of Copenhagen and Aarhus. The survey was financed by The Danish Social Science Research Council and the data was collected by 'Gallup Markedsanalyse A/S'. The response rate is not reported.

Table 1

Gender Differences in Attitudes, 1971-1979-1990. Percent Tolerant Attitudes [a]

		Men	Women	M - W
	1971			
1.	When the country is facing economic crisis it would be best to have a strong man taking power	47	29	18**
2.	Parties going against the welfare state should be banned	54	39	15**
3.	Radio and TV should not lend themselves to the expression of extreme viewpoints	60	48	12**
4.	Parties supporting socialism should be banned	81	69	12**
5.	The authorities should keep better check on tourists entering the country	25	17	8**
6.	Foreign workers should not be allowed to force Danes out of their jobs	11	8	3
	1979			
1.	When the country is facing economic crisis it would be best to have a strong man taking power	56	43	13**
2.	Radio and TV should not lend themselves to the expression of extreme viewpoints	64	55	9**
7.	When a country faces serious problems, democracy falls short	39	30	9**
8.	Foreign workers should have the same right to their own way of life and culture as other people	43	39	4*
9.	We have to be more on guard against indoctrination in schools	13	10	3
10.	Violent crimes should be punished more severely than today	7	5	2
11.	Groups not accepting the democratic system have to put up with the police keeping an eye on them	22	21	1

	1990			
1.	When the country is facing economic crisis it would be best to have a strong man taking power	62	60	2
10.	Violent crimes should be punished more severely than today	9	9	0
12.	It's better to fight crime with prevention and counselling than with harsh sentences	24	26	-2
13.	The government spends too much money on refugees	55	58	-3
14.	Immigration is a threat to our national character	41	45	-4
N^b	1971	639	663	
	1979	900	1014	
	1990	459	515	

a) 'Agree completely' and 'agree somewhat' to tolerant statements or 'disagree completely' and 'disagree somewhat' to intolerant statements.

b) The percentages are computed on the basis of the number of respondents answering the questions. Therefore the N's change a little from item to item.

Data: Election surveys 1971, 1979, and 1990.

* Significant at the .05 level
** Significant at the .01 level

connection with censorship, the banning of political parties, and control of foreigners. Both the range of women's intolerance and the gender differences are larger than those found by Stouffer in 1955.

However, the table also shows that the situation has changed completely during the past twenty years. In 1979, women were still less tolerant than men, even if the differences had decreased, but in 1990 the gap closed. There are no differences in the tolerance or liberalism of men and women. This closing of the gender gap is solely the result of women becoming more tolerant. If we look at the only item asked in all three surveys, namely the one about a strong man taking power, we can see that both men and women have become more tolerant during the 1970s and 1980s. However, the development has been much stronger for women than for men, raising women to the level of men.

The concept of 'tolerance' and its operationalization

In the tradition of Stouffer, political tolerance is generally defined as 'a willingness to 'put up with' those things one rejects or opposes' (Sullivan, Piereson and Marcus 1982, 2) or as 'a willingness to apply such procedures - the right to speak, to publish, to run for office - on an equal basis to all' (Sullivan, Piereson and Marcus 1979, 781).

In recent years a lot of effort has been put into creating more valid and reliable operationalizations of tolerance. Sullivan, Piereson and Marcus have claimed that the measure of tolerance should be content-free, especially if we want to compare over time (Sullivan, Piereson and Marcus 1979 and 1982), whereas Gibson tends to conclude that tolerance is a more universal dimension and that differences in operationalizations are unimportant, as the correlates of tolerance are almost identical regardless of the measure used (Gibson 1992).

Moreover, Gibson and Bingham argue that 'tolerance traditionally has been considered broader in scope' than support for opposition rights (speech, assembly, and associations' (Gibson and Bingham 1982). Taking such a broader concept of tolerance as starting point, they included attitudes towards phenomena as diverse as majority rule, civil liberties for political, social, and ethnic minorities, police enforcement and free abortion. Although they singled out several different dimensions of tolerance, their overall conclusion was that all dimensions were strongly interrelated and formed a common syndrome of tolerance (Gibson and Bingham 1982). Similar results have been obtained from Danish studies (Gaasholt and Togeby 1992). Against the background of Gibson et al.'s analyses one can conclude that even if it would be preferable to distinguish between different more precisely defined sub-dimensions of tolerance, it is acceptable to work with an operationalization of the broader and more diffuse concept.

As shown in Table 1, Danish election surveys have, since 1971, contained a few items which together tap a rather broad concept of tolerance, including attitudes towards majority rule, civil liberties, police enforcement and immigrants. To make things even worse, only one single item is repeated in all three surveys, making it necessary to vary the operationalization of tolerance from one survey to another. According to Przeworski and Teune this is an acceptable procedure in comparative research, however, especially when comparing relationships between systems. In that case it is acceptable to use equivalent indicators instead of identical indicators (Przeworski and Teune 1970). The remaining problem is, therefore, to establish the equivalence.

The 'tolerance items' of all three surveys have been subjected to scale analysis, using the procedure proposed by Mokken[3] (Mokken 1971), with rather similar results. In 1971 the six items shown in Table 1 formed a scale with a weak unidimensional structure (Loevinger's H = .33, Cronbach's alpha = .59), suggesting that they stem from a common attitude syndrome if not from a single dimension. The unidimensionality is a little stronger for the seven items in 1979 (Loevinger's H = .34, Cronbach's alpha = .67) and the 5 items in 1990 (Loevinger's H = .39; Cronbach's alpha = .65). The item involving a strong man taking power appears in all three scales, and the content of the other items does not differ much from survey to survey. In all three cases we deal with items covering a broad or diffuse concept of tolerance or liberalism. Thus, it should be safe to conclude that it is acceptable to build indices of these items in order to compare the relationship between gender and tolerance over the three years.

For each year a simple additive index is constructed, varying between 0 and 6 in 1971, between 0 and 7 in 1979 and between 0 and 5 in 1990. Measured by Pearson correlations, the relationship between gender and tolerance amounts to .23 in 1971, to .15 in 1979 and to .01 in 1990 with women as most intolerant. These combined measures also show that a considerable gender gap in tolerance in 1971 has disappeared in 1990.

But what does it actually mean that men in 1971 have a higher score on tolerance than women? As shown in Table 1 it does not mean that men are tolerant and women intolerant. Both men and women give a surprisingly high number of intolerant answers, but women more often than men. Nor does it necessarily mean that women act more intolerant than men. The relationship between attitudes and behavior is far from perfect in the case of tolerance (Sullivan, Piereson and Marcus 1982, ch. 2). But in a country such as Denmark, where political tolerance is part of the dominant political culture, a gender difference in tolerance means that women are not as well integrated into the dominant and official political culture as men, and that they, therefore, are less inclined to express tolerant views.

---

[3] The scaling procedure used in this paper is that of R. J. Mokken, which is an alternative to the Guttman scaling. Whereas Guttman scaling is based on a deterministic model, Mokken's procedure is based on a probabilistic response model, or latent structure model. Instead of the coefficient of scalability used in Guttman scaling to evaluate the scale, Mokken uses Loevinger's coefficient of homogeneity as a measure of unidimensionality. Loevinger's H ranges from 1 to -1 and conventionally a coefficient above .50 is regarded as indicating a strong unidimensional structure, a coefficient between .40 and '.49 a medium strong structure, and a coefficient between .30 and .39 a weak structure (Mokken 1971).

Political tolerance in Denmark 1971

Not all citizens are exposed to the dominant norms of society to the same degree. And since norms of tolerance are difficult to understand, citizens vary in the degree to which they learn tolerance. As Duch and Gibson point out 'this in turn leads to the hypothesis that greater social integration results in greater political tolerance, at least within democratic polities' (Duch and Gibson 1992: p.240; cf. Stouffer 1955; Lipset 1960; McClosky 1964). It is therefore plausible that the theories developed to explain women's weaker integration into the political system also explain their lower tolerance.

In recent years, three theories have prevailed: the structural explanation, the situational explanation, and the socialization theory (Orum et al. 1974; Welch 1977; Jennings 1983; Clark and Clark 1986; Welch and Thomas 1988; Bennett and Bennett 1993). The aim is now to examine whether some, or any, of these theories explain Danish women's greater intolerance or lack of liberalism in the beginning of the 1970s, or whether other theories are necessary.

The structural explanation takes its point of departure in the fact that women do not have as many social resources, e.g. education, position, and training, as men. Generally speaking, higher education inculcates the general principles of democracy and tolerance and also furnishes the psychological resources necessary for the practice of democracy and tolerance, such as self-esteem, political trust, political interest, and a sense of political efficacy. Furthermore, in general, women are placed at a lower position in the labour force than men, and earn less money, making them more alienated and economically insecure (Pateman 1989), and probably also more intolerant. It is possible to test the structural explanation by controlling the original gender difference in tolerance for such factors as school education, professional training and occupation. If women's lower tolerance can be explained by their lower position in the social structure of society, the control should eliminate the gender difference.

Education is generally perceived as one of the most important determinants of tolerance and liberalism, and it also has a strong impact in this study. While there are conflicting views about the interpretation of this relationship, no one denies that education is highly related to tolerance (Stouffer 1955; Davis 1975; Jackman 1978; Nunn et al. 1978; Hyman and Wright 1979; Jackman and Muha 1984; Sniderman et al. 1984; Engesbak and Todal Jenssen 1991). In Denmark in 1971 men's level of education was higher than women's, and this difference might, therefore, explain the gender gap in tolerance. Table 2 shows, for groups of men and women defined by their school education, the percentage scoring high on tolerance (at least three tolerant answers to the six items from Table 1). The control for school education reduces the gender difference, but not much, because only very few people are in the highest category. More than 80 percent of the population are placed in the lowest educational category, and the gender difference here is almost as large as the difference in the whole population. Thus, school education does not explain the gender difference.

Table 2
Tolerance by School Education and Gender, 1971.
Percent Tolerant[a]

	Men	Women	M - W
Low education	51	30	21**
Medium education	72	57	15*
High education	94	(86)	(8)
All	57	35	22**

a) At least three 'tolerant' answers *to* the six items from Table 1.

(): The N's are between 10 and 29.

Data: Election survey, 1971. (The N's are in the appendix).

* Significant at the .05 level
** Significant at the .01 level

Perhaps the most interesting finding is that the magnitude of the gender difference varies with educational levels. The higher the level of education, the lower the gender difference in tolerance. In the highest educational group which, admittedly, is very small, we find only a small difference between men and women.

Table 3 shows the results when the gender difference is controlled for the other structural factors: professional training, occupation, and age. All three factors are related to gender, including age, since women live longer than men. As expected, all three factors are also related to tolerance, even when controlled for school education. Age does not reduce the gender differences, which are almost identical in all age groups. The patterns regarding professional training and occupation resemble the one already shown for school education. The gender difference in

Table 3
Tolerance by Socioeconomic Factors and Gender, 1971. Percent Tolerant [a]

	Uncontrolled			Controlled by age and school education [b]		
	Men	Wo-men	M - W	Men	Wo-men	M - W
21-29 years	59	39	20	56	35	21**
30-39 years	66	46	20	62	46	16**
40-49 years	61	34	27	60	35	25**
50-59 years	56	36	20	57	37	20**
60-69 years	46	28	18	48	32	16**
70 + years	38	18	20	40	22	18*
Professional training: none	50	28	22	52	31	21**
vocational	57	44	13	57	42	15*
theoretical	90	79	11	72	69	3
Unskilled workers	47	20	27	49	20	29**
Skilled workers	54	-	-	54	-	-
White collars: public sector	79	66	13	70	56	14
White collars: private sector	65	54	11	57	47	10
Self-employed	60	(40)	20	59	(39)	(20)
All	57	35	22	56	36	20**

a) At least three 'tolerant' answers to the six items from table 1.
b) MCA-analysis. The relationship between age and tolerance is only controlled by school education.

Data: Election survey, 1971. (N's are in the appendix).

* Significant at the .05 level
** Significant at the .01 level

tolerance is reduced somewhat, but not decisively. At the same time, however, the magnitude of the gender difference is strongly determined by professional training and occupation. Almost no differences appear between men and women with a theoretical (college) education, whereas strong gender differences appear between people without any professional training and especially among unskilled workers. Women at the bottom of the occupational hierarchy have the lowest scores in political tolerance, as should also be expected in accordance with resource theory.

Women's lower position in the social hierarchy does not explain their lower tolerance. (A simultaneous control for all structural factors only reduces the original gender relationship from .23 to .19). But it is conspicuous that very high and very low resources are especially significant for women. The most resource-rich women do not differ much from their male counterparts, whereas women with fewest social resources deviate from all other groups of men and women by their lack of tolerance and liberalism. So even though structural factors do not abolish the gender gap, they are important for an understanding of it.

The situational explanation points to the special restrictions on women's lives due to their obligation towards home and family. In particular, women with responsibility for small children have few social contacts, little free time, and, consequently, a more restricted field of interest. The result is that women, especially in the early days of marriage, are further removed from political life than men, have less interest in politics, and participate less. Riesman's comments about women's cultural role of protecting the young, which suggest differences in priorities between men and women, are also relevant. In any case, as a result of their greater distance from politics, mothers and homemakers should have less tolerant political attitudes. If women's lower level of tolerance is explained by their connection with children and family, we should find large differences between women according to their family situation, whereas there should be no differences between men and women without family ties.

Table 4 shows the relationship between gender and tolerance, this time controlled for situational, or family, factors. The first observation is that neither marriage, homemaking, nor children have the expected relation to tolerance among women. Divorced women are most tolerant, and single women least, with married women falling in between. Correspondingly, housewives and pensioners fall in between the two groups of working women, unskilled workers and white-collar workers, with the unskilled workers as most intolerant. The table clearly demonstrates that employment per se does not make women more tolerant, but that special kinds of employment might. As Stouffer also found, female workers are less tolerant than other groups.

With regard to children, women without children are most tolerant, but the tolerance rises slightly with an increasing number of children, and, in general, the differences are small. Furthermore, in neither case does the control for family factors reduce the gender difference. (A simultaneous control for all family factors reduces the original gender difference from .23 to .20). Thus, the situational explanation does not gain any support from the data.

Table 4

Tolerance by Family Factors and Gender, 1971. Percent Tolerant [a]

	Uncontrolled			Controlled by age, school education [b]		
	Men	Women	M - W	Men	Women	M - W
Single	56	27	29	53	26	27**
Married/cohabiting	58	36	22	56	37	19**
Divorced/separated	(61)	51	(10)	(64)	48	(16)
Widowed	(35)	24	(11)	(48)	35	(13)
Children: none	55	34	21	57	40	17**
1	58	30	28	56	29	27**
2	63	39	24	56	35	21**
3 +	53	41	12	49	36	13
Housewives	-	33	-	-	34	-
Pensioners	42	23	19	51	33	18**
White collars	71	60	11	62	54	8
Unskilled workers	47	20	27	50	21	29**
All	57	35	22	56	36	20

a) At least three 'tolerant' answers to the six items from table 1.
b) MCA-analysis.

Data: Election survey, 1971. (N's are in the appendix).

* Significant at the .05 level
** Significant at the .01 level

The third explanation claims that women's greater distance from political life is a result of *the gender specific socialization* of children, which relates politics to the male role, and not to the female. Women are less politically involved, have a lesser developed sense of political efficacy, and are also less tolerant, because, from early childhood, they have learned not to take an interest in or be involved in politics. A direct empirical test of this theory is difficult, but an indirect test might do: if an apolitical socialization in childhood and adolescence accounts for women's intolerant views, we should find strong associations between political involvement and tolerance, and these associations should not be eliminated when controlled for structural and situational factors. On the other hand, the gender difference in tolerance should be eliminated when controlled for political involvement.

In Table 5, the relationship is controlled for political involvement, represented by factors such as political interest, political knowledge, and political efficacy. In all three cases, the relationships between political involvement and tolerance are strong, prior to the control for social resources. After control for age and education, the associations are weaker, but not much. Political interest, knowledge, and efficacy have a strong relationship with tolerance among both men and women, a relationship not explainable by differences in social resources such as education. Equally important, however, is the fact that, this time, the gender difference in tolerance is really reduced. Considerable gender gaps still remain, but they are much smaller than before. (A simultaneous control for the involvement factors reduces the original relationship from .23 to .09). Low political involvement could, therefore, be responsible for part of women's greater intolerance. And, as shown, this low political involvement is not caused by structural or situational factors. Together, this gives some support to the socialization theory.

So far the conclusion is easy to draw. The most important reason for women's lower tolerance in Denmark in 1971 seems to be their low political involvement. Women were less interested in politics, felt less efficacious, and knew less about politics. Altogether, these characteristics explain more than half the gender difference. Part of this low political involvement is explained by women's having fewer social resources, primarily their lower level of education. But most of the difference in political involvement is apparently due to the different socialization of men and women, in which men are assigned a political role and women an apolitical. But not all the gender difference in tolerance is explained by the above factors. Therefore, we must conclude that other aspects of female upbringing and of women's lives contributed to women's less tolerant attitudes.

A point of departure for understanding this difference might be the theory of a specific female culture, formulated by Nordic social scientists (Ås 1975 and 1982; Halsaa Albrektsen 1977). This theory claims that men and women live in very

Table 5
Tolerance by Political Involvement and Gender, 1971. Percent Tolerant [a]

	Uncontrolled			Controlled by age, school education [b]		
	Men	Women	M - W	Men	Women	M - W
Political interest:[c]						
low	36	23	13	38	28	10**
medium	57	39	18	53	35	18*
high	72	55	17	69	56	13**
Political efficacy:[d]						
low	35	23	12	37	25	12**
medium	57	38	19	56	40	14**
high	71	54	17	67	54	13*
Political knowledge:[e]						
low	22	14	8	25	17	8*
medium	51	36	15	52	36	16**
high	73	57	16	69	56	13**
All	57	35	22	56	36	20

a) At least three 'tolerant' answers to the six items from table 1.
b) MCA-analysis.
c) Constructed on the basis of three items asking the respondent to evaluate his or her own political interest.
d) Measured by an additive index based on three of the traditional efficacy items: 'Sometimes politics is so complicated that people like me do not understand what is going on', 'I know so little about politics that I should not vote', 'So many other people vote at a general election that it does not matter much whether I vote or not'.
e) Measured by an additive index based on ten items.

Data: Election survey, 1971. (N's are in the appendix).

* Significant at the .05 level
** Significant at the .01 level

different economic, social, and cultural worlds. Women live in the private sphere, i.e. the family, whereas men live in the public sphere, i.e. the workplace and the political system. The female culture is characterized by sensitivity, orientation towards others, compassion, and empathy, but also by object-identity, passivity, and dependence on others. It is important to note that the female culture includes both positive and negative qualities. The social norm-system also differs between men and women in the sense that women are not as familiar as men with abstract political principles such as democracy or political tolerance.

The theory of female culture has been used to explain differences between men and women in the area of political participation, but it is equally suited to explain gender differences in political tolerance. In 1971, women were less tolerant than men because they lived in an apolitical culture guided by other moral principles than the political culture of men. A quality of this fourth explanation is that it offers us an understanding of a fact which has, up until now, puzzled social scientists; namely that women were at the same time both empathic and intolerant.

In contrast to the first three theories, which all refer to the characteristics of the individual woman, the theory of a female culture refers to women collectively. It claims that women as a group, regardless of their individual education, employment or political involvement, are more intolerant than men. For analytical reasons, women's low political involvement has been separated from the specific female culture, but they are actually two sides of the same phenomenon. While the concept of 'female culture' underlines the fact that we are dealing with a collective quality encompassing all women, a quality which is transmitted from one generation of women to the next, one of the defining qualities of this female culture is that it is apolitical.

The development from 1971 to 1990

It is a problem that the above conclusion, concerning the causes of women's less tolerant and liberal views, makes little allowance for the possibility of a rapid change. If gender differences in political tolerance are primarily attributed to women's upbringing and to the different political socialization of men and women, then the situation should be rather stable. But as already shown in Table 1, the situation did indeed change rapidly. In less than two decades women became just as tolerant and liberal as men. What has happened?

Something in the above findings indicates the possibility of breaking the existing cultural pattern. Tables 2 and 3 showed that, not only did the small groups of very resource-rich women with a long education reach the same level of tolerance as men in general, but even the level of the most resource-rich men. A long, theoretical education seems to provide a form of adult socialization capable of changing the intolerance inherent in female culture and socialization. Radical changes in women's social resources may, therefore, result in a general lowering of their intolerance.

As Table 6 shows, a strong increase in women's social resources occurred during the 1970s and 1980s. The educational level of men also increased, but not as much as women's. In the 1971 study, only two percent of women had completed school at the highest level, compared with 21 percent of women in the 1990 study. In 1971, only 29 percent of the women had some kind of professional training, while in 1990, 57 percent had, and about half of these had completed the equivalent of a college education. In the same period, almost all Danish women had joined the labour force. If we disregard pensioners, about half of the women were housewives in 1971, whereas this only applies to four percent of the women in 1990. But the composition of the female labour force also changed, because the growth in employment was limited to white collar jobs. In fact, the number of unskilled female workers declined during the time of the general increase in female employment. In general, the female workforce had far more resources in 1990 than twenty years earlier.

Women's political involvement has also increased during recent years, but at first sight this is not as impressive as the increase in social resources. The strong gender gap in political interest in 1971 has been reduced, but not totally eliminated, in 1990. And there are no changes with regard to political efficacy. These results are surprising, because other studies have shown that the political participation of women has increased strongly and that Danish women today participate at the same high level as Danish men. However, also in these other studies, the self-reported political interest of women is relatively low (Table 7). Women are, apparently, integrated into mass political activities, but still lag behind men in self-confidence and in having a sense of political efficacy (similar results are shown for the US by Beckwith (1986, 148 and 153)). The results raise the question of the validity of political efficacy as an indicator of political involvement, however. In any case, Danish women have, beyond a doubt, been much more politically involved during the 1970s and 1980s

Table 6
Changes in the Composition of the Danish Population, 1971-1990. Percent

		1971		1990	
		Men	Women	Men	Women
School education:	low	79	84	48	42
	medium	15	14	32	37
	high	6	2	20	21
Professional training:	none	47	71	33	43
	vocational	45	22	44	34
	theoretical	8	7	23	23
Occupation:	Unskilled workers	24	17	11	13
	Skilled workers	18	2	15	4
	White collars: public	11	10	15	24
	White collars: private	14	9	22	23
	Self-employed	15	3	11	6
	Pensioners	15	18	19	21
	Housewives	0	39	0	4
	Students	3	2	7	5
Political interests:*	low	25	47	31	43
	medium	33	33	45	41
	high	42	20	24	16
Political efficacy:	low	15	31	12	24
	medium	63	59	59	61
	high	22	10	29	15

a) The operationalization has changed from one study to the other.
Data: Election surveys, 1971 and 1990. (N's are shown in the appendix).

than previously, and also much more integrated into political life. How do these developments relate to the development in tolerance?

Table 7

Changes in Political Participation, 1979-1987. Percent

	1979		1987	
	Men	Women	Men	Women
Participation in party meetings	9	4	7	5
Participation in union meetings [a]	42	33	46	47
Participation in grass-root activities	30	25	29	31
High and medium political interests	72	54	65	56
N	893	876	848	909

a) Only measured for employees.
Data: Election surveys, 1979 and 1987, and the Mass survey, 1979.

Let us start by looking at the relationship between tolerance, school education, and gender (Table 8). As already mentioned, in the population at large the gender gap of 1971 has disappeared in 1990. Generally speaking, the differences have also disappeared in each of the three educational groups. The development has, therefore, been largest for women with the lowest education. The increase in women's social resources has not erased the gender gap, but the increasing tolerance of the least educated women has. In 1971, well-educated women had already reached the level of men, and by 1990 this also applies to other groups of women. The unexplained difference from 1971 has disappeared by 1990.

We gain a more precise illustration of the development by looking separately at the item about a strong man taking power, an item repeated identically in all three surveys (Table 9). The table shows that all groups in Danish society have moved in a more tolerant or democratic direction. This applies to both men and women and to all educational groups. But the increase in tolerance has been most impressive for the least educated women. And this is really a surprising result because, in general, women with a low level of education have been left behind by the development of the 1970s and 1980s, when education became a more and more important social factor. This suggests a profound cultural change during this period, integrating all women into the dominant political culture, which had previously been reserved for men and the few women with many resources. Education is still an important determinant for tolerance, but has less influence on women today than twenty years ago.

Table 8
The Relationship Between Gender and Tolerance by School Education, 1971 and 1991. Pearson's r

	1971	1990
School education: Low	.24**	.06
Medium	.14*	.01
High	.06	.03
All	.23**	.01

* Significant at the .05 level.
** Significant at the .01 level.

Data: Election surveys, 1971 and 1990. (N's are shown in the appendix).

Table 9
'A Strong man taking power', by School Education and Gender, 1971 and 1990. Percent Tolerant [a]

	Men			Women		
	1971	1990	Difference	1971	1990	Difference
School education: low	45	53	8	26	52	26
medium	46	65	19	41	58	17
high	72	81	9	64	75	9

a) 'Agree completely' and 'agree somewhat'.

Data: Election surveys, 1971 and 1990. (N's are shown in the appendix).

The other explanatory factors in Table 10 all tell more or less the same story. The unexplained differences have, generally speaking, disappeared. In some groups men are most tolerant, in other groups women, but the differences are in almost all cases

Table 10

The Relationship a) between Tolerance and Gender by a Number of Explanatory Factors b), 1971 and 1990

	1971	1990
20-29 years	.17**	.06
30-39 years	.16**	.01
40-49 years	.29**	-.03
50-59 years	.23**	.07
60-69 years	.22**	.09
70+	.20*	.02
Professional training: none	.24**	.01
Vocational training	.15*	.07
Theoretical schooling	.02	-.07
Unskilled workers	.32**	-.02
White collar: public sector	.15	.08
White collar: private sector	.09	.04
Self-employed	.10	-.13
Pensioners	.22**	.06
Single	.28**	.01
Married/cohabitating	.21**	.02
Divorced	.22	-.10
Widowed	.13	.15
Political interest: low	.16**	.04
medium	.11*	-.05
high	.16**	.01
Political efficacy: low	.15**	.04
medium	.17**	.03
high	.16*	-.08
All	.21**	.03

a) The entries are Beta-coefficients. The relationships are controlled for age and school education. A positive correlation signifies that men are the most tolerant.
b) The 1990 election survey includes fewer variables than the 1971 election survey, restricting the possibility for comparisons.

* Significant at the .05 level.
** Significant at the .01 level.

Data: Election surveys 1971 and 1990. (N's are shown in the appendix).

Table 11
The Development of Feminist Attitudes among Married and Cohabitating Women from 1965 to 1987

	Opposition to a traditional division of work	Support for a traditional division of work
1965 Married women should not take employment if this results in a man becoming unemployed	17	83
The wife has to take care of the house and children	20	80
It is only natural that the mother does most of the childcare	9	91
1987 In periods with a high level of unemployment men have more right to employment than women	82	18
It is best for the family if the husband is the breadwinner and the wife takes care of the home and family	74	26
Today, it is most fair that husband and wife share the housework equally	95	5

Data 1965: Noordhoek and Smith, 1970. N = 2,610.
Data 1987: Election survey. N = 366.

negligible. And the largest gains in tolerance have always occurred among the leastresource-rich women, e.g. women without professional training or unskilled female workers. It is, furthermore, conspicuous that all generations have experienced the same development. If, for instance, we look at the generation in its fifties in 1971 and in its seventies in 1990, the relationship between gender and tolerance has diminished from .23 in 1971 to .02 in 1990.

These results clearly demonstrate that the increased resources of the individual woman do not explain the development from 1971 to 1990. The gender gap in tolerance has not disappeared because more women have obtained more educational or other individual social resources, or because more women have become politically involved. The decisive change has taken place within all educational categories and within all involvement categories. Not as individuals, but as a group women have become more resource-rich, more politically involved, and more tolerant. The female culture has changed.

It is not possible, on the basis of the two data-sets analyzed here, to present a direct measurement of the changes in the female culture, and we therefore run the risk of reducing the concept of culture to a residual. However, other data makes it possible to find indications of a cultural shift. Women's growing political participation, as documented in Table 7, is one indicator. Another is a strong change in gender role attitudes among married women in Denmark. Table 11 shows that, in the mid 1960s, a large majority of married women supported a very traditional division of work between men and women, whereas, at the end of the 1980s, an equally large majority rejected the same position. The women of the 1960s asserted that their first duty was to the family, while the women of the 1980s expressed a strong engagement in life outside the home, and demanded that men should share the household chores. This clearly demonstrates that the wall between the lives of women and men has broken down during the 1970s and 1980s.

Discussion and conclusion

There were fairly large gender-based differences in political tolerance in Denmark in the early 1970s. On the basis of the above analysis, the conclusion is that these gender differences should be explained by differences in political involvement and by a specific female culture. As we suspect these differences to be rooted in early gender socialization, they should be relatively stable and difficult to change. There were, however, a few examples of women deviating from the general women's culture, namely women with a comparatively very high level of education, which suggests that low political tolerance is not necessarily a characteristic of women.

By 1990, the difference in tolerance between men and women had completely disappeared in Denmark. In the light of the above analysis, this rapid development is surprising. During recent decades, women have obtained more social resources and have become more politically involved, but these changes at the individual level do not explain the rising tolerance. The decisive factor seems to be a collective cultural change, by which especially women with few resources have become more tolerant. During this process the so-called unreduced difference between men and women has also disappeared.

Therefore, what has happened is neither the development expected on the basis of the situation in 1971 - i.e. that more and more women obtained sufficient educational resources to break the dominant pattern - nor the one foreseen by Nunn et al., i.e. that higher education and greater gender equality would lead to more diverse and complex experiences, especially in the younger generations of women, resulting in higher political tolerance (Nunn et al. 1978, ch. 7). Instead, all women, regardless of their individual experiences, education, and age, have become more tolerant, indicating a comprehensive cultural change.

In this chapter, the unreduced gender difference in tolerance of the 1970s has been explained by the coexistence of two different political cultures: a female culture and a male culture. The female culture, encompassing both positive and negative qualities, was determined by women's responsibility towards the family and by their restricted roles as wives and mothers. The point is that all women - with a few exceptions - shared this culture, regardless of their actual situation, i.e. regardless of their marital status, mothering experiences, participation in the labour market, education, or political activity. Women were, in general, less politicized than men, and, therefore, voiced less tolerant views. Men lived in a more politicized political culture and voiced - in accordance with the dominant norms - more tolerant views. The conclusion of this paper is that, today, these separate political cultures have merged, resulting, among other things, in women being more politicized and more tolerant. Another part of the story, not told in this article, is that the male culture has also changed during the same period. This leads us to the question of how such a profound change could take place in less than twenty years?

It is not possible to point to any single explanation. A number of factors seem to have interacted to produce the new situation. For one thing, Danish society has, in general, become more democratic and less authoritarian over the last twenty years. The youth revolt of the late 1960s and 1970s has probably influenced the Danish society more than most other countries. The structures of decision-making have changed both on the more intimate level (in schools, in places of work), and on the political level. Many decisions have been decentralized, and grassroots activities have taken over from more hierarchical and bureaucratic organizations. More people have practiced democratic decision-making in their everyday lives. If it is true that political participation has an educational effect (Pateman 1970), the Danish population should have moved in a more democratic and tolerant direction. However, this change may have affected men and women almost equally even if the changes on the level of participation have been larger for women than for men.

Another general development in Danish society has been the rising level of education (cf. Table 6). In this area, however, the changes have doubtlessly been much greater for women than for men, resulting in an equal level of education for men and women in the younger generations. The change in the collective level of women's resources is important, not the rising level of resources of individual women. In 1971, well-educated women constituted a negligible minority of all women, and were unable to influence the general female culture. In 1991, well-educated women may still be a minority, but the younger generations of women, in particular, possess large educational resources, and who can say that daughters cannot influence their mothers (cf. Sapiro 1991)? In 1971, about half the female population were gainfully employed, many in low-status jobs (cf. Table 6). Today, almost all women work outside their homes, many in interesting and challenging jobs. In 1971, almost all women identified themselves exclusively with their roles as mothers and homemakers, whereas women in 1990 identify themselves equally with their job and their home. Women are no longer primarily defined by the family. And to complete the story, during the same period, men have become more involved in family matters (Togeby 1994). As a result of these developments, the wall between women's and men's lives has broken down, and, at the same time, the political culture of men and women has merged.

However, it is still puzzling that these strong changes have taken place during such a relatively short period. It would probably not have happened at all had it not been for the intense political upheavals and strong political mobilizations which took place in Denmark in the 1970s. Both the modes of participation and the party system changed fundamentally. Two groups were mobilized during this period: the new middle class and the women. Women became much more politically active, much more left-wing, and much more feminist (Togeby 1994) and rejected the traditional division of roles between men and women (cf. Tables 7, 8 and 11). Basically, the breakdown of the specific women's culture was caused by the changing conditions of women in Danish society, but the social movements of the 1970s, including the women's movement, provoked a speeding-up of the development.

It is remarkable that the changes have been sufficiently comprehensive to affect all generations of women. This is really a case of adult socialization replacing old cultural norms and customs by new ones. Even women not personally experiencing great changes in their lives have participated in the collective learning process. And while this has definitely been headed by resource-rich women and the younger generation, it has gradually encompassed all groups of women in Danish society.

References

Baxter, S. & Lansing M. (1983), *Women and Politics. The Visible Majority.* Revised edition. Ann Arbor: The University of Michigan Press.

Beckwith, K. (1986), *American Women and Political Participation. The Impacts of Work, Generation and Feminism.* New York: Greenwood Press.

Bennett, L. L. M. & Bennett, S. E. (1993), 'Changing Views about Gender Equality in Politics: Gradual Change and Lingering Doubts', in Duke, L. L. (ed.): *Women in Politics: Outsiders or Insiders?* Englewood Cliffs, N.J.: Prentice Hall.

Bobo, L. & Licari, F. C. (1989), 'Education and Political Tolerance. Testing the Effects of Cognitive Sophistication and Target Group Affect', *Public Opinion Quarterly*, 53:285-308.

Carroll, S. J. (1989), 'Gender Politics and the Socializing Impact of the Women's Movement', in Siegel, R. S. (ed.): *Political Learning in Adulthood.* Chicago: The University of Chicago Press.

Clark, C. & Clark, J. (1986), 'Models of gender and political participation in the United States', *Women and Politics*, 6:5-24.

Conover, P. J. (1988), 'Feminists and the Gender Gap', *Journal of Politics*, 50:985-1010.

Cook, E. A. & Wilcox, C. (1991), 'Feminism and the Gender Gap - A second look', *Journal of Politics*, 53:1111-1122.

Davis, J. A. (1975), 'Communism, Conformity, Cohorts and Categories: American Tolerance in 1954 and 1972-731', *American Journal of Sociology*, 81: 491-513.

Deitch, C. (1986), 'Sex differences in Support for Government Spending', in Mueller, C. M. (ed.): *The Politics of the Gender Gap. The Social Construction of Political Influence.* Newbury Park: Sage.

Duch, R. M. & Gibson, J.L. (1992), 'Putting up' with fascists in Western Europe: A Comparative, Cross-Level Analysis of Political Tolerance', *The Western Political Quarterly*, 45:237-73.

Engesbak, H. & Todal Jenssen, A. (1991), 'Utdanningens mange fasetter: Hvorfor er høyt utdannede mer positive til innvandrere enn lavt utdannede?', Paper, Nordisk Sosiologkongress, Trondheim.

Gaasholt, Ø. & Togeby, L. (1992), 'Interethnic Tolerance, Education, and Political Orientation: Evidence from Denmark'. Paper, Annual Scientific Meeting of The International Society of Political Psychology, San Francisco.

Gibson, J. L. (1992), 'Alternative Measures of Political Tolerance: Must Tolerance Be 'Least Liked?'', *American Journal of Political Science*, 36:560-577.

Gibson, J. L. & Bingham, R. D. (1982), 'On the Conceptualization of Political Tolerance', *American Political Science Review*, 76:603-620.

Gilens, M. (1988), 'Gender and Support for Reagan. A Comprehensive Model of Presidential Approval', *American Journal of Politics*, 32:19-49.

Goertzel, T. G. (1983), 'The Gender Gap: Sex, Family Income and Political Opinions in the Early 1980s', *Journal of Political and Military Sociology*, 11:209-22.

Golebiowska, E. A. (1992), 'Modern and Traditional Values and Political Tolerance'. Paper, Annual Meeting of the International Society of Political Psychology, San Francisco.

Halsaa Albrektsen, B. (1977), *Kvinner og politisk deltakelse.* Oslo: Pax.

Hyman, H. H. & Wright, Ch. R. (1979), *Education's Lasting Influence on Values.* Chicago: University of Chicago Press.

Jackman, M. R. (1978), 'General and applied tolerance: does education increase to racial education?', *American Journal of Political Science*, 22:302-24.

Jackman, M. R. & Muha, M. J. (1984), 'Education and Intergroup Attitudes: Moral Enlightment, Superficial Democratic Commitment, or Ideological Refinement?', *American Sociological Review*, 49:751-69.

Jennings, M. K. (1983), 'Gender Roles and Inequalities in Political Participation: Results from an Eight-Nation Study', *Western Political Quarterly*,

Jennings, M. K. & Farah, B. G. (1990), 'Gender and Politics: Convergence and Differentiation?', in Risto Sänkiaho, et al.: *People and their Polities.* Helsinki: The Finnish Political Science Association.36:364-85.

Jennings, M. K. & Niemi, R. G. (1981), *Generations and Politics. A Panel Study of Young Adults and their Parents*. Princeton: Princeton University Press.

Kaase, M. (1989), 'Mass Participation', in Jennings, M. K. et al.: *Continuities in political action*. Berlin: Walter de Gruyter.

Lipset, S. M. (1960), *Political Man*. London: Heinemann Educational Books.

McClosky, H. (1964), 'Consensus and Ideology in American Politics', *American Political Science Review*, 58:361-82.

McClosky, H. & Brill, A. (1983), *Dimensions of Tolerance*. New York: The Russell Sage Foundation.

Mokken, R. J (1971), *A Theory and Procedure of Scale Analysis*. The Hague & Paris: Mouton.

Noordhoek, J. A. & Smith, Y. (1979), *Familie og udearbejde*. SFI's studie no. 19. København.

Nunn, C. Z., Crockett, H. J. Jr. & Williams, J. A. Jr. (1978), *Tolerance for Nonconformity*. San Francisco: Jossey-Bass Publishers.

Orum, A. et al. (1974), 'Sex, Socialization and Politics', *American Sociological Review*, 39:197-209.

Pateman, C. (1970), *Participation and Democratic Theory*. Cambridge: Cambridge University Press.

Pateman, C. (1989), *The Disorder of Women*. Stanford: Stanford University Press.

Przeworski, A. & Teune, H. (1970), *The Logic of Comparative Social Inquiry*. New York: Wiley-Interscience.

Riesman, D. (1956), 'Orbits of Tolerance, Interviewers, and Elites', *Public Opinion Quarterly*, 20:49-73.

Sapiro, V. (1983), *The Political Integration of Women*. Urbana: University of Illinois Press.

Sapiro, V. (1991), 'Feminism: A Generation Later', *The Annals of the American Academy of Political and Social Science*, 515:10-22.

Shapiro, R. Y. & Mahajan, H. (1986), 'Gender Differences in Policy Preferences: A Summary of Trends from the 1960s to the 1980s', *Public Opinion Quarterly*, 50:42-61.

Sniderman, P. M., Brody, R. A. and Kuklinski, J. H. (1984), 'Policy Reasoning and Political Values: The Problem of Racial Equality', *American Journal of Political Science*, 28:75-94.

Stouffer, S. A. (1955), *Communism, Conformity and Civil Liberties*. Garden City, N.Y.: Doubleday.

Sullivan, J. L., Piereson, J. E. & Marcus, G. E. (1979), 'An Alternative Conceptualization of Political Tolerance: Illusory Increases', *American Political Science Review*, 73:233-249.

Sullivan L. J., Piereson, J. E. and Marcus, G. E. (1982), *Political Tolerance and American Democracy*. Chicago: The University of Chicago Press.

Togeby, L. (1994), 'The Political Implications of the Increasing Number of Women in the Labour Force', *Comparative Political Studies*, forthcoming.

Verba, S., Nie, N. H. & Kim, J. (1978), *Participation and Political Equality. A Seven-Nation Comparison*. Cambridge: Cambridge University Press.

Welch, S. (1977), 'Women as Political Animals? A Test of Some Explanations for Male-Female Political Participation Differences', *American Journal of Political Science*, 21:711-730.

Welch, S. & Thomas, S. (1988), 'Explaining the Gender Gap in British Public Opinion', *Women and Politics*, 8:25-44.

Ås, B. (1975), 'On Female Culture', *Acta Sociologica*, 18:142-161.

Ås, B. (1982), 'Tilbakeblikk og sideblikk på begrebet kvinnekultur', in Haukaa, R. et al. (ed.): *Kvinneforskning: Bidrag til samfunnsteori*. Oslo: Universitetsforlaget.

Appendix
Number of Persons Scored on Tolerance in Different Categories in the Election Surveys of 1971 and 1990

	1971		1990	
	Men	Women	Men	Women
All	634	636	455	505
20-29 years [a]	138	118	92	81
30-39 years	129	124	89	119
40-49 years	117	122	103	126
50-59 years	107	110	70	65
60-69 years	98	95	60	72
70 + years	45	67	41	42
School education:				
low	501	528	218	214
medium	97	95	147	185
high	36	14	90	106
Professional training:				
none	297	449	152	219
vocational	286	144	199	170
theoretical	51	43	104	116
Number of children:				
none	288	289		
1	127	122		
2	129	147		
3 +	88	74		
Single	81	48	85	52
Married/cohabitating	507	481	325	361
Divorced/separated	18	35	25	27
Widowed	26	68	20	65

Unskilled workers	149	108	50	66
Skilled workers	116	13	67	20
White collar: public sector	67	61	67	123
White collar: private sector	91	57	100	114
Self-employed	95	20	49	29
Pensioners	96	112	87	107
Housewives	0	247	0	19
Students	20	16	34	28
Political interest: low	158	292	138	216
medium	211	213	207	209
high	265	131	110	80
Political efficacy: low	89	193	52	116
medium	408	378	270	313
high	137	65	133	76
Political knowledge: low	68	159		
medium	313	330		
high	253	147		

a) Following the official voting age the youngest age group in 1971 is 21-29 years old whereas in 1979 and 1990 it is 18-29 years old.

Data: Election surveys, 1971 and 1990.

Political language

Lauri Karvonen, Göran Djupsund and Tom Carlson

Introduction

This section of the book deals with political language. The basic question is whether systematic differences exist between men and women in their use of political language. The theoretical starting point is the hypothesis that groups behave differently depending on their relative size. Has the political language used by women as compared to men changed as the activity and representation of women in politics has increased over time?

The present part of the book attempts to highlight this question in two different contexts of postwar Scandinavian politics. First, a highly *formalized* linguistic context is examined, as parliamentary debates in postwar Norway are at the center of attention. Second, a wholly different field of political language is scrutinized; individual election campaigns, a consequence of the Finnish candidate-centered electoral system not found elsewhere in Scandinavia, offer an interesting possibility to compare the language use of men and women in politics. This second context is, of course, much less formalized than the first one. More significantly, while the first context has remained almost completely unaltered over the years, the methods and techniques of election campaigns have *changed* radically in the postwar period. In sum, the study covers a wide spectrum of phenomena related to political language and communication.

These two empirical analyses involve varying data sets and methods. These will be discussed separately for each of the cases.[1]

---

[1] The empirical analysis of parliamentary debates in Norway was carried out by Lauri Karvonen; Göran Djupsund and Tom Carlson did the study on Finnish election campaigns. The same division of labour applied to the draft versions of the present text.

The extent of women's representation

Drude Dahlerup has discussed the significance of the 'critical mass' of women's representation for the form and content of politics at large. Largely on the basis of Rosabeth Moss Kanter's work, she analyzes the effect of the relative size of the minority on the minority's working conditions. Moss Kanter identified four types of situations according to the relative size of the minority (Dahlerup 1988:280):

- The *uniform group* is totally dominated by one group; the social and cultural patterns of this group have a pervasive impact throughout the organization.

- In the *skewed group* the size of the minority is below 15 percent. Here, the representatives of the minority have the role of 'tokens' who are discouraged from expressing the special needs and characteristics of the minority, and who are unable to form alliances with each other.

- In the *tilted group* with a minority representation up to 40 percent, the minority becomes strong enough to influence the culture of the organization at large. Moreover, the representatives of the minority are numerous enough to form alliances with each other.

- The *balanced group* (with ratios within 60:40) is characterized by the predominance of structural and personal factors rather than by interaction patterns conditioned by type (such as race and gender). In other words, the position of the two groups is so self-evident that such mechanisms as tokenism or minority alliances are no longer functional.

Dahlerup notes that the representation of women in Scandinavian politics has definitely passed into the third type of situation; the representative assemblies in Scandinavia are 'tilted groups', where women politicians constitute a significant minority. In most other countries, 'uniform' or 'skewed' groups are the rule. Dahlerup goes on to discuss the possible impact of the 'critical mass' of women's representation on politics. She identifies changes in the reaction to women politicians, changes in the performance and efficiency of women politicians, changes in political culture, changes in the political discourse, policy changes, and changes in women's power. Of particular interest for our study is that given the increased representation of women in politics, the expectation is that 'the tone will be softer in politics', and that 'shorter speeches' and 'less formal language, more to the point' will increasingly characterize the political culture (pp. 288-89). Moreover, the agenda of politics itself will be extended to comprise issues not previously considered to be of a political nature (pp. 291-92).

When did women's representation pass the various critical stages in Scandinavian politics? Table 1 depicts the development since the introduction of universal suffrage.

Table 1
The percentage of women MPs in 20th century Scandinavia.
Averages for decades

	Denmark	Finland	Norway	Sweden
Before 1910	-*)	11		
1910s**)	3	10	0	
1920s	2	9	1	2
1930s	2	7	1	3
1940s	5	11	5	8
1950s	9	15	6	13
1960s	11	16	9	14
1970s	18	23	20	21
1980s	29	31	32	32

*) Indicates that universal suffrage was not yet effective
**) One election in Denmark, six elections in Finland, two elections in Norway

Finland was long an international exception thanks to the comparatively strong representation of women in the parliament, originating from the early introduction of universal suffrage. It was not until the 1970s that roughly similar levels of women's representation were reached throughout Scandinavia. All in all, growth has been considerable during the past three decades. With the partial exception of Finland, women's representation in Scandinavian politics might be divided into three periods: a uniform male culture prior to World War II, a 'skewed' situation until the 1960s, and women as a significant minority (a 'tilted' situation) since the 1970s.

Linguistic differences between men and women

General aspects
The question of linguistic differences between men and women touches on one of the most basic sexual stereotypes. 'Everybody knows' that men and women talk in different ways, usually meaning that women are supposed to talk more and use different ways of expressing themselves than men. More often than not, saying this also implies that male language is superior to female language: men are supposed to speak more precisely and objectively than women, whose language is emotional and tends to 'drift away from the essentials'.

Far from confirming all elements of this classical stereotype, research on male and female language indeed points to some rather systematic differences between the sexes. Women use a simpler and a more concrete language than men, whose usage favors abstractions. Women's language seeks to identify the persons concerned, whereas men employ objective expressions which avoid personal considerations. Women use emotional expressions and refer to emotions considerably more frequently than men. Female language is more empathic, and the flow of communication is characterized by reciprocity; women frequently use expressions that are intended to produce confirmations of consent. Unpleasant things are expressed in an indirect way. Men are more inclined towards a one-way communication, they convey messages rather than engage in a dialogue. This generally gives them a better capacity for authority-oriented situations: men command, lecture and issue statements more naturally than women (Holm 1982:107-110; Adams and Ware 1979:496-498; Lautamatti 1988:186).

Stated in this shorthand manner, these basic observations may appear somewhat banal; they certainly represent only the most typical statistical averages, which conceal a great deal of cross-cultural and individual variation. Nevertheless, they seem to confirm that it may be interesting to inquire into linguistic differences between the sexes in the field of politics as well.

Parliamentary language
While there is a wealth of literature concerning general linguistic differences between women and men, systematic empirical analyses of political language certainly do not abound. As for Scandinavia, Kerstin Thelander's dissertation (1986) is to date the only major study in the field. Furthermore, Esko Vierikko's thesis (1974) on parliamentary language in Finland also pays systematic attention to differences between male and female politicians.

Thelander analyzed both the perceptions of Swedish politicians about the language of politics and the actual linguistic usage of different groups of politicians. Fifty-six members of the Swedish Parliament and 16 local councillors were interviewed. The language spoken in Parliament in 1978-79 by those same 56 MPs was then analyzed as evidenced in the Parliamentary Records. The findings were contrasted with a comparative sample from 1952.

The opinions of the interviewees were largely similar to the generalized differences between men and women which were briefly presented above: women were claimed to use a less complicated, more concrete and more personal language than men. It is all the more interesting to note that Thelander's linguistic analysis of authentic political language by no means offered a straightforward corroboration of these impressions. Female local politicians were found to match these impressions best. As for MPs, however, Thelander found that female political language had become increasingly complex over time; in 1978-79, women politicians were found to use a *more* complicated language than their male colleagues. The author concluded that female MPs apparently adjusted to an existing linguistic norm and became even more loyal representatives of that ideal than their male counterparts (pp. 160-163). In other words, political language stood out as a *professional jargon* which women fully adopted once they entered into the field of parliamentary politics.

This impression is strongly reinforced by an earlier study by Esko Vierikko. Vierikko studied the language of Finnish Members of Parliament in the late 1960s in two different situations: informal language use (interviews) was contrasted with formal language, i.e. speeches at the plenary sessions of the parliament. He found a strikingly consistent pattern. In informal situations, female politicians used a clearly less complicated language than men. They used fewer nouns, adjectives and numerals but more pronouns and subject terms; on the average, they also used shorter words than their male colleagues. In formal situations, however, this order was completely reversed. In their parliamentary speeches, female MPs used an official and complicated language which stood in a clear contrast to their unofficial usage. Thus, for instance, when Vierikko calculated the average length of words for informal and formal situations for 11 different categories of speakers, women MPs ranked eleventh in informal situations and first in formal situations (p. 219). Sex explained differences in language use far better than any other variable, be it education, age or party affiliation (pp. 313-314). Women were extremely conscious of the context in which they spoke, and when appearing in the formal parliamentary role they apparently chose a strongly status-oriented linguistic posture (cf. Adams and Ware 1979:495).

These two studies offer an interesting contrast to the general findings concerning linguistic differences between men and women. At least in the political field, women appear to be highly *context-conscious*. Politics is a trade with a special language; more often than not, women fully adopt these special linguistic patterns once they have entered into the role of politician.

Campaign language

Within the broad tradition of election studies many focus on the campaign substance of both parties and candidates. Surprisingly little interest has, however, been devoted to gender-based differences. Among studies that pay attention to political advertising we can point only to two that have scrutinized the question of gender: the study by Benze and Deqlerq on candidates in television spot-ads in the USA (1985) and Vatanen's study concerning ads in local radio broadcasting in Finland (1988).

Benze and Declerq compare the contents of male and female spot ads in election campaigns between 1980 and 1983. They find more similarities than differences between the ads of males and females. Both male and female candidates chose to play down their party affiliations and mainly to name important issues rather than to stress their own standpoints. Specific group references were generally used to the same extent by men and women although men referred to more general segments of the electorate somewhat more often. Candidates of both sexes used negative advertising in their campaigns. Women more often attacked the standpoints of their opponents while men more often focused in on their competitors' personalities and performance (pp. 280-283). The only significant difference that Benze and Declerq found concerned the images of the candidates. Female candidates are more often than not the object of 'stereotyping in several areas, most notably they are viewed as not as tough as male candidates and lacking competence or experience for an office'. They are, furthermore, seen as 'more compassionate than male candidates as well as more honest' (pp. 279-80).

Benze and Declerq note that female candidates face a dilemma: whether to fight the perception of lacking toughness and competence by choosing a rather male style of campaigning, thus taking the risk of being seen as 'too tough and hence strident and bitchy', or clinging to the existing female style (p. 283; cf. Dahlerup 1988:289). The study shows that the vast majority of female candidates chose the latter strategy. An indicator of this is that toughness was stressed in male campaigns three times more often than in female ones. At the same time, women stress compassion and warmth more than twice as often as their male colleagues. Finally Benze and Declerq note that male and female candidates treat competence, experience and performance in quite a uniform manner (p. 283).

Vatanen's results are strikingly similar to those of Benze and Declerq. Female candidates in Finland display a strategy which is largely similar to that of their colleagues in the USA. The overall impression seems to be that women have little to gain by stressing firmness, strength and toughness. The picture of a strong and firm female politician is not regarded as attractive to voters. On the other hand Vatanen found that if one leaves the firm-soft dimension aside, the female and male candidates are very much alike. Women and men both stress their independence, activity and competence in a rather similar manner (pp. 72-73).

Policy sectors

A fairly consistent pattern of roles between male and female politicians can be discerned throughout the Western world. Some policy sectors are characterized by a high degree of activity by women politicians, whereas they are under-represented in others even given their limited share of seats in representative assemblies. Social welfare questions, education and child care are typically among the first type of issues, whereas defense, foreign policy and economic policy are male spheres of politics (Vallance and Davies 1986:66-67; Sinkkonen and Haavio-Mannila 1981:204-205; Thelander 1986:121). In a third type of issue, women's issues *par excellence* - equal pay, sexual harassment - often only women display any activity (Skard and Haavio-Mannila 1983:111, Skeije 1991:239-40). Again, these differences are well-known, and it is as such not original to state them.

From the point of view of our study, however, it is quite important to pay systematic attention to possible inter-sectoral variation in political language. It is, as Thelander (loc.cit.) notes, quite possible that female politicians use a different language just because they talk about different things than men. Consequently, differences in political language may depend on the fact that 'different sectors talk differently'. Certainly, an important potential change in the language of politics may be that increased activity on the part of women has led to the introduction of a wholly new type of issue, which requires a language different from those of traditional policy sectors. It is, however, equally imaginable that there is a systematic difference between men and women *within* various policy sectors as well.

Furthermore, as Sinkkonen and Haavio-Mannila have demonstrated in the case of the Finnish Parliament (1981:212-214), the sectoral specialization of women politicians is at least to some extent time-specific. Issue specialization may at least to some degree be a function of the development of women's political representation at large.

Empirical analysis I: parliamentary debates in Norway

The general question on which this section focusses is whether there are systematic differences in the content of parliamentary speeches between women and men members of Parliament. Do women and men speak of different *things* (issues, policy sectors) and do they speak in different *ways* (style and orientation)? Are these differences generally valid or do they vary according to sector? Do these differences grow or diminish with the increase of women's representation in politics?

Data

The empirical data consists of parliamentary debates in the Norwegian *Storting* in 1956 and 1986/87 as published in the annual Parliamentary Record (*Stortings-tidende*). The aim is to uncover linguistic differences between male and female MPs and the possible impact of the growth of women's representation on these differences. For this purpose, the selection of the MPs studied aimed at, to the extent possible, eliminating the effects of other variables, such as party affiliation, constituency, age and occupation. The starting point was the thirteen women MPs that participated in the 1956 *Storting*. They were first assigned 'male counterparts' who resembled them as much as possible as to party affiliation, region and age[2]. Their activity and profiles on various policy *sectors* were compared. Thereafter, the linguistic *content* in the speeches of these women politicians was compared with that of men participating in the same debates. Here, it was not possible to take into account party affiliation and other background variables. It was deemed more interesting to compare men and women who spoke on the same issues than to compare 'similar' men and women regardless of which issues they addressed.

For the 1986/87 sample also, these 13 women MPs from 1956 constituted a point of departure. Since the rationale of a longitudinal analysis was to determine whether women politicians acted differently in a situation where women's representation was substantial, it was important to consider a group of women MPs which would

---

[2] A smaller sample was taken in order to check whether *organizational position* (committee memberships, chairmanships etc.) made a difference. The results did not point to any difference whatsoever, as compared to the sample based on the above-mentioned factors. Consequently, this factor was not considered in the further analysis.

resemble the 1956 group as closely as possible as concerns party affiliation, constituency, age and occupation. Again, male counterparts were assigned to these women MPs for the analysis of sectoral activity and linguistic patterns.

Sectors and issues

The analysis distinguished between three general and one specific policy sector. These were largely based on the survey of Nordic research on women in the Scandinavian parliaments presented by Skard and Haavio-Mannila (1983:106-113). *Reproduction* pertains to social policy (family, health, drugs and alcohol, housing and social security), education and cultural policy, and environmental and consumer policy. *Production* covers transport and communication, construction, industry, business, agriculture and fishing, forestry, finance and economic policy, taxation and fiscal regulation, energy and regional policies. *System maintenance* includes criminal policy and law enforcement, foreign and defense policy, the political and administrative systems, the position of minority and interest groups and the general political, administrative and legal relations between individual citizens and the government. Finally, special attention was paid to *women's issues*, which included questions touching upon female dominated groups, institutions and professions, women's health, women's position in marriage and work life, sex roles, prostitution and pornography.

In 1956, the 13 women MPs and their male 'counterparts' spoke on 311 different occasions. Women spoke 94 times, whereas the thirteen men were registered for 217 speeches and questions. This is partly, but not solely explained by the fact that half of the women MPs studied were deputy members who were not present throughout the parliamentary period. Even if this is taken into consideration, it can be concluded that women were generally less active than men in the parliamentary debates.

Thirty years later, this was no longer the case. Of the 489 speeches included in the sample, women accounted for 267 and men for the remaining 222. As for the distribution according to policy sectors, there was no such clear-cut change over time:

Table 2
The activity of women and men MPs on various policy sectors in 1956 and 1986
Percentages

Sector	1956			1986		
	Women	Men	All	Women	Men	All
Reproduction	46.8	10.1	21.2	44.9	22.5	34.8
Production	23.4	47.5	40.2	25.8	54.9	39.1
System mainten.	17.0	42.4	34.7	22.2	22.1	22.0
Women's issues	12.8		3.9	7.1	0.5	4.1

In the 1950s as well as three decades later, women MPs display significantly higher activity than men in the sphere of reproduction. By the same token, issues pertaining to 'production' continue to be a male-dominated field. As for system maintenance, the leveling-off of the differences is largely due to women's increased activity in the field of foreign policy, an area in which women MPs were almost completely passive in the 1950s. It may seem surprising that the attention paid to women's issues has not risen over the thirty year period. It should be remembered, however, that the 1986 sample only comprises about one-fourth of all women MPs, whereas the 1956 data covers all women in the *Storting*. Women's issues were naturally raised and discussed by other women MPs besides those included in our sample for 1986. Nevertheless, one might have expected a visible change on this point over the period studied.

All in all, our data point to continuity rather than change as regards issue specialization among women and men MPs in Norway. They confirm the observations of several other scholars on this point. The growth of women's representation has *not* changed the basic patterns characteristic of women and men.

Linguistic patterns
This study does not concern language at large but *political* language. In other words, the chief aim of the study is not to inquire whether men and women speak differently in general but to look for possible differences pertaining to important categories of political communication. Four such categories found in the literature were used as instruments of classification in a content analysis of the parliamentary speeches:

• *Orientation*. Who are the recipients or beneficiaries of policies and politics? Whose problems are politicians trying to solve (cf. Karvonen and Rappe 1991: 245-46; Borg 1964:162-184)? Here, the main distinction is between a *concrete* and an *abstract* orientation. Statements referring to concrete groups of individuals and their problems were classified as representing a concrete orientation. 'The people', 'farmers', 'single mothers', 'pensioners' and 'students' are typical examples of statements with a concrete orientation. As for abstractions, 'the system', 'the State', 'the development', 'the economy', 'the cultural milieu' and 'the economic situation' are some frequent expressions classified as representing an abstract orientation. Various types of orientation lie somewhere in between these two extremes. 'Northern Norway', 'the schools', 'local government authorities' and 'cultural organizations' are some examples. These were left unclassified.

• *Arguments*. What kinds of reasons were presented as arguments for or against a certain policy, a standpoint or an opinion? The study distinguished between three different types. *Realism* denotes arguments which expressedly stress that which is possible to achieve rather than what is desirable: 'given the current economic situation we must...'; 'we all want peace but...'; 'given this time frame...' etc. *Acceptability* refers to popular will, public opinion or some overarching value: 'this is the clearly expressed view of the majority of our people'; 'it would be incompatible with our tradition of local self-government' etc. *Consistency* refers to compatibility with earlier policies and decisions and the consistent application of rules, principles and guidelines: 'given the fact that we have invested millions in this system, it is only logical that...'; 'if these groups have been granted this right, others must also be entitled...'etc. (cf. Jaatinen 1991:49-50).

• *Propaganda*. Political persuasion is not solely a matter of rational argumentation. More subtle techniques are frequently used to persuade people without their necessarily being aware of the fact that they are the object of persuasion. In a classical study from the early years of propaganda research (Lee and Lee 1939), a number of propaganda techniques ('tricks of the trade') were presented. Three of these were used as indicators in the present study. *Name calling*, 'giving an idea a bad label - is used to make us reject and condemn an idea without examining the evidence' (Lee and Lee 1939:23-24): 'this waste of the taxpayers' money'; 'these anti-democratic features' etc. *Glittering Generality*, 'associating something with a 'virtue word' - is used to make us accept and approve the thing without examining the evidence' (Ibid.).: 'international solidarity demands'; 'this just and fair proposition' etc. *Testimonial* 'consists of having some respected or hated person say that a given idea or program or product is good or bad' (Ibid.): 'as was aptly pointed out by the Chairman'; 'Hitler was an eager advocate of such practices' etc.

- *Metaphor.* During recent years, many scholars have stressed the importance of metaphor for political language (e.g. Petersson 1987; Heradstveit and Björgo 1992:66-74). Metaphors not only constitute an instrument of expression; they also reflect more general views of politics and society and overall patterns of thought. Palonen (1991:14) has pointed out that the distinction between metaphors that have their origins in *mechanistic* notions and those that are of an *organic* origin is potentially interesting from a political science point of view. Examples of the former are references to society and politics as a machine ('the government machinery'), vehicles ('the man at the helm') or arguments using the laws of physics ('equilibrium', 'centrifugal tendencies') as illustrative instruments. Organic metaphors refer to the human body ('social disease', 'we need a strong hand'), animals, plants and organic processes ('flourishing economy'; 'rooted in a belief'). Many such metaphors are naturally quite commonplace and are used in an unreflected way; at the same time, they may tell us something about the 'deep structures' of the minds of the speakers.

Any content analysis of this kind rests on qualitative judgements. What is regarded as 'concrete or abstract orientation', a certain type of argument, propaganda or metaphor is in the final analysis dependent on how the researcher interprets his categories operationally. In this sense, any content analysis will necessarily be a 'soft' approach. At the same time, the very rationale behind this kind of a systematic analysis is to try to reduce large and complicated bodies of empirical material to manageable proportions. In this endeavor, a quantitative form of presentation is a natural instrument.

Operationally, this study records the occurrence of words, expressions and other speech patterns which represent the categories described above. The basic *unit of analysis* is the individual politician speaking in Parliament. The *recording unit* is any word or expression that qualifies for one of our categories. The aim was to calculate the *relative frequency* with which these different categories occurred in the parliamentary speeches. This frequency was measured in terms of occurrence per 100 centimeters of text column.[3] The Norwegian parliamentary record is published on close-printed double-column pages. The material analyzed here consists of two speeches by each of the 26 women MPs included in the study[4] plus a similar set of speeches by men participating in the same debates. The total amount of text included is 3723 centimeters of column, corresponding to roughly 165 columns of text.

Table 3 reports the overall results of the content analysis. The figures denote the relative frequency of each category calculated using the following formula:

$$f = (ot/cmt) \times 100$$

where f = relative frequency, ot = the total number of times a certain category occurred in women's or men's speeches, cmt = the total number of centimeters of column in women's/men's speeches. Thus, saying that the value for 'concrete orientation' for women MPs in 1956 was 9.9 means that such expressions occurred on the average 9.9 times per 100 centimeters of column.

The differences are, generally speaking, fairly small. The occurrence of the various categories of content is on the same general *level* for both women and men. Most of the coded units for women as well as for men concern 'orientation' and 'propaganda', whereas the kinds of 'arguments' that were sought in this study occur to a fairly limited extent in the speeches of both women and men. There is a slight overall increase in the use of the two types of 'metaphors', but the general level of frequency is still fairly low.

Women MPs display a 'concrete orientation' somewhat more often than their male colleagues. This difference was, however, slightly larger in 1956 than in 1986. As for 'abstract orientation' our data indicate that the reasonably clear difference found in 1956 has disappeared altogether. A closer look at various policy sectors indicates, however, that this is largely due to the fact that 'abstract orientation' has increased for women only as concerns what was termed 'production' above: in 1956 the

---

[3] Each specific word or expression was recorded only *once each speech*; in many cases, the speakers used the same expression a large number of times. This would have distorted the results. Consequently, our data report the occurrence of *different* categories of content for each speech.

[4] Four of the 1956 women MPs made only one speech in Parliament, which is why the 1956 sample is somewhat smaller than the 1986 one.

Table 3
Various categories of content in the speeches of women and men MPs in Norway, 1956 and 1986. Relative frequencies per 100 centimeters of text column

		1956		1986	
		Women	Men	Women	Men
Orientation	Concrete	9.9	6.9	6.7	4.8
	Abstract	4.3	9.3	6.6	6.4
Arguments	Realism	0.2	1.0	0.4	0.9
	Acceptability	1.7	1.1	0.7	0.9
	Consistency	0.9	0.2	0.4	0.9
Propaganda	Name calling	1.3	0.6	1.9	2.5
	Glittering generality	2.3	2.5	2.2	3.0
	Testimonial	5.2	7.0	2.2	2.9
Metaphors	Organic	1.9	0.8	3.5	1.9
	Mechanistic	1.7	1.5	4.8	2.0

relative frequency of 'abstract orientation' in this sector was 8.0 for women and 12.0 for men; thirty years later, the corresponding figures were 16.3 for women and 8.9 for men (see *Appendix*). In other words, when discussing economic matters women MPs today appear '*plus royaliste que le roi*'.

The frequencies for the various types of arguments are so low that no conclusions can be drawn. As for propaganda techniques, one may note that the internal frequencies for the three types of propaganda have changed somewhat over time. Interestingly enough, there is a slight increase in the frequency of 'name calling'; in other contexts, this rather aggressive propaganda technique was found to have become considerably less frequent (Karvonen and Rappe 1991:258). Moreover, references to other debaters, speakers etc. ('testimonials') - a rather natural phenomenon in parliamentary debates - have decreased over time.

Finally, women MPs employ both types of metaphors somewhat more frequently than men. The frequency has more than doubled for women and there is a slight increase for men as well.

In sum, differences between women and men MPs were found to be less than dramatic. The reasonably clear difference for 'orientation' - women displaying a more concrete orientation than men - has diminished somewhat over time. Women continue to use the two types of metaphors somewhat more than men. All in all, however, one is struck by the similarity rather than the differences. If anything, our data point to increasing uniformity in language use over time.

Empirical analysis II: election campaigns in Finland

Do women and men differ in the way in which they communicate with their voters? Is there a female campaign style that clearly differs from that of male candidates?

To begin with we would like to emphasize two characteristics of the elections that form the context of the campaigns studied. First, the Finnish regulations concerning elections underline the position of the individual candidate. While the voters in other Nordic coutries vote for party lists the Finnish voter casts his/her ballot directly for a particular candidate. The total number of votes determines a party's share of seats in the parliament; there is no rank-ordering of the candidates within the party. The candidate with the largest number of votes takes the first seat, the one with the second largest number gets the second seat, and so on. Second, developments during the last decades have increasingly underlined the position of the individual candidates in relation to the parties (Pesonen 1991). Thus it seems obvious that a study of the candidates' advertising activity does not concern itself with a marginal phenomenon in the world of politics but rather with a research field of growing importance.

Data
The channels between candidates and their voters are numerous. The methods for getting a message through have steadily developed towards an ever higher degree of refinement. This study limits itself to newspaper ads. The weakness of this approach naturally lies in the many channels left out. On the other hand, newspaper ads have

always been a major form of political advertisement, a fact that gives us a good basis for longitudinal comparisons (cf. Mintz 1986:181).

Our study covers advertising in connection with the parliamentary elections of 1962, 1975 and 1991. Helsingin Sanomat, by far the largest daily in Finland, was used as data source. This paper has no official ties to any of the political parties. For this reason, and because of the large circulation of the paper, it is a major advertising forum for candidates from all parties.

An inquiry into the advertising activity showed that the bulk of the ads appeared during the final week before the elections. Hence this week was chosen as the period from which the main empirical data was gathered.

Table 4
Political newspaper-ads in 1962, 1975 and 1991

	1962	1975	1991
Total number of political ads[1]	16994	8805	12586
Percent of total advertising volume	14.4	6.1	5.9
Percent of total volume of political ads			
Male ads	42.9	42.3	37.0
Female ads	6.4	17.2	23.9
Gender-neutral ads	50.7	40.5	39.1

[1] Centimetres of column

Some characteristics of the campaigns

Three trends in the table merit attention. First, the total number of political ads decreased during this period. This is largely explicable in terms of the increasing importance of new channels (radio, television) for communication between candidates and voters. The downward trend applies both to the total volume of political ads and to their share of all advertisements in the paper. The share of ads solely selling female candidates has risen from 6.4 to 23.9 percent. As was shown earlier the number of female MPs and candidates has grown steadily during this period. The growth of female advertising matches this more general trend fairly well. Generally, women MPs seem to win their seats with a somewhat smaller number of newspaper ads than men.

The third feature concerns the relative position of candidates as compared to parties in the campaigns. As was expected the emphasis placed upon individual candidates has increased. This is evident in the decreasing share of the gender-neutral ads. These have normally been party-ads where the party sells either itself or a larger number of candidates of both sexes.[5]

The intensity of the campaigns is the final general aspect surveyed here. Are the campaigns fairly evenly spread over a longer period of time? Is it possible to identify peaks of intensity? If so, how close to election-day do these peaks occur? One might argue that a high intensity close to election-day implies a strong emphasis on individual candidates and their personalities. Or vice versa, a long and evenly spread campaign can be a sign of a strong position for the political parties. Once again, any differences between female and male campaign designs are of special interest.

The campaigns were studied during the fortnight preceding the elections. Considering the fact that the total number of political ads has decreased over time one might say that the general pattern of intensity is rather stable. The advertisement campaigns clearly culminate at a rather late stage and form a two-day peak consisting of the first election-day and the day before.

Who - men or women - advertises most in the two last days before the election? A high share of advertising here indicates that a candidate focuses to a higher degree on attracting undecided voters at the very end of the campaign.

Table 5
Campaign intensity (Percentage of ads published during the last two days)

	1962	1975	1991
Male ads	50.6	46.0	54.7
Female ads	43.6	55.5	65.2
Gender-neutral	47.5	43.8	58.0

[5] In order to check all tendencies mentioned above not only the volume but also the number of ads were studied. This was done for the entire set of ads as well as for women and men separately. The results acquired were largely identical with the findings presented here.

There seems to be an ever stronger ad-peak during the last two days. Moreover, female candidates today, as opposed to earlier days, peak their campaigns even more than their male colleagues.

The general features of campaigning in newspapers can be summarized as follows. The newspapers seem to have lost their predominant position as channels for political communication in connection with elections. The number of political ads as well as their share of the total volume of advertising has decreased steadily during the period studied. A tendency to peak the campaigns has strengthened over the years; this applies especially to female campaigns. Generally speaking, however, rather limited evidence was found of gender-specific campaign patterns. Thus we might conclude that in spite of the growing number of female MPs and candidates the predominant pattern has prevailed. Female candidates have largely been socialized into roles and patterns formed during years of massive male dominance.

Communication in candidates' newspaper ads
The period highlighted in this section entailed major structural changes in all Nordic countries. This applies especially to Finland where the changes in the demographic and the economic basis of society took place much later and dramatically faster than in the neighbouring countries. It goes without saying that these structural changes have effected political life in many ways.

With a slight simplification one might argue that up to the 1960s the electorate was rather clearly divided between the parties. To a large extent this division followed the traditional left-right axis. The main criteria according to which the voters took stands under different party-banners were social status and occupation. Much of the basis for these cleavages withered away in the intense societal change that started in the early 1960s and continued beyond the mid-1970s. From the parties' point of view the situation was new and awkward. Their traditional segments of support either ceased to exist or were no longer to be relied upon. In order to maintain the level of support already achieved they had to orient themselves toward new segments of voters. The centripetal movement among the voters was thus matched by changes among the parties, in their programs and standpoints. It is no exaggeration to say that almost all parties adopted a catch-all strategy (Martikainen and Yrjönen 1991:55-63; Sänkiaho 1991).

Looking at this structural development from a gender point of view the following would seem particularly important. A vast proportion of the women left their homes and entered the labour market. This development was greatly enhanced by the rapid and sizeable growth of the public and service sectors (for data, see the chapter on trade unions in this volume). Women not only entered the labour market, they did this from a steadily stronger position as their average level of education rose rapidly. Today the majority of first-year students at Finnish universities are women. A further change, which is not as easy to pinpoint but which still has to be considered is the debate on social values and the weakening of traditional gender-roles.

All in all we might say that the changes in the electorate have presented the parties with new challenges. The parties have tried to respond by playing down their ideological role and by loosening their ties to more specific segments of the population (cf. Karvonen and Rappe 1991). As a result, the position of individual candidates has been strengthened further.

Still, only limited attention has been paid to the new position of the female half of the electorate and the question of whether and how the parties have tried to deal with this situation. Three main options seem available to the parties. First, they may try to engage a larger number of female candidates. Second, they can change the way in which their candidates address themselves to the female voters. Finally, their female candidates may have developed a specific style of campaigning and communication.

As to the first strategy we have already shown that the parties have increased the number and proportion of female candidates rather considerably. The following inquiry into the development of the style and contents of candidates' campaigns will try to shed light on the use of the two latter strategies.

The message conveyed through newspaper ads can be described along two dimensions and combinations of these. First, the ads can be verbal in a traditional sense. The candidates use words to tell who they are, what they stand for and what goals they pursue. This part of the message opens up fairly easily to traditional forms of content analysis; consequently, these kinds of methods were employed in this part of our study. The second dimension focuses on visual elements in the ads. To put it differently: ads where the visual element is clearly dominant are far more problematic in a methodological respect. Here, we start out by looking for different iconic signs (photographs, pictures, drawings) as the communicative element. In semiotic terms we look at the ads as structures of meaning where these iconic signs collaborate with verbal signs (words) in conveying a certain message.

The major feature in the development of political ads during the two last decades has been the steady growth in the use of pictures. According to Pekonen, photographs have come to dominate while the position of written messages has diminished. Programmatic standpoints have been replaced by short slogans (Pekonen 1986:49; Pekonen 1989:139). Barthes argues that the photograph of a candidate contains a message of some profound and irrational aspects beyond everyday politics. As such a picture does not tell us anything about the candidate's political aims;

instead it helps to form a kind of personal relationship between the candidate and the voter (Barthes 1970:169).

The strong visual element in ads can also be seen as a way of emphasizing the emotional rather than the rational aspects of politics (cf. Fibiger 1981:167). Earlier research shows that female language in general terms is more emotional than that of men. Thus we might expect female candidates to take to a more visualized style of campaigning than their male colleagues. Along with testing this assumption against our empirical data, we will try to answer questions concerning the contents of the messages in the ads. What are the messages that the iconic and verbal signs try to communicate? Furthermore, do female and male messages display systematic dissimilarities?

The empirical analysis consists of two parts. To begin with we shall focus, using traditional techniques of content analysis, on the verbal aspects of the ads. At the second stage further light is shed on the visually oriented communication and the images of the candidates. The latter endeavour is based on a semiotic-oriented analysis of the meaning of signs.

Sectors and issues
Do male and female candidates differ as to the questions that they try to place on the agenda of parliamentary elections? Do women more than men stress issues that belong to certain policy-sectors? Have there been any changes in these patterns over time?

The same classification of policy sectors as in the previous analysis of parliamentary speeches - production, reproduction, system maintenance and women's issues - is used here to study these questions in the light of newspaper ads. Since the character of ads differs in many important ways from that of speeches, it proved necessary to use one further category, 'no sector'.

The first empirical findings that deserve comment concern this category. Rather surprisingly we found that the tendency not to mention any concrete issues was strong and relatively stable over the years. The share of ads which named no issues was about 50 percent in both 1962 and 1991. The expectation thus falsified was that the banging on the issue-drum would have been much louder in the 1960s than thirty years later. Table 6 contains those ads that mention one or several issues.

With due caution paid to the the small number of cases, the following trends may be pointed out. First, politicians seem to have shifted their orientation in a quite radical way. In the 1960s the emphasis was on issues relating to production. By the 1990s and these questions were almost entirely replaced by issues dealing with the reproductive functions of society. This tendency applies to candidates of both sexes but it is, notably enough, stronger among women. Eight out of ten issues put forward by women relate to reproduction. This in turn might indicate that female candidates actually pursue a strategy aimed mainly at the female voter.

Table 6
Policy sectors in political newspaper ads in 1962 and 1991 (percent, n=76)

Sector	1962			1991		
	Women	Men	All	Women	Men	All
Reproduction	28	25	26	80	47	67
Production	50	54	52	4	42	20
System maintenance		21	12	8	11	9
Women's issues	22		10	8		4

It is also worth mentioning that although candidates generally do mention issues in their ads, few of them express anything like explicit views on these issues. The general tendecy, valid for both sexes at both points in time, is that candidates apparently try to avoid taking definite standpoints.

Pointing at certain issues is one, albeit rather indirect, way of appealing to different segments of the electorate. A more straightforward strategy is to name the addressee of a message. Our analysis started out by asking whether any more or less well-defined groups at all were mentioned. After this it was determined whether the group in question could be seen as 'general' ('every Finn..', 'responsible citizens..'), 'particular' ('wage-earners', 'farmers') or as being dominated by women.

Table 7
Group orientation in political newspaper ads in 1962 and 1991 (percent, n=76)

	1962		1991	
	Women	Men	Women	Men
Group orientation exists	68	68	47	32
No group orientation	32	32	53	68

The general trend seems to be a declining interest among the candidates in linking themselves to any particular segments of voters. This applies especially to the male candidates. Among those politicians who display a more distinct orientation the direction is generally towards loosely defined groups, such as wage-earners. At the same time the extent to which female politicians focus on female voters is low and almost unaltered over time.

Visual communication

Communication in ads is not solely based on language and the use of verbal signs. The message is also conveyed by iconic signs such as photographs. Studies of language in political campaigns have to be expanded to include also these iconic signs (cf. Pekonen 1989:142). The fact that visual communication has rapidly gained ground at the expense of traditional verbal messages underlines the importance of this additional perspective. Pictures can not anymore be seen as mere decorations. They carry meanings and are a central factor in the process of political opinion formation. According to the semiotician Roland Barthes, the special rhetorical technique of the photograph emanates from the lack of cultural codes on the denotative level. One might say that recognizing the motive equals knowing it in real life. On the basis of this analogy, photographs are experienced as more or less self-evident. Yet photographs contain one further level, a connotative level founded on cultural conventions. Different photographic techniques, poses, attributes, objects chosen as motives etc. all constitute signs that are linked to certain meanings in a given cultural context (Barthes 1986a and 1986b).

The extensive use of photographs of candidates indicates, according to Barthes, a strong belief in the persuasive powers of the photograph (Barthes 1970:169). A systematic study of the phenomenon certainly seems in order.

Have male and female politicians in fact adopted different styles of visual communication? Previous research on the perception of candidates and their pictures has pointed to certain aspects as particularly interesting. These aspects would seem equally interesting from a gender point of view. Consequently, seven different visual categories obtained from previous research are used in the following empirical analysis.

- *Overall visual impression.* Iconic signs have a strong position in campaign-related electoral discourse today. Correspondingly, verbal signs have lost their previous predominant position. This might also be interpreted to mean that emotions are getting the upper hand of rationality, if not in the minds of voters, at least in the messages sent by politicians. The questions that were highlighted empirically were whether this tendency can be seen also in this context and whether gender makes a difference in this regard.

Conclusions about the overall impression were based on a gradual sequence of four categories. Ads totally dominated by text were classified as 'verbal'. Ads displaying iconic as well as verbal signs were classified as 'verbally oriented' when the verbal share of text was substantial and as 'iconic-oriented' when non-verbal signs dominated. When the message was conveyed nearly purely by non-verbal signs one may speak of 'iconic' ads.

- *The angle of the picture.* Research done in the field of visual esthetics has pointed to the importance of camera-angles in creating different meanings (Moriarty and Popovich 1991:374). As for candidate photos, two techniques are underlined. Where the picture is taken en face, the purpose is to establish an open relation that inspires confidence. Pictures of candidates looking straight into the camera, into the eyes of the voter, are good examples of this practice (Barthes 1970:170-71; Sallinen-Kuparinen 1987:130). The second technique aims at creating an impression of a candidate with great visions, the right choice for the future. This image is created by using somewhat different camera-angles. The camera closes in on the candidate either from one side or preferably slightly from below. Here the candidate's eyes do not focus on the lens. Instead they seem, in a noble way, to wander off into the distant future (Barthes op.cit.).

- *The size of portraits.* Here the question is how large a part of themselves the candidates show in the pictures. Without going further into the semiotic connotations of different portrait sizes we simply distinguish between 'head and shoulders', 'half-figure', and 'whole-figure' pictures.

- *Facial expression.* Previous studies have clearly shown the importance of facial expressions when it comes to creating a positive image (e.g. Bull and Hawkes 1982; Rosenberg et al 1986; Moriarty and Popovich 1991). At least in commercial ads a smile reflects an endeavour to create a friendly relation to the receiver; the smile is a pleasant and friendly greeting (Choe et al 1986:122; Knuuttila 1991: 129). In their study of commercial ads Choe et al concluded that women tend to smile often and broadly whereas men generally restrict themselves to more neutral expressions (Choe et al, op.cit.). The present analysis distinguishes between neutral expressions, strict smiles and broad, open smiles.

- *Dress*. Several studies have shown that a particular way of dressing also constitutes a choice between meanings that one wishes to communicate (e.g. Reed 1984). On this point, a simple dichotomy is used in the present study. On the one hand we look for candidates who try to live up to the traditional myth of how a politician should look. These candidates dress in a sober and traditional manner. On the other hand we also try to identify those candidates who attempt to present themselves as an alternative to the traditional politicians. In order to reduce the gap between politicians and 'ordinary people' these candidates pursue many avenues. An attempt to dress more casually, like most people do, may be one of these ways.

- *Company*. Usually photographs in candidate ads show only the candidate. In some cases, however, the candidate is accompanied by other people. The aim is to link the candidate to more or less well-defined groups of voters. A picture showing the candidate among workers at a shipyard is a clear sign that this candidate wishes to attract working-class voters. Bringing other people into the photographs may also serve other goals, for instance to underline the candidate's adherence to certain values such as the importance of the family. We distinguish between three categories, the candidate alone, groups related to occupations, persons without apparent social affiliation, and family-related groups.

- *Context*. The setting of the political picture can be organized in many ways in order to evoke certain associations (Sallinen-Kuparinen, op.cit.). Where contexts can be observed we distinguish between those that underline competence (offices, the parliament etc.), contexts relating to special segments of voters (factories, farms, shipyards etc.) and finally environments that relate to unconscious feelings of freedom or leisure (a beach, a river etc.).

Traditional methods of content analysis applied to visual communication would face severe problems related to both the coding process and the reliability of the results (Jensen 1991:37; Moriarty and Popovich 1991:375). Largely similar to the analysis of parliamentary speeches above, a 'soft' approach was chosen; consequently the element of interpretation is of paramount importance. It goes without saying that the role of interpretations varies according to the type of question and categories under focus. Of course, a classification of overall visual impression depends to a high degree on interpretation, whereas determining a camera angle does not involve a strong interpretative element.

Table 8 presents results on five of the seven dimensions. Two of the dimensions 'company' and 'context' did not vary either over time or between men and women. The photos usually showed only the candidate and this was done in a setting with none or very few and neutral attributes.

Table 8
Visual communication in political newspaper-ads in 1962 and 1991
(percent, n = 76)

	1962		1991	
Category	Female	Male	Female	Male
Overall visual impression				
Verbal				
Verb.orient.	74	79	47	42
Icon.orient.	26	21	47	42
Iconic			6	16
Angle				
En face	84	58	100	100
Sideways	16	42		
Size				
Head & should.	94	94	84	88
Half-fig.		6	16	12
Whole-fig.	6			
Expression				
Neutral	37	63		11
Strict smile	37	31	37	52
Broad smile	26	6	63	37
Dress				
Sober	100	94	63	74
Casual			11	20
Other		6	26	6

Generally, changes over time seem greater than the differences between male and female ads. Moreover, differences between men and women seem to decrease over time. A comparison of ads today with those of the 1960s points to the following in particular: the modern candidate looks us straight in the eyes with a broad smile.

He/she does not talk as much anymore, and the promises made are few. Today candidates want to be chosen for who and what they are.

Who, then, are they and what do they want to tell us about themselves? Why should we pick a particular candidate among many others? Do female self-portraits differ from those of male candidates? These questions, all related to the concept and phenomenon of 'image' will be the object of our final analysis.

Images

According to Nimmo and Savage, 'image' stands for '..a human product which consists of a multitude of conceived characteristics.. which some object, event or person mediates from itself' (Nimmo and Savage 1976:8). Here the focus is on personal attributes that the candidates claim to possess and also communicate to the voters. The political ad offers a great number of ways in which the hallmarks of able and trustworthy politicians can be mediated to the voters. The words in the ad, primarily those used to describe the candidate, stand out as perhaps the most important signs. The issues chosen and the ways in which they are presented also tell a great deal about image aspirations.

The toolbox for image-builders also contains a vast variety of iconic signs. These signs are, regardless of cultural connections, more open to interpretation. They can, for instance, be used in a catch-all strategy vis-à-vis the voters.

The challenge facing the image-building candidate is considerable. He has to find the right words and pictures. The signs chosen have to work not only on a general level but also, and especially, in relation to the voters to whom the signs are sent. Further, choosing signs that are individually good is not sufficient. It is even more important to find the right and fruitful mix of verbal and iconic signs. This is especially true when it comes to newspaper ads where the first overall impression is formed in a reading process which is hasty and rather superficial.

Our approach to the study of images contains both qualitative and quantitative elements. It is a sort of methodological compromise. We start out by looking at words and expressions which are classified into nine categories. At the next stage we try to interpret iconic signs and combinations of these as well as verbal signs. Similarly, the characteristics found in this way are given values connected to these categories. The classification scheme used is a slightly modified version of the one originally developed by Benze and Declerq (1985). The categories are as follows:

- 'Competence/Experience' encompasses signs that are linked to competence and different aspects of skills and experience.

- 'Warmth/Compassion' includes signs that stress human warmth, cordiality and compassion.

- 'Performance/Activity' comprises signs by which candidates underline their ability to be active and efficient political decision-makers.

- 'Honesty/Trustworthiness' is a fairly straightforward category containing signs by which the candidates try to establish themselves as particularly honest and worthy of the voters' trust.

- 'Family references' simply denotes signs alluding to the candidates' families, parenthood etc.

- 'Group identification' contains candidates who have underlined their affiliation to some particular group of citizens.

- 'Independence/Bravery' focuses on signs by which candidates try to picture themselves as independent and as persons that stick to their own views whatever the circumstances.

- 'Strength/Toughness' contains signs that are linked to firmness, strength and endurance.

- 'Other signs' is a residual category for candidate ads exhibiting signs that do not match any of the categories above.

It is quite clear that there are differences as well as similarities between the images presented by female and male politicians. The main result is, however, that the similarities clearly overshadow the differences. This holds true to such a large extent that one can speak of a general image for politicians.

Nevertheless, there are minor differences that deserve comment. Looking at the 'soft' image features as a whole (warmth/compassion, family) one may note that these have been used mainly by women and that this tendency grows stronger over time. For female politicians, the use of these soft signs increases from 9 to 24 percent. By contrast, none of the male candidates wanted to present themselves as in any way 'soft' in 1962 and only five percent did so in 1991.

There is, however, a clearly dual element in the way in which the image of women politicians has evolved. The increased use of soft signs is accompanied by an even stronger emphasis on 'harder' features. In 1962 only two percent of the female signs were hard in the sense that they stressed either Independence/Bravery or Strength/ Toughness. The corresponding share of male signs was 15 percent. By the 1990s 22 percent of the signs used by women are hard while the figure for male politicians has risen to a mere 16 percent.

Table 9
Characteristics of image in political newspaper-ads
*1962 and 1991 (percent)**

| | 1962 | | 1991 | |
Category	Women	Men	Women	Men
Competence/Experience	37	41	34	47
Warmth/Compassion	7		14	5
Performance/Activity	11	20	8	14
Honesty/Trustworthiness	19	5	4	12
Family reference	2		10	
Group reference	11	11	8	
Independence/Bravery	2	2	12	9
Strength/Toughness		13	10	7
Other signs	11	7	2	7

* *Number of signs classified: female ads 1962 = 56, 1991 = 50; male ads 1962 = 54, 1991 = 43*

The development as a whole seems to reflect a dilemma mentioned earlier. Are the chances of winning office better if a candidate relies on fairly traditional female values? Or does the world of politics require that women convert to a more manly style? Today, female politicians in general try to live up to expectations based on a traditional, thus also male-dominated role model for politicians. But at the same time, it is more common among female than male politicians to soften up this image. As an example of this approach we might mention an ad where a female candidate declares that 'it takes firmness to promote soft values'. The picture in the ad also shows both types of characteristics; the softness is connoted by a broad smile' and a brightly flowered scarf, the firmness by a huge stone wall in front of which the woman stands.

Summary and conclusions

The main findings of this study can be summarized as follows:

- The sectoral specialization of women MPs has remained largely unaltered over the thirty year period comprised by our study. Women are still 'overrepresented' in welfare issues ('reproduction') and 'underrepresented' within the hard core of economic policies ('production'). The substantial increase in the number of women MPs has not changed this pattern. Apparently, the strengthened position of women has not encouraged them to bridge this traditional gap between men and women; nor has it inspired the male MPs to do so. The striking lack of activity on the part of men in 'women's issues' indicates that the predominant attitude is still that these issues are the exclusive domain of women MPs;

- In campaign advertisements there was almost no gap between men and women as regards the main sectors in 1962: both women and men focused on 'production' and 'reproduction' to about equal degrees. Thirty years later, both men and women focused much more on reproduction. Overall, however, the gap between women and men had widened: women were clearly more dominant in the area of reproduction issues, whereas issues pertaining to 'production' had all but disappeared from their campaign ads. Meanwhile, specific 'women's issues' were still only to be found in ads presented by female candidates;

- The linguistic content of parliamentary speeches revealed only minor differences between women and men. Moreover, the results pointed towards increasing similarity between women and men MPs over time;

- Both group orientation and visual communication in campaign ads demonstrated similarity rather than major differences between women and men candidates. All in all, the changes found over time were common to women and men; women and men politicians seem to partake of the same general pattern of change over time;

- As regards images created by campaign ads, the similarities were found to overshadow the differences between women and men. Nevertheless, female candidates used expressions of warmth and compassion as well as family references clearly more frequently than men. Moreover, the differences here were found to be on the increase. However, parallel to this, the frequency of 'harder' features in female campaign ads was found to have increased over time. Female campaigning therefore created a dual image of 'softness accompanied with sufficient toughness'.

The overall impression is that the similarities between female and male politicians were by far larger than the differences. It is particularly interesting to note that this impression holds true also for the 1990s regardless of the fact that the number and proportion of female politicians today is much greater than thirty years ago. Women politicians of the 1950s and 1960s entered into a world where a role model for politicians was well-defined; they adopted this model to a large extent. The relative size of the female group surely accounts for a major part of this successful socialization of women into a predominantly male sphere. As long as women politicians were still a small group (a 'skewed' situation in Moss Canter's terms), it was next to impossible for female candidates to succeed if they did not whole-heartedly accept the role model offered. This meant that later on, when the proportion of women had grown (a 'tilted group'), a large share of these women were already socialized into the prevailing role and pattern of behaviour. In other words, the image of a female politician had already been formed. To question this image would have been tantamount to questioning those female politicians who adhered to this role model. The predominant behaviour was thereby probably seen as neutral in relation to gender although its foundations lay in an era clearly dominated by male politicians. Seen in this developmental perspective the absence of overwhelming differences between women and men in politics is perhaps not surprising.

Yet differences do exist, and although the pattern over time and across sectors is not uniform, they have generally been relatively stable. Women still bear the sole responsibility for placing 'women's issues' on the political agenda; what there is of activity on the part of male politicians is entirely marginal. They retain their 'overrepresentation' when it comes to issues related to welfare policies. Correspondingly it is they who to a large extent stand for 'soft' forms of political communication. At the same time, they display activity in traditionally 'male' sectors and increasingly attempt to create an image of competence and toughness in their campaigns.

All in all, therefore, the political language of women displays a dual character. Women try to stand for those things that are normally associated with the traditional (male) role of a politician. In addition, they shoulder a responsibility for issues and forms of communication that men politicians rarely touch upon. If the question is put bluntly, i.e. have women changed the language of politics, the answer must be 'no'. Rather, they are faced with a double workload well-known to them from other walks of life.

APPENDIX. Various categories of content in the speeches of women and men MPs in Norway, 1956 and 1986. Relative frequencies for three different sectors (frequency per 100 centimeters of text column)

'Reproduction'

		1956		1986	
		Women	Men	Women	Men
Orientation	Concrete	6.0	5.1	8.2	7.3
	Abstract	1.9	3.2	3.3	5.3
Arguments	Realism	0.3	0.9	0.2	0.5
	Acceptability	1.3	0.6	0.4	0.8
	Consistency	0.9	0.3	0.6	1.2
Propaganda	Name-calling	1.3	0.6	1.1	1.8
	Glittering generality	1.6	2.0	2.4	0.2
	Testimonial	6.2	7.5	1.7	2.0
Metaphors	Organic	0.9	0.3	1.7	1.6
	Mechanistic	2.6	1.3	4.4	1.6

'Production'

		1956		1986	
		Women	Men	Women	Men
Orientation	Concrete	10.0	7.9	5.1	2.1
	Abstract	8.0	12.0	16.3	8.9
Arguments	Realism	0.3	0.5	0.9	0.8
	Acceptability	2.9	2.0	0.9	0.8
	Consistency	0.6	0.0	0.0	0.4
Propaganda	Name-calling	1.6	0.0	1.3	2.5
	Glittering generality	2.5	1.7	2.7	5.1
	Testimonial	4.8	6.4	0.9	2.5
Metaphors	Organic	2.2	1.7	4.6	2.9
	Mechanistic	2.2	2.0	2.7	3.4

'System maintenance'

		1956		1986	
		Women	Men	Women	Men
Orientation	Concrete	3.3	9.3	5.6	2.6
	Abstract	3.3	19.8	5.6	5.7
Arguments	Realism	0.0	0.0	0.4	1.6
	Acceptability	0.6	0.0	0.8	1.0
	Consistency	0.6	1.1	0.4	1.0
Propaganda	Name-calling	0.6	0.0	3.0	3.7
	Glittering generality	4.0	4.6	1.6	2.6
	Testimonial	8.0	4.6	3.5	4.3
Metaphors	Organic	1.3	0.0	5.1	1.0
	Mechanistic	0.0	1.1	6.3	1.6

Bibliography

Parliamentary record

Kongeriket Norges 131. ordentlige Stortings forhandlinger *1986-87, 9. del inneholdende register til forhandlinger i Stortinget og dets avdelinger.* Oslo: A/S O. Fredr. Arnesen Bok- og Akcidenstrykkeri, 1987.
Stortingstidende inneholdende 100. ordentlige stortings forhandlinger 1956. Forhandlinger i stortinget, parts A and B. Oslo: Centraltrykkeriet, 1956.
Stortingstidende inneholdende 131. ordentlige stortings forhandlinger 1986-87. Forhandlinger i stortinget, parts A, B and C. Centraltrykkeriet Österås A/S, 1987.

References

Adams, K.L. and Ware, N. C. (1979), 'Sexism and the English Language: The Linguistic Implications of Being a Woman', in Freeman, J. (ed.): *Women: A Feminist Perspective.* Palo Alto, Ca.: Mayfield Publishing Company.

Barthes, R. (1970), *Mytologier.* Stockholm: Bo Cavefors förlag.

Barthes, R. (1986a), 'The Photographic Message', in Barthes, R.: *Image-Music-Text (Essays).* New York: Hill & Wang.

Barthes, R. (1986b), 'The Rhetoric of the Image', in Barthes, R.: *Image-Music-Text (Essays).* New York: Hill & Wang.

Benze, J. and Declerq, E. (1985), 'Content of Television Spot Ads for Female Candidates', *Journalism Quarterly*, Vol. 62, 2:278-283, 288.

Borg, O. (1964), *Suomen puolueideologiat. Periaateohjelmien sisältöanalyyttinen vertailu sekä katsaus niiden historialliseen syntyprosessiin.* Helsinki: Valtiotieteellinen yhdistys.

Bull, R. and Hawkes, C. (1982), 'Judging Politicians by Their Faces', *Political Studies*, Vol. 30, 1:95-101.

Choe, J.H., Wilcox, G. and Hardy, A. (1986), 'Facial Expressions in Magazine Ads: A Cross-Cultural Comparison', *Journalism Quarterly*, Vol. 63, 1:122-126, 166.

Dahlerup, D. (1988), 'From a Small to a Large Minority: Women in Scandinavian Politics', *Scandinavian Political Studies*, Vol. 11, 4:275-298.

Fibiger, B. (1981), 'Danish Election Campaigns in the Seventies', in Rosengren, K.-E. (ed.): *Advances in Content Analysis*. London: Sage Publications.

Heradstveit, D. and Björgo, T. (1992), *Politisk kommunikasjon*. Oslo: Tano.

Holm, G. (1982), *Et hjerteanliggende. Kvinder. Samfund. Lokalpolitik*. Köbenhavn: Kommunetryk.

Jaatinen, P. (1991), 'Poliittisten puolueiden 'vihertyminen'', in Kanerva, J., (ed.): 'Suomalaisten puolueohjelmien retoriikasta', *University of Jyväskylä, Department of Political Science, Publications* 63:42-55.

Jensen, K.B. (1991), 'Humanistic Scholarship as Qualitative Science: Contributions to Mass Communication Research', in Jensen, K.B. and Jankowski, N., (eds): *A Handbook of Qualitative Methodologies for Mass Communication Research*. London: Routledge.

Karvonen, L. and Rappe, A. (1991), 'Social Structure and Campaign Style: Finland 1954-1987', *Scandinavian Political Studies*, Vol. 14, 3:241-259.

Knuuttila, S. (1991), 'Hymyn ja naurun sukupuoli - sensitiivisen mainonnan ilmeanalyysia', in Lehtonen, K. (ed.): *Mainoskuva - mielikuva*. Helsinki: Valtion painatuskeskus.

Lautamatti, L. (1988), 'Naiset neuvottelupöydän ääressä', in Laitinen, L. (ed.): *Isosuinen nainen. Tutkielmia naisesta ja kielestä*. Helsinki: Yliopistopaino.

Lee, A. and Lee, E. (eds) (1939): *The Fine Art of Propaganda*. Published by the Institute of Propaganda Analysis. New York: Harcourt, Brace and Company.

Martikainen, T. and Yrjönen, R. (1991), 'Vaalit, puolueet ja yhteiskunnan muutos', *Tilastokeskus, tutkimuksia* 178. Helsinki.

Mintz, E. (1986), 'Newspaper Advertising In Canadian Election Campaigns', *Journalism Quarterly*, Vol. 63, 1:180-185.

Moriarty, S and Popovich, M. (1991), 'Newsmagazine Visuals and the 1988 Presidential Election', *Journalism Quarterly*, Vol. 68, 3:371-380.

Nimmo, D. and Savage, J. (1976), *Candidates and Their Images*. St. Monica: Good Year Publishing.

Palonen, K. (1991), 'Näköispatsaista käsitetaiteeseen puolueohjelmissa', in Kanerva, J. (ed.): 'Suomalaisten puolueohjelmien retoriikasta', *University of Jyväskylä, Department of Political Science, Publications*, 63:6-16.

Pekonen, K. (1986), 'Imagon merkitys modernissa politiikassa', in Nousiainen, J. and Wiberg, M. (eds): 'Kansalaiset ja politiikka 1980-luvun Suomessa', *Annales Universitatis Turkuensis*, ser. C., tom. 57:36-60.

Pekonen, K. (1989), 'Symbols and Politics in the Modern Situation: the Problem and Prospects of the 'New'', in Gibbins, J. (ed.): *Contemporary Political Culture: Politics in a Postmodern Age*. London: Sage Publications.

Pesonen, P. (1991), 'Puolueen ja edustajaehdokaan painottuminen äänestyspäätöksissä', *Politiikka*, Vol. 33, 2:98-105.

Petersson, O. (1987), *Metaforernas makt*. Stockholm: Carlssons.

Reed, B. (1984), 'A Fashion Guide to Winning Elections. Clothes Make the Politician', *Legislative Policy*, Vol. 3, 1:37-40.

Rosenberg, S., Bohan, L., McCafferty, P. and Harris, K. (1986), 'The Image and the Vote: the Effect of Candidate Presentation on Voter Preference', *American Journal of Political Science*, Vol. 30, 1:108-127.

Sallinen-Kuparinen, A. (1987), 'Televisioesiintyminen, mediaretoriikka ja poliittinen vaikuttaminen', *Politiikka*, Vol. 29, 2:120-132.

Sinkkonen, S. and Haavio-Mannila, E. (1981), 'The Impact of The Women's Movement and Legislative Activity of Women MPs on Social Development', in Rendel, M. (ed.): *Women, Power and Political Systems*. London: Croom Helm.

Skard, T. and Haavio-Mannila, E. (1983), 'Kvinner i parlamentene', in Haavio-Mannila, E. et al., (eds): *Det uferdige demokratiet. Kvinner i nordisk politikk*. Oslo: Nordisk Ministerråd.

Skjeie. H. (1991), 'The Rhetoric of Difference: On Women's Inclusion into Political Elites', *Politics and Society*, 2:233-263.

Sänkiaho, R. (1991), 'Puolueiden kannatajakunnan rakenne', in *Kansanedustajain vaalit 1991*, Tilastokeskus: Vaalit 1991:2. Helsinki.

Thelander, K. (1986), *Politikerspråk i könsperspektiv*. Uppsala: Liber.

Vallance, E. and Davies, E. (1986), *Women of Europe. Women MEPs and Equality Policy*. Cambridge: Cambridge University Press.

Vatanen, L. (1988), 'Kansanedustajaehdokkaiden paikallisradiomainonnasta vuoden 1987 eduskuntavaaleissa', *Oy Yleisradio Ab, suunnittelu- ja tutkimusosasto, tutkimusraportti*, 3. Helsinki.

Vierikko, E. (1974), *Parlamenttikielen sanasto- ja lauserakenteesta*. Unpublished Licentiate Thesis, University of Oulu.

Part VI

Beyond Scandinavia

Caught in the 'virgin trap': Nicaragua as a cultural contrast

Einar Berntzen

'*With the Virgin on our side we will smash the bourgeoisie*' (Deighton 1983:147)

Introduction

It is said that *cultural traditions* affect the political position of women. Patriarchal norms make it difficult for women to break with the prevailing attitudes and become involved in matters traditionally regarded as men's business. But different milieux may harbour different attitudes towards different forms of political activity. As a contrast, here we are going to deal with the struggle and development of women within a *matriarchal* structural context. Nicaragua is characterized by a *matrifocal* family structure, which, with the possible exception of the almost matriarchal tradition in eastern Finland, is mainly *lacking* in the Nordic countries.[1] Although eastern Finland constitutes an 'exotic' ingredient within the Nordic context, it is not typical of the Nordic countries in an international comparative perspective. Furthermore, to the extent that the structural position of women in eastern Finland can be termed 'matriarchal', it is not accompanied by a corresponding cultural ideological tradition. The peaceful mobilization of women in the Nordic countries came early and gradually became stabilized and institutionalized. In this context the mobilization led to a strengthening of a new political role for women in terms of formal political positions. In Nicaragua, on the other hand, the mobilization of women was late, intense and unstable. The struggle and activity of women inside the Sandinista Revolution provided a stepping stone for the emancipation of women in

---

[1] According to Haavio-Mannila (1970) and Skard & Haavio-Mannila (1985:49-50), a special situation has characterized the position of women in eastern Finland since ancient times: because hunting, fishing and trading journeys and later forestry made men stay away from home for long periods of time, women found themselves alone, with responsibility for home, children and farms. Consequently, women were less oppressed and more able to become involved in political activity than elsewhere in Finland. Women were more often voted into parliament than in western Finland.

Nicaragua but did not lead to a similar strengthening of a new political role for women in terms of formal political positions. Our thesis is that this is mainly due to different *cultural* traditions, i.e. the tenacity of Catholic *marianismo*, the veneration of the traditional role of women as mothers, in Nicaragua. The struggle for the emancipation of women in Nicaragua has taken place within a context marked by a combination of revolution, male chauvinism and a kind of matriarchate.

We therefore start by giving a brief sketch of the Latin American gender culture and the position of women within it.

The cultural tradition

Latin American women participate in nearly all nondomestic spheres of national life to a lesser extent than men (Schmidt 1976-1977; Chaney 1979). This widely documented generalization stems from the structurally subordinate position of women in Latin American society and suggests why women face greater barriers to participating in politics than men. Women are first located in the private sphere of the home (*en la casa*) by the sexual division of labour, while men are first located in the public sphere outside the home (*en la calle*). The sexual division of labour in production builds upon women's subordination in the sphere of reproduction. Women's role in reproductive activities thus constitutes a major barrier to their involvement in nondomestic political action. In Latin America, patriarchal attitudes both reflect and reinforce the subordination of women and their relegation to the domestic sphere. These attitudes, which represent 'ideal' configurations held by both men and women, are summarized by Schmidt (1976-1977:244):

- The sexual division of labour reflects natural differences between men and women
- Women's identity comes through their relationship with men
- Women achieve their highest fulfillment as wives and mothers
- Women are childlike
- Women are apolitical

Patriarchal attitudes operate most profoundly at the familial level and are relatively constant across class lines. The patriarchal model of Latin American family structure is characterized by male control over most activities related to the outside world (*calle*). Within the domestic sphere (*casa*), however, women maintain considerable control through their acknowledged expertise in child rearing and discipline and other household activities. Stevens (1973) states that females wield great power in traditional Latin American families through *marianismo,* the cult of female spiritual superiority. She argues that Latin American women have contributed to the myth of 'machismo' because it offers them certain benefits such as autonomy in the domestic sphere and ability to emotionally coerce, if not downright control, family members. While Stevens views emotional coercion as a form of power, a more compelling argument is that women have to resort to such indirect techniques because they are generally denied direct exercise of power. Even sexually stratified societies provide some avenues for female influence and checks on male prerogatives. However, Stevens explains why Latin American women have a stake in maintaining the traditional familial patterns that strengthen their control of the domestic sphere: the domestic sphere represents the single area in Latin American society where females are acknowledged experts, and women operate relatively autonomously and exercise considerable authority, particularly over children, within this area. Roman Catholicism provides religious legitimation for Latin American family structure. The patriarchal models of family structure and of feminine behaviour represent traditional ideals which facilitate gender stratification and inhibit women's participation in the public sphere. Such models have been undermined by the examples of women who are heads of households or professionals in charge of men.[2] However, at the national level, the formal pattern of male dominance still prevails. The legal status of women in most Latin American civil codes is based upon *patria potestad,* which gives men property rights over wives and children (Chinchilla 1990:380).

Men thus predominate in public activities, as occupational and educational statistics readily indicate. Women similarly participate less in conventional political activities. Women generally vote less frequently than men, as voting studies of a number of countries have found (e.g. Schmidt 1975). Women's limited involvement in conventional politics provides evidence of the lack of women in the public sphere. Conventional politics, however, are limited as an indicator of feminine political participation in Latin America. First, the majority of women did not gain suffrage until after World War II (Jaquette 1976:222). Legal entry of a new group into an electorate has historically been associated with abnormally low voter turnout for group members (Schmidt 1975:480). Second, abstention from conventional politics may be regarded as a political act in Latin America, a refusal to participate in a

---

[2] Only if economic pressures make it impossible to stay home are women to work outside the home, and then only to supplement the family income. Thus it happened that despite the traditional ideal that the women's place is in the home, Nicaraguan women entered the labour market. Mass poverty and 'male abandonment of their families left Nicaraguan women with no alternative but to leave home for jobs.

system that represents only priviledged minorities (Jaquette 1976:233). Finally, much political behaviour in Latin America occurs outside the formal political process. While women have only recently participated in large numbers in the public 'sphere' of revolution and protest, they have constantly influenced politics through their position in kinship networks and their political socialization of children.

Thus, if we define politics as the social institution that constitutes the management of all the (smallest) units of a society, and given that in Latin America this unit is the family, we see that in a world of machismo and marianismo[3] politics becomes the task of the man.

The Latin American woman is above all *mater dolorosa*, the suffering mother. It is the fate of the woman to endure irresponsible, violent and unstable men and carry the burden of maintaining the home and of raising the children. However, she will by being a mother, and by silent sacrifice, obtain a higher moral status than the man. The simple virgin who became the living God's mother is a powerful symbol for women - and men - in Latin America. The most famous of the continent's virgins is Mexico's 'Virgin of Guadalupe'. As Nicaragua's national deity, the 'Absolutely Pure Virgin of the Conception' is on a par with Mexico's Guadalupe. Thus, Nicaragua's most important saint is a woman.

Nicaragua is thus in many ways a matrifocal society. Such societies are characterized by extremely unstable relations between couples, a predominance of single mothers, a mother or grandmother as the *de facto* head of the household, and loosely attached men in unstable work situations, either unemployed or working as migrant workers.[4] The fact that 'the family' in reality means 'the mother plus children' is *de facto* acknowledged in official statistics. At the beginning of the 1980s, 60 percent of all households in the capital of Managua and 34 percent of all Nicaraguan households were female headed (Molyneux 1985a:247).

---

[3] In Latin America the concepts of 'machismo' and 'marianismo' are used to refer to the set of values and complex of ideas surrounding these ideal gender roles. *Marianismo*, which requires women to be virtuous and humble, serves to support the male regime of machismo. *Machismo*, a system of male superiority and dual standards, exists in traditional Nicaragua in an extreme form. Dual standards greatly restrict women's freedom and make them highly accountable to men, who, in turn, enjoy freedom of movement and action with virtually no accountability.

[4] Nobody can give a proper answer as to why Nicaraguan men have children with different women and then wander between their different families. It may be a pattern from the sixteenth century when the Spanish *conquistadores* took several women from the indigenous population. It may also have its roots in the plantation system with a proletariat of seasonal workers who were forced to move around ih the country to harvest cotton, sugar, bananas and coffee (Killander-Braun 1990:312).

The fact that the family lacks a male head is reflected in the Nicaraguan Constitution of 1987. In the proposed Constitution the family was given the status of a 'fundamental core of society' and defined as a married or unmarried couple with children. This led to protests from single mothers who felt that they and their children also constituted families and that they were equally as legitimate cores of society even though they did not live together with a man. In the final version of the Constitution this definition was withdrawn, and as a result the 'fundamental core' was not defined at all.

In Catholic Nicaragua, women have traditionally been associated with the figure of Virgin Mary, the pure and virtuous mother. By adopting this ideal of woman, called *marianismo*, Nicaraguan women strongly identify with the image of the devoted mother (Seitz 1992:164).

The central place occupied by the maternal figure in life is underlined religiously through the celebration of *la purisima*. Virgin Mary is the quintessentially good mother, she is absolutely *pure*. This purity is a kind of honour or moral capital that a woman gains by becoming a mother. She probably gains more and more of it the better a mother she is and the better the children (the sons?) behave themselves. And when a son does something great or dies for a great cause, his mother becomes a 'mother of a hero and martyr' (Ekern 1989).

In what sense can the revolution be said to have contributed to the emancipation of women in Nicaragua? In many respects the participation of women in the revolution implied a break with the traditional role of women in Nicaraguan society described above.

But to what extent did the revolution contribute to the promotion of women's interests? In order to clarify the issues to be discussed below, we shall first briefly delineate three conceptions of women's interests. According to Molyneux (1985a:232) these are: women's interests, strategic gender interests, and practical gender interests.

Women's interests

Since women are positioned in a variety of ways (e.g. according to class, ethnicity, and gender) it is difficult to generalize about the interests of women. What we need is to specify how various categories of women are affected differently as a consequence of their social positioning and their chosen identities. On the other hand, it can not be denied that women have certain general interests in common. These can be called gender interests. Gender interests can be either strategic or practical.

Strategic gender interests

These interests are linked to overcoming women's subordination, such as the abolition of the sexual division of labour, the attainment of political equality by removing institutionalized forms of discrimination, and the adoption of adequate measures against male violence and control of women. Strategic gender interests are the ones most frequently considered by feminists to be women's 'real' interests (Molyneux 1985a:233).

Practical gender interests

These interests arise from the concrete conditions of women's positioning within the sexual division of labour. Practical interests are usually a response to an immediate perceived need, and they do not generally entail a strategic goal such as women's emancipation or gender equality. For example, since women, as a consequence of the sexual division of labour, are primarily responsible for their household's daily welfare, women have a special interest in domestic provision and public welfare. These practical interests do not in themselves challenge the prevailing forms of gender subordination, even though they arise directly out of them. This means that a state may gain the support of women by satisfying either their immediate practical demands or certain class interests, or both, but it may do this without advancing their strategic objective interests at all. With these conceptual distinctions in mind, I shall now consider how the Sandinistas have formulated women's interests, and how women have fared under their rule.

The Sandinista Revolution

The presumption that war and revolution are in some sense 'men's work' has been widely held. The sexual division of labour and the demands of the traditional female roles of wife and mother were presumed by scholars and male revolutionaries alike to preclude female involvement in combat operations of revolutionary organizations (Reif 1986:147-151). To the extent that women participated in guerrilla operations at all, it was presumed that their involvement was confined to support roles as cooks, nurses, and 'keepers of the home fires', or as clandestine providers of food, sanctuary, or intelligence to male guerrillas. This image of female involvement in guerrilla insurgency was not without basis in fact. Linda Reif (1986) argues that prior to the Sandinista revolution, women were not involved in large numbers in combat operations of Latin American insurgencies, with the possible exception of the

Tupamaros guerrillas of Uruguay. The leaders of these supposedly progressive movements were themselves not immune to gender role stereotyping in their pronouncements on the proper role of women in the revolution:

> *'But also in this stage (the guerrilla struggle) a woman can perform her habitual tasks of peacetime: it is very pleasing to a soldier subjected to the extremely hard conditions of life to be able to look forward to a seasoned meal which tastes like something... The women as cook can greatly improve the diet and, furthermore, it is easier to keep her in these domestic tasks; (such duties) are scorned by those (males) who perform them; they are constantly trying to get out of those tasks in order to enter into forces that are actively in combat' (Guevara 1969:87).*

During the rebellion against Somoza the participation of women was extensive. At the time of the victory of the revolution in 1979 almost a third of the active Sandinistas were women (Molyneux 1985a:227; Killander-Braun 1990:313). Women held positions as commanders of everything from small combat units to full battalions. This was epitomized in Dora María Tellez's role as Commander Two in the seizure of the Presidential Palace by the guerillas in 1978. At the final battle of León, four of the seven Sandinista field commanders were women (Reif 1986:158). Evidence such as this clearly challenges us to modify existing theories of Third World revolution in order to account for the phenomenon of non-élite women serving in large numbers as revolutionary combatants. This is especially compelling as many of these women participants were mobilized independently of their husbands, fathers, brothers, and boyfriends; they did not simply follow males into the hills.

By which processes is one subgroup of non-élite insurgent combatants, i.e. female heads of households, mobilized for participation, independently of their spouses? Agro-export-led development has affected the stability of rural social structures in Central American countries. Changes in these structures have created conditions that are conducive to the emergence of revolutionary insurgencies. But to explain the mobilization of non-élite women for political opposition, we must examine the particular impact of these economic and demographic changes on the stability of the family unit and on the status of non-élite women.

Rapid economic, social, and demographic transformations and crises often disrupt the stability of the family unit, leaving the woman with sole responsibility for the support of herself and her children. Left alone to cope with their family's economic distress, women have sought relief through participation in various popular organizations that emerged in Central America under the banner of 'liberation theology'. The popular organizations in which women were involved became targets of regime repression, and women participants became victims of that repression.

Faced with the prospect of death, imprisonment, or other forms of violence at the hands of the regime, women (like men) became more willing to join insurgent organizations, if for no other reason than to avoid becoming victims of state-sanctioned repressive violence.

Land ownership became increasingly concentrated as peasant subsistence cultivators were displaced from the land and their plots absorbed into large commercial estates. In Nicaragua, the share of the rural population that was landless stood at 33.8 percent in 1971, the largest rate of landlessness in Central America at that time (Mason 1992:68). The cash crops that were introduced into Central America (cotton, coffee), involve less labour-intensive production characteristics than the subsistence crops they displaced. Cattle ranching has been estimated to be 7 to 20 times less labour intensive than other forms of agricultural land use (Mason 1992:69). Central American countries did experience a period of industrial growth during the 1960s, but the number of new jobs created was far from sufficient to absorb either the displaced rural population or the growing number of new entrants into the working age population.

Faced with severe deprivation and frequent risks of subsistence crises, displaced peasant households have had few options by which to relieve their economic distress. Emigration to other countries or to other regions in the country provides one alternative.

Rural families are often destabilized by the necessity of the male leaving the family for long periods of time in search of work. Often, temporary absence ends up as permanent abandonment. This leaves the woman as the head of the household with full responsibility for both the subsistence needs of the family as well as the household responsibilities that traditionally have been regarded by males as 'women's work'. Pressures leading to male spouse abandonment and female participation in the labour market are greatest among the landless and those with insufficient land. In Nicaragua during the 1970s, at least half and perhaps as many as three fourths of all farmers controlled land in amounts that were insufficient to provide the family with subsistence security. The proportion of women classified as economically active grew from 14 percent in 1950 to 22 percent in 1970, and to 29 percent by 1977 (Mason 1992:74). As a consequence of economic pressures and political violence the number of female-headed households in Central America has increased dramatically. In Nicaragua in 1978, an estimated one third to one half of all families were female headed. With their husbands gone, rural women often find it necessary to migrate to urban areas, where entry into the informal sector of the urban economy provides the most readily available means of earning subsistence for their families. In

Nicaragua the number of women employed in services quadrupled between 1950 and 1980.

Concentrated in urban *barrios*, abandoned by their husbands, and faced with the risks of subsistence crisis posed by the limited occupational opportunities available in the informal sector, urban women have become frequent participants in the grass roots popular organizations that emerged and spread throughout Central America in the 1960s and 1970s.

Out of these efforts a number of women's organizations came into being. In 1977 the Association of Women Confronting the National Problem (*Asociación de Mujeres ante la Problamática Nacional*, AMPRONAC) was formed in Nicaragua, constituting the first broad based women's organization in that country. At its inception, it included large numbers of middle-class women. AMPRONAC conducted petition drives, organized hunger strikes, and held mass meetings at a time when no other organization would do so out of fear of repressive consequences. As the preponderance of its support base shifted to poor women, many of whom had experienced repression more directly than their middle-class colleagues, AMPRONAC began to confront the regime more directly. As the fighting in Nicaragua escalated, AMPRONAC members began engaging in more direct support of military operations, although still covertly. Finally, in 1978, AMPRONAC announced its support for FSLN, and many of the middle-class members left the organization. Still, by the time of the Sandinista victory, AMPRONAC had as many as 8,000 members (Molyneux 1985b:145).

Experience in AMPRONAC helped poor women break out of their fatalistic indifference to political activity to which the traditional household division of labour and cultural norms of *machismo* had condemned them. Through AMPRONAC they were able to participate in collective action, to develop leadership and organizational skills, and to gain heightened awareness of the possible political remedies for their economic plight. These experiences served them well later as participants in the FSLN.

For the first time Nicaraguan women were allowed to play a prominent role. The revolution recognized them as subjects of their own and as political creatures.

After the victory, some leading functions were occupied by women: Doris Tijerino became Minister of Health and Leticia Herrera led the Sandinista Defence Committees (CDS) before she became vice-president of parliament (*Asamblea Nacional*) in 1984. Violeta Barrios de Chamorro became one of the five members of the governing Junta until she left this body in April 1980 for political reasons.

In spite of these and other examples it has never been a goal in itself in Nicaragua after the revolution to get more women into leading governmental positions. Suffrage, which women had gained in 1955, now became real at parliamentary and presidential elections. Women won 40 percent of the seats in the *Asamblea Nacional* in 1984, but in the government there were only two female ministers and just a handful of other top positions in government were filled by women. None of the nine *comandantes* in the *Dirección Nacional* of the FSLN were women. At the 1990 elections women constituted only 19 percent of the parliamentary representatives. By contrast, the presidential election was won by a woman: Violeta Barrios de Chamorro (Collinson 1990:189).

In a situation in which revolution and civil war made material improvements of the conditions of women impossible, it was particularly by the securing of women's rights through the legal system that the revolution meant a breakthrough. During the elaboration of the new Constitution people had an opportunity to exert influence on its contents through open popular meetings (*cabildos abiertos*) around the country. The Constitutional Commission held separate meetings with different groups, including women. The result of these open meetings was a Constitution that contains more than ten articles which refer explicitly to the rights of women. The Constitution of 9 January 1987 establishes complete equality between men and women (e.g. a woman could earlier be sentenced for adultery against her husband, but not vice versa). Men and women gained equal rights and duties in the home and in relation to the children. The medieval father-right law, *patria potestad*, was replaced by the Law of Nurturing, which mandates shared parental responsibility (*guardia compartida*) (Chinchilla 1990:380). Maltreatment and abuse of women became subject to legal prosecution if the woman herself denounced it. Women could not be denied a job or be fired because of pregnancy. Women were also given a legal right to maintenance for the children. These are all examples of measures aimed at the promotion of *strategic gender interests*.

On the other hand, the Constitution is mute when it comes to women's right to abortion. The present law on abortion is from 1974 and allows abortion only for certain medical reasons. The FSLN leadership was divided over the proposition that the liberation of women should extend to control over their reproductive functions. Speaking at a Face the People meeting sponsored by AMNLAE, the Nicaraguan women's federation, Daniel Ortega opposed abortion and sterilization, saying that a woman who 'aspiring to be liberated', does not reproduce, 'negates her own continuity, the continuity of the human species' (quoted in Chinchilla 1990:387). Some FSLN members opposed abortion because of the lack of resources caused by the contras war, or because of the alleged complexity of the operation. Former Minister of Culture, Ernesto Cardenal, believed Nicaragua needed a larger population, and therefore opposed abortion (El Estiliano 1989:4).

But there remained an enormous difference between the rights of women on paper and their realization. For example, through the agrarian reform women were granted the same rights as men to acquire land and to become independent members of cooperatives, as well as equal pay for equal work. In spite of this only six percent of the women are independent members of cooperatives. The remaining women work together with their men and receive a salary, but do not have the same right to education as the other members and do not have the right to participate in the decision-making process.

In 1982 the war against the *contras* started in earnest. Compulsory military service for all men was introduced in 1983. For women it was made voluntary. A huge number of young men were sucked into the defence apparatus and women began to find their way into the labour market, adult education, the universities and political life. Five years after the revolution, 42 percent of all women in the cities were employed and 33 percent of those living in the countryside. Women constituted 53 percent of all students, and 67 percent of the members of the Sandinista Defence Committees (Killander-Braun 1990:314).

The war had particularly far-reaching consequences for women in the countryside. Here they became extremely important for agricultural production, where they constituted 40 percent of the work force. The revolution needed the women and production needed the women as long as the men were at war. To defend the new position of women in the rural work force, the Union of Agricultural Workers (*Asociación de Trabajadores del Campo*, ATC) played an important part. As more and more men became engaged in the war, the number of female members of the ATC increased. In 1983 women constituted 40 percent of ATC members (Collinson 1990:44).

More than the revolution, it was thus the *war against the contras* (1981-88) that contributed to speed up the realization of the rights of women. Like wars elsewhere, the war in Nicaragua led to increased female full-time participation in jobs they were previously barred from. The official recognition that 'women now fed the nation' resulted in particular women's issues and demands being given official priority. The need to solve women-specific problems and to increase production in the war economy forced trade unions to take women's issues seriously. The main problem remaining was now, as before, the unequal sexual division of labour within the family.

Women's organizations

When AMPRONAC was formed in the autumn of 1977 by FSLN members, its main task was not to work for women's liberation, but to draw more women into the struggle against Somoza. In 1979 30 percent of the guerrilla fighters were women. After the revolution disagreement arose within the FSLN as to the need for a special women's organization in *Nicaragua Libre*. The new women's organization, AMNLAE (*Asociación de Mujeres Nicaraguenses Luísa Amanda Espinoza*[5]), was not founded until August 1979, and its status was as one of the FSLN's many mass organizations. Despite official proclamations to deal with special women's problems, the main task of the AMNLAE was to incorporate women into the solution of the general tasks of the revolution.

The spokeswoman for the official point of view, i.e. that there was no need for a separate organization for women, was none other than Rosario Murillo, president Daniel Ortega's wife. In 1985 the FSLN maintained that the time was not right to focus on the particular problems of women. Bayardo Arce, one of the main ideologues of the FSLN, said that in a situation of war against the contras it was not a good strategy for women to focus on women's problems but that the strategically important thing for women was the survival of the Sandinista revolution.

It is therefore no wonder that the AMNLAE did not place greater demands on the men. The AMNLAE was no doubt the leading force with regard to the legal rights that women have gained through the new Constitution. But when it comes to demanding the participation of men in domestic work AMNLAE has been a non-offensive and toothless organization. As late as 8 March 1987 the slogan was: *Juntos en todo*, together in everything. Women shall fight for their emancipation together with men, not against them.

The turning point came with the FSLN *Proclama* about women in 1987. The *Proclama* was regarded as an official recognition of the particular problems of women. The *Proclama* recognized that women struggled with their own problems because of their gender and that their struggle was legitimate within the revolution. Women's issues could not be postponed because of the war.

This sudden change in the official attitude to the daily problems of women was due to the social and economic consequences of the war against the *contras*. With so

---

[5] Luísa Amanda was a young peasant woman who was killed in 1970. She was the first woman óf the FSLN to die in battle.

many men mobilized, the productivity of women, in particular in the cash-crop sector, was necessary for the survival of the revolution. It was necessary to remove obstacles such as child care and family responsibility that prevented women from increasing their work productivity. The work with specific female problems within the Union of Agricultural Workers (ATC) had borne fruit. The increase in coffee production in 1985-86 as a result of this strategy had convinced the FSLN that the solution to women's problems was not idealistic but pragmatic. Thus, the *Proclama* does not mean that the FSLN had suddenly 'seen the light'. The commitment to a 'militant critique of *machismo*' came in response to *pragmatic* concerns that women's discontent about their daily lives might weaken their strategic role in defense and thus jeopardize the war effort. Later developments confirmed that there were certain similarities between the Nicaraguan war-time mobilization of women and other war-time national emergency mobilizations of women, after which women have been returned to their domestic sphere. Nicaraguan women's newly-found role in the workforce was partly reversed towards the end of the 1980s when the war against the contras drew to a close. Women's entry into the more secure areas of the workforce proved to be more a symptom of war than a permanent change in the economic landscape. Indeed, the military service law guaranteed all demobilized soldiers the right to get their jobs back again.

In addition, as a consequence of the economic collapse caused by the war, and the subsequent need for national cost-cutting measures, women's security in the workplace suffered in particular. In 1988 and again in January 1989, thousands of state workers (mainly urban) were made redundant in a process known as *compactación*. The first round of cuts in 1988 affected office workers in the oversized revolutionary bureaucracy and there were steady complaints that many more women than men were dismissed (Colinson 1990:33). In 1989 the second round of *compactación* was not only more widespread but, in some cases, appeared to be *targeted* at women. The evidence shows that organization and trade union participation were crucial for women to defend their position in the workforce. A salient example is the female workforce on the banana plantations, which rose to constitute over 50 percent of the total workforce during the 1980s. Provided full backing by the national ATC union, the *bananeras* persuaded the management in April 1989 to ensure that any workers made redundant should be comprised of equal numbers of men and women (Colinson 1990:34). At the beginning of 1989 a new government policy known as *concertación* ('harmonization') was introduced to improve co-operation between the country's producers and the government. Under this new social contract, various concessions were granted to private employers and landowners. Some employers were treating *concertación* and *compactación* as one and the same thing and took advantage of the opening to dismiss pregnant women and make female staff redundant.

At any rate the *Proclama* contributed to increasing the pressure against the AMNLAE. The organization changed its name to MOMLAE (*Movimiento de Mujeres Nicaraguenses Luísa Amanda Espinoza*). The change of name was not purely cosmetic. Whereas the AMNLAE was an FSLN mass organization, MOMLAE is supposed to be a broad women's movement free from male and/or narrow political ties.

But modern women's organizations such as MOMLAE have great difficulties in reaching out to Nicaraguan women. Well-educated élite women within the MOMLAE leadership speak a language totally different from that of most non-élite women. It is above all the highly educated women who are active within the women's movement and within trade unions such as e.g. the CONARPO, the Nicaraguan Union of Public Employees. With respect to women's mass organizations it was therefore organizations of a totally different type that were to become dominant.

'The Committees of Mothers of Heroes and Martyrs' or the return of marianismo

We have seen how the participation of women in production, to fill the void left by the men who had to participate in the war against the contras, led to a temporary breakthrough for specific women's issues.

But the war against the contras also led to a strengthening of the traditional role of women: women as *mothers*. The symbol of motherhood was appropriated by both the revolution and the opposition. In a context in which families are headed by the mothers in the absence of the fathers, the mother/child relation (and in particular the mother/son relation) assumes a far greater emotional and economic importance. Motherly sacrifices and women's daily struggle for the survival of their children become recognized and worshipped.[6] It is thus typical that the first woman who was awarded the Carlos Fonseca medal[7] was Doña Lidia Saavedra de Ortega, the *mother*

---

[6] Parts of this section rely on Ekern's excellent article on the importance of Nicaragua's female Patron Saint (Ekern 1989).

[7] Carlos Fonseca is the founder of the FSLN and the chief ideologue. Consequently, the medal which carries his name is the highest distinction in the FSLN hierarchy of orders and titles.

of Daniel Ortega. It happened on the occasion of the 25th anniversary of the foundation of the FSLN on 10 November 1987.[8] *Comandante* Tomas Borge, the oldest of the nine *comandantes*, made the speech saying that the medal was awarded to Mrs. Saavedra '(because she) stood up against the enemy and was fully on a par with her fighting companion. (And who) is also our mother because she is the mother of three of our brothers, among them a martyr' (Ekern 1989:122).[9] Ekern (1989) goes on to wonder whether the Sandinistas deliberately wanted to convey the impression that president Ortega was the saviour of the nation by dressing his mother up in shining white and awarding her the highest distinction for her merits as the most prominent mother of heroes and martyrs.

Thus, the largest women's organization in Nicaragua was not the AMNLAE but the 'Committees of Mothers of Heroes and Martyrs' (*Madres de Héroes y Mártires*). They consisted of all women who lost one or more sons either during the revolution of 1979 or during the subsequent war between the Sandinistas and the *contras*, and who were willing to step in line with the FSLN. However, the Committees were not independent organizations in the sense that they took their own initiatives. This function was taken care of by the FSLN mass organization for women, the AMNLAE, now the MOMLAE. The Committees' most important task was to channel the grief over the lost sons against persons and groups that the FSLN wanted to brand as counter-revolutionaries.

Until the FSLN decided to negotiate with the *contras* every single encouragement to dialogue made by the Church or opposition parties was regularly countered with a series of interviews with the mothers of heroes and martyrs in the Sandinista newspapers. The message was clear, it was inadmissible to negotiate with 'the murderers of our sons'. The national leadership of the FSLN would subsequently join 'the people' in appropriate offical communiqués (Ekern 1989).

With similar regularity the opposition newspaper *La Prensa* would summon the mothers as their witnesses of the truth. If the Sandinistas could not negotiate for any other reason, they could at least do it for the sake of 'ending the sufferings of the mothers'. The political parties exploited the mothers as a front to underline their own messages.

---

[8] November 10th is also the memorial day for the death of Carlos Fonseca.

[9] Daniel's brother Humberto is also a revolutionary *comandante*, whereas a third brother was killed in 1979 and is therefore a martyr.

It is in this perspective that we must consider the election of Violeta Chamorro as president of Nicaragua in 1990.[10] Violeta Barrios de Chamorro is the widow of a hero and a martyr. Her husband, Pedro Joaquín Chamorro, was murdered by Somoza's National Guard on 10 January 1978. It was not Violeta the woman but *Violeta the mother*, who had made peace within her own family[11], who was elected president to create peace and reconciliation also within the greater family: the nation (Vargas 1991:79). She represented *the cause of the mothers*: they wanted their sons back from the war. Hence, her main electoral promise was the abolition of the draft. Many, especially women, voted for an end to the military draft and continued deaths of their children.

Conclusion: 'what difference does a revolution make?'

By way of conclusion, I would like to stress two comparative aspects. First, the Nordic cases demonstrate that *stability matters*. In the Nordic context the mobilization of women and the realization of their demands have become *institutionalized*. In the Nicaraguan context, by contrast, we have shown that in spite of the revolution and considerable progress in the work to better the position of women in Nicaragua, it was the consequences of the civil war rather than the revolution that led to a breakthrough for the political demands of women. However, this did not result in a permanent strengthening of a new political role for women measured in formal political positions as in the Nordic countries. For example, the percentage of female parliamentary deputies declined from an internationally impressive 40 percent in 1984 to only 19 percent in 1990. The increased participation of Nicaraguan women in the workforce as a consequence of the civil war has likewise been partly reversed after the war. The issues and demands Nicaraguan women mobilized to promote have to a far lesser extent been institutionalized.

Second, the Nicaraguan case shows that *culture matters*. The cultural impact of the Sandinista revolution was at best ambiguous with respect to the *machismo* dimension.

---

[10] On February 25, 1990, Nicaraguans went to the polls to freely elect a president, vice-president, and deputies to the National Assembly for the second time in their history as an independent republic. Violeta Barrios de Chamorro, the candidate of the National Opposition Union (UNO), a loose coalition of 14 parties, obtained 55 percent of the vote, compared to 40.9 percent for Daniel Ortega, the incumbent president supported by the FSLN.

[11] Among Violeta Chamorro's children, one son, Pedro Joaquín Chamorro Jr., joined the contras, whereas another son and a daughter assumed prominent positions within the Sandinista regime.

The war certainly enhanced *machismo*, but also led to an increased emphasis on the importance of women, but then as *mothers*. The Committees of Mothers of Heroes and Martyrs was by far the largest and most important women's organization in the country. Women can be organized and do organize themselves, but as *mothers*. It is hardly a coincidence that it was *mothers*, not 'women', who demonstrated on the Plaza de Mayo in Buenos Aires and in front of the presidential palace in Guatemala City.

With the virgin on their side Nicaraguan women may have smashed the bourgeoisie to a certain extent, but they still seem to be trapped within the cultural tradition of *marianismo*. The 'virgin trap' is there as a reality. On the other hand, the extensive involvement of women in politics and social affairs cannot be rolled back altogether. Having experienced a degree of collective power and influence unknown to them throughout their history, it seems likely that Nicaraguan women will fight hard to preserve the gains they have achieved so far, and even create the necessary ideological infrastructure that enables them to push their emancipation further ahead. Nicaragua will therefore for many years to come display a peculiarly dual situation combining culturally determined traditionalism and female activism created by the special conditions of the Sandinista revolution and the subsequent civil war.

References

Chaney, E. M. (1979), *Supermadre: Women in Politics in Latin America*. Austin: University of Texas Press.

Chinchilla, N. Stolz (1990), 'Revolutionary Popular Feminism in Nicaragua: Articulating Class, Gender, and National Sovereignty', *Gender & Society*, Vol. 4, 3:370-397.

Colinson, H. (ed.) (1990), *Women and Revolution in Nicaragua*. London and New Jersey: Zed Books Ltd.

Deighton, J. et al. (1983), *Sweet Ramparts: Women in Revolutionary Nicaragua*. London: War on Want and Nicaragua Solidarity Campaign.

Ekern, S. (1987), Street: *Culture and Politics in a Nicaraguan Neighbourhood*. Bergen: Department of social anthropology, University of Bergen.

400   *Women in Nordic Politics*

Ekern, S. (1989): 'Den absolutt rene jomfruen', *Internasjonal Politikk*, nr. 4-6:115-131.

Ekern, S. (ed.) (1990), *Fra geriljaseier tilpresidentvalg. Nicaragua fra revolusjonen i 1979 til valgene i 1990*. Publikasjon nr. 4. Oslo: Institutt for menneskerettigheter.

El Estiliano, C. (1989), *News from the NICA School in Esteli*. Cambridge, Mass.: Febr. 1989.

Frühling, M., Nyberg, J. and Sandberg, S. (1990), *Nicaragua - De första tio åren*. Stockholm: Carlssons.

Guevara, Che (1969), *Guerrilla Warfare*. New York: Vintage.

Haavio-Mannila, E. (1970), 'Sex Roles in Politics', in *Scandinavian Political Studies*, Vol. 5:209-240.

Hillson, J. (1989), 'Controversy Sharpens Over Women's Rights in Nicaragua', *El Estiliano. News from the NICA School in Esteli*. Cambridge, Mass., February:4.

Jaquette, J. S. (1973), 'Women in Revolutionary Movements in Latin America', *Journal of Marriage and the Family*, 35:344-354.

Jaquette, J. S. (1976), 'Female Political Participation in Latin America', in Nash, J. and Safa, H. (eds): *Sex and Class in Latin America*. New York: Praeger.

Killander-Braun, L. (1990), 'Kvinnan och revolutionen', in Frühling, M. et al. (ed.): *Nicaragua - De första tio åren*. Stockholm: Carlssons.

Mason, T. D. (1992), 'Women's Participation in Central American Revolutions: A Theoretical Perspective', *Comparative Political Studies*, Vol. 25, 1:63-89.

Molyneux, M. (1985a), 'Mobilization Without Emancipation? Women's Interests, the State, and Revolution in Nicaragua', *Feminist Studies*, Vol. 11, 2:227-254.

Molyneux, M. (1985b), 'Women', in Walker, T. (ed.): *Nicaragua: The First 5 Years*. New York: Praeger.

Reif, L. L. (1986), 'Women in Latin American Guerrilla Movements. A Comparative Perspective', *Comparative Politics*, Vol. 18, 2:147-169.

Schmidt, S. W. (1975): 'Women in Colombia: Attitudes and Future Perspectives in the Political System', *Journal of Inter-American Studies and World Affairs*, 17:465-489.

Schmidt, S. W. (1976-1977), 'Political Participation and Development: The Role of Women in Latin America', *Journal of International Affairs*, 30:243-260.

Seitz, B. J. (1992), 'From Home to Street: Women and Revolution in Nicaragua', in Bystydzienski, J. M. (ed.): *Women Transforming Politics. Worldwide Strategies for Empowerment*. Bloomington: Indiana University Press.

Skard, T. and Haavio-Mannila, E. (1985), 'Mobilization of Women at Elections', in Elina Haavio-Mannila et al. (eds): *Unfinished Democracy. Women in Nordic Politics*. Oxford: Pergamon Press.

Stevens, E. P. (1973), 'The Prospects for a Women's Liberation Movement in Latin America', *Journal of Marriage and the Family*, 35:313-321.

Vargas, O. R. (1991), *Adonde va Nicaragua. Perspectivas de una revolución latinoamericana*. Managua: Ediciones Nicarao.

Contributors

Christina Bergqvist, researcher, Department of political science, Uppsala University, Sweden.

Einar Berntzen, assistant professor, Department of Comparative Politics, University of Bergen, Norway.

Tom Carlson, assistant researcher, Department of political science, Åbo Akademi, Finland.

Göran Djupsund, associate professor, Department of political science, Åbo Akademi, Finland.

Lauri Karvonen, professor, Department of comparative politics, University of Bergen, Norway. Adjoint professor, Department of political science, Åbo Akademi, Finland.

Ulf Lindström, professor, Department of comparative politics, University of Bergen, Norway.

Per Lægreid, professor, Department of administration and organization theory, University of Bergen, Norway. Senior researcher, Norwegian Research in Organization and Management, Bergen, Norway.

Richard E. Matland, assistant professor, Department of political science, University of Houston, Texas.

Kristin Morken, research assistant, Department of comparative politics, University of Bergen, Norway.

Maria Oskarson, lecturer, Department of political science, University of Gothenburg, Sweden.

Nina Cecilie Raaum, assistant professor, Department of comparative politics, University of Bergen, Norway.

Per Selle, professor, Department of comparative politics, University of Bergen, Norway. Senior researcher, Norwegian Research in Organization and Management, Bergen, Norway.

Jan Sundberg, professor, Department of political science, University of Helsinki, Finland.

Lise Togeby, senior lecturer, Department of political science, University of Aarhus, Denmark.

Bjarne Øymyr, senior executive officer, Norwegian Social Science Data Services, University of Bergen, Norway.